The Roster
of the
GENERAL SOCIETY OF THE WAR OF 1812
1989

and

Supplement to the 1989 Roster

Compiled and Edited by
Dennis F. Blizzard

CLEARFIELD

The Roster of the General Society of the War of 1812: 1989
Originally published Mendallhall, Pennsylvania, 1989
Copyright © 1989 by
The General Society of the War of 1812, Inc.
All Rights Reserved.

Supplement to the 1989 Roster
Copyright © 1999 by
The General Society of the War of 1812, Inc.
All Rights Reserved.

Reprinted, two volumes in one, with the permission of
The General Society of the War of 1812, Inc.
for Clearfield Company, Inc. by
Genealogical Publishing Co., Inc.
Baltimore, Maryland
1999

International Standard Book Number: 0-8063-4866-6
Set Number 0-8063-4865-8

Made in the United States of America

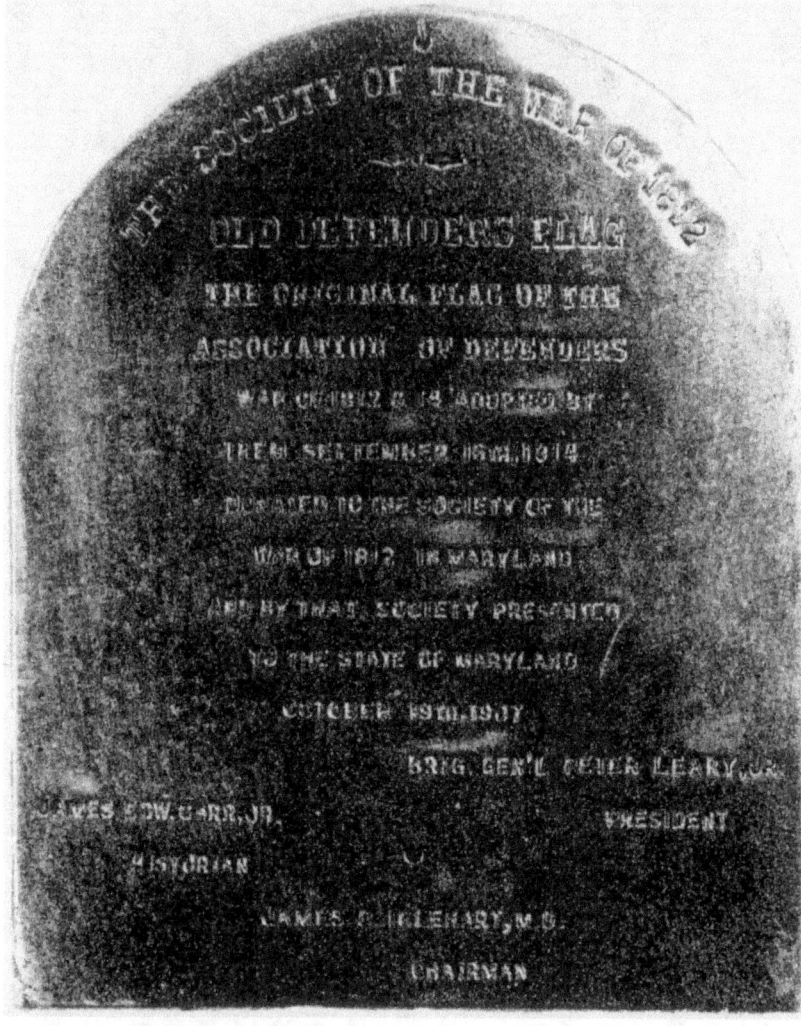

Legend: The Society Of The War Of 1812, Old Defenders' Flag, The Original Flag Of The Association Of Defenders, War of 1812 & 1814 Adopted By Them September 16th, 1814, Donated To The Society Of The War Of 1812 In Maryland, And By That Society Presented To The State Of Maryland October 19th, 1907, Brig. Gen'l Peter Leary, Jr., President, James Edw. Carr, Historian, James D. Inglehart, M.D., Chairman *(Courtesy of Richard N. Hambleton, Annapolis, MD)*

GENERAL SOCIETY of the WAR OF 1812

"The General Society of the War of 1812 derives its antiquity and standing as a veteran organization from two sourses; one, the Society of the War of 1812 in Maryland, founded, as the "Defenders of Baltimore," on the Battlefield of North Point, September 14, 1814 by participants in that engagement; the other, the Society of the War of 1812 in the Commonwealth of Pennsylvania, organized at Independence Hall, Philadelphia, January 9, 1854 by the Pennsylvania veterans of that war."

1972 REGISTER
p. iii

The greatest happiness of the thinking man is to have fathomed what can be fathomed, and quietly to reverence what is unfathomable.

Goethe

THE ROSTER
of the
GENERAL SOCIETY OF THE WAR OF 1812
1989

Compiled and Edited by
Dennis F. Blizzard

With an Introduction by
John W. W. Loose
Publication Committee
Donald G. Beetem
Clement D. Erhardt, Jr.
F. Wynne Paris
Forrest R. Schaeffer

(Real measures were taken to reproduce names and data as discernible from original manuscripts. The publisher accepts no responsibility for omissions, misstatements, or other inaccuracies which may appear or may not appear in this book. Archives and Records Depository, 230 N. President Ave., Lancaster, PA 17603.)

DEDICATED TO SAMUEL R. SLAYMAKER II
SECRETARY GENERAL 1975-1986
PRESIDENT GENERAL 1987-1989

FOREWORD

Today's General Society of the War of 1812 is an exceptionally active organization. Within the past year, for example, it has been represented at historical functions in England, Canada, and in most of the twenty-two states which include its autonomous affiliates.

When the organization was founded in 1814 it was concerned mainly with the rights of veterans and the upkeep of their graves. Later, it encouraged research and the preservation of historical data, including memorials to patriots of that era of our national history. Its primary concern now is the cherishing, maintenance, and extension of the institutions of American freedom; the fostering of love of country; and intelligent patriotism through improved understandings of the War of 1812 and its results, the better to perpetuate the high ideals for which this country was meant to stand.

Some may feel that the care and maintenance of these ideals are more than at best perfunctory ceremony or at worst an exercise in pro forma jingoism. In the deepest sense these acts should evoke memories of patriots' struggles—often under very trying conditions—to, and if necessary die, in hopes that the efforts would make a difference in the on-going trials of the United States. By our acts we are reminded that they have, indeed, made a difference, and we can feel better for it.

On February 16, 1980, when as Secretary General addressing the District of Columbia Society on the topic of "Patriotic-Hereditary Societies: Their Challenge in the '80's" I pointed out that these societies were faced with a twin threat to their wellbeing, if not to their existence. First, it became increasingly difficult for many of us to interest our children in our societies. And when we lose them, the lifeblood will be drained from said societies. They were not 'relevant,' the kids told us..."

In rueing the grim possibilities of the future of these societies, with reference especially to our children, I discussed Dr. Henry Kissinger's book, *White House Years*. His feeling relative to the disgust and disappointment of American students as they demonstrated against our foreign policy and military involvement in Indo-China, allowed that the breakdown of the established ideals and values of their elders had undermined respect for patriotism and familism. Youth saw the older generation as cut loose from traditional attitudes and goals in politics and in personal lifestyles. Dr. Kissinger evaluated our developing generation as in an emotional state of organized anger. Fortunately, institutionalized and public reactions evolve quickly in modern culture.

In ten years we have seen many changes for the better on the national scene. There is no question about the American public's becoming more attuned to things patriotic. This has been pretty much agreed to by spokesmen of both political parties. Space will not permit an exploration of the probable reasons. But they are there and bode well for the future of societies such as this. True, the "spirit of malaise" of which President Carter spoke in 1979 has occasionally given way to displays of conspicuous consumption and gross materialism by some who pass for role models. And there have been too many instances of unspeakable venality in business and government. But things are looking up in general—particularly in schools. There is new-found interest in American history. Ten years ago R.O.T.C. courses were all but disbanded on a great number of campuses. Today they are considered "in" on many, as shown by this Society's presentation of 239 awards in R.O.T.C. competitions during 1988.

We are ready for a new patriotism and happily announce what I described in the Board Meeting of March 4, 1989 as "... the most historically worthwhile project which the Society has ever undertaken, *The General Society of the War of 1812 Roster*—an ancestor index record."

Likewise, we are ready for a substantive new approch to the efforts of magnifying the historical role played by the patriots of the War of 1812 in the American experience. Having participated in momentous events in honor of the War of 1812 in the United Kingdom, Canada, Michigan, Texas, Minnesota, Kentucky, New Jersey, Maryland, the District of Columbia, Georgia, Louisiana, Pennsylvania, and New York it is positive that the General Society is on the "cutting edge" of an expanded recognition with an ever-increasing set of purposes. This new enthusiasm opens 1989 with official representation in Belgium to commemorate the 175th anniversary of the signing of the Treaty of Ghent.

March 10, 1989

S. R. Slaymaker II
President General

Respectfully, former President General Slaymaker's Foreword has been included. His enthusiastic anticipation of the publication of "The Roster" was known to all. Even though this part of the book had not gone to press at the time of his demise, the benefit of his thoughts for the Society has been preserved.

PREFACE

The experience of completion of all of one's ambitions is reserved for only a few people. Who has not begun some work, only to have to set it aside short of the goal? The ages abound with unfinished tales and chronicles initiated by an obscure scribe which are left to be found and later concluded by the pen of an distant counterpart. The formation of this book characterizes such a situation.

Early in this century an unknown member of our Society commenced a roll which would catalog the members and their 1812 *propositi* from the time of the founding near the end of the past century. The task was surely difficult because well regulated admission and numbering systems were not then in use. The first enroller ended his efforts, as accurately as the records at hand permitted, around the year 1914.

Sometime later another indexer, with different style and form, moved the inventory into the fourth decade of the current century. His system also suffered omissions, duplicated entries, transposed names and incorrect numbering. But fault should not be laid in the face of diligence given freely of one's time and mind.

When the Society's archives were removed from Washington to Lancaster, an indifferent looking sheaf of papers caught the attention of Counsellor General Loose, who recognized the cogency of these abortive efforts. The erstwhile unknown and unfinished pages were forwarded to me for advice. That nothing should be considered nor proposed until the entire Society be enrolled and serious effort be made for accuracy and totality was my report. I also recommended that if several years were given to the task which it readily could require, the Society would have the makings of a unique volume worthy of publication at the time of the 1989 anniversary year of the war's end and the Treaty of Ghent.

An eager and supportive signal to procede was accorded by the Board of Directors and for more than two years the compiling and editing progressed. The process brought forth much primary, but obscure, data: some all but forgotten and some misinterpreted over the years. The re-readings and study of original materials provided a perspicuous insight into the attitudes and practices of the Society in its formative period.

It would be absurd to promulgate the claim that the details now brought together in the finalized text are, or could be, without error. We have dealt with records maintained variously by both faithful and careless custodians during more than a hundred years. The work has been done in the setting of an objective and meticulous historian, although the effort drew not upon any thesis or dialectic. Presented not as merely a mundane research syllabus nor only as an abstracted reference tool, it is hoped that the finished roster will abide for the thoughtful Society member as a link to the genesis of an honorable compatriotship which grants a birthright from the patriots to their descendants: a privilege, not by law but by hereditary continuity.

Attesting to the Society's unimpeachable antiquity, this work features the names and service of veterans of the War of 1812 who were bona fide founders and members of the Society. Thus instituted by participants in the war it commemorates, the General Society of the War of 1812, like the Cincinnati, Aztec, and Loyal Legion, was recognized and covered by War Department regulations governing the wearing of its insignia on military uniforms.

Mechanically, the book has been arranged to provide the most flexible access for the user. Following a section devoted to War of 1812 veterans and their service records, is the main body of the membership set chronologically. Two indices are incorporated to give reference to The Roster. The first index offers alphabetically the names of every member admitted through April 15, 1989 and refers to his General Society four digit filing number. The second index includes all eligible *propositi* and refers to the General Society four digit filing number of the application on which each *propositus* is documented. Although more difficult to achieve, this system is superior to a single mixed index. Name styles on original papers are used as thereon given.

In entries which show multiple ancestors, the first one listed is from the original application: others which follow are from supplementals. The constitutional provision regarding failure of lineal descent, . . . *one collateral descendant may be admitted to represent the said participant* . . ., causes instances in which a female is named as the "ancestor." Neither the roster nor the ancestor index shows any *propositus* to be in the collateral condition. The originally filed application will demonstrate the single collateral claim permitted in Article VI.

Acknowledgement of the highest order is accorded to Mr. John W. W. Loose, without whose faithful assistance and advice the material for the book could not have been amassed for use. As a scholar, archivist, and a long-time General Society officer, he made a tremendous contribution to this work. The diligent input of Mrs. Germaine Rooney, as typist and reader, brought the dim history into legible copy. Her gentle nature in the heat of summers' work kept the motion going.

Messrs. Clement D. Erhardt, Jr., Forrest R. Schaeffer, Donald G. Beetem, and F. Wynne Paris were the constant support division by always keeping the objective set on producing a creditable publication by 1989. Nothing was ever asked of them that was not quickly and completely provided.

Lutherville, Maryland *Dennis F. Blizzard*
April 15, 1989

CONTENTS

Foreword vii
Preface ix
Preamble xii
Officers of the General Society 1
Meetings of the General Society 5
Introduction 7
Original Veteran Marker 12
Veteran Members 15
The Roster 21
Chronicles of State Societies 139
Archival Sources 153
Member Index 157
Ancestor Index 205

PREAMBLE
TO THE CONSTITUTION OF THE
GENERAL SOCIETY OF THE WAR OF 1812

WHEREAS, in the Providence of God, victory having crowned the forces of the United States of America, in upholding the principles of the Nation against Great Britain in the conflict known as the War of 1812; we the survivors and descendants of those who participated in that contest, have joined together to perpetuate its memories and victories; to collect and secure for preservation rolls, records, books and other documents relating to that period; to encourage research and publication of historical data, including memorials of patriots of that era in our National history; to care for and, when necessary, assist in burying actual veterans of that struggle; to cherish, maintain and extend the institutions of American freedom, and foster true patriotism and love of country.

OFFICERS
GENERAL SOCIETY OF THE WAR OF 1812
1989

MR. CLEMENT D. ERHARDT, JR.
President General

(VACANT)
Deputy President General

District Deputy Presidents General
MR. HOMER F. DEAN, NEW ENGLAND
MR. RUSSELL BEMENT, JR., MIDDLE ATLANTIC
MR. DENNIS F. BLIZZARD, CHESAPEAKE
MR. WILLIAM C. KNIGHT, CAROLINAS
MR. MONCURE C. O'NEAL, SOUTHERN
MR. JOHN P. CAVOROC, GULF
MR. L. JACKSON SHAW, OHIO VALLEY CENTRAL
MR. BURTON L. SHOWERS, GREAT LAKES
MR. B. ALLEN YOUNG, WESTERN

Vice Presidents General
MR. JOSEPH W. SLEDGE, JR., ALABAMA
MR. LEE E. BISHOP, JR., CALIFORNIA
MR. THOMAS C. ETTER, JR., DISTRICT OF COLUMBIA
MR. CHARLES A. TINGLEY, FLORIDA
MR. ROBERT B. ARNOLD, GEORGIA
MR. RICHARD E. CAREY, ILLINOIS
COL. BENJAMIN H. MORRIS, KENTUCKY
MR. JOHN R. CAVAROC, LOUISIANA
COL. SAMUEL A. RITTENHOUSE, MARYLAND
MR. JAMES W. SIMMONS, MASSACHUSETTS
MR. DONALD M. D. THURBER, MICHIGAN
MR. JOHN H. JONES, MINNESOTA
MR. ROY W. WILKINSON, JR., MISSISSIPPI
MR. RICHARD A. SCUDDER, NEW JERSEY

MR. RICHARD B. SHULL, NEW YORK
MR. HUGH B. JOHNSON, NORTH CAROLINA
MR. ROBERT E. GRIM, OHIO
MR. F. SHUNK BROWN, III, PENNSYLVANIA
MR. C. BATTLE SHAW, JR., TENNESSEE
MR. JOSEPH M. CLARK, JR., TEXAS
MR. JUDSON P. MASON, SR., VIRGINIA
MR. B. ALLEN YOUNG, WISCONSIN

MR. DENNIS F. BLIZZARD
Vice President General—Publications

MR. DONALD G. BEETEM
Vice President General—Public Relations

MR. B. ALLEN YOUNG
Vice President General—Military Awards

MR. FORREST R. SCHAEFFER
Secretary General

MR. CLEMENT D. ERHARDT, JR.
Treasurer General

MR. F. WYNNE PARIS
Registrar General

MR. RAYMOND B. CLARK, JR.
Genealogist General

MR. MYRON C. BANKS
Judge Advocate General

MR. RICHARD E. CAREY
Historian General

DR. JOSEPH V. HOPKINS
Surgeon General

REV. DR. G. HALL TODD
Chaplain General

COL. H. HARDING ISAACSON
Marshal General

MR. JOHN W. W. LOOSE
Counselor General

MR. B. ALLEN YOUNG
Executive Administrator—Members-at-Large

COL. STEWART B. McCARTY, JR.
Assistant Secretary General

MR. THOMAS C. ETTER, JR.
Assistant Treasurer General

MR. ALBERT B. SNAPP
Assistant Registrar General

(VACANT)
Assistant Genealogist General

MR. GRIFFITH F. PITCHER
Assistant Judge Advocate General

B. GEN. WILLIAM B. GOLD, JR.
Assistant Historian General

DR. PHILIP W. BERNSTORF
Assistant Surgeon General

REV. DR. GEORGE G. MERRILL
Assistant Chaplain General

REV. CANON EDWARD N. WEST
Assistant Chaplain General

MR. JAMES F. VILLERE
MR. CHARLES J. SINNOTT
MR. JOSEPH D. CLARK, JR.
MR. ROBERT B. OSBORNE
MR. CLOVIS H. BRAKEBILL
DR. CLYDE E. NOBLE
MR. JUDSON P. MASON, SR.
Assistant Marshals General

OFFICERS EMERITI

MR. STANLEY D. KOLB
MR. MALCOLM DE LA HOUSSAYE
MR. JOHN W. W. LOOSE
MR. EDWARD C. BEETEM, II
MR. NICHOLAS D. WARD
Past Presidents General

B. GEN. FRANCIS WOOLFLEY
District Deputy President General

Officers

MR. HOWARD W. WISEMAN
District Deputy President General

MR. S. VANNORT CHAPMAN
Judge Advocate General

R. ADM. F. PAULL MITCHELL
Registrar General

MR. HOWARD B. BURGESS
Assistant Registrar General

MR. RICHARD C. SCHLENKER
Vice President General, Membership-at-Large

MR. JOHN A. PENTZ
Vice President General

STATE PRESIDENTS
1989

Alabama
MR. EDWARD T. DOUGLASS, JR.

California
MR. DENNIS W. SIMPSON

District of Columbia
MR. RICHARD C. SCHLENKER

Florida
MR. JOE B. CLARK, JR.

Georgia
MR. ROBERT B. ARNOLD

Illinois
MR. RICHARD E. CAREY

Kentucky
DR. THOMAS L. RILEY

Louisiana
MR. CURTIS P. ROME, JR.

Maryland
MR. W. KING BARNES, JR.

Massachusetts
MR. JAMES M. SIMMONS

Michigan
MR. DONALD J. PENNELL

Minnesota
MR. CURTIS J. OLIVER

Mississippi
MR. GERALD P. GUICE

New Jersey
MR. RUSSELL K. DUTCHER, III

New York
MR. THOMAS H. LIPSCOMB, III

North Carolina
MR. JERRY L. HIGGINS

Ohio
MR. KEITH D. ASHLEY

Pennsylvania
MR. MARCELLUS H. MCLAUGHLIN, JR.

Tennessee
MR. L. JACKSON SHAW

Texas
DR. ROBERT L. KURTH

Virginia
MR. WILLIAM H. HUME

Wisconsin
MR. WILLIAM H. RODDIS

MEETINGS
OF THE
GENERAL SOCIETY OF THE WAR OF 1812

1894, April 14. *Congress Hall*, Philadelphia, Pa.

1895, June 19. *Carpenter's Hall*, Philadelphia, Pa.

1896, June 19. *Second Regiment Armory*, Philadelphia, Pa.

1898, June 21. *Select Council Chamber*, Baltimore, Md.

1900, June 30. *Merion Cricket Club*, Haverford, Pa.

1902, June 20. *Faneuil Hall*, Boston, Mass.

1904, June 17. *State House*, Philadelphia, Pa.

1906, June 16. *Cosmos Club*, Washington, D.C.

1908, June 20. *Hotel Belvedere*, Baltimore, Md.

1910, June 25. *Champlain Club*, Cliff Haven, Plattsburgh, New York.

1912, October 12. *Historical Society of Pennsylvania*, Philadelphia, Pa.

1914, September 12. *Hotel Belvedere*, Baltimore, Md.

1916, September 16. *Copley-Plaza*, Boston, Mass.

1918 (No meeting held because of the World War.)

1920, June 12. *Great Falls (Va.)*, Washington, D.C.

1922, October 7. *Fraunce's Tavern*, New York City

1925, June 6. *Historical Society of Pennsylvania*, Philadelphia, Pa.

1928, September 12. *Hotel Southern*, Baltimore, Md.

1930, September 13. *Town Hall*, Weymouth, Mass.

1932, October 1. *Mayflower Hotel*, Washington, D.C.

1934, September 22. *Berkeley-Carteret Hotel*, Asbury Park, N.J.

1936, September 26. *Thayer-West Point Inn*, West Point, N.Y.

1938, October 1. *Warwick Hotel*, Philadelphia, Pa.

1940, September 28. *Hotel Sheraton*, Boston, Mass.

1942, September 26. *Princeton Inn*, Princeton, N.J.

1944, September 23. *Hotel Biltmore*, New York City.

1946, September 28. *Hamilton Hotel*, Washington, D.C.

1948, September 11. *Hotel Southern*, Baltimore, Md.

Meetings

1950, September 30. *Hotel Benjamin Franklin*, Philadelphia, Pa.

1952, September 19. *Grosvenor Hotel*, New York City

1954, September 24. *Hotel Bellevue*, Boston, Mass.

1956, September 14. *Lord Baltimore Hotel*, Baltimore, Md.

1959, January 6. *St. Charles Hotel*, New Orlean, La.

1960, September 22. *Hotel Barclay*, Philadelphia, Pa.

1962, September 21. *Hotel Claridge*, Atlantic City, N.J.

1964, September 11. *Hotel Sheraton Belvedere*, Baltimore, Md.

1966, September 17. *University Club*, Washington, D.C.

1968, September 20. *Hotel Biltmore*, New York City

1970, September 25. *Hotel Benjamin Franklin*, Philadelphia, Pa.

1972, September 9. *Lord Baltimore Hotel*, Baltimore, Md.

1975, February 1. *Royal Sonesta Hotel*, New Orleans, La.

1978, September 23. *Hotel Brunswick*, Lancaster, Pa.

1981, October 3. *Holiday Plaza*, Burlington, N.J.

1984, September 8. *Cross Keys Inn*, Baltimore, Md.

1987, January 10. *Royal Orleans*, New Orleans, La.

INTRODUCTION

by
JOHN W. W. LOOSE

During the 1840s and 1850s veterans of the War of 1812, especially those living in the Northeast, held meetings and encampments. In addition to the usual camaraderie of old comrades in arms, such meetings seemed to have as a purpose the marshaling of strength to secure legislation favorable to the veterans. Pensions were on the minds of many veterans as they gathered to recount the battles they had fought to confirm and make permanent the independence of the United States of America. The centennial of American Independence stirred renewed interest in our heritage in 1876. Because the ranks of aging veterans had begun to thin rapidly by this time, their sons and grandsons took up the patriot cause. Many Americans perceived a serious threat to American institutions and values caused by hordes of immigrants—many without any knowledge of or sympathy with our political and economic traditions—flocking to our shores during the last quarter of the nineteenth century. Their interest in preserving American traditions thus heightened, Americans between 1876 nd 1910 organized patriotic hereditary societies whose membership requirements were based on proof of descent from an ancestor who rendered significant service, usually military, in time of crisis to the nation. As the end of the nineteenth century approached, state associations entered a new phase. National or general societies were formed to bring harmony, uniformity, efficiency, and strength to the numerous state societies. Moreover, an organizational structure of this nature would be analogous to the federalism of the national and state governments. Nothing could be more typically American!

Thus it was that surviving veterans of the War of 1812, meeting in general convention at Independence Hall in Philadelphia on 9 January 1854 organized *The Society of the War of 1812*, and elected Joel B. Sutherland as its president. From that date until 10 November 1890, five surviving veterans served as president of the Society. On 8 January 1891 John Cadwalader, grandson of Brigadier General Thomas Cadwalader who commanded the "Advance Light Brigade" of the Pennsylvania Militia in 1814–1815, was chosen to head the Society. At once the organization began preparations for incorporation in the Commonwealth of Pennsylvania. A constitution and by-laws were drawn up. The charter that was presented to the Court of Common Pleas in Philadelphia was approved, and articles of incorporation were granted by decree of that Court on 19 November 1892. Although the charter states the name of the association is the *Society of the War of 1812*, the constitution that accompanied the charter clearly indicates in Article I that "The Society shall be known as the *General Society of the War of 1812*." Throughout the constitution the name "General Society" is used. The fourth provision in the charter states "This Society, seated and located in the City of Philadelphia, State [sic] of Pennsylvania, United States of America, shall have the right to constitute, warrant, authorize and recognize one branch of the Society of the War of 1812, in each State or Territory of the United States." At that time the Society had 53 veteran members and 253 descendant members.

At the Fortieth Annual Meeting of the Society, held in the old U.S. Senate Chamber in Philadelphia, on 19 February 1894, the secretary reported 57 gentlemen residing in 14 states had been admitted to membership during the previous year. The minutes of that meeting state "During the past year the long mooted project of organizing branches of the Society in other States has assumed a new phase, and in due time you will be called on to determine whether it is expedient to aid in the formation of a National Society, composed of delegates from several States." Having laid claim to the "General Society" name in its constitution and its intention to form state societies in its charter, the Philadelphia organization was ready to invite kindred groups in other states to become affiliated with the "General Society." To accomplish this, a conference committee was appointed.

Negotiations were commenced with the Maryland association which had evolved from *The Defenders of Baltimore*, formed on 14 September 1814 following the successful defense of Baltimore. As early as 1841 a movement was in the wind to form a national veterans' organization for holding national encampments, defraying funeral expenses of impoverished veterans, and providing for the education and moral instruction of their children. Baltimore was the site of a national encampment of veterans from Maryland, Pennsylvania, Virginia, and the District of Columbia on 14 May 1842. One result of this gathering was the formation of the *Association of the Defenders of Baltimore in the War of 1812*. The seventeen-day conclave ended with a huge parade which was reviewed by the President of the United States, John Tyler; and Chief of Staff, General Winfield Scott.

The "Old Defenders," their numbers now greatly diminished by deaths, admitted sons and descendants to carry on the traditional activities and ceremonies annually to commemorate the Defense of Baltimore. On 23 October 1893, following discussions with the Pennsylvania Society of the War of 1812, the Marylanders were incorporated as *The Society of the War of 1812 in the State of Maryland*. The Pennsylvanians, functioning as the General Society, had prepared a "Basis of Union" which each state society was expected to adopt as a condition to affiliation with the *General Society of the War of 1812*. *The Society of the War of 1812 in the State of Maryland* adopted the "Basis of Union" in 1894 and became the second state society in the General Society. Owing to the founding date of the *Defenders of Baltimore* on 14 September 1814, the General Society through its Maryland state society affiliate takes that date as the origin of its existence. Like the Pennsylvania state society, the Marylanders had veterans as presiding officers from 1814 to 1888. Its first two presidents, termed "military commanders," were Major General Samuel Smith, the hero of Baltimore's defense; and Major General George H. Steuart. In all, eleven veterans headed the Maryland organizations, ten of them being commissioned officers, prior to affiliation with the General Society. Many commissioned officers since affiliation have served as president.

Turning their attention toward New York, the conference committee ran headlong into a problem. Veterans of the War of 1812 in New York expressed interest in forming a state society that would become affiliated with the General Society; indeed, several of the General Society's founders lived in New York. However, an organization did exist in that state. On 3 January 1826 *The Military Society* of the War of 1812 had been formed by veterans of that war. As its numbers decreased, it consolidated with the *Veteran Corps of Artillery in the State of New York*, an organization that had its origin on 25 November 1790, only seven years after the formation of *The Society of the Cincinnati*. The style used by the association since then has been *The Veteran Corps of Artillery, State of New York, Constituting The Military Society of the War of 1812*. When descendants of veterans of the War of 1812 were admitted in 1892, the style used in the articles of incorporation was simply the *Society of the War of 1812*. Membership eligibility requirements differ for both components, and the Military Society's requirements are similar to but not identical to those established for affiliates of the General Society. To surmount this obstacle, veterans in New York formed an association which was incorporated 6 July 1896 as the *Society of the War of 1812 in the State of New York*. The General Society granted the group a charter on 12 February 1897. A suit in equity was begun by the Veteran Corps of Artillery/Military Society seeking that the new organization be enjoined from using the name *Society of the War of 1812 in the State of New York* owing to the confusion that the similarity of names would cause. The New York Supreme Court agreed with the older society, and on 8 September 1900 ordered a change of name. The resulting style was *The Society of the Second War with Great Britain in the State of New York*, less formally known as "The New York Division of the General Society of the War of 1812." Numerous efforts have been made without success to unite the two organizations. There is extensive overlapping of membership, and cordial relations exist despite resistance to suggestions for merger.

During the time discussions were being held in Philadelphia between the Pennsylvania and Maryland societies, representatives from veterans' groups in Massachusetts and Connecticut were in attendance. On 4 April 1894 the Society of the War of 1812 in the Commonwealth of Massachusetts was founded and on 10 September 1894 the Society was incorporated. Connecticut formed its Society on 5 April 1894 with incorporation following the next day. Immediately these four state organizations became the "charter members" of the *General Society of the War of 1812* which had sprouted from the side of the *Society of the War of 1812 in the Commonwealth of Pennsylvania*. It should be noted the General Society's incorporation is derived from that of the Pennsylvania organization. The General Society, two years in the planning, became a reality on 14 April 1894 at Independence Hall.

A group of veterans and descendants in Ohio formed the *Society of the War of 1812 in the State of Ohio* on 8 January 1895 and were admitted to the General Society shortly thereafter. Forty one members were recruited during the next three years, and then the association became dormant. The General Society revoked its charter, effective 1 January 1911. Renewed interest resulted in reorganization on 27 August 1988, and the charter was returned.

In September 1895 the *Society of the War of 1812 in the State of Illinois* was organized and incorporated. It then was chartered by the General Society. Veterans and their descendants living in and near the national capital founded the *Society of the War of 1812 in the District of Columbia* on 18 April 1896. Many of the founding members were members of the Pennsylvania and Maryland societies whose professional and political responsibilities kept them close to the federal government. The organizational meeting was held at the home of General Adolphus Washington Greeley who was elected the first president of that state society. The General Society presented the District of Columbia society with its charter on 19 June 1896.

Meanwhile, the *Society of the War of 1812 in the State of New York* (later renamed *The Society of the Second War with Great Britain in the State of New York*) was able to add to its rolls 24 members who were in addition to the 12 members holding membership in the Pennsylvania and Massachusetts societies. The New York organization was admitted to the General Society on 12 February 1897.

The Society of the War of 1812 in the State of New Jersey was chartered by the General Society on 21 June 1898, having been organized on 25 February 1898.

In 1901, the *Society of the War of 1812 in the State of Delaware* was established with 20 charter members, most of them Pennsylvanians or Marylanders. Within two or three years the Delaware organization became inactive, owing, probably, to the proximity of the two most senior affiliates of the General Society, Pennsylvania and Maryland. Its charter was revoked effective 1 January 1911.

For a period of twenty-five years no additional societies were chartered. Efforts were made to organize state societies in Virginia and Colorado without success. To add to our historical perspective it may be useful to ponder some of the early membership statistics:

State Society	1911	1912	1914	1915	1916	1920	1922
Pennsylvania	212	201	224	211	213	189	218
Maryland	110	112	140	129	130	101	94
Massachusetts	39	44	54	54	46	41	42
Connecticut	24	24	26	24	24	22	24
Illinois	23	25	38	41	32	35	40
District of Columbia	43	44	44	40	40	40	46
New York	61	64	71	75	75	71	70
New Jersey	31	33	40	38	41	43	46
Total	543	547	637	612	601	542	580

In 1926 the *Society of the War of 1812 in the State of Missouri* was founded by members from the Illinois society. Never having more than 15 members, the Missouri group became dormant after two years. Interest in reviving the Missouri Society is underway at present.

In 1929 the *Society of the War of 1812 in the State of Indiana* was organized with 27 members. Although the Society became inactive after World War II, the extraordinary longevity of some of its members prevented its total demise, and it, too, is experiencing a renewal of interest.

The General Society, in an effort to accommodate those eligible persons whose residence was far removed from an organized state society, created a membership-at-large class in 1935. Eventually, it was anticipated, enough members-at-large in a given area could become the nucleus of a new state society. Moreover, this group could receive into its membership men who had belonged to a state society no longer operating.

On 4 May 1946 the *Society of the War of 1812 in the State of Michigan* was chartered. For many years this group has been held together through the heroic efforts of a few devoted members, and now has begun to show new life.

The last major battle of the War of 1812 occurred near New Orleans where General Jackson vanquished the British troops. In 1951 an organizing campaign took place, and by 8 January 1952—137 years to the day after the American victory—the *Society of the War of 1812 in the State of Louisiana* was chartered.

Within the month following, the Society was incorporated. Today the Louisiana society has the largest membership of any state society in the General Society. Its activities are the highlight of the New Orleans social season.

While nurturing the formation of the Louisiana Society, the late William Henry Pitcher, President General 1956-1960, encouraged the development of state societies in Alabama, Texas and Kentucky. During 1958 organization occurred, and on 8 January 1959 the General Society presented charters to the *Society of the War of 1812 in the State of Texas*, the *Society of the War of 1812 in the State of Alabama*, and the *Society of the War of 1812 in the Commonwealth of Kentucky*. The untimely death of G. Glenn Clift, Kentucky's state historian, and organizing president of the Kentucky Society, hampered the growth of that society.

Gentlemen in North Carolina began organizing a society in 1970, and on 13 March 1971 the General Society presented a charter to the *Society of the War of 1812 in the State of North Carolina*, Florida, to which many northerners flee to avoid the ravages of winter, seemed to be a state where numerous members, including the late President General Pitcher, took up residence. Organization occurred in 1980-1981. By March 1982, the General Society was able to grant charters to Florida, Virginia, Wisconsin, and Minnesota state societies. The *Society of the War of 1812 in the State of Georgia* was chartered on 14 September 1983. The following year the *Society of the War of 1812 in the State of Tennessee* was chartered. Mississippi gentlemen had been trying heroically to form a state society for many years, and finally, in January 1987, their efforts resulted in being chartered by the General Society. The *Society of the War of 1812 in the State of Mississippi* is now a reality, making that state society the twenty-fifth chartered by the General Society, and the twenty-fourth active state society.

Objectives of the General Society were indicated in its first constitution. Among them were the collection and preservation of rolls, records, books, and documents relating to the War of 1812. Through gradual accretion a small collection represented the realization of that goal. Unfortunately, the General Society did not have a headquarters in which its library and archives could be housed. As officers changed, the records and books frequently were lost. Since 1986 the General Society has been able to maintain an archives at the Lancaster County (Pa.) Historical Society. The very small collection of books will grow, it is hoped, into a representative War of 1812 library.

Marking the graves of veterans of the War of 1812 was an early activity of the General Society; the first markers were placed in 1902. They were cast in finegrain bronze and were approximately twelve inches high, exclusive of supporting rod. They cost $1.50 each! In 1904 the National Society, U.S. Daughters of 1812, was given permission to use the General Society's markers. After 1914 the U.S. Daughters of 1812 used its own markers. Approximately thirty years ago the General Society marker—its cost now was $55—became unavailable. Within the last year a new and less expensive General Society "star" marker was designed and manufactured.

Original Veteran Marker

GRAVE MARKER OF THE GENERAL SOCIETY OF THE WAR OF 1812
ADOPTED AT THE BIENNIAL MEETING IN BOSTON, MASSACHUSETTS, JUNE 20, 1902

THE ROSTER
of the
GENERAL SOCIETY OF THE WAR OF 1812
with the
GENERAL SOCIETY FILING NUMBERS
1892 TO 1989

HISTORY with its flickering lamp stumbles along the trail of the past, trying to reconstruct its scenes, to revive its echoes, and kindle with pale gleams the passion of former days.

Winston Churchill

Roster of Membership
BEGINNING 19 NOVEMBER 1892

Veteran Members

ALLEN, GEORGE R., aged 100 years, 6 months. Norwood, N.Y.
  Private. Served 1 year, 6 months. Company Commander, Captain Robinson, New York Militia. In battles of Ogdensburg, New York, 1812, and Lundy's Lane, Canada, 1814.

AMES, DAVID H., aged 100 years, 8 months. Jerseyville, Ill.
  Corporal. Served 1 year. Company Commander, Captain Hovey; Regimental Commander, Colonel Thomas B. Benedict, New York Militia. In battle at Ogdensburg, New York, 1812.

AMICK, JACOB, aged 100 years, 1 month. High View, Va.
  Private. Served one year. Company Commander, Captain F. I. Marston, Thirty-first Virginia Regiment, Colonel Taylor, Commanding. At bombardment of Fort McHenry, Maryland, 1814.

BLAIR, DAVID, aged 95 years, 6 months. Charity P.O., Gallia Co., Ohio.
  Corporal. Served 6 months. Company Commander, Captain Samuel Meulah, Ohio Militia. (Youngest of four brothers who served).

BUFFINGTON, STEPHEN, aged 98 years, 6 months. Swansea Centre, Mass.
  Private. Served 1 month. Company Commander, Captain John Hood, Massachusetts Militia. Stationed at Fort Phoenix, Fair Haven, Massachusetts.

BURROUGHS, WILLIAM, aged 100 years, 6 months. Mountainberg, Ark.
  Sergeant. Served 1 year. Company Commander, Captain Stevens Griffith. Guarded Indian warriors.

16 Veteran Members

CLEVELAND, MOSES, aged 93 years, 6 months.   Dubuque, Iowa.
    Orderly. Served 3 months under his father, Colonel Augustine Cleveland.

COFFMAN, JOSEPH, aged 90 years, 6 months.   Millsap, Parker Co., Texas.
    Drummer. Served 4 years. Company Commander, Captain W. Sumpter, Seventh Regiment, United States Light Infantry. In battle at New Orleans, Louisiana, January 8, 1815.

COON, HEZEKIAH, aged 95 years, 6 months.   Boonesboro, Boone Co., Iowa.
    Private. Served 8 months. Company Commander, Captain Lemuel Potter. Regimental Commander, Colonel Daniel Wright.

CRONK, HIRAM, aged 104 years, 11 months.   Ava, N.Y.
    Private. New York Militia, Captain Fuller's Company, 157th Regiment (Westcott's) Infantry. Served in defense of Sackett's Harbor, N.Y.

CURL, JARROT, aged 97 years, 2 months.   Whitfield, Hickman Co., Tenn.
    Sergeant. Served 7 months. Second Regiment Mounted Volunteers, Colonel Thomas Williamson, Commanding. In battles at New Orleans, Louisiana, December 23, 1814, and January 8, 1815.

CYPHER, JOHN, aged 96 years, 6 months.   Farmer's Creek, Lapeer Co., Mich.
    Private. Served 3 months. Company Commander, Captain Joseph Petre, Michigan Volunteers.

DALLY, ABRAM, aged 97 years, 6 months.   Brooklyn, N.Y.
    Adjutant. Served one year. Company Commander, Captain Andrews, Eleventh Regiment Heavy Artillery. Stationed at Fort Gansevoort, New York. In battle at Lundy's Lane, Canada, 1814.

DROMILLARD, JOSEPH, aged 96 years, 6 months.   Gallipolis, Ohio.
    Fife-Major. Served 2 years. Company Commander, Captain Chum. Regimental Commander, Colonel Robert Safford, Ohio Volunteers. Brigade Commander, General Edward W. Tupper, 1812.

FRANKLIN, ANDREW, aged 100 years.   Burlington, Coffey Co., Kan.
    Private. Served 3 years. Company Commander, Captain Armstrong. Corps Commander, General Scrogden. In battles at Fort Stephenson, Ohio, July, 1813; and Lundy's Lane, Canada, 1814.

FRITZ, MICHAEL, aged 95 years, 6 months.   Friedensburg, Schuylkill Co., Pa.
    Private. Served from September 2, 1814, to March 5, 1815, in Captain Peter Snyder's Company, Second Regiment, (Lieutenant Colonel Adam Ridsher, Commanding), First Brigade, Pennsylvania Militia.

GARDENHIER, GEORGE W., aged 95 years, 6 months.   Meigs Post Office, Tenn.
    Private. Served 1 year. Company Commanders, Captain John Childs and Lieutenant Paul Childs.

Veteran Members 17

GILMORE, WILLIAM, aged 93 years, 6 months.   Montezuma, Cayuga Co., N.Y.
Private. Served 1 year. Company Commander, Captain Bassett. Regimental Commander, Colonel Bloom. Corps Commander, General McClure, New York Militia.

HAINES, WILLIAM JACK, aged 104 years, 6 months.
Memorial Home, St. Louis, Mo.
Private. Served in Captain Gregory's Company, Tennessee Militia. Participated in battle of New Orleans, Louisiana, January 8, 1815.

HENDRON, JOEL, aged 98 years, 6 months.   Spring Water, Livingston Co., N.Y.
Private. Served 1 year. Company Commander, Captain Chester Barrow, New York Militia.

HIGGINS, SAMUEL C., aged 98 years, 6 months.   West Gorham, Maine.
Private. Served 44 days. Company Commander, Captain Barnabas Higgins, Maine Militia.

HOOPER, JAMES, aged 89 years, 6 months.   Baltimore, Md.
Coxswain. Served 3 years on United States Schooner "Comet," Captain Boyle, United States Navy. Cruising in Chesapeake Bay watching British fleet, 1814.

KLOCK, ABRAHAM, aged 91 years, 6 months.   Brier Hill, St. Lawrence Co., N.Y.
Private. Company Commander, Captain Jacob Failing, New York Militia.

LEVY, IRA, aged 93 years, 6 months.   Mt. Vernon, Kennebec Co., Maine.
Private. Served 6 months. Company Commander, Captain Bailey. Regimental Commander, Colonel Wool. Corps Commander, General Hampton, 1813.

LOOMIS, ROBERT, aged 95 years, 6 months.   Liverpool, Medina Co., Ohio.
Sergeant. Served 2 years. Company Commander, Captain Jared Ingersoll. Regimental Commander, Colonel Ethan Allen. In battle at Fort Erie, Canada, 1814.

LOVETT, ERASTUS, aged 96 years.   Rome, Bradford Co., Pa.
Private. Served in Pennsylvania Militia.

LUMBERSON, JOHN, aged 89 years, 9 months.   Baltimore, Md.
Drummer. Company N, First Baltimore Company of Artillery, Captain Charles Pennington. In Battle of Baltimore, September 12 to 14, 1814. Remained in U.S. Army until 1834.

MCCOY, DAVID, 103 years, 6 months.   Redlands, San Bernardino, Cal.
Corporal. Served 2 years. Company Commander, Captain Thomas McGilton. Regimental Commander, Colonel Williams. Corps Commander, General William Henry Harrison. In battle of the Thames, Canada, 1813. (Saw Tecumseh slain.)

18 Veteran Members

MICKLEY, DANIEL, aged 97 years.   Waynesboro, Franklin Co., Pa.
  Sergeant. Served 30 days. Company Commander, Captain Miller, Pennsylvania Militia. First Company fired on by the British in the attack on Baltimore, Maryland, 1814.

MILLER, CHARLES, aged 97 years, 6 months.   Booneville, Oneida Co., N.Y.
  Private. Company Commander, Captain Whitmore, New York Militia. In battle at Sackett's Harbor, New York, 1813.

MOORE, MICHAEL, aged 92 years, 6 months. Lieutenant United States Army.
  20 Seventh Avenue, Brooklyn, N. Y.
  Musician. Served through the war in Captain John Sproul's Company, Thirteenth Regiment, United States Infantry.

MORRIS, HENRY, aged 93 years, 6 months.   Port Chester, N.Y.
  Drummer. Served 1 year. Company Commander, Captain Brett. New York Militia. Served in Block House in the Narrows, New York Harbor, New York.

MURRAY, JOHN, aged 90 years, 6 months.   Boothby, Maine.
  Private. Served 1 year. Company Commander, Captain William M. Reed, Maine Militia.

NYE, CORNELIUS, aged 96 years, 6 months.   Fairfield, Somerset Co., Maine.
  Musician. Served 1 year. Company Commander, Captain Ansel Tobey, Maine Militia.

ORSBURN, DAVID, aged 100 years, 6 months.   Tupper's Plains, Ohio.
  Drummer. Served 6 months. Company Commander, Captain William Hull; Regimental Commander, Colonel Dobbins; Corps Commander, Major General Jacob Brown, United States Army.

OSGOOD, JANNA, aged 98 years, 6 months.   Dundee, Yates Co., N.Y.
  Private. Served 1 year. Company Commander, Captain Levi Dunnie, New York Militia.

PACKARD, SAMUEL, aged 90 years, 6 months.   Rockland, Maine.
  Drummer. Served 1 year. Company Commander, Captain Samuel Tolman, Maine Militia.

PARKS, DAVIS, aged 103 years, 6 months.   Fowler, Clinton Co., Mich.
  Private. Served 1 year. Company Commander, Captain Roswell Lyster, New York Militia.

PEAVEY, JOHN W., aged 95 years, 6 months.   Braintree, Vt.
  Private. Company Commander, Captain Nathaniel Gilman, New Hampshire Militia. Served at Portsmouth, New Hampshire, guarding United States stores.

PHILLIPS, HENRY, aged 100 years. Versailles, Cattskill Co., N.Y.
    Private. Company Commander, Captain Pollard, Independent Indian Company. In action six (6) times on Canadian border; Major General Peter B. Porter, Commanding, 1813–1814.

PIERCE, DYER, aged 101 years, 6 months. Belvidere, Boone Co., Ill.
    Ensign. Served 6 months. Company Commander, Captain Abraham Smith. Served on Canadian frontier.

PITKIN, JOHN, aged 98 years, 6 months. Mount Vernon, Ohio.
    Private. Served 3 years. Company Commander, Captain G. Spencer, Thirtieth Regiment United States Infantry.

POOR, BENJAMIN, aged 91 years. Raymond, N.H.
    Musician. Served in Captain Samuel Shackford's Company, New Hampshire Militia, 1812–1815.

RAY, LEONARD, aged 96 years, 6 months. Beltic, Texas.
    Private. Served 2 years, 7 months. Company Commander, Captain Winslow, Twenty-fourth Regiment United States Infantry, Major Frank Armstrong, Commanding.

RICHARDS, ISAAC, aged 99 years, 6 months. East Machias, Maine.
    Private. Served 3 years. Company Commander, Captain James H. Winslow, Maine Militia.

ROOT, ANON, aged 98 years, 6 months. Whitewater, Wis.
    Private. Served 1 year. Company Commander, Captain Briggs.

SCRUTON, MILES, aged 99 years, 6 months. Merrill, N.H.
    Private. Served 1 month. Company Commander, Captain William Cousins, New Hampshire Militia.

SEXTON, ISAIAH B., aged 87 years, 6 months. Sparta, Kent Co., Mich.
    Waterboy. Served 6 months. Company Commander, Captain Moses Waters, New York Militia.

SIMPSON, PRESLEY, aged 96 years, 6 months. Paris, Bourbon Co., Ky.
    Private. Served 3 months. Company Commander, Captain John De Bell; Regimental Commander, Colonel A. T. Mason; Douglas Brigade, Virginia Militia. In battle at Fort McHenry, Maryland, 1814.

SMART, EDWARD, aged 94 years, 6 months. North Dixmont, Maine.
    Sergeant. Served 1 year. Company Commander, Captain J. Dow; Lieutenant, James Field; Ensign, Nathaniel Muncy; Maine Militia.

SMITH, ELEAZAR, aged 94 years, 6 months. Alexandria, Grafton Co., N.H.
    Private. Served 1 year. Company Commander, Captain Nathan Johnson; Regimental Commander, Colonel Edward Sites. Also served in Captain Joshua Marrium's Company, New Hampshire Militia.

20 Veteran Members

SPARROW, HARVEY, aged 100 years, 6 months. Orleans, Barnstable Co., Mass.
Private. Served 8 months. Company Commander, Captain Moses Higgins, Massachusetts Militia.

SPINNEY, THOMAS, aged 91 years, 6 months. Bay Point, Sagadahoc Co., Maine.
Private. Served 1 year. Company Commander, Captain Richard Hagan; Regimental Commander, Colonel Andrew Reed; Corps Commander, General William King, Maine Militia.

STOUGHT, JACOB, aged 103 years, 6 months. Dadeville, Tallapoosa Co., Ala.
Private. Served 1 year. Company Commander, Captain John McLean, Alabama Volunteers.

STURTEVANT, THOMAS M., aged 92 years, 6 months. Madison, Morris Co., N.J.
Private. Served 1 year. Company Commander, Captain George Ashbridge, New York Militia.

TAYLOR, JORDAN, aged 99 years, 6 months. Buckingham Court House, Va.
Private. Served 1 year. Company Commander, Captain George Booker; Brigadier General Robert B. Taylor's Brigade, Virginia Militia.

TINTO, FREDERICK, aged 98 years, 6 months. Alder Creek, Oneida Co., N.Y.
Private. Served 1 year. Company Commander, Captain Rudolf Root, New York Militia. In battle at Sackett's Harbor, New York, 1813.

TOWNLEY, JAMES, aged 92 years, 6 months. Chili, Coshocton Co., Ohio.
Drummer. Served 3 years. Company Commander, Captain Martin; Regimental Commander, Colonel Phillips, Pennsylvania Volunteers.

WELSH, WILLIAM, aged 94 years, 4 months. Baltimore, Md.
Private. Maryland Militia Independent Blues, Captain Levering, Fifth Regiment, Colonel Sterett. In Battle of Baltimore, September 12, 1814.

WILLIAMS, DAVID J., aged 98 years. Saratoga, N.Y.
Private. Served in New York Militia.

WOOD, JABIN, aged 98 years, 6 months. So. Richland, Oswego Co., N.Y.
Private. Served 1 year. Company Commander, Captain Alvin Smith. In battle at Sackett's Harbor, New York, 1813.

YANCEY, WILLIAM, aged 91 years, 6 months. Daphne, Ala.
Drummer. Served 4 years. Company Commander, Captain Gilbert C. Russell; Regimental Commander, Colonel Purdy. (His father served in same Company.)

YOUNG, NATHANIEL, aged 99 years, 6 months. Linnaeus, Aroostook Co., Maine.
Musician. Served 1 year. Company Commander, Captain Bailey, Maine Militia.

The Roster

MEMBER	ANCESTOR	GEN. SOC. NO.
Hay, Peter Stuart	Hay, Peter	0001
Reilly, Andrew Jackson	Reilly, Paul	0002
Chase, Thomas	Chase, Thomas C.	0003
Johnson, John C.	Johnson, Samuel	0004
Ludington, Marshall Independence Day	Ludington, Zalmon	0005
Hay, William Henry Odenheimer	Hay, Peter	0006
Hay, Maldom	Hay, Peter	0007
Freeburger, Alexander Cooper	Cooper, Robert	0008
Griffith, Louis Philip	Griffith, Howard, Jr.	0009
Miller, Lewis H.	Miller, Andrew	0010
Hadel, Albert Kimberly	Kimberly, Nathaniel	0011
Downs, Samuel Addison	Neven, Thomas	0012
Smith, Robert T.	Smith, Benjamin B.	0013
Hyland, James	Hyland, Henry M.	0014
Cadwalader, John	Cadwalader, Thomas	0015
Reilly, George Francis	Reilly, Paul	0016
Reilly, Paul	Reilly, Paul	0017
Roe, Fayette Washington	Roe, Isaac	0018
Roe, Francis Asbury	Roe, Isaac	0019
Sharpe, Alfred Clarence	Snider, Nicholas	0020
Towle, George Francis	Towle, Joseph	0021
Penrose, George Hoffman	Hoffman, William	0022
Corbusier, William Henry	Myers, Stephen Sloat, Alexander	0023
Spencer, William Gardner	Spencer, Silas	0024
Garrard, Joseph	Garrard, Daniel	0025
Howe, Henry Smith	Sias, Nathaniel	0026
Trenchard, Edward	Trenchard, Edward Barclay, John Mortimer	0027
Allen, Louis Joseph	Stremback, Jacob, Jr. Stremback, Jacob, Sr.	0028
Nichols, Maury	Maury, Abraham	0029
Davenport, Richard Graham	Davenport, Isaiah Graham, George Watson, James	0030
McDowell, William Osborne	Osborne, Enos A.	0031
Rice, Edmund	Rice, Edmund	0032
Long, Oscar Fitzalan	Mabie, Jacob	0033
Webster, Leroy Charles	Webster, John Adams	0034
Bellas, Henry Hobart	Smith, William Rudolph Anthony, Thomas Anthony, Joseph, Jr.	0035

MEMBER	ANCESTOR	GEN. SOC. NO.
Greely, Adolphus W.	Greely, John Balch Cobb, Samuel	0036
Burbank, Clayton Sullivan	Burbank, Sullivan	0037
Frost, Timothy Prescott	Frost, Timothy Moore	0038
Dallas, Alexander J.	Dallas, Alexander James	0039
Remington, Cyrus Kingsbury	Remington, Shadrach	0040
Averill, Henry Ketchum, Jr.	Averill, Henry Ketchum, Sr. Platt, Zephaniah Pitt	0041
Roe, George	Roe, Isaac	0042
Walworth, Hiram	Walworth, Hiram	0043
Wilcox, Reynold Webb	Webb, Reynold	0044
Carr, Camillo Casatti Cadmus	Koontz, John	0045
Wood, Benjamin Franklin	Wood, James	0046
Church, William Conant	Conant, John	0047
Allen, Theodore Lathrop	Allen, Moses	0048
Brooke, John Rutter	Brooke, William	0049
Johnson, Alfred B.	Steele, James	0050
Green, Richard Henry	Green, Richard Todd, William W.	0051
Green, William Webb	Green, Richard	0052
Glentworth, James	Glentworth, James	0053
Clark, Arthur Wellington	Houghton, Ralph Clark, John R.	0054
Murray, Charles Henry	Billings, Andrew Seymour, Hezehiah Murray, Elinu Murray, Dauphin	0055
Westbrook, Frederick Edward	Westerbrook, C. D. Westerbrook, Frederick	0056
Colles, Christopher John	Colles, James	0057
Hoyt, Henry Martyn	Hoyt, Ziba	0058
Abbott, Charles Wheaton, Jr.	Abbott, Joel	0059
Morgan, Appleton	Appleton, James	0060
Alexander, John S.	Alexander, Hugh	0061
Corliss, Augustus Whittemore	Corliss, Ebeneza	0062
Tupper, Tullius C.	Tupper, Charles	0063
Paulding, Charles Henry	Russell, Isaac F.	0064
Hobart, David McKnight	Hobart, Nathaniel Potts Smith, William Rudolph Anthony, Joseph	0065
Hoff, Wm. Bainbridge	Bainbridge, William	0066
Hoff, Arthur Bainbridge	Bainbridge, William	0067
Viele, Sheldon Thompson	Viele, John L. Barton, Benjamin	0068
Bullus, Wm. Ellison	Bullus, John	0069

MEMBER	ANCESTOR	GEN. SOC. NO.
Brooke, John	Brooke, Jesse	0070
Brooke, Benjamin	Brooke, Jesse	0071
Bristol, Henry Brevoort	Brevoort, Henry B.	0072
Dudley, Edgar Swartout	Dudley, Peter	0073
Swartwout, Egerton	Swartwout, Robert	0074
Swartwout, Satterlee	Swartwout, Robert	0075
Eldredge, Edward H.	Eldredge, Oliver	0076
Allen, Edward Gray	Strembeck, Jacob	0077
Collins, Holdridge Ozro	Van Etten, Anthony	0078
Moore, John W.	Mooers, Benjamin	0079
Henry, John William	Kearney, John A.	0080
Willey, Wm. Lithgow	Willey, John	0081
Sanno, James Madison Johnston	Sanno, George Michael	0082
Coe, Charles Pierson	Coe, Darius	0083
Turner, James Varnum Peter	Turner, William	0084
	Turner, Peter	
	Turner, Daniel	
	Turner, Henry Edward	
Taylor, James Lookerman	Taylor, John Bradford	0085
Hollander, Elmer Rand	Baldwin, Charles North	0086
Davis, Augustus Plummer	Davis, Jacob	0087
Winne, Robert L.	Winne, Francis D.	0088
O'Neill, James Wilkes	O'Neill, John	0089
Otto, John	Otto, Jacob S.	0090
Pope, James Worden	Johnson, James	0091
Moore, Harry Thornton	Haws, Joel	0092
Comegys, Wm. Henry	Comegys, Cornelius Parsons	0093
Swayer, James Estcourt	Sawyer, Horace Bucklin	0094
Bryan, Charles Page	Bryan, William	0095
Heyl, Edward Miles	Heyl, Philip	0096
Penrose, Charles Wilkinson	Hoffman, William	0097
	Brown, Jacob	
Voorhies, Gordon	Voorhies, Peter Gordon	0098
Burdett, Charles Lewis	Prescott, Lewis	0099
Van Duersen, Wm. Walter	Van Duersen, William, Jr.	0100
Baker, George T.	Hunt, Ebenezer	0101
Heyl, Charles Heath	Heyl, Philip	0102
French, Wm. Freeman	Beach, Samuel, Jr.	0103
Hammond, Andrew Goodrich	Ripley, Franklin	0104
Morgan, James Henry	Morgan, Avery	0105
Henry, James Malcolm	Kearney, John A.	0106
Keys, Alexander Brooks	Brooks, Alexander Scammell	0107
	Brooks, John	
Benham, Henry Hill	McNeil, John	0108

MEMBER	ANCESTOR	GEN. SOC. NO.
Porter, John Biddle	Biddle, John	0109
Alden, Charles Henry Jr.	Alden, Charles Henry	0110
Von Schrader, Frederick	Bissel, Daniel	0111
Lewis, Albert Nelson	Lewis, Elisha	0112
Sanford, George Bliss	Sanford, Hervey	0113
	Sanford, Elihu Jr.	
Horton, William Edward	Clarke, William	0114
Atkinson, Benjamin Walker	Atkinson, Henry	0115
	Walker, Benjamin	
Jackson, Charles B.	Sitcher, Andrew	0116
Philbrook, Charles Frederick Bacon	Philbrook, Alfred Spooner	0117
	Philbrook, Benjamin	
	Sly, John, Jr.	
	Sly, John	
	Bacon, Jonathan	
Shubrick, Edward Rutledge	Shubrick, Edward Rutledge	0118
Wallace, Herbert Fairfax	Brooke, William	0119
Baird, Henry Carey	Baird, Thomas James	0120
Webster, Edmund Kirby	Smith, Joseph Lee	0121
Sutherland, Charles	Sutherland, Joel B.	0122
Mason, Theodorus Bailey Myers	Myers, Mordecai	0123
Wetherbee, Winthrop	Holden, Moses	0124
Gordon, Ray Tompkins	Tompkins, Daniel D.	0125
Fowler, Edward Sydney	Fowler, Gilbert Odgen	0126
	Belknap, Chauncey	
Appleton, Daniel Fuller	Appleton, James	0127
Williams, Charles	Randall, Josiah	0128
Stull, Adam Arbuckle	Stull, Adam	0129
	Delaney, Jacob	
Hoffman, Alexander Wm.	Hoffman, William	0130
Parker, Montgomery Davis	Davis, Amasa	0131
Hughes, Henry Douglas	Hughes, Edward	0132
Barbour, Charles Justin	Dart, Reuben	0133
	Jennings, Jonathan	
Hayden, Horace Edwin	Hayden, Horace H.	0134
	Robinson, Nicholas Nixon	
	Manlove, John	
	Robinson, Benjamin Hazel	
	Hawes (House), John	
Ford, John Donaldson	Ford, John	0135
Biddle, John	Biddle, John	0136
Sparhawk, Charles Wurts	Sparhawk, Thomas	0137
	Vanuxem, Lewis Clark	
Muhlenberg, Francis Benjamin	Muhlenberg, Peter, Jr.	0138
Buffum, Wm. Mansfield	Buffum, James R.	0139
	Swan, Benjamin	

The Roster 25

MEMBER	ANCESTOR	GEN. SOC. NO.
Townsend, James Hill	Mead, Artemus	0140
Haight, Frederick Everest	Cook, Joel	0141
Garlington, Ernest Albert	Garlington, Christopher	0142
MacDonald, Malcolm	MacDonald, John	0143
	Hyde, John	
Hodgkins, Joseph Wilson	Bubier, John	0144
Sparhawk, John, Jr.	Sparhawk, Thomas	0145
	Vanuxem, Lewis Clark	
Adams, Robert, Jr.	Hart, William H.	0146
Mills, Stephen Crosby	Crosby, Stephen	0147
Gardner, Asa Bird	Bentley, John	0148
Ambrose, Paul	Oliver, Paul Ambrose	0149
Frazer, Persifor	Cave, Thomas, Jr.	0150
Wessells, Charles H.	Wessels, John	0151
Frick, Albert W.	Frick, Jacob	0152
Leidy, Philip	Leidy, Philip	0153
Wood, Charles Ogden	Wood, John	0154
Warren, Henry Dexter	Roby, Joseph Warren	0155
Daneker, William H.	Daneker, John Jacob	0156
Bristow, Frank Henry	Sickles, Daniel	0157
		0158 Void
		0159 Void
		0160 Void
Poore, Benjamin Andrew	Poore, Andrew	0161
Robe, Charles Franklin	Robe, Roswell	0162
McClellan, John	McClellan, John	0163
Clement, Charles Maxwell	Clement, Evan C.	0164
Hoffman, Eugene Baker	Hoffman, William	0165
Hoffman, Charles Wheeler	Hoffman, William	0166
Reip, Alfred H.	Reip, Henry	0167
Wright, John Randolph	Wright, John	0168
Reip, Thomas Henry	Reip, Henry	0169
Schminke, Frederick William	Schminke, George	0170
Warner, John Edwin	Warner, Andrew E.	0171
Christhilf, Edward	Christhilf, Harry	0172
Taylor, Clifford	Taylor, William	0173
Carr, James Edward Jr.	Wright, John	0174
Deal, John Thomas Jr.	Stewart, Thomas	0175
Morling, Frank L.	Watts, Thomas B.	0176
Merrikin, David Welles	Merrikin, Joseph R.	0177
Primrose, Samuel Fletcher	Hush, Samuel	0178
Chambers, Robert Marion	Chambers, John McLaughlin	0179
Long, Wm. Frederick	Long, Jesse	0180

MEMBER	ANCESTOR	GEN. SOC. NO.
Carr, Alfred Jarrett	Wright, John	0181
Mills, Ezekiel Jr.	Mills, Ezekiel, Sr.	0182
Howard, Ernest	Wright, John	0183
Long, Samuel Burkett	Long, Jesse	0184
Hough, John Edward	Sumwalt, John T.	0185
Sadtler, Howard Plitt	Sadtler, Philip B.	0186
Watts, Benjamin	Watts, Nathaniel	0187
Buckingham, Charles Wesley	Buckingham, Levi	0188
Nicoll, Benjamin Brevard	Nicoll, Thomas	0189
Dutton, Thomas Waltham	Dutton, John	0190
Hall, Joseph Cotton	Hall, Joseph	0191
Mills, George Albert	Mills, Ezekiel, Sr.	0192
Smith, Asa H.	Smith, Benjamin B.	0193
Marr, William G.	Merrikin, Joseph	0194
Marr, Robert E. L.	Merrikin, Joseph	0195
Ord, Edward. O. C.	Ord, James	0196
MacKinley, William E. W.	Gibson, John	0197
	Trumbo, Matthias	
	Scofield, Thomas E.	
Potter, William	Bower, Jacob	0198
Viven, John Ludlow	Viven, John	0199
Snyder, George Duncan	Snyder, Simon	0200
Keim, Beverley Randolph	Randolph, Thomas Beverley	0201
Wetherill, Alexander Macomb	Macomb, Alexander	0202
Mackenzie, George Norbury	Mackenzie, Thomas	0203
	Downing, Howell	
Lowry, Nathan Parks	Dutton, John	0204
Townsend, Rufus M.	Boyd, George	0205
Sproat, Harris Elric	Sproat, James William	0206
Sadtler, Charles Herbert	Sadtler, Philip B.	0207
Easter, Arthur Miller	Klein, Lewis	0208
	Miller, Daniel	
Warner, George E.	Warner, Andrew E.	0209
Lowry, Robert Kelly	Dutton, John	0210
	Lowry, James	
Read, John Joseph	Read, Samuel J.	0211
Case, David Brainard	Scott, William G.	0212
Wood, Marshall William	Marshall, Joseph	0213
Lindesmith, Eli Eashington	Lindesmith, Daniel	0214
Gregg, Levi Laertes	Parish, Levi Hardin	0215
Nash, Charles Wesley	Davey, Hugh	0216
Contee, Richard	Contee, John	0217
Ford, Thomas G.	Darling, James	0218
Anderson, Thomas McArthur	McArthur, Duncan	0219

The Roster 27

MEMBER	ANCESTOR	GEN. SOC. NO.
Rockenbach, Samuel Dickerson	Hannah, William	0220
Alden, Charles Henry	Alden, Charles Henry	0221
Vanuxem, Louis Clark	Vanuxem, Louis Clark	0222
Henry, John Francis, Jr.	Gale, Peter	0223
Watmough, James Horatic	Watmough, John Goddard	0224
Potter, Thomas, Jr.	Bower, Jacob	0225
Backus, Brady Electur	Backus, Electur Malloy	0226
Bulloch, Joseph G.	Lewis, John	0227
Whyte, Wm. Pinkney, Jr.	Whyte, Joseph Pinkney, William	0228
Barrett, John L.	Barrett, John M.	0229
Collins, Charles Lee	Coffin, Robert Stevenson	0230
Rawle, William Brooke	Rawle, William, Jr.	0231
Johnson, Harvey	Johnson, James	0232
Burton, Chester Warren	Burton, Hiram Burton, Simon Burton, Salmon Burton, Simon, Jr. Burton, William Millett, Samuel	0233
Wetmore, Wm. Boerum	Boerum, William	0234
Blunt, Stanhope English	Blunt, Mark S.	0235
Burgin, George Horace	Burgin, John Lentz, Jacob	0236
McNair, Thomas Speer	McNair, Thomas	0237
Reynolds, William Butler	Reynolds, John	0238
Medairy, George Roberts	Medairy, John	0239
Biddle, Wm. Shepard, Jr.	Biddle, John	0240
Nichols, Henry Kuhl	Nichols, Francis Bonde	0241
Nichols, George Frederick	Nichols, John Lynde, Joanathan	0242
Briggs, Frank Harrison	Briggs, Thomas Otis	0243
Brooks, Francis Mark	Brooke, Nathan	0244
Evans, Ellwood Waller	Waller, William	0245
Goodwin, Charles Ridgely	Goodwin, Robert Norris	0246
Medairy, Jacob Henry	Medairy, John	0247
Dulany, John Mason	Dulany, Samuel	0248
Dulany, William Mason	Dulany, Samuel	0249
Green, Thomas Neving	Neving, Thomas	0250
McCurley, Felix	McCurley, Felix Graham, William	0251
McCurley, James Wallace	McCurley, Felix Fowble, William Graham, William Gould, James	0252

MEMBER	ANCESTOR	GEN. SOC. NO.
Tufford, Walter H.	Tufford, Philip	0253
Chenoweth, Alexander Crawford	Crawford, William Bradford	0254
Pennypacker, Samuel Whitaker	Whitaker, Joseph	0255
Paulding, Tattnall	Paulding, Hiram	0256
Jones, Richmond Legh	Jones, Jehu	0257
Rhoades, Lyman	Harsen, Cornelius	0258
Bailey, Joseph Trowbridge	Bailey, ——	0259
Hains, John Power	Jenkins, William Smythe	0260
Halbertstadt, Baird	Baird, Thomas J.	0261
Woodward, Edwin Tully	Woodward, Theodore	0262
Boughter, Francis	Reichart, John Berry, John	0263
Egle, William Henry	Von Trupel, John	0264
Baker, George Livingston, Jr.	Armistead, George	0265
Rea, Samuel	Rea, John	0266
Lee, Edward Clinton	Lothrop, Thomas	0267
Rupp, Henry Wilson	Wilson, John	0268
Snyder, Frederic Antes	Synder, Simon	0269
Robe, Lucien Stevens	Robe, Roswell Burnham, George W.	0270
Spencer, Wm. Chetwood	Spencer, Oliver Hatfield	0271
Bonnaffon, Ferdinard Victor	Bonnaffon, Anthony	0272
Bonnaffon, Sylvester, Jr.	Bonnaffon, Anthony McClintock, Joseph Allen	0273
Gill, Wm. Harrison	Gill, William Lowry	0274
Dudley, Augustus Palmer	Dudley, Patrick	0275
Gresham, John Chowning	Dunaway, Rawleigh	0276
Worth, William Scott	Worth, William Jenkins	0277
Webb, DeWitt	Webb, John	0278
Wessells, Henry Walton	Palmer, Chillion	0279
Keen, Gregory Bernard	Hutton, John Galt	0280
Horn, Tiemann Newell	Horn, Joseph	0281
Addison, Taylor	Armstrong, Peter	0282
Webster, Frank Daniel	Severance, Benjamin	0283
Sener, Samuel Miller	Fick, Adolph Christian	0284
Albaugh, Jacob	Albaugh, William	0285
Davis, Charles Luken	Davis, Isaac	0286
Mercur, Rodney Augustus	Davis, John	0287
Bouldin, Augustus	Bouldin, John	0288
Cassard, William L.	Cassard, Gilbert	0289
Hooper, James	Veteran	0290
Taylor, Clarence Wills	Crain, Richard More Taylor, William	0291

MEMBER	ANCESTOR	GEN. SOC. NO.
Whipple, Charles Henry	Wright, Benjamin	0292
Laughter, William Hunt	Laughter, John L.	0293
DeYoung, Charles Zadoc	DeYoung, Isaac	0294
Zieber, Eugene	Zieber, Isaac	0295
Pool, Wellington	Pool, William	0296
Cassard, Jesse L.	Cassard, Gilbert	0297
Baker, George Livingston	Beals, Henry	0298
Wakeman, Jessup	Hull, Lyman	0299
Ward, Aaron	Ward, Aaron	0300
Ripley, Winfield Scott, Jr.	Ripley, Uriah	0301
	Perham, Jonathan	
Norwood, Randolph	Norwood, John	0302
Morris, Galloway Cheston	Cheston, James	0303
Denis, Augustus Henry	Carmick, Daniel	0304
Myers, Joseph A.	Goodard, Charles	0305
Sadtler, Christopher Columbus	Sadtler, Philip B.	0306
Curl, Jarrott	Veteran	0307
Wilson, John Appleton	Wilson, Thomas	0308
Merwin, Walter Lee	Merwin, Miles	0309
Pinkerton, Samuel Stanhope Smith	Pinkerton, John White	0310
Haverstick, George Henry	Musser, George	0311
Wright, Jacob Ridgway	Wright, Joseph	0312
Turpin, Morley Bebee	Bebee, James C.	0313
Wayne, William	Wayne, Isaac	0314
Green, James Oscar	Burham, James	0315
Chapman, Paul Goddard	Chapman, Ebenezer	0316
Jackson, Alfred Baury	Jackson, Samuel	0317
	Baury, Frederick	
Oliver, Charles Augustus	Oliver, William George	0318
Hurd, Rukard	Duncan, Alexander	0319
Burgin, Herman	Lentz, Jacob	0320
	Herman, John Caner	
Warner, Culbreth Hopewell	Warner, Michael	0321
Reynolds, Charles Ambrose	Reynolds, John	0322
Coffman, Joseph	Veteran	0323
Cadwalader, Charles Evert	Cadwalader, Thomas	0324
Noyes, James Atkins	Noyes, Daniel Rogers	0325
Noyes, Charles Phelps	Noyes, Daniel Rogers	0326
Wickersham, Robert O'Neill	O'Neill, Robert	0327
Stevens, William Coppee	Stevens, William	0328
Stevens, John Conynham	Stevens, William	0329
Heaton, John Edward	Jennison, Levi	0330

MEMBER	ANCESTOR	GEN. SOC. NO.
Fitch, Edward Sherman	Fitch, Joseph Pratt	0331
	Jones, Daniel	
Chauncey, Harry David	Stevenson, John E. W.	0332
Lamping, William	Starr, William	0333
Sadtler, John Philip Benjamin	Sadtler, Philip B.	0334
Farrington, Charles Lincoln	Farrington, Elijah	0335
Brown, Dudley Parrish	Dudley, William	0336
French, Louis Mardenbrough	Beach, Samuel Jr.	0337
Delafield, Augustus Floyd	Delafield, Edward	0338
Bradley, Cyrus Sherwood	Hull, Lyman	0339
Hamilton, Alexander	Hamilton, John Chruch	0340
Swartwout, John Henry	Swartwout, Robert	0341
		0342 Void
Beatty, Franklin Thomason	Beatty, James	0343
Galloupe, Charles Wm.	Gallop, Isaac	0344
Binney, Amos	Binney, Amos, III	0345
Collamore, John Hoffman	Binney, John	0346
Philbrook, Charles Calhoun	Philbrook, Benjamin	0347
James, George Frank	James, Samuel	0348
Frisbee, Franklin Senter	Butterfield, Joseph	0349
Bowen, Hessa Emery	McDaniel, Matthew	0350
Galloupe, George Augustus	Gallop, Isaac	0351
Higgins, Samuel C.	Veteran	0352
Franklin, Andrew McKee	Veteran	0353
Nye, Cornelius	Veteran	0354
Philbrook, Alfred S.	Philbrook, Benjamin	0355
Smart, Edward	Veteran	0356
Smith, Eleazer	Veteran	0357
Turner, John Clock	Turner, Charles	0358
Andrews, William Taylor	Richards, Ambe	0359
Dickey, Philip Sadtler	Sadtler, Philip B.	0360
Welsh, William	Veteran	0361
Bransby, John C.	Weaver, John	0362
Danaker, Edwin Thomas	Danaker, John Jacob	0363
Craddick, Joseph N.	Craddick, Joseph	0364
		0365 Void
Stickney, George Henry	Stickney, Henry	0366
Norris, Alex Wilson	Swoyer, John	0367
	Stine, George	
Sands, James Thomas	Sands, James	0368
Duane, Russell	Duane, William	0369
Skiddy, Wm Wheelwright	Skiddy, William	0370
Houston, Henry Howard	Houston, Samuel Nelson	0371

The Roster 31

MEMBER	ANCESTOR	GEN. SOC. NO.
Houston, Samuel Frederic	Houston, Samuel Nelson	0372
Derr, Andrew Fein	Derr, Michael	0373
Hart, Byerly	Byerly, John	0374
Wright, George Riddle	Wright, Joseph	0375
Rupp, Henry G.	Wilson, John	0376
Dickey, Charles Herman	Sadtler, Philip B.	0377
Hill, Thomas	Hill, Thomas Gardner	0378
Hill, Samuel Emory	Hill, Thomas Gardner	0379
Strobel, Albert Perigo	Strobel, John Peter	0380
Bulkeley, Morgan Gardner	Morgan, Avery	0381
Cadle, Henry	Cadle, John	0382
Parrish, James Hagerty	Parrish, William Sheaves, Robert	0383
Parrish, William Tippett	Parrish, William Sheaves, Robert	0384
Dorcy, Benjamin Holladay	Downe, Nathaniel H.	0385
O'Neill, James Busick	Busick, John	0386
Marston, John	Marston, John	0387
Boggs, Francis Henry	Boggs, Alexander Lowry	0388
Conrad, James Madison Monroe	Conrad, David	0389
Warfield, Edwin	Watkins, Gassaway	0390
Wilson, John James	Wilson, James	0391
Maloney, James Aloysius	Grady, Anthony	0392
Wade, Samuel Henry	Samble (Sipley), Thomas Wade, Zepheniah Allen, Robert Davis, James	0393
Hill, Nicholas Sluby	Hill, Thomas Gardner	0394
Iglehart, James Davidson	Davidson, James	0395
Cobb, Charles H.	Cobb, Josiah	0396
Dulany, John Highenbotham	Dulany, Samuel	0397
Randall, Watson Beale	Taylor, Lemuel Watson, Thomas Randall, Beale	0398
Dulany, Wm. James Clarke	Dulany, Samuel	0399
Tucker, James Armstrong Owens	Hill, Thomas Gardner	0400
Cole, Robert Clinton	Cole, William	0401
Jones, Hugh Burgess	Jones, Wm. Robinson	0402
Bobart, Charles Carroll	Bobart, Charles Carroll	0403
Peters, Winfield	Furlong, William	0404
Ives, Francis Joseph	Semmes, Raphael	0405
Brice, Philip Howard	Brice, Nicholas	0406
Miner, Sidney Roby	Ross, William	0407
Stevenson, James Madison	Stevenson, John E. W.	0408

32 The Roster

MEMBER	ANCESTOR	GEN. SOC. NO.
Cromwell, Charles	Cromwell, Nathan	0409
O'Neill, Hugh Lewis	Busick, John	0410
Forbush, Wm. Curtis	Forbush, Asa	0411
Jordan, Scott	Jordan, John	0412
Hatcher, Robert Stockwell	Hatcher, Archibald	0413
Manigault, Gabriel E.	Manigault, Charles	0414
Gehring, John George	—	0415
Reed, John Ludovicus	Reed, Henry Ludovicus	0416
Dennis, James Teackle	Wilson, Thomas	0417
Wood, Philip Bryson	Wood, John	0418
Morrell, Edward deVeaux	Powel, John Hare	0419
Ellis, Edward Dimick	Chapman, Asa	0420
Woodman, Clarence Eugene	Woodman, Stephen	0421
Dewey, Hiram Todd	Dewey, Jeremiah	0422
Dewey, George Eugene	Dewey, Jeremiah	0423
Dewey, Hiram Stapleford	Dewey, Jeremiah	0424
Morgan, John Hurst	Berry, John	0425
Culver, Francis Barnum	Appleby, John	0426
Hulse, William Brinkett	Hulse, John	0427
Holloway, Reuben Ross	Ross, Reuben	0428
Shoemaker, Michael Myers	Steiner, Henry Shoemaker, Robert	0429
Lee, Howard Hall Macy	Ford, George W.	0430
Bowen, James Barton	Rensselaer, Cooms	0431
Grannis, George Washington	Grannis, Alva	0432
Warren, Henry Joseph	Raymond, George Bromley	0433
Seymour, Origen Storrs	Sanford, Elihu Jr. Sanford, Hervey	0434
Reid, Samuel Chester	Reid, Samuel Chester	0435
Hastings, Henry	Hastings, Walter	0436
Pearson, Joseph Hiram Starr	Marston, Charles	0437
Soule, Frederick William	Mason, Henry	0438
Gill, Nicholas Rufus	Gill, Stephen	0439
Gill, Robert Lee	Gill, Stephen	0440
Gill, Roger Taney	Gill, Stephen	0441
Cole, John Carroll LeGrand	Hayes, Walter Cody	0442
Wright, George Bohan	Wright, Spencer	0443
Brinkerhoof, Roeliff	Brinkerhoff, George R.	0444
Pendleton, Edmund	Pendleton, Nathaniel Greene	0445
Calhoun, John Franklin	Calhoun, Daniel (David)	0446
Mercur, James Watts	Davis, John	0447
Wilkinson, Ogden Dungan	Wilkinson, Elisha	0448
McCormick, Robert Laird	White, Hugh	0449

The Roster 33

MEMBER	ANCESTOR	GEN. SOC. NO.
O'Neill, Charles Frank	Busick, John	0450
Jones, Stockton White	Eakin, Samuel Hunter	0451
Avery, Frank Montgomery	Avery, Ebenezer, 3rd.	0452
Matlack, John Rugan, Jr.	Vandever, Wm.	0453
Massey, Henry Vogdes	Vodges, Jacob	0454
Townsend, Thomas Gerry	Townsend, Daniel S.	0455
Este, Charles	——	0456
Gard, Daniel Hosmer	Dunsmoor, Phineas	0457
Ward, Hurbert Herrick	Follett, Martin Dewey	0458
Davidson, Robert Mason	Davidson, Robert	0459
Johnston, Lee Ralston	Johnston, William	0460
Johnston, Charles Calvin	Johnston, William	0461
Munson, Marvin Morgan	Munson, Augustine	0462
Conrad, Townsend Nelson	Conrad, David	0463
Saffarrans, George Coolidge	McCartney, John	0464
Massey, Frank Hogan	Vogdes, Jacob	0465
Gilmore, Tiffin	Gilmore, William Young	0466
VanDuersen, Wm. Walter	VanDuersen, William Jr.	0467
Nelson, William Wallace	Nelson, Benjamin	0468
Turney, Omer Asa	Winchester, Johnadab	0469
Gaumer, Daniel H.	Gaumer, Daniel Barrett, John	0470
Swearingen, Thomas Townsley Van	Swearingen, James Strode	0471
Binney, Arthur	Binney, Amos, 3rd. Binney, John	0472
Gage, Seth Newton	Arnold, Seth Shaler	0473
Sayres, Edward Stalker	Humes, Samuel	0474
Damon, Albert Forster	Damon, Joseph	0475
Damon, Edwin Adams	Damon, Joseph	0476
Reid, Henry Nelson	Goldsberry, Thomas	0477
Hatfield, Henry Reed	Hatfield, Adam	0478
James, John Faraday	Hubbs, Zebulon Townsend	0479
Spangler, Tileston Fracker	Spangler, Jacob	0480
Rankin, John Hall	Jefferies, John	0481
Robbins, Howard Sumner	Robbins, Josiah	0482
Binney, William Greene	Binney, Amos, 3rd. Binney, John	0483
Weeks, John Wingate	Weeks, John Wingate	0484
Blaisdell, Frank Moses	Bladisdell, Moses	0485
Adams, William Porter	Davis, Eliphalet	0486
Flint, Wyman Kneeland	Gregg, William Martin, Wait	0487
Roberts, Charles Bailey	Rich, Reuben	0488

34 The Roster

MEMBER	ANCESTOR	GEN. SOC. NO.
Keplinger, John Bernard	Keplinger, Michael	0489
Miffling, James	Mifflin, John Ross	0490
Faber, Willis Henry	Faber, Samuel	0491
Haddock, Stanley Brickett	Shinn, John, Jr.	0492
Laubenstein, Ezekias	Fritz, Michael	0493
Schultz, Bernard Van Horne	VanHorne, Isaac Darlington, Meredith	0494
Patterson, Wm. Houston	Patterson, Robert	0495
Davidson, Robert Mason	Davidson, Robert	0496
Aldrich, Orlando Wesley	York, Stephen	0497
Ward, Harry Parker	Follett, Martin Dewey	0498
Brinkerhoff, Roecliff	Brinkerhoff, George R.	0499
Ward, Hurbert Herrick	Follett, Martin Dewey	0500
Franklin, Robert Scott	Swearingen, James Strode	0501
Darrow, Walter Nicholas Paine	Darrow, Leavitt	0502
Woltz, James Mitchell	Hoddy, Robert Hoddy, Richard Hoddy, John Shepherd, John Shepherd, David	0503
Norton, Thomas Herbert	Horsford, Jedaiah	0504
		0505 Void
Wright, George Mitchell	Wright, Alpha	0506
Elliott, Thomas Ireland	Bunting, John	0507
Carr, William Edwin	Wright, John	0508
Brown, Willis	Prindle, Eleaxer	0509
Packard, Ambrose	Packard, Ambrose	0510
Hall, Bordman	Hall, Frye	0511
Jordon, William Meserve	Porter, Stephen	0512
Lumberson, John	Veteran	0513
Rice, Lewis	Brigham, Nathaniel	0514
Green, Frank Delaplaine	Green, Isaac	0515
Rogers, Archibald	Drummer, Stephen	0516
Yeager, Frederick Musser	Yeager, Daniel	0517
Halberstadt, George Howell	Baird, Thomas James	0518
Stamford, Llewellyn M.	Beach, Peter	0519
Noble, Henry Harmon	Noble, Ransom McNeil, Charles	0520
Hyde, James Clarence	Clark, Norman	0521
Hyde, Raymond Newton	Clark, Norman	0522
Patterson, Robert	Patterson, Robert	0523
Pepper, Edward	Cave, Thomas	0524
McCulloch, Champe Carter, Jr.	McCulloch, Wm. Horsley	0525
Frazer, James Patriot Wilson	Steele, John, Jr.	0526

The Roster 35

MEMBER	ANCESTOR	GEN. SOC. NO.
Frazer, Reah	Steele, John, Jr.	0527
Brewster, Henry Colvin	Brewster, Elisha Belcher	0528
Benjamin, Marcus	Hough, Ezra	0529
MacDonough, Rodney	MacDonough, Thomas	0530
	Hackstaff, William Greene	
Brown, Harold Atherton	Prindle, Eleazer	0531
Rogers, Edward Sidney	Fisher, Messenger	0532
	Harriman, James	
	Nickerson, Warren	
	Fletcher, William	
Woodard, Theron Royal	Perkins, John, Jr.	0533
Young, E. Weldon	Young, William	0534
Martin, Harry Culver	Monmonier, Francis	0535
Comegys, Benjamin Bartis	Comegys, Cornelius Parsons	0536
McCain, George Nox	Rockefeller, Henry	0537
Jarves, Deming	Jarves, Deming	0538
Burt, Andrew Sheridan	Gano, John S.	0539
Follett, Edgar Austin	Follett, Martin Dewey	0540
	Wright, Spencer	
Lakee, Eugene	Kendall, Johnson	0541
Dickey, John Lincoln	Peterson, Martin	0542
Clark, Alonzo Howard	Carnes, John	0543
VanDyke, Harry Weaton	Edson, Joseph	0544
		0545 Void
Coe, Henry Clark	Coe, Adam Simmons	0546
Johnson, James Bowen	Johnson, Jeremiah	0547
Smith, Ormond Gerald	Smith, Moses Rogers	0548
Webb, Henry Randall	Randall, Henry Knapp	0549
Watkins, John Elfreth	Elfreth, John	0550
		0551 Void
Chambers, Charles Houghtaling	Chambers, Ralph	0552
Chambers, Walter Lee	Chambers, Ralph	0553
Fretz, John Edgar	Johnston, David	0554
Bolles, Charles Harrington	Bolles, Frederick D.	0555
Shirley, Rufus George	Gautier, John Sinclair	0556
	Sidell, John, Jr.	
Wilson, John Sanford	Wilson, John Sanford	0557
Marine, William Matthew	Knowles, William	0558
Johnson, James Bowen	Johnson, Jeremiah	0559
Noel, Jacob Edmond	Noel, Jacob	0560
Walton, H. Harrison	Walton, Nathaniel	0561
Buchanan, William Insco	Buchanan, George	0562
Baker, William Spohn	Baker, George Nice	0563
Carleton, Horace Morrison	Morrison, Jonathan	0564

36 *The Roster*

MEMBER	ANCESTOR	GEN. SOC. NO.
McCulloch, Robert Lemmon	Gleim, Christian	0565
Robeson, John Terrell	Robson, Robert Amsy	0566
Clark, Alonzo Howard	Carnes, John	0567
Smith, Frank Birge	Birge, Cyrus	0568
Henry, John William	Kearney, John A.	0569
Watkins, John Elfreth	Elfreth, John	0570
Howard, William Hanson	——	0571
Wilson, Frank Stedman	Wilson, Andrew	0572
Cox, Edwin Birchard	Cox, Matthew	0573
Cox, William Emerson	Cox, Matthew	0574
Winlock, William Cranford	Winlock, Joseph	0575
McMaster, George Hunter	McMaster, John	0576
Sill, Harold Montgomery	Dunlap, Sallows	0577
Rhinelander, Philip	Rhinelander, Wm. Christopher	0578
Watkins, John Elfreth, Jr.	Elfreth, John	0579
Winlock, Wm. Crawford	Winlock, Joseph	0580
Calder, Charles Grant	Grinnell, Moses	0581
Stewart, James Edmundson	Stewart, George H.	0582
Reynolds, Wm. Butler	Reynolds, John	0583
Birkhaeuser, Theodore Kelso	Armstrong, Samuel	0584
Chambers, Elias Hullfish	Chambers, Ralph	0585
Baird, James Mercer	Cooper, Francis	0586
VanDyke, Harry Weston	Edson, Joseph	0587
Coleman, Leighton	Coleman, John	0588
Baker, George Comstock	Comstock, Peter	0589
Graves, Henry Duncan	Graves, Jeremiah	0590
Miller, Sylvester Barton	Miller, Thomas	0591
Jones, Nathan Henry	Blish, Daniel Jones, Nathan	0592
Beckwith, George Henry	Mooers, Benjamin Hazen	0593
Cady, Hiram Walworth	Mooers, Benjamin John	0594
Larkin, Orrell Town	Larkin, Elam	0595
King, Charles Alfred Ely	Ely (Eli), George	0596
Nichols, Thomas Brainerd	Nichols, Levi	0597
Sheldon, Henry Luther	Sheldon, Samuel Sheldon, Walter	0598
Weed, George Standish	Standish, Matthew Mead, Smith Roberts, John	0599
Erwin, James J.	Morrow, William	0600
Brown, Walter Scott	Brown, Levi	0601
Wadhams, Frederick Eugene	Wadhams, Luman Cole, Samuel	0602
Ridgate, Thomas Howe	Ridgate, Benjamin Cornick	0603

MEMBER	ANCESTOR	GEN. SOC. NO.
Joy, William Francis	Joy, Francis	0604
Allen, Crawford Carter	Allen, Howard	0605
Arnold, Allen	Lowd, Allen	0606
Chandler, Frederick Emerson	Henderson, Daniel	0607
Bull, Robert Berry	Berry, John	0608
Hayden, Charles Leslie	Hayden, Horace H.	0609
Rothermel, John Jacob	Fick, Adolph Christian	0610
Hord, Arnold Harris	Hord, Elias Armstrong, Robert Armstrong, John	0611
Griffith, Wm. Herrick	Griffith, Joshua	0612
Jenkins, Francis deSales	Jenkins, Edward Jenkins, John I.	0613
Jenkins, Edward Austin	Jenkins, Edward Jenkins, John I.	0614
Peck, John Ama	Peck, John A.	0615
Holcombe, John Marshall	Johnson, Nathan	0616
Holmes, George James	Holmes, Bartlett	0617
Whitney, Eli	Dalliba, James	0618
Hyde, Frank Charles	Clark, Norman, Jr.	0619
Lockhart, Jacob Trumbull	Lockhart, Thomas	0620
Slocum, James Edward	Kendall, Johnson	0621
Tootle, Milton, Jr.	Subte, Lewis	0622
Nevers, Edward	Liswell, Thomas	0623
Douglas, Archer Wall	Brown, Thomas	0624
Cox, James William	Cox, Thomas	0625
Baker, Laurence Clark	Comstock, Peter	0626
Bernard, Alfred Duncan	Gore, George	0627
Saxton, Henry Dearborn	Clary, Ethan Allen	0628
Elder, William Henry	Elder, Basil Spalding	0629
Fogg, Arthur Lloyd	Fogg, Nathan	0630
Townsend, Thomas Gerry	Townsend, Daniel S.	0631
Hester, Jacob	Hester, John Dipolt	0632
McCurdy, Irwin Pounds	McCurdy, Alexander Doty, Nathaniel	0633
Yeager, James Martin	Yeager, Jacob	0634
Glass, James Gamewell	Glass, John	0635
Kelly, William Dunham	Sage, Hezekiah, Jr.	0636
Cook, Joseph Tottenham	Tottingham, Joseph	0637
Bonnaffon, Sylvester, III	Bonnaffon, Anthony	0638
Hand, Billings Learned	Hand, Samuel	0639
Payne, Daniel Safford French	French, Joel	0640
Peck, William Noble	Noble, Daniel	0641
McKelvey, William James	Scofield, Jacob Smith	0642

MEMBER	ANCESTOR	GEN. SOC. NO.
Warren, Albert Marshall	Marshall, Jonathan	0643
Wadhams, Albion Varet	Wadhams, Luman	0644
	Cole, Samuel	
Hough, Pliny Miles	Sumwalt, John T.	0645
Boucher, Charles	Boucher, Henry	0646
Murphey, Elijah Warriner	Murphey, Elijah	0647
Burroughs, James DeForris	Goodrich, Silas	0648
Knott, Aloysius Leo	Knott, Edward	0649
Bascombe, Western Radford	Kearney, Stephen Watts	0650
Foster, Volney William	Foster, John C.	0651
Allen, John Vincent	Allen, John	0652
Kelly, Luther Sage	Sage, Hezekiah, Jr.	0653
Johnston, John Alexander	Sweeney, Daniel	0654
Greve, Charles Theodore	Emery, John	0655
Pierce, George Francis	Pierce, Lewis	0656
Edge, Nelson James Harrison	Edge, Isaac, II	0657
Daly, Martin Ordway	Daly, James	0658
	Tolman, Robert Pierce	
Hess, Frank Judson	Hess, Denis	0659
Shoemaker, James Duncan	DeForest, Philip	0660
Cowen, Benjamin Rush	Cowen, Benjamin Sprague	0661
Buck, George Hickman	Buck, Benjamin	0662
Gardner, George Clinton	Gardner, Charles Kitchell	0663
Culver, Charles Mortimer	Rodman, Joseph	0664
Barrell, Harry Ferdinand	Wood, John	0665
Runyan, Forrest Mitchell	Runyan, Joseph	0666
Shoemaker, Harvey	Hester, John Dipolt	0667
Shoemaker, Joshua Lippincott	Hester, John Dipolt	0668
Shoemaker, Owen	Hester, John Dipolt	0669
Robeson, Fielding Tecumsch	Robeson, Robert Amay	0670
Crowell, Samuel Babcock	Babcock, Samuel, Jr.	0671
	Babcock, Samuel, Sr.	
Darrach, Edgar	Darrach, Thomas Bradford	0672
McCullough, Robert A.	———	0673
Vickers, Wm. Handy Collins	Vickers, Joel	0674
	Wilmer, John Williamson	
Mason, Theodorus Bailey Myers	Myers, Mordecai	0675
Robinson, Herbert Fulwiler	Mahan, Alexander	0676
Parsons, Charles Sumner	Parsons, John	0677
Ball, Flamen, Jr.	Follett, Oran	0678
Keim, DeBenneville Randolph	Randolph, Thomas Beverly	0679
Estes, Frederick Anson	Goodwin, Tristam	0680
Hayes, George Charles	Hayes, Joseph	0681

The Roster 39

MEMBER	ANCESTOR	GEN. SOC. NO.
Schermerhorn, Frank Earl	Benton, Samuel	0682
Alford, George Willaim	Gilder, Reuben	0683
Kiersted, Andrew Jackson	Kiersted, Lake	0684
Leary, Peter, Jr.	Leary, Peter	0685
Robinson, Edward Augustus	Tuck, Levi	0686
Owens, Edward Burneston	Owens, Joseph	0687
	Buck, Benjamin	
Arthurs, Edward Ferguson	Ferguson, William	0688
Gaither, Alfred	Gaither, Henry	0689
Harrison, Thomas	Harrison, Gustavus	0690
	Magruder, George	
Talbott, Hattersly Worthington	Talbott, Richard	0691
Neilson, Robert Musgrave	Neilson, Robert	0692
McNeal, Joshua Vansant	McNeal, James	0693
Clark, Augustus Taylor	Aldrich, Thomas Canby	0694
Birckhead, Lennox	Birckhead, Hugh	0695
Condit, Oscar Halsted	Condit, Jothan	0696
Hunt, Adelbert Bancroft	Moulton, Abel	0697
Barrell, Joseph E. M.	Wood, John	0698
Lardner, James Lawrence	Lardner, Lynford	0699
Baird, William Mercer	Cooper, Francis	0700
Satterlee, Herbert Livingston	Wilcox, DeLafayette	0701
Hull, William	Wheeler, Joseph	0702
Beale, Charles Frederick Tiffany	Beale, Chester	0703
Johnson, Joseph Taber	Johnson, Jeremiah	0704
Gard, Wordsworth	Dunsmoor, Phineas	0705
Caldwell, Newton W.	Stone, Oliver	0706
Holden, James Cotton	Holden, Horace	0707
Jones, W. H.	Carter, Ephriam, Jr.	0708
Weeks, Wm. Raymond	Weeks, Wm. Raymond	0709
Dewey, George	Dewey, Simeon	0710
Bromley, John Lewis	Bromley, Lewis	0711
Rusk, Jacob Krebs, Jr.	Rusk, George	0712
Richardson, George Eliot	Richardson, Alford	0713
Richards, Jeremiah	Richards, John	0714
Richards, Charles Spielmann	Richards, John	0715
Skinner, Henry Whipple	Whipple, John	0716
Denman, Abram C., Jr.	Halsey, Jacob B.	0717
Parkhurst, Charles Dyer	Tanner, Christopher	0718
Schauffler, Wm. Gray	Reynolds, Samuel	0719
Jones, Albert Sydney	LaTourrette, Peter	0720
Hall, John William	McComas, Nicholas	0721
Thornton, James Brown	Thornton, James Brown	0722

MEMBER	ANCESTOR	GEN. SOC. NO.
Branch, Henry	Harris, Benjamin James	0723
Branch, Charles Henry Hardin	Chiem, Richard Henry	0724
	Harris, Benjamin James	
Kirkman, George Wyckerly	Walker, William	0725
McCormick, W. Laird	White, Hugh	0726
McCord, James Hamilton	Field, John	0727
Baker, George Fales	Rush, Lewis	0728
Alford, Reuben Gilder	Gilder, Reuben	0729
Wadsworth, Charles, Jr.	Wadsworth, Elijah	0730
Crowell, James Gardner	Babcock, Samuel, Jr.	0731
	Babcock, Samuel, Sr.	
Walton, George Edward Cooper	Cooper, Francis	0732
Hinds, Ernest	Hinds, Byram	0733
Hargett, Douglass Henry	Burns, James	0734
Bates, Theodore Cornelius	Bates, Obadiah	0735
Amee, Albert Francis	Amee, Jacob	0736
Lunt, William Wallace	Curtis, Lebbeus	0737
Galloney, Frank Hutchinson	Kirkpatrick, David	0738
Eastwick, Charles Henry	Eastwick, Thomas	0739
Douglass, Robert Dunn	Douglass, George	0740
Douglass, Robert Graham Dunn	Douglass, George	0741
Douglass, Benjamin Dun	Douglass, George	0742
Comegys, Edward Tiffin	Comegys, Cornelius Parsons	0743
Corwin, David Rittenhouse Porter	Corwin, David, Jr.	0744
Dunlap, Sallows	Dunlap, Sallows	0745
Whitney, Eugene Walcott	Pierce, Presevied	0746
Teale, Charles Edward	Teale, John Cranmer	0747
Willard, James LeBarron	LeBarron, James	0748
Keith, Solomon Lorin	Keith, Solomon	0749
Hawkins, Elijah	Hawkins, Elijah	0750
Riggs, Manfred Moses	Riggs, Moses	0751
Harrison, Carter	Russell, William	0752
Burnett, Willard Elmer	Gale, Charles	0753
Wall, Alfred Clements	Clements, Reuben	0754
Burbank, Charles Decker	Burbank, Peter	0755
Fisk, Charles William	Ball, Cyrus	0756
	Ten Broeck, John	
Richards, George Herbert	Kays, Samuel	0757
	Richards, Cyrus George	
Conover, Arthur Van Derveer	Read, Samuel J.	0758
Bates, William Graves	Bates, Levi	0759
Fotterall, Stephen Blakely	Fotterall, Stephen Egan	0760
Clarkson, John Van Boskerck	Van Boskerck, John	0761

The Roster 41

MEMBER	ANCESTOR	GEN. SOC. NO.
Evans, Frank Brooke	Evans, James	0762
	Berrell, Jeremiah	
Ashmead, William Harris	Graham, Thomas	0763
Brandel, Littleton Chandler	Brandel, William	0764
Sadtler, Charles Edward	Sadtler, Philip B.	0765
Obertenffer, Reece Marriner	Moulder, John Nicholson	0766
Obertenffer, Herman Freytag	Moulder, John Nicholson	0767
Porter, Augustus Drum	Reed, William	0768
Hall, Harrison	Hall, James	0769
Tilden, Albert Colburn	Tilden, Luther	0770
Cronk, Hiram	Veteran	0771
Neilson, George Peabody	Neilson, Robert	0772
Brown, George Edward	Brown, Amasa	0773
Curtis, Hanford Lorenzo	Curtis, Ebenezer	0774
Seavey, Fred Hannibal	Fernald, Josiah	0775
Henry, William Louis	Henry, Stephen Chambers	0776
Wyeth, Huston	Morris, Presley	0777
Woodward, M. Stevens	——	0778
Deadman, William Fiske	Deadman, William	0779
Holden, Edward Packard	Holden, Horace	0780
Pendergast, James Lynch	Lynch, James	0781
Kennedy, Francis Sudlow	Kennedy, Ebenezer Briggs	0782
Redman, John Lyne	Redman, John	0783
Megaw, Fred Holmes	Ford, Isaac	0784
Ransom, Porter Virgil	Morgan, Lodowick	0785
Nichols, James Allen	Nichols, Levi, Jr.	0786
	Walbridge, Solomon	
Buckenham, John Edgar Burnett	Huston, John, Jr.	0787
Hedges, Job Elmer	Brittin, William	0788
Williams, Charles Collier	Williams, Robert Pearce	0789
Pear, Albert Marston	Fuller, Daniel	0790
Freeman, William	Clarke, Thomas	0791
Lake, Richard Pinkney	Lake, George	0792
	Lake, Washington	
Craiger, Sherman Montrose	Vanderslice, Edward	0793
Burton, LeGrand Stirling	Germain, Stephen	0794
Brown, Henry Kirk Bush	Udall, James	0795
Holland, Joseph	Holland, Jonah	0796
Thomas, Frank Warner	Sprague, Joshua	0797
	Thomas, Andrew	
Judson, William Pierson	Pierson, Philo	0798
Wadhams, Albion James	Wadhams, Luman	0799
Fairchild, Benjamin Clyde	Fairchild, Benjamin Smith	0800
	Morhous, Michael	

42 The Roster

MEMBER	ANCESTOR	GEN. SOC. NO.
Cameron, Edward Madison	Cameron, James	0801
Cox, Frederick Joseph	Cox, Thomas	0802
Payne, Charles Rockwell	French, Joel	0803
Huffmaster, James Taylor	Huffmaster, Joseph	0804
Cadwalader, John	Cadwalader, Thomas	0805
Wells, Guy Everett	Wells, Benjamin	0806
Stacey, Edward Porter	Stacey, Sam Sewell	0807
Hutchins, Nathan Harrington	Hutchins, John	0808
Longfellow, James Griffith	Parvis, Joseph	0809
Thompson, Gilbert	Gilbert, Judson	0810
		0811 Void
		0812 Void
Hutchins, Arthur Briley	Hutchins, John	0813
Simmons, Wellington Gerowe	Simmons, Noble	0814
Parvis, William Thomas	Parvis, Joseph	0815
Hutchins, Charles Lewis	Hutchins, John	0816
Beatty, Frank Edmund	Beatty, James	0817
Hutchins, James Anderson	Hutchins, John	0818
Hutchins, Daniel Voshell	Hutchins, John	0819
Elliott, John Stadden	Stadden, John	0820
Hutchins, William Voshell	Hutchins, John	0821
Beatty, John Wood	Beatty, James	0822
Woodman, Andrew Jackson	Woodman, Stephen	0823
Ferris, David Brainard, Jr.	Ferris, Jacob, Jr.	0824
Buckey, Mervyn Chandos	Packett, John	0825
Pentz, Franklin Eldridge	Pentz, Daniel	0826
Pentz, Wm. Fletcher	Pentz, Daniel	0827
McDonald, Isaiah Heylin	McDonald, William	0828
Ellis, William	Waller, Jonathan	0829
Newell, William Clayton	Dunlap, Sallows	0830
Jones, Constant Eakin	Jones, Edward Peters Eakin, Samuel Hunter	0831
Herrick, Clinton Bradford	Metcalf, Charles	0832
Averill, Charles Sidle	Averill, Stephen Noble	0833
Lawrence, Frederick Kendall	Kendall, Johnson	0834
Reid, William Magraw	Reid, John Charles	0835
Garnsey, John Henderson	Henderson, Daniel C.	0836
Reed, Thomas	Reed, Thomas	0837
Talbott, Otho Holland Williams	Talbott, Richard Williams, Otho Holland	0838
Talbott, Hattersly Worthington, Jr.	Talbott, Richard Williams, Otho Holland	0839

MEMBER	ANCESTOR	GEN. SOC. NO.
Wesson, James Leonard	Nye, Abraham	0840
Hand, Augustus Noble	Hand, Samuel Noble, Ransom Northrup, Samuel Gould, John	0841
Lyman, Silas Brownson	Lyman, Silas	0842
Townsend, Thomas Gerry	Townsend, David S.	0843
Francis, Charles Spencer	Rogers, William	0844
Nellis, William Jacob	Nellis, Joseph Peter	0845
Chambers, George Brown	Chambers, Perdue	0846
Webb, John Sidney	Randall, Henry Knapp	0847
Brodhead, Robert Packer	Brodhead, Garrett, Jr.	0848
Danker, Albert	Harrison, Frederick	0849
Anderson, James Blythe	Anderson, Oliver Blythe, James	0850
Barnes, William Edgar	Barnes, Joseph Goff	0851
Metcalfe, John Elias	Metcalfe, Charles	0852
Beitler, Lewis Eugene	Marklee, Conrad	0853
Dashiell, Nicholas Leeke	Dashiell, Henry Harris, Benton	0854
Hastings, Arthur Chapin	Burr, Timothy	0855
Sumner, William Henry	Sumner, Henry Payson	0856
Sherman, Fred Henry	Sherman, Humphrey French, Joel	0857
MacArthur, Arthur	MacArthur, Charles Guilderoy	0858
Radford, Harry Vincent	Radford, Jeremiah Smith	0859
Richards, Williams Stiger	Richards, John	0860
Pond, Ashley	Pond, Ashley Pond, Benjamin	0861
Pond, Levi Sheldon	Pond, Ashley Pond, Benjamin Hinckley, Nathaniel	0862
Brown, George Levi	Brown, Levi	0863
Brown, Friend Abner	Brown, Levi	0864
Weitzel, Eben Boyd	Weitzel, George	0865
Denis, George Jules	Carmick, Daniel	0866
Lynde, Francis Engle Patterson	Patterson, Robert	0867
Bickford, Robert Sloane	Sloane, Samuel	0868
Harris, Walter St. George	Harris, Jonathan Beckwith, Elisha	0869
Drown, John Wilson	Shaw, Abraham	0870
Prince, Levi Bradford	Prince, William Robert	0871
LaMont, Harvey Murray	Warren, Orlando Edgar	0872
Davis, Chester Wyman	Coy, Alvin	0873
Buckey, Thomas William	Hite, James	0874

MEMBER	ANCESTOR	GEN. SOC. NO.
Fox, Wm. Carlton	Fox, Augustus Carlton	0875
Willis, William Nicholas	Willis, John	0876
Meigs, Henry Benjamin	Meigs, Luther	0877
Rutter, Wm. Ives, Jr.	Hobert, Robert Enoch Smith, William Rudolph Anthony, Joseph	0878
Dilks, Walter Howard	Hyland, Stephen	0879
Knight, Franklin Comly	Knight, Joseph	0880
Metcalfe, Clinton James	Metcalfe, Charles	0881
Whish, John David	Palmer, David Denham	0882
Baker, Roy Ball	Baker, David	0883
Needham, Charles Willis	Needham, Calvin	0884
Nichols, Willard Atherton	Atherton, Abel Willard Weeks, Lemuel	0885
Peale, Augustin Runyon, Jr.	Peale, Charles Linneaeus	0886
DeYoung, Bertram Isaac	DeYoung, Isaac	0887
Darrach, Henry	Gobrecht, Christian	0888
Boyce, Albert Page	Page, James	0889
Williams, Arthur	Sanno, George Michael	0890
Huffmaster, Isaiah Hayman	Huffmaster, Joseph	0891
Huffmaster, H. Taylor	Huffmaster, Joseph	0892
Lilly, John	Lilly, William	0893
Anderson, Charles Henry	Anderson, James	0894
Cameron, Frederick Ward	Cameron, James	0895
Ainsworth, Danforth Emmit	Ainsworth, Danforth	0896
Danker, Walton Stoutenburgh	Harrison, Frederick	0897
Beall, William Marbury	Beall, Lloyd	0898
Boyd, James Knox Polk	Rust, Samuel	0899
Bissell, Charles M.	Bissell, Daniel	0900
Rosebrock, Alden Ivan	Gotham, John	0901
Lorton, Alfred Hathaway	Lorton, Lewis R.	0902
Somervell, William Howe	Scrivener, John	0903
Clark, Samuel	Clark, David	0904
Bissell, Thomas Teed	Bissell, Daniel	0905
Smith, Edward Levi	Brown, Levi Graves, Luther	0906
Lord, Calvin	Russell, Samuel Hooper	0907
Wallace, Hamilton Stone	Brooke, William	0908
Merrill, Charles Warren	Spaulding, James	0909
Hills, Elbridge Romeyn	Hills, Elijah	0910
Hellick, Chauncey Graham	Hellick, Jacob	0911
Boston, Leonard Napoleon	Bacon, Septimus	0912
Henry, Reginald Buchanan	Buchanan, James	0913

MEMBER	ANCESTOR	GEN. SOC. NO.
Brown, James Edgar	Brown, Samuel Byrne	0914
Klock, George Ferdinand	Klock, George T.	0915
Mountain, William	Paynter, Lemuel	0916
Field, Thomas Yardley, Jr.	Robinson, Jonathan Jehu	0917
Brookes, George Deshield	Brookes, John	0918
Snyder, Charles E.	Knickerbocker, James	0919
Marine, Richard Elliott	Knowles, William	0920
Marine, Madison	Knowles, William	0921
Deshon, George Durfee	Durfee, Daniel, Jr.	0922
Cornell, George Augustus	Cornell, Henry	0923
Kenly, William Watkins	Kenly, Edward Watkins, Gassaway	0924
Merritt, James Black, III	Merritt, Benjamin	0925
Banks, George Washington	Stow, Daniel	0926
Warne, Edward Paul Brey	Warne, Elisha Spring	0927
Hay, Southard	Hay, Peter	0928
Sloan, John Hope	Hope, Robert	0929
Behm, John William	Helmbold, George	0930
Harris, Thomas Cadwalader	Harris, Thomas	0931
Waring, William Emory, Jr.	Leary, Peter	0932
Waring, Benjamin Harrison	Beard, John	0933
Diggs, Ross Miles	Diggs, Beverly	0934
Taylor, Benjamin Franklin	Taylor, Robert	0935
England, Charles	Middleton, Richard	0936
Blue, Victor	Blue, John	0937
Blue, Rupert	Blue, John	0938
Akin, Henry Charles Robeson	Robeson, Thomas	0939
Hopkins, Alfred Francis	Johnson, Alfred, Jr. Johnson, Alfred	0940
Bauer, Frederic Gilbert	Blake, William Shute, John William	0941
Blair, Irving James	Blair, Ezekiel	0942
Adams, Washington Irving Lincoln	Briggs, Edward D.	0943
Alford, Albert Gallatin	Alford, Ami	0944
Phifer, Robert Smith, Jr.	Hunt, Eustace	0945
McDonald, William Bartholow	Perkins, John	0946
Kaufman, John Williams	Kaufman, Jonathan	0947
Fitzpatrick, Wm. Claude	Fitzpatrick, Rene	0948
Sheib, Samuel Henry	Elbert, Samuel	0949
Landstreet, John	Landstreet, John	0950
Collins, Edwin Barnes	Collins, Eben Hall	0951
Scherck, Henry Joseph	Marks, Alexander	0952

MEMBER	ANCESTOR	GEN. SOC. NO.
Moyer, Nevin Wilberforce	Moyer, Daniel	0953
Estes, Webster Cummings	Estes, Benjamin Hall	0954
Spear, Harry William	Wilson, John	0955
Rouse, Francis Willis, Jr.	Rouse, Peregrine	0956
Keim, George deBenneville	Mitchell, Henry	0957
Linnard, George Brown	Linnard, William	0958
Quackenbush, Claire Courtney	Quackenbush, Isaac F.	0959
Baughman, Greer Harry	Greer, George	0960
Baughman, Charles Christian	Greer, George	0961
Baughman, Emilius Allen	Greer, George	0962
Langhorne, Charles McIndoe	Langhorne, Maurice	0963
Jordon, Charles Philander	Jordan, John	0964
Cooke, William Dewey	Trout, Joseph	0965
	Stribling, Erasmus	
	Waddell, Littleton	
MacDonald, John Stuart	Younker, Francis	0966
Rinehart, Thomas Warden	Roney, William	0967
Rinehart, Evan Urner	Roney, William	0968
Bell, Ola Walter	Snell, John Jacob	0969
Bradford, John	Bradford, John	0970
	Armistead, George	
Babcock, William Henry	Babcock, Lodowick Stanton	0971
Fleming, Allison Sweeney	McFerran, John	0972
Stewart, Ambler Jones	Bay, Thomas	0973
Pinkney, Townsend	Gautier, Samuel John Sinclair	0974
Whyte, Isaac Hezekiah	Mengle, Peter	0975
Green, Robert McCay	Green, Isaac	0976
Botsford, Stephen Jason	Freeman, Samuel	0977
Abert, William Stone	Abert, John James	0978
Tarr, Frederick Crey	Crey, Frederick	0979
Mahool, John Barry	Biays, James	0980
Holden, Edward Packard, Jr.	Holden, Horace	0981
Currier, Charles Otis	Legg, Otis	0982
Smith, L. Bertrand	Smith, Ambrose	0983
Miller, Elmer Pliny	Miller, Pliny, Jr.	0984
Pettingell, Frank Hervey	Pettingell, Cutting	0985
Battis, Edward Clarence	Battis, John	0986
Phebus, Joseph Scott	Phebus, John	0987
	McVay, Jacob	
Middlebrook, Louis Frank	Middlebrook, Robert, Jr.	0988
		0989 Void
Straight, Charles Tillinghast	Avery, Elisha	0990
Lenore, Clifford	Leonor, Lewis	0991

MEMBER	ANCESTOR	GEN. SOC. NO.
Bowers, William	Bowers, Henry	0992
Crawford, Henry Victor	Crawford, Moses	0993
Holden, Horace	Holden, Horace	0994
Williamson, Thomas Wilson	Green, Charles Bosley	0995
Ford, Henry Jones	Jones, Uriah	0996
Beatty, John Edwin	Cole, James Alexander	0997
Throckmorton, Charles Woodson	Throckmorton, Josiah	0998
Hotchkin, Walter Bryant	Hotchkin, Eliphalet	0999
Barratt, Norris Stanley	Dill, Robert	1000
Fisher, James Henry	Sparks, Samuel	1001
Handy, John Curtis	Matthews, William	1002
Read, Charles French	Hull, William	1003
Metcalf, Willis Charles	Metcalf, Charles	1004
Johnson, Lucius Warren	Bell, Holly	1005
Parker, Edward Hegeman	Hegeman, Daniel	1006
Kellogg, George Casper	Averill, Henry Ketchum, Sr. Kellogg, Lorenzo	1007
Westfall, John Henry	Wright, Daniel	1008
Cassard, John	Cassard, Gilbert	1009
Alford, Newell Gilder	Gilder, Reuben	1010
Goodrich, William	Cocke, John	1011
Scott, John Morin	Scott, John Morin	1012
Newell, Edward Harvey	Dunlap, Sallows	1013
Kidder, George Sherman	Kidder, Maynard	1014
Wells, Frederick Howard	Wells, William, Jr. Wells, William, Sr.	1015
Morgan, Daniel Taylor	Edie, David	1016
Dold, William Elliot	Dold, Samuel Miller	1017
MacChesney, Nathan Wm.	MacChesney, Nathan	1018
Camp, Charles David	Camp, Cyrus Talmage	1019
Dallam, Harry Gough	Gough, Harry Dorsey	1020
French, Chester Lee	French, William	1021
Hite, Drayton Meade	Hite, James Madison	1022
Cathcart, Asbury Roszel	Cathcart, Robert	1023
Blackwood, Norman Jerome	Smith, Joseph Lee	1024
Bradford, Samuel Webster	Kell, Thomas	1025
Summers, Walter Penrose	Green, Charles Bosley	1026
Houghton, Ira Holden	McMurray, Samuel	1027
Grindall, Charles Sylvester	Armstrong, Thomas Grindall, John Gibson	1028
McDowell, Ralph Walker	Dean, Joseph, II	1029
Ziegler, Walter Macon Lowrie	Patterson, James	1030
Powell, Washington Bleddyn	Powell, William	1031

48 The Roster

MEMBER	ANCESTOR	GEN. SOC. NO.
Stevens, William Kerper	Stephens, George	1032
McCain, Donald Rockefeller	Rockefeller, Henry	1033
Bell, William Hemphill	Johnson, Seth	1034
Truman, Henry Hertel	Mead, Shadrach	1035
		1036 Void
Duvall, Richard Mareen	Waring, Francis	1037
	Duvall, Barton	
Pleasanton, Frank Rodney	Mitchell, Henry	1038
Ziegler, Jacob Stanley	Patterson, James	1039
Shreffler, Benjamin Franklin	Shreffler, John	1040
Flower, John Sebastian	Flower, Gustavus	1041
Henderson, Charles Franklin	Henderson, Peter	1042
Baker, Henry Gardner	Sanford, Ruben	1043
Byrd, James Edward	Sheldon, James	1044
Strobel, James William	Strobel, John Peter	1045
Daniels, Joseph	Daniels, Joseph	1046
Young, Jared Wilson	Young, John	1047
Lowe, John Williamson	Boerstler, Jacob	1048
	Boerstler, Charles G.	
Pritchard, Arthur John	Stewart, John I.	1049
Levy, Jefferson Monroe	Levy, Uriah Phillips	1050
Parker, Francis Hubert	Ayer, Herbert	1051
Peck, Paul Noble	Noble, Daniel	1052
Reese, Howard Hopkins	Cassard, Gilbert	1053
Maynadier, Thomas Murray	Bond, Thomas E.	1054
Hildt, John C.	Hildt, John	1055
Hildt, Thomas	Hildt, John	1056
Cherbonnier, Andrew Victor	Cherbonnier, Pierre	1057
Peck, Theodore Safford,	Safford, Hiram	1058
Noble, John Harmon	Noble, Ransom	1059
	Sherman, Humphrey	
	French, Joel	
Nye, Bartlett	Moore, Noadiah	1060
McLellan, Hugh	Moore, Noadiah	1061
Maltbie, William Henry	Van Deman, Henry	1062
Somervell, Woodruff Marbury	Scrivener, John	1063
Foster, Clarence Dulany	Dulany, Samuel	1064
Hancock, James Etchberger	Despeaux, John	1065
	Etchberger, William	
Kemp, Edwin Faxon	Gray, John	1066
Sellers, Edwin Foote	Beebe, Ebenezer	1067
Kaylor, Adrian Roy	Smith, Frederick	1068
Armstrong, Harold Rodney	Spering, Henry	1069

The Roster 49

MEMBER	ANCESTOR	GEN. SOC. NO.
Easter, James Miller	Klein, Lewis	1070
Claghorn, Wm. Crumby	Claghorn, John William	1071
Carr, Lovell Henry	Lovell, Harles Sheaffe	1072
Kemp, Isaac	Felter, John P.	1073
Brumfield, Jerome Edgar	Brumfield, William	1074
McComas, Henry Angle	McComas, Zaccheus Onion	1075
Dell, Thomas Medairy	Mills, Ezekiel	1076
Dickerman, Frank Elliott	Harris, Oliver	1077
Turner, Everett Pendleton	Turner, John Bryant	1078
Richards, Frederick Barnard	Richards, Joseph	1079
Hastings, Arthur Chapin, Jr.	Burr, Timothy	1080
Hastings, Orlando Burr	Burr, Timothy	1081
Fisk, Arthur Aylmer	Ball, Cyrus	1082
	Ten Broeck, John	
Dailey, Harry	Bay, Andrew	1083
Osgood, Everett	———	1084
Stahl, John Henry, Jr.	Stahl, Harry	1085
Orem, John Henry, Jr.	Schuchtts, John Henry	1086
Banning, Kendall	Banning, Calvin	1087
Caldwell, Francis Gustavus	Caldwell, James St. Clair	1088
Brinton, Howard Futhey	Futhey, Robert	1089
DeYoung, Arthur	DeYoung, Isaac	1090
Fotterall, Wm. Foster	Fotterall, Stephen Egan	1091
Danenhower, Edward Bushell	Godman, Samuel	1092
Appleton, Charles Brooks	Appleton, Benjamin Barnard	1093
	Brooks, Charles	
Clark, Byron Nathaniel	Gove, Enos Sanborn	1094
Miller, John Henry	Smithsom, Gabriel	1095
Pennington, Josias	Pennington, Josias	1096
Amee, John	Amee, Jacob	1097
Pearson, Arthur Emmons	Benjamin, Jesse	1098
Litchfield, Wilbur Jacob	Rhodes, Ezekiel	1099
Beal, Francis Leavett	Beal, Caleb	1100
	Souther, Nathan	
Manrose, Ernest Fitch	Risley, James	1101
Wood, Edward Allen	———	1102
Prentiss, William	———	1103
Hisky, Thomas Foley	Shipley, William	1104
Hall, William Anderson	Hall, James	1105
Naylor, Emmett Hay	Hay, Daniel	1106
McGaw, George Keen	McGaw, John	1107
Leland, Edmund Francis	Daniels, Joseph	1108
Heckler, Charles Edwin	Strong, William A.	1109

50 The Roster

MEMBER	ANCESTOR	GEN. SOC. NO.
Van Gilder, William C.	——	1110
Ingram, Finis S.	Ingram, Thomas	1111
Douglass, George L.	——	1112
Hall, Ross	——	1113
Wheeler, Arthur D.	——	1114
Purkhiser, Edward Grant	Rush, Thornton	1115
Wortman, Glen R.	——	1116
Monnette, Orra Eugene	Scribner, Samuel, Jr.	1117
Semple, Frank, Jr.	Blair, Alexander	1118
Lott, James Filmore	Stewart, Robert	1119
Ovenshine, Samuel	Ovenshine, Jacob	1120
Scott, John Fulton Reynolds	Scott, John	1121
Briggs, Herbert	Burnett, Stephen Grover	1122
Zimmerman, Charles Ballard	Zimmerman, Joseph	1123
Brown, Harry Webster	Lazell, Sylvanus	1124
Cool, Joseph Gilbert	Griffin, Stephen	1125
Leland, Amory	Daniels, Joseph	1126
Kraner, Albert Ludlow	Scott, Andrew	1127
Booth, Charles Maclay	Maclay, John	1127A
Hume, Edgar Erskine	Glover, John Bryant, Hiram Shumate, John Hume, Charles Crist, Jacob Jett, Stephen	1128
Collmus, Charles Carroll, Sr.	Collmus, Levi	1129
Colbert, Edwin Abbott	Hayes, Walter Cody	1130
Royse, William Coates	Dickson, John Nichol, John	1131
McDonnell, Austin McCarthy	Massie, John Whitney	1132
Perkins, George Henry, Jr.	Perkins, John	1133
Hall, Summerfield Davis	Perkins, John	1134
Dukes, Alexander Thompson	Neilson, Robert	1135
Glentworth, Theodore, 3rd.	Wentz, Jacob	1136
Guthrie, Harry Jones	Lowry, Job T.	1137
Royer, John Whittier	Hobart, Enoch	1138
Walmsley, James Armineous	Burroughs, James	1139
Shreve, Milton William	Shreve, Israel	1140
Stevens, George Beckwith	Stevens, Joseph Lowe	1141
Huddleson, James Howard	Stockton, John Cox	1142
Thompson, Marshall Putnam	Putnam, Samuel	1143
Walworth, Arthur Clarence	Nason, Leavitt	1144
Talbot, Archie Lee	Robbins, Asa, Jr. Smith, Samuel	1145

The Roster 51

MEMBER	ANCESTOR	GEN. SOC. NO.
Crowninshield, Bowdoin Bradlee	Crowninshield, Benjamin W.	1146
Reifsnider, John Milton	Zacharias, Daniel	1147
Harris, William Hall	Harris, David	1148
Riggs, Clinton Levering	Riggs, Elisha	1149
Boyce, Hayward Easter	Page, James	1150
Robertson, George Sadtler	Sadtler, Philip Benjamin	1151
Phillips, George Thomas	Phillips, Benjamin	1152
Tudbury, Warren Chamberlain	Breed, Holton Johnson	1153
Gardner, Charles Frederic	Gardner, Edward	1154
Barbour, Lucius Barnes	Barbour, John, Jr.	1155
Bristor, Joseph Whiteridge	Bristor, George	1156
Biays, Tolley Alexander	Biays, James, Jr.	1157
Hobart, Thomas Duncan	Hobart, Robert Enoch	1158
Holstein, Otto	Gilman, Nathaniel, III	1159
Corson, Alan	McPherson, Henry Hendley	1160
Bonnell, Russell	Oliver, Paul Ambrose	1161
Zook, Erle Will	Baxter, William	1162
Wood, Walter Aaron	Wood, Aaron Wood, Thaddeus Mead Delano, Jesse	1163
Jenkins, Michael	Jenkins, William	1164
Smith, George Louge	Hampton, Thomas	1165
Hendrick, John Buford, Jr.	Clark, Christopher	1166
Van Horn, Arthur	Soule, Howland	1167
Burroughs, Charles Frederick	Burroughs, Enoch Cannon, William	1168
Richardson, George Lynde	Richardson, John Lynde, Jonathan	1169
Foster, Romulus Adam	Foster, Adams Burch, Richard	1170
Hale, Ledyard Park	Hale, Benjamin	1171
Parker, Arthur Caswell	Parker, William	1172
Tuckerman, Alfred	Gibbs, George	1173
Harrington, Arthur Clark	Scotes, Norton Hodsdon, Isaac	1174
Sharp, Alfred Elliott	Bloomer, Daniel	1175
Berry, Thomas Lansdale	Emory, John King Beck	1176
Bissell, Benjamin	Webster, John Adams	1177
Mohler, Isaac Wimbert, Jr.	Adams, Alexander	1178
Bruce, Oliver Herman	Bruce, Robert	1179
Linville, Charles Hardesty	Linville, James M.	1180
Van Horn, John Albert	Soule, Howland	1181
Shepard, Benjamin	Sturtevant, Thomas	1182
Dunkel, Joel Ambrose	Dunkel, John	1183

MEMBER	ANCESTOR	GEN. SOC. NO.
Harrington Harrison Loring	Harrington, Simon	1184
Smith, Harry Pattison	Frisbie, Levi Smith, John Larrabee, Benjamin	1185
Smith, Walter Frank	Frisbie, Levi Smith, John Larrabee, Benjamin	1186
Shriver, Alfred Jenkins	Jenkins, Edward	1187
Allen, Francis Burke	Burke, Francis	1188
Osborn, Stuart Rae	Barber, Noah	1189
Galibraith, Wm. Ayres	Davenport, William	1190
Perry, James DeWolf	Perry, Raymond Henry Jones	1191
Bierbower, James Culver	Garrard, James Kennedy, Washington Carey, William	1192
Kay, Wm. DeYoung	DeYoung, Isaac	1193
Capp, Seth Bunker	Tucker, Benjamin	1194
Frazer, John	Cave, Thomas	1195
McIntyre, Allan Fellows	Dunham, Shubael	1196
Montgomery, Eugene Miller	Montgomery, William	1197
Jenkins, Benjamin Wheeler	Jenkins, Felix	1198
Hall, Clayton Colman	Hall, Thomas William	1199
Smith, Frank Edmond	Smith, John Larrabee, Benjamin	1200
Stetson, Francis Lynde	Hascall, Ralph Stetson, Reuben	1201
Osborne, Horace Bond	Condit, Stephen	1202
Stockton, Richard, 6th.	Stockton, Robert Field	1203
Merrill, John Lenord	Dodge, Robert	1204
Huckel, William Gulager	Huckel, Francis	1205
Scott, George Eyster	Scott, John	1206
McNamee, Charles	Holmes, Israel	1207
Bonniwell, Eugene Cleophas	Capes, William	1208
Scott, John, Jr.	Scott, John	1209
Quackenbos, Henry Forest	Jack, John	1210
Busch, Miers	Boyle, Philip	1211
Moore, Arthur Allison	Gault, James	1212
Reno, Jesse Wilford	Reno, Lewis Thomas Reno, Benjamin	1213
Parker, Alvin Mercer	Bloodgood, Aaron	1214
Parker, Joseph Brooks Bloodgood	Bloodgood, Aaron	1215
Sahm, William Knopp Tridel	Tridel, John	1216
Buker, Horace Edward	Buker, Jonah	1217
Magruder, Caleb Clark, Jr.	Magruder, Thomas	1218

MEMBER	ANCESTOR	GEN. SOC. NO.
Stowell, Wm. VanNess	Stowell, Ration Levings	1219
Henshaw, Alonzo Norton	Norton, Carlos Alonzo	1220
Raborg, Edward Livingston, II	Raborg, Christopher, II	1221
Brevoort, Charles P.	——	1222
Sicussatt, St. George Charles Leakin	Leakin, Sheppard Church	1223
Campbell, John Deveny	Campbell, Thomas	1224
Safford, Ralph Kirkham	Mix, Elijah	1225
Lay, William	Crittenden, William Gatewood	1226
Caldwalader, Thomas Francis	Caldwalader, Thomas	1227
Stewart, Andrew	Howell, Joshua Ladd	1228
Emerson, George Douglas	Emerson, Nathaniel	1229
Richardson, James Barbour	Richardson, John Lynde, Jonathan	1230
Hastings, Walcott Brown	Burr, Timothy	1231
Rymers, George Henry	Rice, Ezekial	1232
Holden, James Austin	Holden, Moses	1233
King, John Walden	King, John	1234
Drayton, Samuel	Hillyer, Simon	1235
Sloan, Charles Wortham	Sloan, John	1236
Moore, Malcolm	Gault, James	1237
Perry, James Dewold, Jr.	Perry, Raymond Henry Jones	1238
Weaver, Ethan Allan	Stecher, John	1239
Fackenthal, Benjamin Franklin, Jr.	Adam, Dennis	1240
Allen, Joseph Aloysius	Allen, John	1241
Dartt, John Gregg Lieb	Mitchell, David	1242
Everhart, Lay Hampton	Bowman, Andrew	1243
Evans, Clarence Richard	Collmus, Levi	1244
Hale, Horace Charles	Hale, Benjamin	1245
Warne, William Budd, Jr.	Warne, Elisha Spring	1246
Swearer, Herbert Dayne	Wersler, John Gulden	1247
Muhlenberg, Frank Peter	Muhlenberg, Peter	1248
Newton, Sanford Hamilton	Newton, Alvin	1249
Chase, Ferdinand Walker	Carter, Benjamin	1250
Kelly, Irving Washington	Kelly, James	1251
Armistead, Lewis Addison	Armistead, Walker Keith	1252
Knowlton, Clarence Hinckley	Pettengill, Elisha	1253
Hayes, Philip Cornelius	Hayes, Gaylor	1254
Moore, Daniel McFarlan	Moore, William Walker Moore, John B.	1255
Voorhees, George Van Wickle	Voorhees, John P.	1256
Osborne, Horace Sherman	Osborne, Henry	1257

MEMBER	ANCESTOR	GEN. SOC. NO.
McCowan, Robert Joseph Foster	Shute, Samuel Moore	1258
Southard, Louis Carver	Southard, John	1259
Payne, Harry Francis	Clark, Lathrop	1260
Ellis, Albert Washington	Fish, Lemuel	1261
McLellan, Malcolm Nye	Moore, Noadiah	1262
Thompson, Raymond Webb	Todd, Bernard	1263
Drapier, William Henry	Draper, Gideon	1264
Rea, Henry Robinson	Rea, John	1265
Shoemaker, Henry Wharton	Shoemaker, Henry	1266
Walker, William Samuel Crittenden	Crittenden, William Gatewood	1267
Barton, Wm. Eleazer	Barton, Eleazer	1268
Lyman, Charles Burt	Rhoades, David	1269
Goddard, Leroy A.	Goodard, James	1270
Stahl, Resler Meloy	Stahl, Henry	1271
Nevius, Arthur Seymour	Stahl, Henry	1272
Stahl, Elias Brinton	Stahl, Henry	1273
Reid, Robert Joseph	Reid, Joseph Carmel	1274
Smith, Guy J.	——	1275
Sapp, Frank M.	——	1276
Sapp, E. S.	——	1277
Morrow, James William	Morrow, William	1278
Blinn, William Cady	Blin, Theodore	1279
Warder, Walter	——	1280
Warder, William H.	——	1281
Kern, Charles Everett	Miles, William	1282
Loucks, Frank Horace	Loucks, George G.	1283
Sparks, John F.	Sparks, Solomon	1284
Davis, James William	Davis, Isaac	1285
Bonniwell, Thomas John	Capes, William	1286
Bonniwell, Charles Anthony	Capes, William	1287
Reed, Worth	Reed, Stephen	1288
Hopkins, Robert Hiram	Hopkins, Hiram	1289
Hopkins, John Cook	Hopkins, Hiram	1290
Beckford, Walter Harry	Swan, Nathan	1291
Salmon, Stephen Decatur	Loring, Perez	1292
Stowe, Benjamin Levi	Stowe, Frederick	1293
Andrews, Charles Allen	Andrews, Thomas, Jr.	1294
		1295 Void
Jewett, Charles Timothy	Jewett, Martin Dewey	1296
		1297 Void
Omer, Lewis	Omer, Peter	1298
		1299 Void

MEMBER	ANCESTOR	GEN. SOC. NO.
Moore, Myron Foster	Moore, John, II	1300
Nesbit, Harry Van Tyle	Nesbit, James I.	1301
Heaton, Guilford A.	——	1302
Bixler, Wm. Henry Harrison	Bixler, David	1303
Thompson, Porter Lindsley	Lindsley, Abraham Bradley	1304
Haines, Burton C.	——	1305
Montgomery, Shelley Hoskins	Montgomery, William	1306
Power, Martin John	Boyd, William	1307
Royse, Samuel Durham	Dickson, John	1308
Green, Thomas Edward	Green, Thomas	1309
Turner, Will Sidney	Campbell, Walter	1310
Snyder, Leo Harter	Snyder, William	1311
Herndon, John Goodwin, Jr.	Turner, Robert	1312
	Dale, Adam	
Camp, George A.	——	1313
Woodruff, Cadwell	Woodruff, Joseph	1314
Cromwell, Benjamin Franklin	Cromwell, Oliver	1315
Wetter, John King	Parrish, William	1316
Palmer, William Morgan	Palmer, William	1317
Merrell, Richard I.	Merrell, John	1318
Amick, Jacob William	Klunk, Peter	1319
	Amick, Jacob	
Tompkins, Daniel D.	Tompkins, Daniel D.	1320
Bosson, Frederick Needham	Bosson, Jonathan Davis	1321
Deshon, Percy	Deshon, Daniel, Jr.	1322
Taylor, Thad Talmage	Bruner, Solomon	1323
Danker, Frederick Harrison	Harrison, Frederick	1324
Biddle, Clement	Biddle, Clement Cornell	1325
Davis, Sussex Delaware	Davis, Samuel Boyer	1326
DeForest, Louis Effingham	Lawrence, Watson Effingham	1327
James, Carlton	McCarty, Alfred	1328
	James, Thomas Anson	
Massey, Maurice Richardson	Vogdes, Jacob	1329
Joy, Leslie Wells	Hine, Tamerlane	1330
	Joy, Zelan	
Reichner, Louis Irving	Fraser, James P.	1331
Hogg, William Stetson	Hogg, Samuel	1332
Allen, John Vincent, Jr.	Allen, John	1333
Boddie, John Bennett	Winchester, James	1334
Ellington, Charles Townley	Bond, Elial	1335
Davis, Charles Ross	Tempest, William	1336
Baker, Charles Chaney	Boxley, George	1337
Hall, Reynold Thomas	Crockett, Samuel	1338
	Rumney, John	

MEMBER	ANCESTOR	GEN. SOC. NO.
Simpson, Jay Maxwell	Schuyler, Peter Philip	1339
	Simpson, Joseph	
Moore, Harry Thornton	Haws, Joel	1340
Mills, Rowland Yearley	Mills, Ezekiel	1341
Roane, Samuel Bertrand	Roane, John Jones	1342
Metcalf, Charles Henry	Metcalf, Chandler	1343
Snyder, Russell William	Snyder, Adam Vrooman	1344
Thornell, Lewis Taylor	Taylor, Lewis	1345
Holden, George Meads	Holden, Abel	1346
Winans, Carlton George	Winans, William Wanton	1347
Carr, Henry Lovell	Lovell, Joseph	1348
Huson, Hobart	Miller, Ezra	1349
Darling, Carlos Parsons	Parsons, Luke	1350
Stark, Lloyd Rider	Stark, Jonathan	1351
Crowell, William Sloan	Babcock, Samuel	1352
Tilton, Francis Theodore	Armstrong, Thomas	1353
Shufeldt, William Techumseh	Mullany, James Robert	1354
Yeakle, Walter Atwood	Huston, John, Jr.	1355
McShea, Walter Ross	Barton, William	1356
Nevin, Edwin Channing	Nevin, David	1357
Miller, Philip Schuyler	Schuyler, Peter Philip	1358
McMullin, Nelson VanBuskirk	Henderson, John	1359
Welch, Elwood Stuart	Welch, Daniel	1360
Phillips, George Thomas	Phillips, Benjamin	1361
Davis, Arthur Christy	McCleary, Robert	1362
Blair, Frank Perrin	Blair, James	1363
Dunlap, Walter Eugene Briggs	Dunlap, Josiah	1364
	Dowd (Doud), Samuel	
Holloway, Charles Thomas, II	Ross, Reuben	1365
Brinton, John Willard	Futhey, Robert	1366
Ball, Thomas Hand	Frowert, John	1367
Klunk, Louis William	Klunk, Peter	1368
Eddy, Samuel Schuyler	Schuyler, Peter Philip	1369
Boling, Eugene H.	Smith, Adam	1370
Gurley, William Frank Eugene	Hall, Giles	1371
	Reed, John	
Brown, Bache Hamilton	Clinton, Alexander	1372
Hart, Thomas	Beverly, John	1373
Moulton, George Mayhew	Moulton, Jacob Smith	1374
Focke, Ferdinand Brauns	Smull, Jacob	1375
Focke, Walter David	Smull, Jacob	1376
Agens, Sylvester Halsey Moore	Agens, James	1377
Gurley, George Poulin	Wallace, Thomas Nesmith	1378

MEMBER	ANCESTOR	GEN. SOC. NO.
Miles, Rowland	Miles, Reuben	1379
Page, Carroll Smalley	Smalley, Francis, Jr.	1380
Bryant, Frederick Stewart	Bryant, Daniel Chandler	1381
Shank, Charles Abram	Shank, John	1382
Wilcox, Edwin Howard	Shaler, Ephriam	1383
Page, Proctor Hull	Smalley, Francis, Jr.	1384
Harris, William Hall, Jr.	Harris, Davis	1385
Keogh, Chester Henry	Benjamin, Elias	1386
Stewart, John Trusedale	Brown, David	1387
Jelke, John Faris, Jr.	Frazier, Thomas	1388
Dillon, Arthur Orison	Sheldon, Ichabod	1389
Cox, James William, Jr.	Cox, Thomas Donnell, John	1390
Cox, Thomas Riggs	Cox, Thomas Donnell, John	1391
Simonds, Frederic Pond	Breed, Holton Johnson	1392
McComas, Joseph Patton	McComas, Zaccheus Onion	1393
Thompson, Henry Oliver	Thompson, Henry	1394
Hoffman, Alfred Ayers	Hoffman, Julius	1395
Brown, Gilbert Patten	Poole, Samuel Hall	1396
Cadmus, Eugene Leroy	Cadmus, Thomas	1397
Ackley, Charles Saxton	Ackley, Oliver	1398
Hobart, Robert Enoch	Hobart, Robert Enoch	1399
Roggenburger, Adolphus	Myers, Solomon	1400
Newell, Louis Henry Field	Dunlap, Sallows	1401
Favrot, Joseph St. Clair	Favrot, Philogene	1402
Henkels, Joseph Felix	Snyder, Thomas	1403
Cranford, James William	Cranford, James	1404
Marbury, William Henry	Davis, Samuel Boyer	1405
Webb, Haywood Hutchinson	Randall, Henry Knapp	1406
Sanford, John Lowry	Warner, Michael Sanford, George	1407
Banning, Pierson Worrall	Pierson, Philo	1408
Lewis, George Harlan	Cutter, Joshua	1409
Bay, Charles Andrew	Bay, Andrew	1410
Hutchison, Joseph P.	Pierce, Barnabas C.	1411
Steely, Harlin Melville	Steely, Gabriel Steely, George Hiser, William	1412
Herrick, Samuel	Herrick, Samuel Herrick, Edward	1413
Swords, Robert Stanard	Stanard, John	1414
Osterhoudt, Harvey Jay	Osterhoudt, Simeon	1415
Rowan, Robert Livingston	Armstrong, John Adams	1416

MEMBER	ANCESTOR	GEN. SOC. NO.
Orcutt, Husdon Earl	Minard, Abel	1417
Worthington, Thomas Chew	Worthington, Rezin Hammond	1418
Slayton, William Taft	Slayton, Bucklin	1419
Richardson, Royall Roller	Richardson, Charles	1420
Worthington, Richard Walker	Worthington, Rezin Hammond	1421
Crisler, Lewis Allen	Conner, Andrew	1422
Wallace, Wyndham Stokes	Brooke, William Davis, Samuel Boyer Jones, Edward	1423
Bernard, Richard Constable	Gore, George	1424
Jones, Stockton White	Jones, Edward Peters Eakin, Samuel Hunter	1425
Bristor, Wm. Beverly	Bristor, George	1426
Gray, John Daniel	Tempest, William	1427
Bartlett, John Albert	Bartlett, Ebenezer	1428
Boulden, Charles Newton	Boulden, Nathaniel L.	1429
Greene, Samuel Edward, III	Daugherty, Daniel	1430
Roseboom, Jesse Garretson	Roseboom, Henry	1431
Hamley, Arthur J.	Wilson, Peter	1432
Gridley, Edward Mead	Scott, Jeremiah	1433
Steelman, Hiram	Steelman, Frederick	1434
Cranford, Edward Beamer	Cranford, James	1435
Adams, Arthur	Adams, Daniel	1436
Biays, James Phillip	Biays, James	1437
Turner, George Henry Brown	Lazell, Sylvanus	1438
Clement, Theron B.	Clement, Evan Collins	1439
Clement, Charles Francis	Clement, Evan Collins	1440
Howard, Ezra Elkanah	Howard, James Powell	1441
Godley, Walter	Helmbold, George, Jr.	1442
Stewart, Earl Ruthven	Saddler, William	1443
Shelly, Howard Merrell	McClellan, Hugh	1444
Rupley, George	Rupley, Simon Baxter, William	1445
Crolius, Allen Potter	Walcott, Silas	1446
Getelman, Ralph	Wagener, Henry	1447
Burbank, Abram Lincoln	Burbank, Peter	1448
Harvey, Aylmer O.	Rerick, John	1449
Turner, Huntley Sigourney	Lazell, Sylvanus	1450
Burt, Clarence Edward	French, Ephraim French, Ephraim, Jr. Horton, Simeon	1451
Ellis, Norman Stanley	Fish, Lemuel	1452
Fowler, William Eric	Fowler, John	1453
Collins, George Gordon	Collins, John Alexander	1454

MEMBER	ANCESTOR	GEN. SOC. NO.
Henderson, Charles Griffith	Henderson, Peter	1455
Mitchell, Robert Levis	Mitchell, George Edward	1456
Morley, Charles Sheriff	Keefer, Anthony	1457
Cann, Frank William	Cann, John	1458
Parkhurst, George Comfort	Tanner, Christopher Stockman, Jacob	1459
Ferree, Sheridan	Ferree, Joel	1460
Barrett, John Minot	Barrett, John Miller	1461
Busch, Clarence Marshall	Busch, John Francis	1462
Dennison, Herbert Elmer	Dennison, Isaac	1463
Warren, George Copp	Jackson Isaac	1464
Dayton, Ralph	Hornblower, Josiah	1465
Barry, John Neilson	Neilson, John	1466
Richardson, George Lynde	Richardson, John Lynde, Jonathan	1467
Tschudi, Samuel Werner	Tschudy, Samuel	1468
Hart, Albert Bushnell	Bushnell, William	1469
Harrison, Wm. Preston	Russell, William	1470
Keith, Arthur Leslie	Pringle, John	1471
Orebaugh, David Alvin	Orebaugh, Jacob	1472
Daingerfield, Foxhall Alexander	Daingerfield, Leroy Parker	1473
Benson, Oscar Suter	Garsuch, Thomas	1474
Worthington, Thomas Chew, III	Worthington, Rezin Hammond	1475
Wheeler, Walter Raymond	Bartholomew, Deming	1476
Bonniwell, Eugene Cahill, Jr.	Capes, William	1477
Irwin, Charles Megee	Gwinn, James	1478
Sells, John Davis	Davis, John	1479
Barratt, Thomas Levering	Dill, Robert	1480
Clement, Martin Withington	Clement, Evan Collins	1481
Appleton, Floyd	Appleton, James	1482
Cauffman, Stanley Hart	Badger, Bela	1483
Stewart, Henry Christopher Hand	Helfmeier, Herman	1484
Leland, Charles Thurman	Leland, Thomas	1485
Conkling, Wm. Johnson	Conkling, John Johnson	1486
Hiss, Fielder Israel, Jr.	Hiss, Philip Israel, Fielder	1487
Crane, Wm. Herbert	Crane, Elias B.	1488
Wiegand, William E.	Wiegand, Daniel	1489
Harris, Wm. Barney	Barney, Joshua	1490
Bauer, Louis Hopewell	Shute, John William	1491
Owen, Franklin Buchanan	Lloyd, Edward, IV	1492
Wilkinson, Charles Marion	Wilkinson, Samuel Brannon, Thomas	1493

MEMBER	ANCESTOR	GEN. SOC. NO.
Cornelius, Thomas Reese	Daneker, John Jacob	1494
Turner, Arthur Campbell	Campbell, George Washington	1495
Hammond, Edward	Hammond, Lloyd Thomas	1496
Phillips, Levi Benjamin	Phillips, Benjamin	1497
Thomsen, Rossel Cathcart	Cathcart, Robert	1498
Cromwell, Andrew Grant	Cromwell, Oliver	1499
Webb, Edward Joseph, Jr.	Kelso, John R.	1500
Drayton, Samuel, Jr.	Hillyer, Simon	1501
Tschudy, Harold T.	Tschudy, Samuel	1502
Power, John Leonard	Zollinger, Jacob	1503
Henderson, George Washington	Henderson, Peter H.	1504
Baker, Hamilton Wallace	Brooke, William	1505
Baker, John Mitchell	Brooke, William	1506
Bauer, Charles Humphrey	Shute, John William	1507
Lobdell, Edward John	Lobdell, John	1508
Hisky, John Guido	Shipley, William	1509
Hisky, William George	Shipley, William	1510
Dorrance, Charles Samuel	Dorrance, George	1511
Dorney, Charles Polk	Dove, William Geoghegan	1512
Hughes, Adrian	Hughes, Thomas	1513
Sample, Mathias William	Zimmerman, David	1514
Allen, Thomas Lamb	Allen, William Henry	1515
Busch, Henry Paul	Boyle, Philip	1516
Dilks, Walter Howard, Jr.	Hyland, Stephen	1517
Thomas, Warner Roberts	Fulmer, John	1518
Banks, Clayton French	Stowe, Daniel	1519
Atkinson, Benjamin Walker, Jr.	Atkinson, Henry Walker, Benjamin	1520
Hornblower, Josiah	Hornblower, Josiah	1521
Merseles, Frank Hornblower	Hornblower, Josiah	1522
Hornblower, William	Hornblower, Josiah	1523
Hoffnagle, Herbert Daniel	Hoffnagle, John	1524
Thayer, Corwin Moffat	Thayer, Oppolos	1525
Harris, William Barney, Jr.	Barney, Joshua	1526
Slothower, Henry	Clagett, Elie	1527
Wiegand, William Green	Wiegand, Daniel	1528
Williams, George Washington	Williams, Joseph	1529
Fackenthal, Frank Diehl	Dennis, Adam	1530
Ashby, Bernard	Ashby, Nimrod	1531
Dexter, Henry Clinton	Slocum, Benjamin	1532
Stiness, Edward Clinton Bessom	Stiness, Samuel	1533
Dexter, Theodore Everett	Slocum, Benjamin	1534
Finley, Mark Florus	Finley, William	1535

The Roster 61

MEMBER	ANCESTOR	GEN. SOC. NO.
Finley, Mark Florus, Jr.	Finley, William	1536
Focke, Harry Smull	Smull, Jacob	1537
Leary, Rudolph Williams	Leary, Peter	1538
Miller, Charles Robert	Miller, John	1539
Smith, Francis Scott Key	Key, Francis Scott	1540
Johnson, Boone Van Horn	Johnson, John	1541
Crowell, Samuel Babcock, Jr.	Babcock, Samuel, Jr.	1542
Crowell, John Head	Babcock, Samuel, Jr.	1543
Smith, Jesse Marion	Thompson, Isaac	1544
Stull, Raymond	Stull, Adam	1545
Pearson, Robert Humphreys	Nichols, Robert Humphreys	1546
Drayton, Joseph William	Hillyer, Simon	1547
Winans, James Dusenberry	Winans, William Wanton	1548
Pugh, Alexander Lefever, Jr.	Dudley, Peter	1549
Martin, Wm. Arthur, Jr.	Kip, Henry	1550
Hunt, Brandon Noble	Moulton, Abel	1551
Turner, John Henry	Lazell, Sylvanus	1552
Houck, George Wesley	Houck, John	1553
Houck, Harry Elijah	Houck, John	1554
Davis, Harry Alexander	Norris, John Bradford Davis, William Grant, William	1555
Robinson, Erdis Geroska	Holden, Abel	1556
Parker, George Turner	Atkins, Quintus Flaminius	1557
Gentry, William Richard	Gentry, Richard	1558
Babbitt, Byron Fenner	Babbitt, Amos	1559
Douglas, Archer Wall	Brown, Thomas	1560
Jackson, John Collins	Collins, John Alexander	1561
Brown, James Newton	McLaughlin, James, Jr.	1562
Buckland, Samuel Aldrich	Buckland, Frank	1563
Matthews, James Alonzo	Allison, Hugh	1564
Lewis, Edward McElhiney	Cook, Richard Fielding	1565
Sumwalt, John Wesley Richardson	Danker, John J.	1566
Faidley, Harvey Franklin	Faidley, John	1567
Dexter, Charles Asa	Slocum, Benjamin	1568
Dold, Douglas Meriwether	Dold, Samuel Miller, Sr.	1569
Dold, Wm. Elliott, Jr.	Dold, Samuel Miller, Sr.	1570
Sayre, Lansing Glen Lytle	Newell, Rezon Bryant	1571
Grimke, Frederic Drayton	Walker, Isaac	1572
Reid, James Thompson	Hodges, George Washington	1573
Adams, William Waugh	Hoover, John	1574
Eiler, Homer	Sharrock, Everard	1575
Lord, Frank Howard	Skinner, Daniel	1576

62 The Roster

MEMBER	ANCESTOR	GEN. SOC. NO.
McNair, James Birtley	McNair, Thomas	1577
Duncan, Daniel Lewis	Duncan, Wesley Leland	1578
Kneass, Carl Magee	Kneass, Christian	1579
Ashbridge, Whitney	Nichols, Francis (Boude)	1580
Stewart, Francis Edward	Nicholson, Orson	1581
Boyer, George Washington	Boyer, William	1582
Stockwell, John Wesley, Jr.	Mathias, Griffith	1583
Hitch, David Marshall	Harris, Robert Lacey	1584
Martin, George Kip	Kip, Henry	1585
Martin, Edwin Hulshizer	Kip, Henry	1586
Newkirk, Eugene	Kip, Henry	1587
Owens, Edward Burneston, Jr.	Owens, Joseph Buck, Benjamin Cassard, Gilbert	1588
Reeder, Charles Merrick	Reeder, Charles	1589
Stafford, Morgan Hewett	Lothrop, Ebenezer	1590
Herrick, Robert Webster	Benjamin, Samuel	1591
Richardson, Baury Bradford	Richardson, Charles	1592
Jackson, Wm. Benjamin, Sr.	Bush, William S.	1593
Lanahan, William Wallace	Reeder, Charles	1594
McColgan, Edward	Reeder, Charles	1595
Reeder, Charles Howard	Reeder, Charles	1596
Reeder, Charles Leonard	Reeder, Charles	1597
Reeder, James Dawson	Reeder, Charles	1598
Reeder, Leonard Ben	Reeder, Charles	1599
Reeder, Maurice Lanahan	Reeder, Charles	1600
Webb, William Rollins	Webb, Abner, Jr.	1601
Colbert, Philip Maulsby	Hayes, Walter Cody	1602
Bruce, Pearl Willard	Goucher, Robert	1603
Lewis, Richard Brainard	Lewis, Jonathan	1604
Thorne, Albert George	Dana, Francis	1605
Davis, James Madison	Davis, William	1606
McKinnell, William Wendell Bollman	Bollman, Thomas (Gottlieb)	1607
Reynolds, Frank Starr	Reynolds, Joseph Carter, Daniel	1608
Hooper, James Mason	Mason, James	1609
Stockwell, Herbert Grant	Mathias, Griffith	1610
Stockwell, Joseph Francis	Mathias, Griffith	1611
Donaldson, Francis Adams, Jr.	Landell, George	1612
Henderson, Frank Clarence	Henderson, John	1613
Miles, Benjamin Cottman	Starne, Joseph	1614
Miles, Joseph Starne	Starne, Joseph	1615

MEMBER	ANCESTOR	GEN. SOC. NO.
Shope, Edward Pierce Lentz	Shope, Henry Adam	1616
Shope, Samuel Zimmerman	Shope, Henry Adam	1617
Salmon, Harvey Wallis, III	Wear, Samuel	1618
Holden, Edwin Roy	Holden, Abel	1619
Diggs, Charles Francis	Diggs, Beverly	1620
Packer, Frank Marcus	Packer, George	1621
Macy, Edward Warren	Dewing, Warren Dewing, Timothy	1622
Weeks, Sinclair	Weeks, John Wingate	1623
Beers, Walter Whitney	Beers, Abel	1624
Burtnett, Bertrand Garrison	Burtnett, Daniel	1625
Libby, Henry Mortimer	Burtnett, Daniel	1626
Young, Howard Edward	Weigle, Samuel	1627
Reeder, Clarence	Reeder, Charles	1628
Frazer, Goerge Augustine	Frazer, James	1629
Pratt, Walter Merriam	Lemont, John	1630
Wing, William Arthur	Howland, Joshua	1631
Baldwin, Charles Gambrill	Baldwin, William Henry	1632
Aldrich, Richard Stoddard	Joy, James	1633
Hoffnagle, Harry Herbert	Hoffnagle, John	1634
Snow, Henry	Inloes, William	1635
Mears, Adelbert Warren	Belote, Charles	1636
Mears, Christian Emmerich	Belote, Charles	1637
Read, Harold Comer	Hull, William	1638
Stafford, Russell Henry	Lothrop, Ebenezer	1639
Clarke, George Sharp	Sage, Henry	1640
Danenhower, Edward Bushell	Goodman, Samuel	1641
Winslow, Lorenzo Simmons	Carpenter, Francis	1642
Russell, Lyman Brightman	Russell, Henry Brightman, George Cleaver	1643
Roush, Lyman Plummer	Roush, Henry, Sr.	1644
Currie, William Thomas	Currie, Ezekiel	1645
Dickey, Edmund Sadtler	Sadtler, Philip Benjamin	1646
Reeder, Amos Alphonse	Reeder, Charles	1647
Reeder, Thomas Leonard	Reeder, Charles	1648
Sage, William H.	Robson, Benjamin Ross	1649
Baldwin, Willard Augustine	Baldwin, William Henry	1650
Baldwin, Summerfield, Jr.	Baldwin, William Henry	1651
Pierce, Charles Carroll	Neil, John Glidden Gorham, Barna (Barnabas)	1652
Hanna, Meredith	Hanna, John	1653
Brock, John William	Brock, John, Jr.	1654
Shober, Reginald K.	Shober, Samuel L.	1655

MEMBER	ANCESTOR	GEN. SOC. NO.
Dilks, John Hyland	Hyland, Stephen	1656
Trowbridge, Charles Reuben	Trowbridge, Reuben	1657
Kress, Claude Washington	Kress, Henry	1658
Kress, Palmer John	Kress, Henry	1659
Montgomery, Thomas Lynch	Montgomery, John Crathorne	1660
Balthis, William Leonard	Balthis, George	1661
Kramer, Leighton	Scott, Andrew	1662
Joseph, Rupert Laurens	Hart, Bernard	1663
Wiggin, Burton Howe	Robbins, Asa, Jr.	1664
Becker, John Austin	Shaver, Peter	1665
Porter, Robert Lee, Jr.	Buck, Benjamin	1666
Peice, George	Neil, John Glidden	1667
Taylor, Arthur Rodney	Taylor, James	1668
Hooper, Oliver Furbish	Mason, James	1669
Reeder, Charles Merrick	Reeder, Charles	1670
Clearwaters, John Frederick	Gookins, William, Jr.	1671
Taylor, Blair	Taylor, Robert A.	1672
Schrum, John Luther	Schrum (Shrum), George	1673
Markle, Augustus Robert	Markle, Abraham	1674
Taylor, Harold	Taylor, Robert A.	1674A
Thacker, Henry Heston	Thacker, Allen	1675
Reasoner, Mark Howard	Miranda, Jonathan	1676
Watkins, Oscar Leon	Southard, William	1677
McAlpin, Milo Frederick	Graves, Lucius	1678
McAlpin, Charles Walter	Graves, Lucius	1679
Clearwaters, James Donald	Barnes, James	1680
Schrum, Otto David	Schrum, (Shrum) George	1681
Calvert, George Chambers	Chambers, James	1682
Clearwaters, John Harold	Barnes, James	1683
Hodges, Fletcher	Hill, Joseph, Jr.	1684
Leete, Frederick Deland	Deland, Levi	1685
Morgan, George Edward	Williams, Abner Morton	1686
Richardson, Hervey Bigelow	Richardson, William Hervey	1687
Symmes, Samuel Dunn	Dunn, Nathaniel A.	1688
Miller, Clair LeMoine	George, William, Jr.	1689
Ristine, Harley Thompson	Ristine, Henry	1690
Ristine, Theodore Harmon	Ristine, Henry	1691
Ristine, Warren Henry	Ristine, Henry	1692
Dresser, Frank Estervan	Dresser, Thomas	1693
Glover, Charles Carroll, Jr.	Glover, Charles	1694
Baldwin, John Ashby	Baldwin, William Henry	1695
Markle, Richard Theodore	Markle, Abraham	1696

MEMBER	ANCESTOR	GEN. SOC. NO.
Hastings, Morris Chase	Burr, Timothy	1697
Sherman, William Edgar	Sherman, Aaron	1698
Mackenzie, John Moores Maynadier	Mackenzie, Thomas Downing, Howell	1699
Offutt, Thomas Worthington	Jenkins, Felix	1700
Thomas, Harry George	Thomas, Charles W.	1701
Jones, Robert Copeland	Bowie, Eversfield	1702
TenEyck, Peter Gansevoort	TenEyck, Coenradt	1703
Whipple, Charles Henry	Wright, Benjamin	1704
Kinsey, John Ingham	Young, John Jr.	1705
Stanton, Herbert Charles	Stanton, William, II	1706
Reeves, John Woolson, II	Bancroft, John, III	1707
Forbes, William Innes	Forbes, Murray	1708
Kramer, Albert Ludlow, Jr.	Scott, Andrew	1709
Roberts, Graham	Graham, George	1710
Dell, Charles Squires	Mills, Ezekiel, Sr.	1711
Dell, Samuel Mills	Mills, Ezekiel, Sr.	1712
Dell, Thomas Medairy, Jr.	Mills, Ezekiel, Sr.	1713
Riggs, Richard Cromwell	Riggs, Elisha	1714
Hartman, Ralph William	Chambers, James	1715
Behm, Henry Godley	Helmbold, Goerge	1716
Blessing, Alexander Francis	Boone, Mordecai	1717
Hathaway, Harry St.Clair	Snyder, John C.	1718
Brooke, Francis Mark	Brooke, Nathan	1719
Cochran, Samuel Payntz	Bayless, Benjamin	1720
Parmenter, Elmer Ellsworth	Paramenter, Joseph	1721
Jones, William	Cranston, James	1722
Pond, Walter Hinckley	Pond, Ashley Pond, Benjamin Hinckley, Nathaniel	1723
Hill, John Phillip	Clayton, Philip	1724
Rawlings, James Madison	Rawlings, Benjamin	1725
Mackenzie, George Norbury, IV	Mackenzie, Thomas	1726
Sharp, Alfred Elliott	Boomer, Daniel	1727
Clark, Elmer Sayre	Clark, Samuel	1728
Harrison, George	Harrison, Thomas Edward	1729
Dell, Albert Hampson	Mills, Ezekiel, Sr.	1730
Drown, Charles Lincoln	Lake, Isaac	1731
Southard, Lawrence	Southard, John	1732
Folsom, Wendell Burt	Folsom, Josiah	1733
Frye, Leslie Alva	Hoffman, John	1734
Beals, Donald Marcy	Champion, Sylvester	1735
Roosevelt, Ralph Moross	Roosevelt, Thomas Wilton	1736

MEMBER	ANCESTOR	GEN. SOC. NO.
Perkins, Constantine Marrast	Perkins, Richard	1737
Carman, Travers Denton	Carman, Richard	1738
Hollyday, Thomas Worthington	Worthington, Rezin Hammond	1739
Fish, Roswell Oliver	Champion, Roswell, Jr.	1740
DeWeese, Walter Earl	Wersler, John Gulden	1741
Williams, Herman Warner, Jr.	Dunbar, Hosea	1742
Ryan, Franklin Winton	Ryan, Thomas	1743
Kuper, William Henry	Turner, William	1744
Cummins, Wm. Jennings, III	Cummins, John	1745
Benedict, Charles Emerson	Benedict, Isaac	1746
Moriarty, George Andrews, Jr.	Moriarty, John	1747
Woodman, Walter Irving	Woodman, Moses	1748
Filkins, Douglas C.	Fuller, Moses	1749
Filkins, Daniel G.	Fuller, Moses	1750
Liebmann, August George	McAfee, John	1751
Long, Charles Colfax	Vandenbemden, Joseph	1752
Bonnaffon, Ashton Clagett	Bonnaffon, Anthony	1753
Brown, William Findlay	Shunk, Francis Rawn	1754
Brown, William Findlay, Jr.	Shunk, Francis Rawn	1755
Cadwalader, John, III	Cadwalader, Thomas	1756
Massey, Frank Horgan, II	Vogdes, Jacob	1757
Massey, Jay Richardson	Vogdes, Jacob	1758
Massey, Maurice Richardson, Jr.	Vogdes, Jacob	1759
Ottey, Abram Carter Farr	Trites, John	1760
Tifft, John Alden	Brooke, William	1761
Barton, Lyman Guy	Akin, Abraham, Jr.	1762
	Akin, Martin James	
Larkin, Hanford William	Larkin, Elam	1763
McGarry, Wm. Rutledge	McGarry, William Rodney	1764
Linthicum, John Charles	Linthicum, Abner	1765
McCurley, William Stran	McCurley, Felix	1766
Boswell, Frederick Page	Boswell, Henry	1767
Pitcher, William Henry, Jr.	Porter, Wrixham Lewis	1768
	Fountain, Henry	
Pierce, Arthur Johnson	Lillie, Samuel Shaw	1769
Colman, Paul Fessenden	Fessenden, Thomas	1770
Gardner, Lester Durand	Sweetser, Seth	1771
	Rogers, William	
Chewning, Wm. Jeffries Jr.	Chewning, Reuben	1772
Foreman, Albert Watson	Alden, Ebenezer	1773
Long, James Hall	Rich, Joel	1774
	Rich, John Jr.	
Bronaugh, Frederick Louis	Bronaugh, William	1775

MEMBER	ANCESTOR	GEN. SOC. NO.
Bulkeley, Houghton	Morgan, Avery	1776
Willis, John Edward	McCartney, John	1777
Kenyon, Howard Nathaniel	Kenyon, Samuel Rogers	1778
Brown, George Hollister	Boyd, John	1779
Harding, Charles Trott	Melzard, Benjamin	1780
Adams, Herbert Luther	Trowbridge, Luther	1781
Schryver, Floyd Wade	Wade, Lewis	1782
Cass, Kingman Packard	Kingman, Edward	1783
Meyer, Harold Irving	Stucky, John Rogers, John	1784
McNair, Hugh	McNair, David	1785
Goltz, Carlos Washington	Wakefield, Matthew	1786
Blatchford, Charles Lord	Wickes, Van Wyck	1787
Britigan, William Henry	Lemon, Isaac	1788
Britigan, Herbert Dana	Brown, David	1789
Lord, William Adgate	Lord, Joseph	1790
Coppage, John W.	Deane, Ambrose	1791
Mattern, Edwin Lafayette	Snyder, David	1792
Baldridge, Joseph Evans	Beatty, Hamilton	1793
Brown, Alexander Paul	Shunk, Francis Rawn	1794
Dillenbeck, Clark	Shell, George I.	1795
Green, Robert McCay, III	Green, Isaac	1796
Russell, Charles Jacob	Russell, William, III	1797
Belsterling, Charles Starne	Preston, William	1798
Landon, Herman Robert	Landon, Walsten Tolin, James	1799
Leonard, Laurence	Morin, Josiah	1800
White, Glenn William	Stiles, Joseph	1801
Beals, John David, Jr.	Champion, Henry	1802
Kern, Ralph Donald	Nichols, Zadok	1803
Whitney, Edson Leone	Whitney, Joseph	1804
Norton, Richard Pearson	Norton, Zacheus	1805
Turner, Molyneaux Lawrence	Woodbury, Robert	1806
Baskette, Alvin K.	Owin, James	1807
Linthicum, George Milton	Linthicum, Abner	1808
Haas, William Henry, Jr.	Haas, Samuel	1809
Allison, Albert Crawford Green	Hart, William Watts	1810
Edmundson, Frank Busha	Bateman, Benjamin	1811
Keller, George Troxell	Young, John, Jr.	1812
Kelly, John Alexander	Everett, Joseph	1813
Povenmire, Harlo Monroe	Bobenmoyer, John	1814
Rambo, Ormond, Jr.	Luffberry, John	1815
Williams, Lester James	Porter, Shadrach	1816

MEMBER	ANCESTOR	GEN. SOC. NO.
Hollis, Minot Everett	Hollis, Jonathan	1817
Cromwell, Oliver Colbert	Cromwell, Oliver	1818
Betts, Philander, III	Betts, James	1819
Hall, Wm. Hunt, Jr.	Hall, Edward Pearsall	1820
Porter, David Dixon	Porter, David	1821
Dukehart, Morton McIlvain	Dukehart, Henry V.	1822
Tollerton, Robert Wm.	Gunn, John	1823
Sears, Francis Richmond	Macumber, Ephraim	1824
Moore, Henry Virginius	Cory, William	1825
Morgan, Philip Sidney	Berry, John	1826
Calder, Philip Raymond	Calder, William	1827
Skinner, Maurice Edward	Jones, John	1828
Butler, Gurdon Montague	Butler, Lemuel G. Post, Oliver	1829
Corson, Alan, Jr.	McPherson, Henry Hendley	1830
Corson, Burton Francis	McPherson, Henry Hendley	1831
Morris, Lawrence Johnson	Cheston, James	1832
Sutter, William Henry	Rover, John	1833
Davis, William McCay	McCay, William	1834
Betts, Philander Hammer, III	Betts, James Shirk, John	1835
Brown, Harry Charles	Brown, Stewart (Stuart)	1836
Lord, Wm. Adgate, Jr.	Lord, Joseph	1837
Hooker, Roland Mather	Francis, John Williams, Solomon, Jr.	1838
Whittinghill, George David	Phillips, Solomon	1839
Clark, Dwight	Cotting, William Thomas, Richard	1840
Janney, Mahlon Hopkins	Jameson, William	1841
Cunningham, Carleton Brown	Cunningham, John	1842
Healy, Francis Augustine Alphonsus	Smith, John	1843
Nelson, Richard Douglas	Cole, Barnet	1844
Richards, John Bion	Ramsdell, Abner	1845
Simmons, Manfred Elliston	Simmons, James, Sr.	1846
Sherman, Franklin Chapman	Low, Samuel Sherman, Asaph	1847
Hooker, Thomas Bedell	Williams, Solomon, Jr.	1848
Hooker, Bryan Edward	Williams, Solomon, Jr.	1849
Peirce, George Fales	Neil, John Glidden	1850
Burt, Frank Hunt	Burt, Franklin	1851
Rand, Waldron Holmes, Jr.	Holmes, Nathaniel, Jr.	1852
Klugh, Paul Brown	Jones, Isaac Brown, David	1853

The Roster

MEMBER	ANCESTOR	GEN. SOC. NO.
Pugh, Henry Donne	Dudley, Peter	1854
Smith, Robert Palmer	Smith, John Wheeler	1855
Fitchet, Seth Marshall	Fitchet, James N.	1856
Hollis, Charles William	Hollis, Jonathan	1857
Kemp, Theodore Halsey	Felter, John Polhemus	1858
Kemp, George Washington	Felter, John Polhemus	1859
Webb, Wm. Rollins, Jr.	Webb, Abner, Jr.	1860
Paddock, Edwin Loveland	Paddock, Loveland	1861
Towne, Phineas	Town, Stephen	1862
Badgley, William Walton	Badgley, Aaron	1863
Steele, Frank Bartlett	Hull, William	1864
Rockwell, Paul Ayres	Baldwin, David	1865
Henrici, Max	Benton, John	1866
Jenness, Herbert Leon	Toxier, Stephen	1867
Carty, Alton Burnside	Lugenbeel, Moses	1868
Carty, Roy Franklin	Lugenbeel, Moses	1869
Hume, Edgar Erskine, Jr.	Hume, Charles	1870
Perkins, Mahlon Fay	Perkins, Moses	1871
Schmidt, Manfield	Mansfield, Leonard Dyre	1872
Aller, Harris Coles	Aller, Peter	1873
Garvin, Howard Madison	Burks, Rowland Peartree	1874
Reeves, Howard Gendell	Bancroft, John, III	1875
Smith, Wm. Poultney	Shinn, John	1876
Faxon, Charles Henry	Faxon, Walter Stiles Barnes, Elijah	1877
Hogeboom, Francklyn	Hogeboom, Peter L.	1878
Greely, John Nesmith	Greely, John Balch	1879
Shane, Edward Melburn	Shane, Daniel	1880
Oliver, Henry Addison	Towne, Elijah	1881
Fairbank, Leigh Cole	Fairbank, George	1882
Cairns, Douglas Walker	Bogardus, Robert	1883
Pentz, John Angelo	Pentz, John Joseph	1884
Gould, Lyttleton Bowen Purnell	Berry, John	1885
Myers, Philip	Metcalfe, Thomas	1886
Ijams, George Edwin	Ijams, John	1887
Wilder, William Murtha	Wilder, Sampson	1888
Hooper, Stuart Cator	Brohawn, John	1889
Brower, Ogden	Brower, John Lefoy	1890
Weaverling, Charles Clair	Weaverling, John	1891
Fish, Erland Frederick	Fish, Simeon, Sr. Fish, Simeon, Jr.	1892
Hoffman, Benjamin Rose	Hoffman, Jacob	1893
Morris, Elliston Joseph, Jr.	Cheston, James	1894

MEMBER	ANCESTOR	GEN. SOC. NO.
Regar, George Bertram	Regar, Henry	1895
Swing, Albert Holmes	Swing, Abraham	1896
Ambrose, Thomas	Ambrose, Mordecai	1897
Hurd, Joy Seth	Hurd, Joy	1898
Kendall, Messmore	Goodhue, Joseph	1899
Ketcham, John Lewis	Ketcham, John	1900
Henderson, Branton Holstein	Couch, Philip	1901
Regan, James, III	Ridgate, Benjamin Cornick	1902
D'Enbo, Francis J.	Denbo, Joseph	1903
Pickens, Henry	Read, Sion Spencer	1904
Zoll, Allen Alderson	McMaken (McMahan), Joseph Hamilton	1905
Smull, George Warner	Smull, Jacob	1906
Bottomley, Henry Stone	West, Leonard	1907
Shattuck, Levi Hubbard	Cole, Royal	1908
Sadler, Lucien MacDowell	Fountain, Andrew	1909
Willis, William Clifford	Crane, Elias Crane, John	1910
Dutcher, Henry Redman	Jayne, Benajah (Benaar)	1911
Morgan, Charles Lemon	Lemon, Mathias	1912
Rich, John Allen	Rich, John, Jr.	1913
Orvis, Edwin Waitstill	Orvis, Elihu	1914
Orvis, Homer Waitstill	Orvis, Elihu	1915
Orvis, Warner Dayton	Orvis, Elihu	1916
Orvis, Arthur Emerton	Orvis, Elihu	1917
Plummer, Thomas Parran	Waring, Henry, Jr.	1918
Miller, Burke Hammond	Miller, John	1919
Gardiner, William Howard	Baird, Thomas James	1920
Pinkerton, Paul Price	Pinkerton, William	1921
Dupray, Frederick Hervey	Duprey (Dupray), Thomas	1922
Slavens, Thomas Horace	Slavens, Isaiah Stanley, Page	1923
Towne, John William	Towne, Stephen	1924
Gardiner, Edward Carey	Baird, Thomas James	1925
Hoff, Arthur Bainbridge, Jr.	Bainbridge, William	1926
Kehew, Nox McCain	Rockefeller, Henry	1927
McCain, Donald Rockefeller, Jr.	Rockefeller, Henry	1928
Ligget, Robert Charles	Russell, Henry	1929
Runk, John Ten Broeck	Jeffries, John	1930
Runk, Louis Barcroft	Barcroft, Stacy Brown	1931
Swing, James Truman	Swing, Abraham	1932
Swing, Robert Hamill D.	Swing, Abraham	1933

MEMBER	ANCESTOR	GEN. SOC. NO.
Willis, Conover English	Baldwin, Stephen Crane, Elias Crane, John	1934
Reddish, Craig Leslie	Reddish, Silas	1935
Orvis, Schuyler Adams	Orvis, Elihu	1936
Orvis, Schuyler Adams, Jr.	Orvis, Elihu	1937
Washburn, Lester Allison	Alliston, Dennis	1938
Adare, Charles Henry, Jr.	Raymond, Josiah	1939
Burpee, Washington A., Jr.	Ashmead, Isaac	1940
Mercur, James Watts, Jr.	Davis, John	1941
Helick, Reuben Harold	Hellick (Helick), Jacob	1942
Kohler, Frederic Dudley	Kohler, George	1943
Lamb, Scott Grisell	Lamb, Jacob	1944
Sherron, James Fenton, Jr.	Delaney, Jacob	1945
Warren, Lawrence Seymour	Warren, Benjamin	1946
Merwin, William Walters	Merwin, Miles	1947
Hay, Randall Groves	Hay, Peter	1948
Lyon, John Augustus	Lyon, John S.	1949
Winters, George Edward	Winters, Daniel	1950
Cushman, Seth Wilson	Cushman, Seth	1951
Grubert, Reese Thompson	Thompson (Thomson), William	1952
Beardsley, Harry Judson	Judson, Henry	1953
Gardner, Laurence Russell	Bailty, Jacob G.	1954
Altaffer, Maurice Willard	Altaffer, John	1955
Thomas, Guy Alfred	Nimocks, Rowland	1956
Wilbar, Waldo Morton	Fobes, Joshua, 2nd.	1957
Dana, Edward	Saunders, Samuel Little	1958
Deatrick, Ambrose Winston	Nugent, David McDonald, James	1959
Lloyd, William Henry	Borden, Francis Hopkins, Charles B. Strawbridge, John	1960
Detwiler, David Roy	Breidenthal, Henry	1961
Hampton, Vernon Boyce	Webb, Samuel	1962
Claflin, Leander Chapin	Farrington, Elijah	1963
Packard, Kent	Packard, Hezekiah	1964
Patterson, James Otey	Otey, Armistead	1965
Dana, Harold Ward	Dana, George	1966
Graham, Arthur Butler	Graham, Henry	1967
Boggs, John Lawrence	Lawrence, James	1968
Weld, John Gardner	Curtis, George	1969
Logan, Harry Craig	O'Neale, William	1970
Farmer, Zelah Rice	Farmer, John	1971
Fairbank, Leigh Cole, Jr.	Fairbank, George	1972

MEMBER	ANCESTOR	GEN. SOC. NO.
Musser, Earl Beachy	Myers, Michael, Sr.	1973
Guernsey, Raimund Thomas	Mickley (Mickly), Jacob	1974
Sargent, Edward Rotan	Worcester, Samuel	1975
Sargent, Winthrop, Jr.	Worcester, Samuel	1976
Rambo, Bertram Pierre	Luffberry, John, Jr.	1977
Boden, Harry Clark	Boden, John Newkirk, Matthew	1978
LeMar, Harold Diehl	Lemar, James	1979
Glover, Charles Carroll, III	Glover, Charles	1980
Matheny, Willard Reynolds	Matheny, Charles Reynolds	1981
Willis, Urban George	Willis, James H., Jr.	1982
Day, James Westbay	Day, Morgan	1983
Carey, Lee Cummins	Cummins, John	1984
Huson, Hobart, II	Miller, Ezra Huson, Calvin, Sr.	1985
Colvin, Harold Riley	Crooks William	1986
Hampton, Wm. Judson, Jr.	Webb, Samuel	1987
Moody, Alfred Alric	Moody, Jacob S.	1988
Smith, Elizur Yale	Bulkeley, Joshua	1989
Ansart, Louis Loomis	Ansart, Felix	1990
Whitney, Allan Joseph	Flansburgh, Jacob	1991
Pierce, William Greene	Neil, John Glidden	1992
Rex, Daniel Ferrell	Betz, George Ferrell, Lewis Wells Kemmerer, John Myers, Peter, Jr. Radabaugh, John	1993
Calder, Philip Raymond, Jr.	Calder, William	1994
French, Bruce Hartung	French, Grovey	1995
McIntire, Edward Harding	Alexander, James	1996
Sargent, Winthrop, 3rd.	Worcester, Samuel	1997
Sargent, Samuel Worcester	Worcester, Samuel	1998
VanDeventer, Horace	VanDeventer, Christopher	1999
Cramer, Kenneth Frank	Clark, Ralph	2000
Kileski, Frederic G.	Fletcher, Phineas Parker	2001
Hamilton, George H.	Hamilton, William	2002
Long, Charles R.	Green, Jesse	2003
Sargent, Fitzwilliam, 3rd.	Worcester, Samuel	2004
McCreery, Samuel	McNeir, William	2005
Sturgis, Samuel B.	Sturgis, Nathan	2006
Eshleman, Benjamin	Davis, John	2007
Wolcott, John Dorsey	Cornwell, William	2008
Rice, William Elmer	McCurley, John	2009
Babson, John Capron	Haraden, Nathaniel	2010

MEMBER	ANCESTOR	GEN. SOC. NO.
Gibbs, Frederick Roccofort	Gibbs, Jacob	2011
Weakley, Raymond DeCamp	Swain, Charles W.	2012
Wager, John Philip	Wager, Philip	2013
Scott, George Addison	Jones, Richard Yeaton	2014
Carnrick, Millard	Hilton, John	2015
Brown, William Samuel, Jr.	Brown, Stewart	2016
Walker, Isaac Henry	Walker, Isaac	2017
Scully, Charles Alison	Scott, John	2018
Burpee, Washington A., III	Ashmead, Isaac	2019
Goodridge, Edwin Tyson	Goodridge, Ira	2020
Hinkson, J. T. Ward	Caldwell, Thomas	2021
McCreery, Samuel, Jr.	McNeir, William	2022
Sargent, Compton	Worcester, Samuel	2023
Tower, Charlemagne	Tower, Reuben	2024
Watts, David Miller	Miller, Henry	2025
Page, Thomas Neilson	McCorison, William	2026
Hughes, John Francis, II	Norris, John Bradford	2027
Hughes, Harry A. D.	Davis, William	2028
Anderson, Nils, Jr.	Massie, Peter	2029
Litts, Raymond N. J.	Shields, Thomas	2030
Bielaski, Frank Brooks	Cary, Robert James	2031
Fell, Charles Woodford	Ketcham, John	2032
Martin, Ora Alexander	Reynolds, John	2033
Wurts, John Sparhawk	Noble, John	2034
Claghorn, Charles E., 3rd.	Claghorn, John William	2035
McMichael, Cyrus	Mason, John	2036
Swing, Edward C. K.	Swing, Abraham	2037
Swing, Robert H. D., Jr.	Swing, Abraham	2038
Rolston, Lyon	Coles, James	2039
Colby, Lafayette	Colby, Thomas W.	2040
Dana, Richard Hardy	Saunders, Samuel Little	2041
Carver, Eugene P., Jr.	Pendleton, Phineas	2042
Swift, James Marcus	Swift, John	2043
Bonelli, Louis Henry, Jr.	Breed, Aaron	2044
Weeks, George W., III	Weeks, Stephen	2045
Taylor, Ira Thomas	Taylor, Henry	2046
Clark, Ivor Bach	Hudson, William Leverett	2047
Sanford, William Lanahan	Warner, Michael	2048
Kirk, Charles Gilbert	Gilbreath, Benjamin Wright, Morgan	2049
Brittin, Lewis Hitchcock	Brittin, William	2050
Collins, Charles F.	Jones, William	2051
King, Joseph Choate	King, Benjamin, III	2052

MEMBER	ANCESTOR	GEN. SOC. NO.
Thomas, David, 2nd.	Scheetz, Henry	2053
Hopkinson, Edward, Jr.	Swaim, William	2054
White, Richard Kerr	Kerr, David	2055
White, Thomas Roberts, Jr.	Kerr, David	2056
Pennypacker, Bevan A.	Whitaker, Joseph	2057
Hellick, George Franklin	Hellick (Hellic), Jacob	2058
Hellick, George Franklin, Jr.	Hellick (Hellic), Jacob	2059
Reichner, Morgan S. A.	Fraser, James P.	2060
Metz, Robert E. L.	Berlin, Philip	2061
Densmore, George Ellis	Saunders, Samuel Little	2062
Gibbs, William Frank	Gibbs, Jacob	2063
Montgomery, Hugh E.	Montgomery, John Crathorne	2064
Sykes, A. McKnight	McKnight, John	2065
Howard, Morton	Howard, Maurice	2066
Brown, Henry Paul, III	Houston, Samuel Nelson	2067
Schaff, David S., Jr.	Haynes (Hanes, Haines), John	2068
Brown, Francis Shunk, Jr.	Shunk, Francis Rawn	2069
Hill, Norman Alan	Hill, Thomas, Gardner	2070
Douglass, Rudolph A.A.	Wells, William	2071
Overington, Robert Bruce	Beatty, Henry	2072
Whitney, William R.	Flansburg, Jacob	2073
Mathews, William E.	Sharriot, Abraham	2074
Smith, Stephen DeWitt	Graves, Lucius	2075
Peak, Cassius S.	Allison, Uriah Prigmore, Thomas	2076
Bauer, Richard Wingate	Schute, John William	2077
Hyde, Edward Duncan	Pechin, William	2078
Pentz, Harry G.	Pentz, John Joseph	2079
Englar, David F., Jr.	Metcalfe, Thomas	2080
Pentz, Benjamin H.	Pentz, John Joseph	2081
Brown, Harvey Newton	Brown, George	2082
Parker, Albert	Gridley, Sylvester	2083
Haley, Whitney Watson	Haley, Noah	2084
Williams, Charles Roper	Coleman, Henry Embry	2085
Williams, George B.	Coleman, Henry Embry	2086
Bonniwell, Alfred E.	Capes, William	2087
Bonniwell, Bernard	Capes, William	2088
Bonniwell, Eugene C.	Capes, William	2089
Bonniwell, John Green	Capes, William	2090
Bonniwell, Robert Budd	Capes, William	2091
Cochran, Joseph H.	Allison, William	2092
Perry, Herbert J.	Perry, Jabez	2093
Easby, May Stevenson	Stevenson, Cornelius	2094

The Roster 75

MEMBER	ANCESTOR	GEN. SOC. NO.
Hitch, Marshall D.	Harris, Robert Lacey	2095
Herndon, Richard M.	Turner, Robert	2096
Stockwell, David Hunt	Mathias, Griffith	2097
Clay, William Rogers, Jr.	Clay, Green	2098
Allen, Robert Webster	Coombs, George	2099
	Dickson, John	
Shute, George Cameron	Shute, Andrew B.	2100
Bigelow, William M.	Curtis, Moses	2101
Regar, Gordon R.	Regar, Henry	2102
Major, Ralph H., Jr.	Major, John	2103
Sutcliffe, Richard G.	Gregory, John	2104
Roberts, Harry	Roberts, William	2105
Beckwith, Brainard K.	Mooers, Benjamin	2106
Slingluff, Jesse, Jr.	Slingluff, Jesse	2107
Tracy, Robert C.	Tracy, Dyer, II	2108
Barter, Forest Hermon	Webster, Phineas	2109
Calder, Robert M.	Calder, William	2110
Schaal, Frederick G.	Sibley, Elisha	2111
Seaman, John T.	Smith, Ebenezer H.	2112
Smith, Leroy	Jayne, Morris	2113
Fitler, Dale B.	Fitler, William	2114
Regar, Philip W.	Regar, Henry	2115
Jones, J. Davis	McKnight, John	2116
Jones, Charles M.	duBois, Jeremiah Greenman	2117
Palmer, Frederic Courtland	Palmer, Reuben, Jr.	2118
West, Edward N.	West, Henry	2119
Allen, Covington K., Jr.	Scott, Winfield	2120
Hires, William L.	Hart, William Watts	2121
Herndon, Dale L.	Turner, Robert	2122
Cornman, Frank W., Jr.	Jones, David	2123
Warren, Ulysses Grant, Jr.	Warren, Benjamin	2124
Scott, David J.	Scott, John	2125
Regar, Howard S.	Regar, Henry	2126
Regar, Henry	Regar, Henry	2127
Regar, Newton K.	Regar, Henry	2128
Regar, Clayton	Regar, Henry	2129
Gibble, Isaac O.	Regar, Henry	2130
Clement, James H.	Clement, Evan Collins	2131
Clement, Harrison H.	Clement, Evan Collins	2132
Forbes, William I., Jr.	Forbes, Murray	2133
Forbes, Francis C.	Forbes, Murray	2134
Wiederseim, William C.	Kuns (Koons) (Kuntz), John	2135

MEMBER	ANCESTOR	GEN. SOC. NO.
Burpee, David	Ashmead, Isaac	2136
	Atlee, William Pitt	
Brownfield, Lee B.,II	McCormick, James	2137
Sterling, Montaigu M.	Sterling, Eben	2138
Howard, George S.	Regar, Henry	2139
Lutz, Parke H.	Regar, Henry	2140
Lloyd, James P.	Dunlap, Sallows	2141
Regar, Jason W.	Regar, Henry	2142
Wiederseim, Theordore E.	Koons (Kuns,Kuntz), John	2143
Bispham, Harrison A.	Koons, John	2144
Regar, Ralph E.	Regar, Henry	2145
Regar, Isaac C.	Regar, Henry	2146
Huey, Malcolm S.	Hunt, Simon	2147
Wintringer, George C.	Wintringer, Nathan	2148
Forbes, Charles W.	Forbes, Murray	2149
Hitch, Marshall D.	Harris, Robert Lacey	2150
Fuller, Burdett S.	Fuller, Asaph	2151
Fuller, Byron J.	Fuller, Asaph	2152
Rue, Howard S.	Hanna, John	2153
Rue, Howard S., Jr.	Hanna, John	2154
Rue, William H.	Hanna, John	2155
Rue, John R., 4th.	Hanna, John	2156
Gordon, William R.	Hagler, Benjamin James	2157
Millholland, James H.	Millholland, Robert Douglas	2158
Fitler, Nathan M.	Fitler, William	2159
Elmendorf, Ten Eyck	Elmendorf, Martin	2160
	Ten Eyck, Harmon Hoffman	
Smith, Lloyd D.	Smith, Waitstill	2161
Austin, Richard L.	Austin, Alexander	2162
Fink, Charles E.	Goldsborough, Robert	2163
Collenberg, Henry T., Jr.	Jordan, William	2164
Gans, Arthur D.	Miller, Andrew	2165
Zoll, Allen A., III	McMaken (McMahon), Joseph H.	2166
Holden, James F.	Holden, Abel	2167
Zoll, George C.	McMaken, Joseph H.	2168
Cochran, Joseph A.	Allison, William	2169
McIntire, Alexander R.	Alexander, James	2170
Cornog, David W. L.	Jones, David	2171
Yeakle, Joseph W.	Huston John Jr.	2172
Gibbs, Benjamin	Gibbs, Isaac	2173
Creamer, William H.	Liffberry, John, Jr.	2174
Allen, Philip M.	Cummins, David	2175

MEMBER	ANCESTOR	GEN. SOC. NO.
Whelden, Ford H.	Giddings, Hiram	2176
Hastings, Harold M.	Fillmore, Comfort Day	2177
Baldwin, Frederick J.	Baldwin, Sylvester	2178
Candler, Clarence L.	Boardman, James	2179
Goddard, Calvin H.	Acheson, Thomas	2180
Scott, James K.	Cox, Caleb	2181
Stuart, Harold L.	Bishop, Zepheniah (Phannel), Jr.	2182
Colby, Archie R.	Colby, Thomas W.	2183
Davis, Laurence R.	Perry, Gad	2184
Bender, Addison F., Jr.	Bender, Jacob A.	2185
Esler, Lewis H.	Schlosser, John George	2186
Grimes, George R.	Fite, Caspar	2187
Jacob, Julian H.	Miller, James, II	2188
Melvin, Frank W.	Merritt, John	2189
Sargent, Fitzwilliam	Worcester, Samuel	2190
Scott, Peter D.	Scott, John	2191
Widener, George D.	Elkins (Elkens), George W.	2192
Moorhead, Robert L.	Gordon, Samuel	2193
Springer, Robert G.	Springer, Job	2194
McAlpine, Roderick K.	Graves, Lucius	2195
McAlpine, Roderick K., Jr.	Graves, Lucius	2196
Brooks, Harold C.	Esselstyn, John Brodhead	2197
Edwards, Ray O., Sr.	Russell, George Burr Strevey (Streebery), Peter	2198
Borch, Fred G.	Sharp, Isaac	2199
Stansfield, George J.	Snyder, Adam Vrooman	2200
McIntire, Allyn Brewster	Alexander, James	2201
Deffenbaugh, Goerge S.	Graves, Eliphalet W.	2202
Rider, Charles J.	Hough, Thomas	2203
Dowling, Wilfrid S.	Anderson, John William	2204
Cranford, James Reed	Cranford, John	2205
Whelden, Gilbert Hart	Giddings, Hiram	2206
Whelden, Gilbert Hart, Jr.	Giddings, Hiram	2207
Kolb, Stanley Denmead	Kolb, John William	2208
McComas, Henry Clay	McComas, Henry Gough	2209
		2210 Void
Goodwin-Perkins, Charles A.	Goodwin, John, Sr.	2211
Roberts, Robert Leonard	Vickers, Clement	2212
Mitchell, William A.	Mitchell, George Edward	2213
Martin, Christian Hess	Martin, David	2214
Brautigam, Edward, Jr.	Hornblower, Josiah	2215
Sargent, Gorham P., Jr.	Worcester, Samuel	2216

MEMBER	ANCESTOR	GEN. SOC. NO.
Lloyd, Malcolm, Jr.	Howell, Joshua Ladd	2217
Hepburn, Barry H.	Hayes, Patrick	2218
Hepburn, W. Horace, Jr.	Hayes, Patrick	2219
Camden, Horace P., Jr.	Urwiler, George	2220
Roberts, Robert L., Jr.	Vickers, Clement	2221
Herman, Walter F.	Smull, Jacob	2222
Harrison, John S., 4th.	Harrison, William Henry	2223
Clement, Charles F., Jr.	Clement, Evans Collins	2224
Clement, Henry L.	Clement, Evans Collins	2225
Stuart, Charles J.	Bishop, Zepheniah (Phannel), Jr.	2226
Orcutt, Harry P.	Wood, Enos Nathan	2227
Meade, Thomas W.	Wright, William Alfred	2228
Fernley, George A.	Newkirk, George	2229
Fernley, Thomas A., Jr.	Newkirk, George	2230
Dwier, W. Kirkland	Luffberry, John	2231
Banks, Clayton F., Jr.	Stow, Daniel	2232
LeMar, William B.	LeMar, James	2233
Starling, Guy W., Jr.	Norris, John Bradford	2234
McKinley, Gerald A.	Davidson, Lewis	2235
Aunkst, Straub B.	Aungst, Daniel	2236
Peregoy, Frederick C., Jr.	Buck, Benjamin	2237
Tinges, Charles H.	Webster, John Adams	2238
Stein, Charles F., Jr.	Griffith, Thomas	2239
Bowley, Raymond F.	Churchill, Shepard	2240
Maraspin, Davis G.	Davis, Lothrop	2241
Hardesty, Marion N.	Hardesty, Edward	2242
Miller, Harry E.	Miller, William	2243
Buckles, Frank W.	Lucas, Robert	2244
Brent, Julius H.	Brent, John	2245
Ward, John W., Jr.	Ward, John Wesley	2246
Bliss, Charles J.	Bliss, Francis	2247
Bliss, Maurice H.	Bliss, Francis	2248
Brooke, Edward	Irwin, Matthew	2249
Blinn, Charles P., Jr.	Sargent, Epes Hilton, Morrill	2250
Knox, John	Frushour (Freshour), George	2251
Stoddard, Henry H., Jr.	Day, James	2252
Whelan, Thomas A.	Whelan, Thomas	2253
Townsend, David	Townsend, David S.	2254
Swan, Kenneth F.	Swan, William Lowell, Moses	2255
Cushman, Norman F.	Cushman, Don Alonzo	2256

MEMBER	ANCESTOR	GEN. SOC. NO.
Sillcocks, Henry	Hull, James	2257
Goodwin, William G.	Goodwin, James	2258
Steers, Francis F.	Steers, William	2259
Lee, Leander R.	Taylor, Titus	2260
Kopp, Heber C.	Buvinger, Leonard, Jr.	2261
Rich, William L., Jr.	Rich, Thomas Lathrop	2262
Harris, Joseph N.	Gilberthorp, William	2263
Morse, Richard C.	Donaldson, William	2264
Geer, Herbert W.	Geer, Harris	2265
Tucker, Brison C.	Cumming, Robert	2266
Carswell, Robert M.	Carswell, Robert	2267
Moorhead, Robert G.	Gordon, Samuel	2268
Cook, Ross K.	Cook (Cooke), Adam Ridgway, Andrews	2269
Dodd, Milton C.	Reynolds, Abraham	2270
Dickinson, John	Dickinson, Solomon	2271
Knight, Frederick H.	Knight, Richard	2272
Felton, Samuel M.	Felton, Cornelius Conway	2273
Cecil, Arthur Bond	Owens, Joseph	2274
Hughes, Carroll W., Jr.	Norris, John Bradford	2275
Rieck, Chester E., Jr.	Carlock, Abraham	2276
Wooden, Ernest E.	Huster, Gotlieb	2277
Reed, William B.	Reed, William	2278
Carter, Woodward L.	Carter, Curtis	2279
Lillard, Gerald F.	Lillard, Thomas	2280
Gowen, James Emmet	Winder, Levin	2281
Sutton, James P.	Eckert, Jacob	2282
Wheeler, Harry M.	Wheeler, Thomas	2283
Vincent, Charles R.	Allen, James	2284
Vincent, Charles R., Jr.	Allen, James	2285
Vincent, Patrick T.	Allen, James	2286
Wier, Herbert W.	Wier, John Richard	2287
Carver, Ransom Fuller	Pendleton, Phineas	2288
Bauer, Charles H.	Shute, John William	2289
Owens, William C.	Owens, Joseph	2290
Ijams, George E., Jr.	Ijams, John	2291
Wright, Howard P.	Wright, Benjamin	2292
Brown, Francis S., III	Shunk, Francis Rawn	2293
Ball, Alfred J.	Ball, Israel R.	2294
Merseles, Frank H., Jr.	Hornblower, Josiah	2295
Wiltbank, George E.	Wiltbank, Robert	2296
Constant, Robert F.	Constant, John	2297
Myers, Philip, III	Metcalfe, Thomas	2298

MEMBER	ANCESTOR	GEN. SOC. NO.
Martin, Joseph P.	Pentz, John Joseph	2299
Green, Joseph E., Jr.	Green, Samuel	2300
Shehan, Daniel Edward	Dames, Augustus	2301
Green, Edwin Bernard	Cook, Bernard Henry, Sr.	2302
Parr, Guy Hudson	Rucker, Richard	2303
Rutherford, Milton D.	McClendon, Joel Brown, Joseph	2304
Foster, Dulany	Dulany, Samuel	2305
Christhilf, Stuart, Jr.	Christhilf, Heinrich	2306
Benjamin, James L.	Naseby, John	2307
Stiff, Ashby G.	Stiff, William Nelson	2308
Simmons, James M.	Simmons, James, Sr.	2309
Creesy, George B.	Rea, Ebenezer, Jr.	2310
Wadleigh, Albert P.	Wadleigh, Benjamin Dean	2311
Jackson, William B., Jr.	Bush, William S.	2312
Goodrich, Everett B.	Gardner, David	2313
Warfield, Edwin, III	Watkins, Gassaway	2314
Redding, George Hyde	Redding, Samuel	2315
Peterson, Robert C.	Constant, John	2316
Parr, Lee S.	Blunt, Francis	2317
Stansbury, James E.	Stansbury, Elijah	2318
Hall, George A.	Hall, Martin	2319
Salter, John L., Jr.	Salter, Henry	2320
Richardson, Beale H., IV	Dawson, Thomas Richardson, Genjamin Wimberley, Ezekiel	2321
Rieman, Charles E.	Rieman, Henry	2322
Hopkins, Carroll Creswell	Jones, Hugh Andrew	2323
Reeder, Oliver H.	Reeder, Charles	2324
MacClamroch, James G. W.	Bell, Benjamin	2325
Moore, Pierre Albert	Henshaw, William Slaughter King, John Edwards	2326
McCracken, Robert T.	Wilkins, Robert	2327
Ambler, Frank R.	Smith, Christopher	2328
Ambler, Henry S.	Smith, Christopher	2329
Crowell, Samuel B., III	Babcock, Samuel	2330
Coleman, Bertram D.	Winder, Levin	2331
Taylor, James L., Jr.	Taylor, John Bradford Dyer, William Hay Allen, Shubael Trigg, Stephen	2332
Widener, Peter A. B., III	Thomas, Allen	2333
Elkins, George W., Jr.	Elkins, George W.	2334
Morse, Richard C., Jr.	Donaldson, William	2335

The Roster 81

MEMBER	ANCESTOR	GEN. SOC. NO.
Felton, Samuel M., Jr.	Felton, Cornelius Conway	2336
Young, Edward E.	Young, Jacob	2337
Young, Charles D.	Forster, John, III	2338
George, Thomas S.	Bouldin, Jehu	2339
Ashley, Lawrence I.	Lawrence, Thomas Leggett	2340
Baldwin, Charles E.	Baldwin, William Henry	2341
Christhilf, Stuart M., Sr.	Christhilf, Heinrich	2342
Kolb, Stanley D., Jr.	Kolb, John William	2343
Chittenden, Leslie W.	Lloyd, James, III	2344
Cobb, John Devine, Jr.	Kolb, John William	2345
Kolb, David W.	Kolb, John William	2346
Trueheart, Herbert L.	Buck, Benjamin	2347
Leeming, Leonard B.	Grandy, William	2348
Von der Poel, Peter G.	Ives, Chauncey	2349
Stoughton, Oscar B., Jr.	Brady, Hugh	2350
Anson, Edward Hiram	Anson, Brinton Payne	2351
Swisher, Charles H.	Swisher, Jacob	2352
Cobb, Elliot	Candler, John, Jr.	2353
Hopkins, Henry P.	Chattle, Thomas	2354
Hopkins, Henry P., Jr.	Chattle, Thomas	2355
Dukehart, Thomas V.	Dukehart, Henri Van Arden	2356
Kenyon, Nathaniel C.	Kenyon, Samuel Rogers	2357
Kenyon, Howard N., Jr.	Kenyon, Samuel Rogers	2358
Currie, Edward A., Jr.	Wells, Sheriff	2359
Houston, Harold A.	McCollough, James Brown	2360
Currie, Ulysses B.	Wells, Sheriff	2361
Moore, Henderson A., Jr.	Wells, Sheriff	2362
Shepherd, William E.	Gwynne, David	2363
Rice, William E., Jr.	McCurley, John	2364
Stroud, Howard D.	Wells, Sheriff	2365
Adams, Francis T., Jr.	Darlington, William	2366
Walker, Robert C.	Coleman, Robert L.	2367
Dixon, Fitz-Eugene, Jr.	Elkins, George W.	2368
Barratt, Norris S.	Dill, Robert	2369
Clothier, Isaac H., Jr.	Hallowell, Isaac	2370
Fuller, Edward R.	Fuller, Nathaniel	2371
Ambler, Charles M.	Smith, Christopher	2372
Gold, William B., Jr.	Barnet (Brandt), Michael	2373
Skillern, Ross P.	Porter, James Madison	2374
Johnson, Andrew R., Jr.	Zollinger, Jacob	2375
Sherman, Roy H.	Sherman, Samuel	2376
Ogden, Henry D.	Ogden, Peter Voorhees	2377

82 The Roster

MEMBER	ANCESTOR	GEN. SOC. NO.
Favrot, Henri M.	Favrot, Louis Estevan	2378
Villere, Sidney L.	Villere, Jacques Philippe	2379
Bezou, James F.	Bouligny, Charles J. D.	2380
Villere, James F.	Villere, Jacques Philippe	2381
St. Paul, John, Jr.	de la Houssaye, Louis A.	2382
Barnes, Walter J.	Bankston, John	2383
de la Vergne, Charles E.	Villere, Jacques Philippe	2384
de la Vergne, Hugues J., II	Villere, Jacques Philippe	2385
Deynoodt, Joseph F.	Orso, Zenon	2386
Otis, Walter Joseph	Otis, William	2387
Villere, Ernest C.	Villere, Jacques Philippe	2388
Wilkinson, Hugh M., Sr.	Wilkinson, James	2389
Parker, Herbert C., Jr.	Martin, Joseph Richard	2390
Parker, Herbert C.	Guffin, Andrew	2391
de Kernion, Paul S.	de Kernion, Crispin Charles	2392
Lastrapes, Edwin P.	LeMonnier, Yves	2393
Bayles, Generes D.	Waggaman, George Augustus	2394
Favrot, Clifford F.	Favrot, Louis Estevan	2395
Nott, George W.	Nott, William	2396
Flowers, John R., Jr.	de Chalmette, Ignace de Lino	2397
Hardin, Harry S., Jr.	White, Maunsell	2398
Hardin, Sidney, L.	White, Maunsell	2399
Nicholls, Thomas C., Jr.	Nicholls, Thomas Clark	2400
Favrot, Henry Richmond	Favort, Louis Estevan	2401
White, John Tobin	White, Maunsel	2402
Villere, Henri Francois	Villere, Jacques Philippe	2403
Favrot, Henri Mortimer, Jr.	Favrot, Louis Estevan	2404
de Mont, Edgar Rollins	De Peyster, William	2405
Plauche, Henry	Plauche, Jean Baptiste	2406
Charbonnet, Louis Sidney	Villere, Rene Gabriel	2407
Charbonnet, Emmet Joseph	Villere, Rene Gabriel	2408
Dart, John	Plauche, Henry Urbain	2409
Adams, Lionel	de la Garciniere, Charles Fagot	2410
Lallande, Joseph	Arnoult, Cyril Honore	2411
Pratt, Gerald O'Connor	Henshaw, William Slaughter	2412
Capdevielle, Paul Maine	Miltenberger, Louis Christian	2413
Palfrey, Campbell	Bloomfield, Joseph	2414
Aldige, James George, Jr.	Lepretre, Jean Baptiste	2415
Urquhart, Kenneth Trist	Urquhart, David	2416
Garic, Charles Anthony	Garic, Jean Francois	2417
Plauche, James Joseph, Jr.	Plauche, Jean Baptiste	2418
Legier, John Robert	Newman, Francis	2419

The Roster 83

MEMBER	ANCESTOR	GEN. SOC. NO.
Collenberg, Stewart Neale	Jordan, William	2420
Stafford, Donald Bernard	Calliham, David	2421
Favrot, Joseph St. Clair, Jr.	Favrot, Philogene	2422
Bernard, Joseph Grima	Grima, Barthelemy	2423
Foster, Richard Rushton	Duplessis, Francois, III	2424
Plauche, Walter Flower	Plauche, Jean Baptiste	2425
Maught, Adrien Andrew	Martin, Joseph Richard	2426
de la Vergne, Jules Kristian	Villere, Jacques Philippa	2427
Kock, Edouard James	Lepretre, Jean Baptiste	2428
deColigny, Guerric Gaspard	Cutter, Fitch	2429
Claiborne, Walter Herbert	Claiborne, Ferdinand Leigh	2430
Thompson, William Norton, Jr.	Jones, Roger	2431
Andry, Charles Gilbert	Andry, Michel	2432
Olivier, Felix LaRue	Hebrard, Antoine	2433
Sarpy, Robert Henry	Fortier, Michel, II	2434
Perrilliat, William C.	Claiborne, Ferdinand Leigh	2435
Wisdom, William Bell	Minor, Thomas, II	2436
Monroe, Francis Adair	Adair, John	2437
Messick, Andrew Stewart	Pharr, Robert	2438
Wisdom, Norton Labatt	Minor, Thomas, II	2439
Villere, Walter Peter	Villere, Jacques Philippe	2440
Posey, Henry Tharp	Posey, Thornton	2441
Forstall, Frederick K.	Forstall, Edmond John	2442
Beluche-Mora, Isidro	Beluche, Renato	2443
Weinmann, John Giffen	Love, Robert	2444
Gelpi, Herman Kahle	de la Ronde, Pierre Denis, II	2445
Gelpi, Chester Philip	de la Ronde, Pierre Denis, II	2446
Johnson, Charles Owen	Briggs, Griffin Carter, Parsons	2447
Clement, William Edwards	Clement, Henry	2448
LeCorgne, Robert Edgar, Jr.	Foucher, Pierre	2449
Read, Charles Favrot	Favrot, Louis Estevan	2450
Swigart, Frederic Robert	Duplessis, Francois, Jr.	2451
Forstall, Allen Henry	Forstall, Edmond John	2452
Forstall, Lawrence Peter	Forstall, Edmond John	2453
Forstall, Warren Anthony	Forstall, Edmond John	2454
Forstall, Frederick Joseph	Forstall, Edmond John	2455
Forstall, Earl Louis	Forstall, Edmond John	2456
Perrilliat, Howard A. K.	Claiborne, William C. C.	2457
Provosty, Michel Olivier	Labatut, Jean Baptiste	2458
Seghers, Guy Joseph	Seghers, Dominique	2459
Adams, Lionel, Jr.	delaGarciniere, Charles Fagot	2460
Adams, Orr	delaGarciniere, Charles Fagot	2461

MEMBER	ANCESTOR	GEN. SOC. NO.
Adams, Lloyd	delaGarciniere, Charles Fagot	2462
King, Clifford Alonzo, III	King, Reuben	2463
Wilkinson, William Scott	Wilkinson, James	2464
Means, Edward Barnwell	Pinckney, Thomas	2465
Hadden, Callender F.	Irvine, Callender	2466
Hadden, Callender F., Jr.	Irvine, Callender	2467
Hadden, Richard I.	Irvine, Callender	2468
Hadden, Robert W.	Irvine, Callender	2469
de la Houssaye, Louis P.	de la Houssaye, Louis A.	2470
Freret, Rene Alexis	Duplessis, Francois, Jr.	2471
Kock, Edouard James, Jr.	Lepretre, Jean Baptiste	2472
Hero, Alvin Anthony	Forstall, Edmond John	2473
Baldwin, Gustave B., Jr.	Bouligny, Charles Joseph D.	2474
Walmsley, Hughes Philip	Lewis, James	2475
Long, Edgar Hall	Rich, Joel, Sr. Rich, John, Jr.	2476
Reynaud, Clarence Sidney	Favrot, Louis Estevan	2477
Soule, George	Hogeboom, Peter	2478
Soule, Evan Ragland	Hogeboom, Peter	2479
Provosty, Michel Becnel	Labatut, Jean Baptiste	2480
Young, John Randolph	Forster, John, III	2481
Snyder, Martin P.	Cassin, John	2482
Favrot, Laurence H.	Favrot, Louis Estevan	2483
Bartlett, Walter Manny	Bartlett, Josiah	2484
de la Houssaye, Roy Edward	de la Houssaye, Louis A.	2485
Pipes, William Fort	Pipes, David	2486
Hopkins, Joseph Carroll	Jones, Hugh	2487
Le Gardeur, Rene Joseph	Montegut, Jean Raymond	2488
Lapeyre, Andre Charles	Foucher, Pierre	2489
Lapeyre, Felix Henri	Foucher, Pierre	2490
De Buys, Rathbone Emile	De Buys, Pierre Gaspard	2491
Berl, Charles Waggaman	Waggaman, George Augustus	2492
Bres, Edward Sedley	Seghers, Dominique	2493
Carriere, Olivier P.	Labatut, Jean Baptiste	2494
Puig, Felix Joseph	Labatut, Jean Baptiste	2495
Blythe, Donald Forbes	Ducros, Rodolphe Joseph	2496
Hale, Lawrence Herbert	Labatut, Jean Baptiste	2497
Hall, Francis Compton	Hall, Richard Wilmot	2498
Andry, George Ricau	Andry, Manuel	2499
Charbonnet, Gilbert H.	Rumsey, Stephen	2500
Parlange, Walter Charles, Jr.	Hebrard, Antoine	2501
LaCour, Arthur Burton, Jr.	Bush, Joseph Reuben	2502
Wilkinson, Hugh Miller, Jr.	Wilkinson, James	2503

MEMBER	ANCESTOR	GEN. SOC. NO.
Smith, John Augustine	Smith, Augustine Charles	2504
Favrot, Gervais Freret	Favrot, Louis Estevan	2505
Stibbs, John Henry	Beall, Reazin	2506
Linfield, Robert Paine	Joor, John	2507
Baldwin, Lawrence Jacob	Boulingny, Joseph Dominque	2508
Aldige, James George	Lepretre, Jean Baptiste	2509
Magee, Robert Towles	Towles, Henry	2510
Sinnott, James Butterfield, III	Smith, William	2511
Lafaye, Albert Emory	Baron, Noel Auguste	2512
Lafaye, Edward Emory, II	Baron, Noel Auguste	2513
Maginnis, Donald Ambrose, Jr.	Bush, Joseph Reuben	2514
LaCour, Charles Maginnis	Bush, Joseph Reuben	2515
Eustis, Joseph Bres	Seghers, Dominque	2516
Villere, Pierre	Villere, Jacques Philippe	2517
Eustis, Henry Chotard	Chotard, Henry	2518
Irion, Valentine	Irion, George Anderson	2519
Eustis, Lawrence Bres	Eustis, Abram	2520
Dart, Henry Plauche, Jr.	Plauche, Jacques Henri Urbain	2521
Rapier, George Senac	Des Forges, Louis Hus	2522
Rapier, Edward Desforges	Des Forges, Louis Hus	2523
Pilie, Louis Henry	Pilie, Louis Philippe	2524
Barranger, Garic Kenneth	Garic, Jean Francois	2525
LaBarre, Pierre Francois	Seghers, Dominique	2526
Moyer, R. Kirk	Hoffman, Peter	2527
Michinard, George S.	Dimitry, Andrea	2528
Pilie, Louis Andrieu	Pilie, Louis Philippe	2529
Delery, Frank Benjamin	Lanaux, Charles Julien	2530
Colcock, William Ferguson	Blair, Francis	2531
De Russy, Charles Nolte	De Russy, Lewis Gustavus	2532
Barrow, Mercer	Joor, John	2533
Farwell, Frank Evans	Coldwell, John Campbell	2534
Farwell, Charles A.	Coldwell, John Campbell	2535
Loker, David Cartan, Jr.	Lewis, James Martin	2536
Gibbons, John Francis, III	Jenkins, Benedict Joseph	2537
Olivier, Pierre De V., Jr.	Hebrard, Antoine	2538
Subers, Christopher V.	Hay, Peter	2539
Bickley, Ervin F., Jr.	Felton, John	2540
Cope, Jacob Erdman	Hartzel, Jacob	2541
Jayne, John Kennon	Clement, Evan Collins	2542
Hillery, Andrew F.	Rouse, E. S. S.	2543
de la Vergne, Jacque P.	Villere, Jacques Philippe	2544
Ball, Harold Curtis	Ball, Samson Edward	2545

MEMBER	ANCESTOR	GEN. SOC. NO.
Yates, Emmet Quintard	Spann, John	2546
Shaw, Morgan Langford	Campbell, James	2547
Brousseau, Andre Ringgold	De La Ronde, Pierre Denis, II	2548
Scranton, Lewis Bruce	Crane, Aaron T.	2549
Young, Benjamin Loring	Sewall, Benjamin	2550
Fowler, Samuel Robert, Jr.	Kolb, John William	2551
Parr, Guy Hudson, Jr.	Blunt, Francis	2552
Bordley, John Lawson	Rothrock, John	2553
Middendorf, John William, Jr.	Stone, William	2554
Stein, Charles Francis, III	Griffith, Thomas	2555
Hutchinson, William Brown	Rothrock, John	2556
Weisheit, Joseph Elmer, Sr.	Paddison, Samuel	2557
Klinefelter, George Young	Young, Jacob	2558
Sappington, Thomas Jonas	Sappington, Henry	2559
Sander, George Francis, Jr.	Roberts, John	2560
Boisfontaine, Curtis Rich	Veillon, Joseph Sylvain	2561
Wolford, Thomas Lionel	Bienvenus, Pierre Terville	2562
Eshleman, Sidney St. John, Jr.	Thibaut, Jean Pierre	2563
Eshleman, Benjamin Franklin	Thibaut, Jean Pierre	2564
de la Houssaye, Malcolm L.	de la Houssaye, Louis A.	2565
Chaffe, David Blackshear, Jr.	Hamilton, William	2566
Gamble, Richard Whitaker	Beall, William Dent	2567
Monroe, Malcolm Logan	Adair, John	2568
de la Vergne, Juillac H.	de la Vergne, Hugues	2569
Hebert, Warren Harang	Bouligny, Charles Joseph D.	2570
Thompson, Willard M.	Dickinson, David	2571
Archinard, Pierre Andre	De Alpuente, Francisco B.	2572
Archinard, John Joseph	Gaillard, Pierre	2573
Walls, John Abbet	Walls, Isaac	2574
Stiff, Ashby Gordon, Jr.	Stiff, James	2575
Montgomery, William J., III	Porter, Andrew	2576
Athey, Charles Burch	Jennings, James	2577
Villere, Plauche Francois	Villere, Jacques Philippe	2578
Dunbar, Walter Durke	Henshaw, William Slaughter	2579
Ward, Swan Sullivan	Calliham, John, Jr.	2580
Shannon, Irwin Vick	Irwin, John Lawson	2581
du Fossat, Sidney Louis	Bermudez, Joaquin	2582
de Verges, Edward J.	de Chalmette, Ignace de Lino	2583
de Verges, Edward J., Jr.	de Chalmette, Ignace de Lino	2584
Wilkinson, James III	Wilkinson, James	2585
Jones, Joseph Merrick	Thomas, David	2586
Mallary, Nelson Dagg, Jr.	Dagg, John Leadley	2587

The Roster 87

MEMBER	ANCESTOR	GEN. SOC. NO.
de la Houssaye, Edward A., III	de la Houssaye, Louis A.	2588
Friebely, Howard Eugene	Hartley, Michael	2589
Clement, Alfred Henry	Clement, Henry	2590
Baldwin, David Gilmore, Jr.	Bouligny, Charles Joseph	2591
Story, Henry Clement	Story, Benjamin	2592
Cassard, John Ernest	Vieillon, Joseph Sylvain	2593
Hulse, John Innerarity, III	Hulse, James P.	2594
Lake, James Hammond	Hammond, Elisha	2595
Delery, Joseph Charles, Jr.	Lanaux, Charles Julien	2596
Robinett, Paul McDonald	Simmons, John	2597
Shehan, J. Brooke	Dames, Augustus	2598
Shehan, William Henry	Dames, Augustus	2599
Taylor, Howard Richards	Taylor, Robert	2600
Wolford, Lionel Thomas, Jr.	Bienvenu, Pierre Terville	2601
Armant, Henry Joseph	Villere, Jacques Philippe	2602
Richardson, Horace Kimball	Bisbee, Daniel	2603
Norris, James Biscoe, II	Biscoe, James	2604
Todd, Galbraith Hall	McCrady, William	2605
Wilson, Charles Maurice	Joyce, Thomas Boyce	2606
Dell, Charles Squires, Jr.	Mackenzie (McKenzie), Thomas	2607
	Appold, George	
	Swan, William	
Erichson, Samuel C.	Erichson, Christian	2608
Vanderslice, Franklin F.	Causten, James H.	2609
Anderson, Edward Lane	Anderson, Isaac	2610
Cornwell, Ralph T. K.	Kline, John George	2611
Erdman, George Brown	Mengle, Benjamine	2612
Hires, Charles Edgar	Colby, Jonathan	2613
Rossmann, Edward Albert	Slicer, Andrew	2614
Dinkins, Ladd Augustine	Dinkins, James	2615
Lapeyre, Fernand Stephen	Foucher, Pierre	2616
Seghers, Paul D'Otrenge	Seghers, Dominique	2617
Thompson, Robert Wilkins	Wilkins, Robert	2618
Loose, John Ward Willson	Mathiot, Jacob	2619
Rhoads, Samuel Creadick	Hobensack, George	2620
Town, Charles M.	Town, Thomas	2621
Davis, Conner, Sanders	Brankston, John	2622
Delery, Lucien Carlisle	Lanaux, Charles Julien	2623
Harsh, George Jr.	Hall, William	2624
Shehan, William Henry, Jr.	Dames, Augustus	2625
Newman, Harry Wright	Newman, Horatio	2626
Hudson, Carlton Lee	Hudson, Henry O.	2627
	Doyns, Chichester	

MEMBER	ANCESTOR	GEN. SOC. NO.
Gibbs, Richard DeArmond	Gibbs, Jacobs	2628
deLassus, Louis St. John	Plauche, Jean Baptiste	2629
Eisenhower, Dwight David	Dietrich, Jacob	2630
McCauley, Edwin Douglas	Smith, Lucius	2631
Wogan, Philip Bernard	Labranche, Alexandre	2632
Wogan, Victor Louis, Jr.	Labranche, Alexandre	2633
Fissell, William H.	Fissell, Henry, Jr.	2634
Currier, Ross Hamilton	Ross, Jonathan	2635
Atwood, Henry Estes	Goodwin, Tristram	2636
Pond, Thomas Temple	Pond, Preston	2637
Roth, Edward, Jr.	Lambert, Levi Young	2638
Manning, Richard Charles, III	Smull, Jacob	2639
Cadwalader, Lambert	Williams, Jonathan	2640
Fitzhugh, Howard S., II	Fitzhugh, Philip	2641
Finger, John Whelchel	Meadows (Meadors), Barney	2642
Jones, Robert Copeland, Jr.	Bowie, Eversfield	2643
Townsend, Donald	Towsend, Jeremiah	2644
Hutchison, Rollo Ewing	Morrison, Robert	2645
Wiener, Edward	Anderson, Reuben	2646
Spahr, Boyd Lee	Rockefeller, Peter	2647
Knight, Frederick H., 3rd.	Knight, Richard	2648
Wenrich, Risdon Keeler	Poulson, John	2649
Warren, George Rodney, Jr.	Warren Benjamin	2650
Keen, George Benson	Smith, Sabritt	2651
Brierre, Roland Theodore	Hebrard, Antoine	2652
Freret, Adolphe Schreiber	Forstall, Edmond John	2653
Raub, George R., Sr.	Aultman, William	2654
Wight, Oliver Birckhead	Eichelberger, William	2655
Sutton, Fredus Edmund	Pennington, Fredus	2656
Holden, Irvin	Pentz, Daniel	2657
Harrison, Henry Christopher, Jr.	Harrison, Stephen	2658
Berry, Clarence Melvin	Shawger, J. Philip	2659
Rogers, John Philip	Shawger, Philip	2660
Berry, Clarence Augustus	Shawger, J. Philip	2661
Brinley, Henry DeNyse	Brinley, Henry	2662
Williamson, Edgar, Jr.	Pennington, James	2663
Freret, Frederick George	Forstall, Edmond John	2664
Smith, Erwin Weir, Jr.	Gray, William Fairfax	2665
Lyons, George Dewey, Jr.	Lyon, Asahel Dimic	2666
Starke, Aubrey Harrison	Starke, William B.	2667
O'Hara, V. Winthrop	Condit, Ezekiel Dilley (Dillie), Lewis	2668
Koontz, Amos R.	Graves, Jacob	2669

MEMBER	ANCESTOR	GEN. SOC. NO.
MacCarthy, Howard, Jr.	Harrison, Stephen	2670
Pryor, William Young	Baldwin, Justus	2671
	Bush, Henry C.	
Raub, George R., Jr.	Altman, William	2672
Derbes, Vincent Joseph	Verret, Augustin	2673
deLavergne, Jacques DeB.	De La Vergne, Hugues	2674
Legrand, Edmond G. J.	Pascal, Francois	2675
Dabney, Thomas Ewing	Ewing, Robert	2676
Mott, George H.	DePeyster, William S.	2677
DuBarry, William Hagan	Duane, William	2678
Wiener, Alexander L.	Anderson, Jennifer	2679
Wiener, Edward, 3rd.	Anderson, Bolitha	2680
Turner, Frederick Fairthorne	Updegraff, Abner	2681
Turner, William Howard	Updegraff, Abner	2682
Turner, Ellwood J., Jr.	Updegraff, Abner	2683
Clement, Harrison H., Jr.	Clement, Evan Collins	2684
	Harrison, Joel	
Clement, Martin W., II	Clement, Evan Collins	2685
Clement, James Higbie, Jr.	Clement, Evan Collins	2686
Howard, Morton, III	Howard, Maurice	2687
Howard, Harrison Sabin	Howard, Maurice	2688
Aller, Harris Coles, Jr.	Aller, Peter	2689
Boehringer, Karl Jay	Eby, Jacob	2690
Freed, Willard Musselman	Ruth, Jacob	2691
Patchett, Henry Powell	Hopkins, Elias	2692
Potts, Thomas Alva	Young, Abraham	2693
Bowman, Norwood David	Branner, John	2694
Saylor, Henry Durston, II	Wack, Jacob	2695
Sargent, Winthrop, IV	Worcester, Samuel	2696
Sargent, Samuel Worcester	Worcester, Samuel	2697
Zoll, Allen Alderson, II	McMaken, Joseph Hamilton	2698
McCloskey, Patrick John	Du Bourg, Pierre F. S. C.	2699
Raub, William Henry	Altman, William	2700
Young, Andrew Brodbeck	Young, Jacob	2701
Claflin, Leander Chapin	Farrington, Elijah	2702
Massey, Edgar Wilson	Vodges, Jacob	2703
Creamer, Raymond Kemble	Luffberry, John	2704
Clement, Charles Francis, III	Clement, Evans Collins	2705
Clement, Henry Rawle	Clement, Evans Collins	2706
Clement, John Kay, Jr.	Clement, Evans Collins	2707
Clement, Peter Withington	Clement, Evans Collins	2708
Butler, Thomas Richard	Felton, Cornelius Conway	2709
Clement, John Browning, Jr.	Clement, Evan Collins	2710

MEMBER	ANCESTOR	GEN. SOC. NO.
Robinett, Clifton Harvey	Simmons, John	2711
Clift, Garrett Glenn	Clift, Newton	2712
Butler, James Barnard	Butler, George Pollard	2713
Robinett, Frank Appleby	Simmons, John	2714
Phillips, Charles Alan	Guth, Henry	2715
Casebolt, Edwards T.	Lockwood, John	2716
King, Charles Daly	Bloomer, Thomas	2717
Barnes, Norman	Thomas, Samuel	2718
Eustis, Ernest Lewis, Jr.	Eustis, Abram	2719
Whitlock, Bache McEvers	Emmet, Thomas Addis	2720
Smith, Tevis Clyde, Jr.	Smith, Ransford	2721
Chaney, James Eugene	Chaney, Thomas	2722
Vanderhoof, William W., Jr.	Hopler, Conrad	2723
Ewing, Leslie Hand	Ewing, Jeremiah, Jr.	2724
Weston, Clement Walker	Weston, John Whitney	2725
Hickey, Maunsel White	White, Maunsel	2726
Davidson, Arthur Cleveland	Hamilton, Thomas	2727
Brumbaugh, John Daniel	Huston, John	2728
Koontz, James W., II	Graves, Jacob	2729
Marston, James Graham	Chaytor, Daniel	2730
Dickey, Francis George	Sadtler, Philip Benjamin	2731
Guy, William Burton, Jr.	Graves, Jacob	2732
Bennett, Edgar Harrison	Kemp, Thomas	2733
Adams, James Frederick, IV	Appold, George	2734
Forman, Wm. Harper, Jr.	Montan, Anthony	2735
Berl, Eugene Ennalls, II	Waggaman, George Augustus	2736
Forman, William Harper	Montan, Anthony	2737
Pendleton, Neal Francis	Pendleton, John	2738
Heflin, James Lester	Owens, William	2739
Werst, Harry K.	Stanley, James	2740
Crawford, James Merrill	Scout, Lewis	2741
Lehde, Pendleton Emile	Pendleton, John	2742
Hardin Bayless E.	Singleton, Jechonias	2743
Sanders, Robert Stuart	Adair, John	2744
Holifield, Marvin Bertrie	Holifield, William	2745
Duncan, Charles Yarbrough, Sr.	Young, Benjamin S.	2746
Hall, DeLou Perrin	Hall, Bainbridge	2747
Richardson, William Miller	Taylor, Thompson	2748
Whitesides, Lawson Ewing	Hail, John	2749
Tuttle John William	Tuttle, John	2750
Tullis, Charles Owen	Hutton, Cornelius	2751
Parker, William Alderman	Parker, Zachariah	2752

The Roster 91

MEMBER	ANCESTOR	GEN. SOC. NO.
Frazee, John Henry	Frazee, John	2753
Ordway, Richard Shannon	Stanwood, Ebenezer	2754
Wolford, Charles A. P.	Bienvenu, Pierre Terville	2755
Peck, Carlos Erbine	Peck, Josiah J.	2756
Terrell, Daniel Skidmore	Miltenberger, George	2757
Terrell, John Edward	Miltenberger, George	2758
Gwynne, Abram Evan	Gwynne, David	2759
Gilman, Charles Malcolm B.	Drake, Aaron	2760
Stratton, M. Lawrence	Ellis, Aaron	2761
Lafaye, Albert Emory, Jr.	Baron, Noel Auguste	2762
Benson, John Oregon	Linthicum, Abner Jr.	2763
Davis, Curtis Carroll	Williamson, James	2764
Bauer, Richard Wingate	Fobes, Joshua, 2nd. Horn, Otis Baker	2765
Green, Edwin Bernard, Jr.	Cook, Bernard Henry	2766
Pitcher, Griffith Fontaine	Griffith, Thomas Fountain (Fontain), Henry Porter, Wrixham Lewis	2767
Welch, Robert N.	Gray, Isaac	2768
Gentry, Franklin Marion, II	Gentry, Richard, II	2769
Peterson, Robert Karl	Fletcher, Thomas, Sr.	2770
Stockton, Jack Potter, III	Stockton, Robert Field	2771
Blauvelt, Louis L.	Blauvelt, Jacob I.	2772
Cartier, Roy Anthony	Marin, Evariste Pierre Antoine	2773
Adams, Jeremy Yvon M. du Q.	Des Forges, Louis Hus	2774
Smith, Len Young	Dudley, William	2775
Barratt, Norris Stanley, III	Jones, Jehu	2776
Lewis, Clifford, 3rd.	Kernan, William	2777
Crowell, Robert	Babcock, Samuel	2778
Keogh, Lawrence Knapp	Knapp, Auren	2779
Rareshide, Clarence	Villere, Jacques Philippe	2780
Brousseau, Andre Ringgold, III	White, Maunsel	2781
Van Dine, Warren L.	Brewer, John	2782
Albee, David Dempster	Albee, Samuel	2783
Clemens, Charles Eldon	Gilkyson, Andrew	2784
Van Dyke, Edward James	Lorton, Louis Robert	2785
Holmes, William Henry E.	Beatty, George	2786
Benedict, Purdy Faitoute	Benedict, Joseph Purdy, Isaac	2787
Murphy, Herschel Stratton	Leatherwood, Thomas	2788
Whiteford, Roger Streett, Jr.	Whiteford, Hugh, Jr.	2789
Lehmann, Leslie Sexton	Elbert, Samuel	2790
Moale, John Gray Foster	Moale, Samuel	2791

MEMBER	ANCESTOR	GEN. SOC. NO.
Coleman, E. Richard	Johnson, Samuel	2792
Beetem, Edward Charles, 2nd.	Beetem, Abraham	2793
Shriner, Edward Derr, Jr.	Scholl, Christian	2794
Malone, Edwin Scott, III	Malone, Samuel Pinchum	2795
Early, Clarence Fielding	Smith, Ransford	2796
Stevenson, John McAllister	Chipman, Timothy Fuller	2797
Stephens, Uel, Jr.	Briscoe, Thomas	2798
Barcus, Joseph Garland	McFerrin, James	2799
Goff, Sudduth	Goff, Elisha	2800
Fender, James Wade	Christie, Israel	2801
Fender, Robert, Worthel	Christie, Israel	2802
Seghers, Guy Joseph, Jr.	Seghers, Dominique	2803
Brown, Kennell Philip	Moore, Lewis	2804
Bishop, John Lester	Bishop, Isaac	2805
Pollock, William Franklin	Coburn, James W.	2806
Nichols, Marvin Curtis	Halliburton, Martin	2807
MacArthur, Douglas	MacArthur, Charles Gilderoy	2808
Hughes, Pierre Auguste	Blanchard, Reuben Kimball	2809
Goldsby, Joseph Hugh, Jr.	Edwards, Daniel, Sr.	2810
Peck, Robert McCracken	Wilkins, Robert	2811
Huntington, Frederick W.	Huntington, Samuel Howard	2812
Palmer, Robert Ellis	Dunbar, George Towers, Sr.	2813
Harrah, Eric	Gwynne, David	2814
Gerard, James Watson, II	Gerard, James Watson Claiborne, Ferdinand Leigh	2815
Plauche, Henry Hester	Plauche, Jean Baptiste	2816
Dart, Albert Laplace	Plauche, Jacques Henri Urbain	2817
Carmeron, Arnold Guyot, Jr.	Cameron, John	2818
McCloskey, Walter Stauffer	Bringier, Michel Douradou	2819
De La Vergne, Charles E., Jr.	Villere, Jacques Philippe	2820
Carpenter, William Thomas	Kerr, Samuel	2821
Clinton, Charles Kenneth	Clinton, Alexander	2822
Goodsell, Percy Hamilton, Jr.	Candee, Enos	2823
Mellen, William Henshaw	Stratton, Alpheus	2824
Cope, William C.	Hammond, Thomas	2825
Townsend, Arthur Liston	Carter, Joshua	2826
Wentz, Theodore Hillsley	Stadelman, William, Jr.	2827
Carpenter, William T., Jr.,	Kerr, Samuel	2828
McDonald, Kenneth Madison	Madison, Peyton	2829
Lallande, Sumter Louis	Arnoult, Cyril Honore	2830
Arnoult, Mandeville P., Jr.	Delery, Jacques Monplaisir Chauvin	2831
Legrand, Paul Marie	Pascal, Francois	2832

The Roster 93

MEMBER	ANCESTOR	GEN. SOC. NO.
Todd, James Mulherrin	Kemper, John George	2833
Hyams, Robert Portis, Jr.	Rollins, Richard	2834
Salmon, Clarke	Salmon, Birsdall	2835
Byrne, James de Buys	de Buys, Pierre Gaspard	2836
Delgado, Manuel Odelon, Jr.	Villere, Rene Philippe Gabriel	2837
Roy, John Overton, Jr.	Martin, Joseph Richard	2838
Lafargue, Fleury L. E.	Generelly, Fleury Theotime	2839
Dickson, Helion, Jr.	McWillie, William	2840
Hartson, Maurcie John, Jr.	Bienvenu, Alexandre deVince, II	2841
Adams, Leon	De La Garciniere, Charles Fagot	2842
Hartson, Maurice John, III	Bienvenu, Alexandre de Vince, II	2843
Richardson, Frank Byron, Jr.	Richardson, Rufus	2844
Fortier, Louis Joseph	Fortier, Michel, II	2845
Brown, William Perry, Jr.	Blanchard, Reuben Kimball	2846
Bezou, George Marc	Delery, Jacques Monplaisir Chauvin	2847
Martin, Richard Massie	Lepretre, Jean Baptiste	2848
Strother, James Herschel	Strother, Aaron	2849
Strother, Charles Jackson	Strother, Aaron	2850
Lehmann, Wallace Kemp	Elbert, Samuel Kemp, Joseph	2851
Hambleton, Richard Nicolai	Turner, Nathan	2852
White, William Zebulon	Waters, Zebulon	2853
Elmendorf, Wm. Ten E., Jr.	Elmendorf, Martin	2854
Worthington, Miltenberger, Jr.	Miltenberger, Anthony Felix Smull, Jacob	2855
Spurrier, Oliver Walter	Spurrier, Greenbury	2856
Brice, Carroll Allyn	Brice, Nicholas	2857
Davis, Milton Wickers, Jr.	Griffith, Lyde	2858
Edelen, Crolian William	Spalding, Joseph	2859
Guttery, John McQueen, Sr.	Chappell, Miles	2860
Helick, Reuben Martin	Helick, Jacob	2861
O'Neal, Moncure Camper	Coffee, John	2862
Pirkle, Charles Gaston	DeFriese, Hiram Abiff	2863
Morris, John Delashmutt	Dorsey, Jonathan	2864
Clothier, Isaac H., IV	Hallowell, Isaac	2865
Bradley, John Miller	Curley, Isham, Jr.	2866
Cavaroc, Roger Antoine	Lamothe, Jean-Baptiste	2867
DeRussy, Charles Nolte, Jr.	DeRussy, Lewis Gustavus	2868
Ivy, Robert Eugene	Stovall, John	2869
Desobry, Louis Edward, Sr.	Chinn, Thomas Withers	2870
Andry, William Louis	Andry, Manuel	2871

MEMBER	ANCESTOR	GEN. SOC. NO.
Andry, Allain Charles, Jr.	Andry, Manuel	2872
Goodspeed, Lawrence Archibald	Goodspeed, Levi	2873
Goodspeed, Aloysius Berchmans	Goodspeed, Levi	2874
Gagnet, John Lawson	d'Herbigny, Charles Zenon	2875
Michel, Edouard Jules	Bonaventura y Alpuente, Don Francisco	2876
Ouellette, Arthur Russell	Fiske, Mark	2877
Brower, Walter Scott	Brower, Abraham	2878
Jenkins, Arthur Darwin	Jenkins, William	2879
Collins, Ralph Harry	Collins, John	2880
Johnston, Henry Poellnitz	King Thomas DeVane	2881
Cavaroc, Victor Viosca	Lamothe, Jean-Baptiste	2882
Toca, Roland Garic	Garic, Jean Francois	2883
Richardson, Julius Gray	Gray, Alexander	2884
Andry, Allain Charles, III	Andry, Manuel	2885
Derbes, Clause Joseph	DeLaronde, Pierre Denis, IV	2886
Pascal, Gabriel Louis	Pascal, Francois	2887
Pendleton, Neal F., Jr.	Pendleton, John	2888
Deynoodt, Joseph F., Jr.	Montegut, Jean Raymond	2889
Landry, Stuart Omer	Landry, Simon Julien	2890
Fossier, Albert S.	Labatut, Jean-Baptiste	2891
Geary, Cyril Paul, Jr.	Pascal, Francois	2892
Fischer, Frederick Hall	Wyman, John	2893
Fischer, John Sargent	Wyman, John	2894
Fischer, Frederick Waters	Wyman, John	2895
Walker, John Mort, Jr.	Walker, Joseph	2896
Cadwalader, Gouverneur, Jr.	Williams, Jonathan	2897
Bond, John Russell	Bankston, John	2898
Allen, Thomas Eldridge	Tharpe, Jeremiah Allen	2899
Nicaud, Frederick Harvey	Ducatel, Germain	2900
Orrick, Metcalf	Baker, Joshua	2901
Kratovil, Cortlandt Otto	Raymond, Josiah	2902
Stuart, Russell Allen	Thomas, John	2903
Ordway, Frederick Ira, Jr.	Shannon, William Stanwood, Ebenezer	2904
Thomas, Belton Earp, Jr.	Morris, Garret	2905
Letford, William	Ashley, Wilson	2906
Green, Samuel Alexander, Jr.	Howison, Alexander	2907
Morrison, Benjamin Olivier	Story, Benjamin Saxon	2908
Jones, Robert Randolph	Bentley, James	2909
Pendleton, Reuben Allen, III	Pendleton, John	2910
Brinton, Edward Harvey	Buck, William Richardson	2911
Mulholland, Roye Artice	Mulholland, Hugh	2912

The Roster 95

MEMBER	ANCESTOR	GEN. SOC. NO.
Wehrle, Clarence Sebastian	Brown, Aloysius Lewis	2913
Wilson, Clifford William	Strother, Aaron	2914
Stewart, Frank Ross	Stewart, Simeon	2915
Hays, Reese Henry, Jr.	Long, Benjamin	2916
Douglass, Hiram Kennedy	Spinks, Raleigh Westmoreland, John, Sr.	2917
Goodson, Henry Grady, Jr.	Jackson, William, Jr.	2918
White, Richard David	Kerr, David	2919
McMaster, Fitzhugh	McMaster, John	2920
Nelson, William Jones, Jr.	McConnell, James	2921
Shotts, James Edgar, Sr.	Stone, John	2922
White, Geoffrey Roberts	Kerr, David	2923
Wiener, Alexander Loder, Jr.	Anderson, Jennifer	2924
Wiener, Edward McIntosh	Anderson, Jennifer	2925
Willcox, Robert Irving	Willcox, Oliver Whittlesey, Parnell (Parke)	2926
Smallwood, Grahame Thomas, Jr.	Bush, Oliver Clark, Samuel	2927
Gilbert, Leon Jacques	Scott, John Baytop	2928
Couturie, Maurice Louis	Garidel, Louis Ambroise	2929
Larue, Ferdinand deVesine	Foucher, Pierre Edmond	2930
Moore, Gardere Francis	Bowie, Rezin Pleasants	2931
Labry, Robert Stone	Durel, Jean-Baptiste Newville	2932
Pendleton, Reuben Allen, Jr.	Pendleton, John	2933
Cavaroc, Victor Viosca, Jr.	Lamothe, Jean-Baptiste	2934
Plauche, Henry Hester, Jr.	Plauche, Jean-Baptiste	2935
Plauche, Paul Sidney	Plauche, Jean-Baptiste	2936
Morrison, DeLesseps Story	Story, Benjamin Saxon	2937
Boggs, Thomas Hale	Jones, John Powers	2938
Bowe, Dudley Pleasant	Bowe, Nathaniel	2939
Kyle, Walter James, Jr.	Yoakley, Richard J.	2940
Thompson, Robert Wilkins	Wilkins, Robert	2941
Clement, James Higbie	Harrison, Joel	2942
Brooks, James Taylor	Harrison, Joel	2943
Green, Seymour Ledyard	Wilson, John	2944
Markley, Russell Kindig	Markley, Philip	2945
Roth, Jon Biddle	Wilkinson, James	2946
Breisacher, Karl Gustave, III	DeLaronde, Pierre Denis, IV	2947
Brower, Walter Jordon	Brower, Abraham	2948
Campbell, Lloyd Miles	Burlew, Cornelius	2949
Bezou, Henry Charles	Delery, Jacques Monplaisir Chauvin	2950
Burke, Michael Whittington	Jackson, Wiley	2951

MEMBER	ANCESTOR	GEN. SOC. NO.
Thorp, Wakeman Blanchard	Smalley, Francis	2952
Hansell, Charles Richardson	Hansell, William	2953
Brodnax, Marion Jack	Brodnax, Edward Brooking	2954
Mann, Robert Neville	Daniel, Chisolm	2955
Heckscher, Ledyard Hart	Byerly, John	2956
Clement, Frederick T. J.	Clement, Evan Collins	2957
Kephart, Calvin Ira	Kephart, Jacob	2958
Evans, George Webster	Baker, Conrad, Jr.	2959
Lynch, Cleveland Michel	Bonaventura y Alpuente, Don	2960
Wentz, Theodore Hillsley, Jr.	Stadelman, William, Jr.	2961
Wentz, Timothy Frazer	Stadelman, William, Jr.	2962
Wentz, Christopher Wildner	Stadelman, William, Jr.	2963
Sargent, Winthrop	Worcester, Samuel	2964
Jenkins, Edward Felix	Jenkins, Felix	2965
Stewart, Carl Hoak, Jr.	Robertson, Julius Caesar	2966
Shehan, Robert Joseph	Dames, Augustus	2967
Evans, Frank Barton, Jr.	Evans, James	2968
Blizzard, Dennis Frizzell	Arbaugh (Earbaugh), John Blizzard, William of W.	2969
Querens, Percy Lennard	Ferlot, Antoine	2970
Marquez, Edward Leonhard, Jr.	Lepretre, Jean-Baptiste	2971
Arnold, Harvey Wilson	Rayburn, James	2972
Crowell, John Head	Babcock, Samuel	2973
Quin, Everett Michael	Gulick, John	2974
Bush, Arthur Egbert	Bush, Henry C.	2975
Smartt, Ephraim Herbert	Smartt, William Cheek	2976
Dorman, John Frederick	Beall, Walter, Jr.	2977
Drouilhet, Adrien Francois	White, John J.	2978
Knadler, Robert Warren	Duvall, Bartow	2979
Bealmear, James Irving, Jr.	Bealmear, Francis	2980
Durst, Ross Compton	Durst, John	2981
Klinefelter, Arthur	Klinefelter, Michael	2982
Barnes, William Calvin	Cockrill, Thomas	2983
Smith, Winfield Ross	Brandeberry, Philip	2984
Richard, Albert Earl	Labranche, Alexandre	2985
Whitley, Andrew Rieger	Whitley, William	2986
Querens, Allan Eustis	Ferlot, Antoine	2987
Roberts, Thomas Owen	Gorman, David	2988
Purdy, Thomas L., Jr.	Purdy, Isaac	2989
Chambers, William Ely	Ely, Epaphras Cook	2990
Lowell, James Russell	Lowell, Reuben	2991
Thorne, Samuel, Jr.	Lee, James	2992
Atwood, Lee Brown	Atwood, Solomon	2993

MEMBER	ANCESTOR	GEN. SOC. NO.
Oliver, Norris Schermerhorn	Oliver, William George	2994
Twining, Robert Barber	Twining, John	2995
Brokaw, Roberts Wyckoff	Brokaw, Isaac C.	2996
Pugh, William Nussear S.	Hopper, Daniel Cox	2997
Waters, Samuel Kyle	Streett, John	2998
LeBlanc, Clyde Joseph	DeLaronde, Pierre Denis, IV	2999
Roosevelt, Julian K.	Morris, Charles	3000
Yeager, James Gernerd	Snyder, George	3001
Barker, James Higbie	Harrison, Joel	3002
Burgner, Walter C., III	Jordan, Ephraim	3003
Reichstein, Arthur F.	Withers, Thomas W.	3004
Dougherty, Clifford L.	Bartholomew, Sherman	3005
	Fuller, Simeon	
McCluer, Paul B.	McCluer, Robert	3006
Yokum, Jules DeFazende	DeFazende, Sebastien	3007
King, Frederic D., III	Fell, Robert W.	3008
Derbes, Charles J., Jr.	Martin, Joseph Richard	3009
Demaree, Joseph Paul	Demaree, Samuel	3010
Camp, John Frederick, Jr.	Lacey, Ebenezer	3011
Conkey, Maurice C.	Conkey, Thomas Hamilton	3012
Pierce, Samuel, Jr.	Loring, Perez	3013
	Shaw, Josiah	
Martin Thomas Wesley	Martin, Jesse	3014
Sledge, Joseph W., Jr.	Hobson, Matthew	3015
White, Frank S., III	Murray, David	3016
Barker, Stanley Cline	Burk, Thomas	3017
Rice, Joseph Clarence	McCurley, John	3018
Dickie, Robert Burns, II	Graves, Lucius	3019
Bresee, Wilmer Edgar	Bresee, Harmon	3020
Wood, Charles P.	Spilman, John	3021
Pierce, Richard Donald	Taggart, John	3022
Bryan, Frederic A.	Barney, Joshua	3023
		3024 Void
Green, Richard Ellwood	Cook, Bernard Henry	3025
Lehmann, Brent Dawson	Elbert, Samuel	3026
Woods, Joseph Wheeler	Appleton, James	3027
Taylor, Clement Newbold	Cocke, John	3028
DuBarry, Joseph N., III	Duane, William	3029
Blacklock, Aubrey H., Jr.	Blacklock, Nicholas F., II	3030
Broad, William H. Jr.	Trousdale, William	3031
Fossier, Horace L., Jr.	Labatut, Jean-Baptiste	3032
Bonnet, Eldon Bernard	Landry, Ursin	3033
Collins, Charles, Jr.	Labranche, Alexandre	3034

98 The Roster

MEMBER	ANCESTOR	GEN. SOC. NO.
Roy, Joseph Folse	DeFlaugeac, Antoine P.	3035
Faget, William Edward	Faget, Jean-Baptiste	3036
Devenport, Joseph F.	Devenport, Jean, Jr.	3037
Johnson, Andrew M.	Bennett, Abijah	3038
McCauley, Bishop	Slaughter, Francis T.	3039
Eld, Peter Fuller	Fuller, Calvin Perry	3040
Slaymaker, Samuel C., II	Slaymaker, Henry Fleming	3041
Slaymaker, Samuel R., II	Slaymaker, Henry Fleming	3042
Pharr, Eugene A., Jr.	Pharr (Farr), Henry	3043
Atkinson, Guy	Rathbone, William	3044
Eld, Terry J.	Fuller, Calvin Perry	3045
Gilman, Charles M., Jr.	Drake, Aaron	3046
Smith, Harold Raphael	Townley, Robert, Jr.	3047
Forster, Andrew J.	Decker, Andrew D.	3048
Parsly, Elmer G.	Montanye, Thomas B.	3049
Salmon, Clarke, Jr.	Salmon, Birsdall	3050
Robertson, William C., III	Sparks, Wright Bruce	3051
Derbes, Edward J., Jr.	Pilie, Louis Philippe	3052
Delery, Baldwin Hunter	Delery, Nicolas Chauvin	3053
Couturie, Henry W., Jr.	Garidel, Louis A.	3054
Minge, Jackson C., Jr.	Harrison, William Henry	3055
Pilie, Martin Arnaud	Pilie, Louis Philippe	3056
Tiblier, Thomas Joseph	DeChemilly, Germain D.	3057
Evans, Daniel Goode	Rillieux, Vincent, II	3058
Greene, Norman Joy	Green, Alanson	3059
Parry, Richard	Harris, William	3060
Privett, William K.	Blevins, John	3061
Eshleman, Benjamin, Jr.	Davis, John	3062
Stick, Gordon M. F., Sr.	Fair, Peter	3063
Watson, David Coleman	Coleman, Richard	3064
Stick, Thomas H. F.	Waters, Richard R.	3065
Rapier, George E.	Des Forges, Louis H.	3066
Stick, Gordon, M. F., Jr.	Fair, Peter	3067
Durel, Homer Joseph	Durel, Michel, V.	3068
Livaudais, Jacques A.	De Fazende, Sebastien F.	3069
Tiblier, Sidney L., Jr.	De Chemilly, Germain D.	3070
Norris, Abell A., Jr.	Beall, John of L.	3071
Yeager, Wayne Evans	Snyder, George	3072
Bonnaffon, Charles A.	Bonnaffon, Anthony	3073
Sellers, Nicholas	Caldwell, James	3074
McLeod, Kenneth, Jr.	Cantrelle, Michel B., Jr.	3075
Harper, Marshall L.	LeBeuf, Martial, II	3076

MEMBER	ANCESTOR	GEN. SOC. NO.
Weidner, William D., Jr.	Arnoult, Pierre G.	3077
Massey, Edward M.	Vodges, Jacob	3078
Ashenhurst, James G.	Ashenhurst, Oliver	3079
Ashenhurst, John W.	Ashenhurst, Oliver	3080
Meyer, Paul Rogers	Rogers, John	3081
Barnes, Robert M.	Hill, David Bailey	3082
McMaster, Richard K.	McMaster, John	3083
Vaughan, Edwin Steuart	Steuart, William	3084
Luckett, Robert L.	Crain, John	3085
Hill, Benjamin Jr.	Gifford, William	3086
Brown, Russell	Brown, Ira	3087
Linthicum, George E., III	Linthicum, Charles G.	3088
Scott, Frank Bertram	Hoshall, Jesse, II	3089
Farrington, Douglas F.	Perry, Melatiah B.	3090
Canedy, Albert W.	Canedy, Zebulon L.	3091
Barnes, Wilson K., Jr.	Cockrill, Thomas	3092
Canter, Ashby Hawkins	Canter, Henry	3093
Knapp, Alfred Averill	Barnum, Daniel	3094
Staehle, Jack Carl	Knap, Elijah, II	3095
Head, Glenn Lloyd	Tipton, Solomon Loyd, Eli	3096
Brush, Herbert S., Jr.	Brush, Elijah	3097
Brush, Herbert S., III	Brush, Elijah	3098
Lescure, William J., 3rd.	Mackubin, George	3099
Means, Walker Wilson	Means, George	3100
Macgowan, Bates, Jr.	Shelby, Isaac	3101
Diaz, Ralph Edouardo	Manning, Caleb	3102
Diaz, Abram Henry	Manning, Caleb	3103
Diaz, Walter Palmer	Manning, Caleb	3104
Diaz, Joseph Aurelio	Manning, Caleb	3105
Johness, Allen Henry, Jr.	Chenet, Eugene	3106
Rucker, Henry Cowles, III	Rucker, William B.	3107
Gibson, John McCullough	Gibson, Jacob, II	3108
Robins, Reginald Starr	Peters, Christian G.	3109
Crozat, Edwin Paul	Lafferanderie, Lucien	3110
Denis, Wilfred D., Jr.	Carmick, Daniel	3111
Hoefer, Frederick W.	Trowbridge, Adonis	3112
Hoefer, Richard Allan	Trowbridge, Adonis	3113
Clark, Ephraim Stuart	Clark, Samuel	3114
Miller, James Francis	Miller, Thomas, II	3115
Moss, Clive Arthur	Arthur, Ambrose	3116
Webster, Burnice Hoyle	True, James Hill	3117
Collier, Dudley Foster	Lang, John	3118

MEMBER	ANCESTOR	GEN. SOC. NO.
Collier, Arthur Luke	Lang, John	3119
Chapman, Arthur Stetson	Stetson, Abner, Jr.	3120
Napier, John H., III	Wheat, Joseph	3121
	Tate, James	
	Napier, John Staples	
	Burks, Daniel	
Barrosse, Bertin O.	D'Avezac, Auguste G.	3122
Gibbs, Robert Frederick	Gibbs, Jacob	3123
Ordway, Frederick Ira, III	Stanwood, Ebenezer	3124
Beall, Clarkson J.	Beall, John Hilleary	3125
Johnson, Robert L.	Tappan, George	3126
Estes, John W. J.	Estes, Triplett Thorp	3127
Moylan, Chalres E., Jr.	Gorsuch, George W.	3128
Parrish, William F.	Woodward, Philemon, Jr.	3129
McBride, Robert Martin	McBride, Charles	3130
	Keith, John Lee	
	Martin, Valentine	
Janeway, Augustine S.	Linnard, William	3131
DuBarry, Joseph N., IV	Duane, William	3132
DuBarry, Joseph N., V	Duane, William	3133
Etter, Thomas C., Jr.	Etter, Philip	3134
Wilson, Goerge Fried, Jr.	Miller, Abraham	3135
Rawle, James, 2nd.	Rawle, Francis William	3136
Addison, Joseph, Jr.	Waring, John, Jr.	3137
Michel, Robert Emory	Wood, Matthew	3138
Cornett, Robert F., Jr.	Jordan, Hugh	3139
Sternbergh, Van R., Jr.	Meaders, Barney	3140
Ball, Walter Vancion	Butterworth, Buckley	3141
Baldwin, William M.	Fortier, Jean Michel	3142
Powers, Robert Benjamin	Powers, Avery, Jr.	3143
White, William Warner	Kerr, David, 2nd.	3144
Hoff, William B.	Bainbridge, William	3145
McClain, Frank M., Jr.	McClain, John	3146
Lane, Charles H.	Cahoon (Calhoun), Caleb	3147
Mace, Clarence Eugene	Mace, Henry	3148
Bernard, Guy Francis	DuMontier, Onesiphore B.	3149
Robertson, William C., IV	Sparks, Wright Bruce	3150
Brown, James Henry	Rumph, Jacob, II	3151
Anderson, John Sherburne	Gaulden, Zachariah	3152
Brady, Thomas P.	Richardson, Jared N.	3153
Walton, John M., Jr.	Walton, William	3154
Barnes, Charles M., Jr.	Barnes, Asa	3155
Sustendal, George F.	Chretien, Hyppolite	3156
Chadwick, Winslow J.	Chadwick, James	3157

MEMBER	ANCESTOR	GEN. SOC. NO.
Bezou, Sidney L.	Delery, Jacques M. C.	3158
Deynoodt, Donald A.	Orso, Zenon	3159
Colomb, Charles L., Jr.	Garidel, Louis Ambroise	3160
Hinds, Charles Franklin	Hind, William	3161
Medairy, Bernard J., Jr.	Medairy, John	3162
George, Thomas Stevens, Jr.	Bouldin, Jehu	3163
Barnes, Wilson King	King, Samuel	3164
McClinton, James Selby, Jr.	Sangster, James	3165
		3166 Void
Richards, Earl Morgan	Borzorth, William	3167
Vollmer, John Frederick	Young, Peter	3168
Helms, Paul Edward	Helms, Cadwalader M.	3169
Howard, Robert Morton	Howard, Maurice	3170
Henderson, Branton H., Jr.	Couch, Philip	3171
Atkinson, Alan Watt	Watt, John	3172
Fellows, Leon Wallace	French, Ebenezer	3173
Williams, Leonard D.	Williams, William	3174
Engle, Kline d'A.	Pontius, Henry	3175
Favrot, Richmond G.	Favrot, Luis Estevan	3176
Stockton, Milton A., Jr.	Oliver, Jean Baptiste	3177
Sinnott, Charles J.	Smith, William	3178
Woolfley, Francis A.	Flanders, Joseph	3179
Brown, George McGehee	Wilson, James	3180
Woodruff, Leslie Rae	Woodruff, Jonathan	3181
Scudder, Richard Alan	Johnson, John	3182
	Reeve, Joab	
Sweeney, Henry W. S.	Whitcomb, Lot	3183
Robinson, Bradford,	Bryant, Levi, Jr.	3184
Dolliver, Alan Kemp	Kemp, Joseph	3185
Bushey, Arthur C., Jr.	Bell, Cecelius	3186
Shattuck, Marquis E.	Smith, Asaph	3187
Carriere, Marion F.	Fernandez y Mendoza, Jose Joaquin	3188
Livaudais, Herbert S.	Livaudais, Jean B. E.	3189
Robins, Irvine Ashton,	Brown, Redden	3190
Ramond, Charles Knight	Wells, William John	3191
Yockey, Ross Paul	Alpuente, Don Francisco	3192
Levis, Frederick Hemsley	Rowland, Jonathan	3193
Hopkinson, Francis	Swaim, William	3194
Massey, Jay Richardson, Jr.	Vodges, Jacob	3195
Machold, Roland Morris	Decatur, Ann Pine	3196
Esler, Charles Vansant	Schlosser, John George	3197
Burpee, Jonathan	Ashmead, Isaac	3198
Watson, William A.	Harl, Baldwin	3199

MEMBER	ANCESTOR	GEN. SOC. NO.
Brown, Harry C., Jr.	Brown, Stewart	3200
Robertson, Haywood Lawrence	Baker, John	3201
Neeper, Creed Arbuthnott	Conant, Airs (Ayres)	3202
Magee, John Alexander	Magee, Alexander	3203
Medairy, Bernard John	Medairy, John	3204
Markley, Harvey Curtis	Cooley, Henry	3205
Adams, Harrington	Harrington, Seth	3206
Isaacson, H. Harding	Dupre, Jacques	3207
Burgoon, Norman Aaron, Jr.	Burgoon, Jacob	3208
Krais, Frederick Vernon, Jr.	Lovell, George	3209
Frazier, Griffin Guy	Meredith, Peter	3210
Bonniwell, Donald Raymond	Capes, William	3211
Smith, Carlisle F.	Garr, Benjamin	3212
Meyer, Robert Brooks	Clingman, George Washington	3213
Beall, Wilson Wylie	Beall, Lloyd	3214
Whiteford, Daniel Francis X.	Willingham, James	3215
Buck, James Marshall	Grasty, George	3216
Buck, James Marshall, II	Roberts, Joseph Gill	3217
		3218 Void
Murray, James Anderson, V	Gillette, Jonathan	3219
Wilson, Francis Vaux, III	Potter, Jonathan	3220
Clarke, Francis Mann, Sr.	Hodges, Wilson Blount	3221
Matthews, Harry Z.	Ebur, John Francis	3222
Brooke, William Hill	Brown, Gustavus	3223
Scott, Leon Lake, Sr.	Scott, Abraham, Jr.	3224
Boyd, David Preston, III	Finch, Jonathan	3225
Galvin, Michael J., Jr.	Stevens, Benjamin F.	3226
Clarke, Francis Mann, Jr.	Hodges, Wilson Blount	3227
Hynes, Lee Powers	Powers, Fredrick	3228
Reed, Willis McCook	Ahl, Peter	3229
Clothier, George B.	Hallowell, Isaac	3230
Vollmer, Earl S.	Young, Peter	3231
Vollmer, Earl S., Jr.	Young, Peter	3232
Haskins, George Lee	Allen, Jonathan	3233
Brodhead, Truxtun Read	Beale, George N.	3234
Wadhams, Albion James	Wadhams, Luman	3235
Lessig, Brooke Montgomery	Rush, Philip	3236
Hopkinson, John Joseph	Swaim, William	3237
Poorman, S. Sturgis	Sturgis, Nathan	3238
Poorman, S. Sturgis, Jr.	Sturgis, Nathan	3239
Hopkinson, Francis, Jr.	Swaim, William	3240
Schall, John Hubley, IV	Schall, George	3241

The Roster 103

MEMBER	ANCESTOR	GEN. SOC. NO.
Davis, Edward Lawrence	Peale, Rembrandt	3242
Etter, Thomas Clifton	Etter, Philip	3243
Synder, Martin Avery	Cassin, John	3244
Clothier, Birchard T.	Hallowell, Isaac	3245
Hopkinson, James P.	Swaim, William	3246
Halberstadt, Robert LeConte	Baird, Thomas James	3247
Clothier, William J., 2nd.	Hallowell, Isaac	3248
Henderson, Gerald Van S.	Couch, Philip	3249
Subers, Albert R.	Hay, Peter	3250
Davies, Wallace Evan	Hitch, Hardy Elgit	3251
Gause, Francis Gregory, Jr.	Gregory, Francis Hoyt	3252
Currie, William Roberts	Abernathy, Charles Clayton	3253
Southerland, Henry deLeon, Jr.	Lamb, John	3254
McCaw, John Todd	McCaw, William Henry	3255
Vogtle, Alvin Ward, Jr.	Armstrong, Jesse	3256
Waring, William Hunter	Waring, John	3257
Mann, Eugene Turner, Sr.	Woods, Archibald	3258
McDonald, Walter Smith	Bize, Daniel	3259
Stewart, Donald Franklin	Donaldson, James Lowry	3260
		3261 Void
		3262 Void
		3263 Void
Jacobs, Charles Robinson, Jr.	Kirkpatrick, Andrew	3264
		3265 Void
		3266 Void
Seaman, Wayne DeWitt	Jones, David	3267
Williams, John Kennedy, III	Campbell, John	3268
Walling, Arthur William	Walling, Daniel	3269
Lattimer, John Kingsley	Goldthwaite, Oren	3270
Nolte, Lawrence W.	Sheely, George Washington	3271
Inloes, Joseph Howard	Rolle, Thomas	3272
Erhardt, Clement Dumont, Jr.	Reilly, Patrick	3273
Jett, Robert Samuel, Jr.	Jett, Thomas H.	3274
Jones, Bartlett Braxton	Jones, Bartlett, Sr.	3275
Brathwaite, Peter Lloyd	Borden, Francis	3276
Tower, Lawrence Phelps	Tower, Reuben	3277
Merritt, James Miller	Lynch, Patrick of William	3278
Bristor, William Beverly, Jr.	Bristor, George	3279
Chapman, Samuel Vannort	Webb, William	3280
Walling, Arthur Patrick	Walling, Daniel	3281
Walling, Stephen Patrick	Walling, Daniel	3282
Wells, William John, Jr.	Cain, Mathew	3283

MEMBER	ANCESTOR	GEN. SOC. NO.
Lauck, Gerold McKee	Lauck, Isaac Streit	3284
Soniat, Disney, L., Jr.	Bermudez, Joaquin	3285
Dupuy, Homer Joseph	Dupuy, Aubry	3286
Ward, Frank Anthony, II	Park, Russell J.	3287
Sellers, John Harrison	Sellers, Samuel	3288
Cameron, George Edward	Browne, Hugh	3289
Pratt, Robert Armstrong	Whittum, Daniel	3290
Davis, Robert Hare	Davis, Samuel Boyer	3291
Snyder, John Avery	Cassin, John	3292
Reed, William Edgar	Ahl, Peter	3293
Hires, Charles Edgar, Jr.	Colby, Jonathan	3294
Saylor, Harold Durston, II	Wack, John Jacob	3295
Robb, Eugene Willard K.	Kline, John George	3296
Yardley, John L. M., Jr.	McKim, James	3297
Corson, Alan, 3rd.	McPherson, Henry Hendley	3298
Roak, Christopher Dale	Clement, Evans Collins	3299
Dent, Daniel DuVal	Clement, Evans Collins	3300
Humrichouse, James Walker	Humrichouse, Frederick	3301
Petefish, Russell H.	Petefish, George	3302
Fairbanks, Warren Evans	Fairbanks, David	3303
Humrichouse, Richard Huse	Humrichouse, Frederick	3304
Humrichouse, Christopher Peter	Humrichouse, Frederick	3305
Yardley, Ralph B.	McKim, James	3306
Watson, William Anthony	Harl, Baldwin	3307
Dilks, Charles Day	Hyland, Stephen	3308
Flint, Daniel Waldo Boone	Flint, Daniel	3309
Howard, Joshua Harrison	Howard, Maurice	3310
Brodhead, George Milton	Brodhead, Richard	3311
Blair, William Richardson	Jenkins, Thomas	3312
Brodhead, Frank Chaplain	Brodhead, Richard	3313
Saylor, Henry Durston, III	Wack, John Jacob	3314
Hopkinson, Mark	Swaim (Swain), William	3315
Machold, William Deas	Decatur, Ann Pine	3316
de la Houssaye, Arthur Alexander	de la Houssaye, Louis Alexander, LePelletier	3317
du Mont, John Sanderson	Smith, Walter	3318
Dinkins, Ladd Augustine, Jr.	Dinkins, James	3319
Lapeyre, Paul Martial	Foucher, Pierre	3320
Hopkins, Joseph Vincent, Jr.	Lemonnier, Yves	3321
Baldwin, Albert Sr.	Boulingy, Charles Dominique	3322
Aldige, James George, III	LePretre, Jean Baptiste	3323
Bernard, Thomas Norton	Labranche, Alexander	3324
Charbonnet, Clayton Joseph	Rumsey, Stephen	3325

The Roster 105

MEMBER	ANCESTOR	GEN. SOC. NO.
Carriere, Lyle Francis	Fernandez y Mendoza, Jose Joaquin	3326
Eustis, Henry Chotard, III	Chotard, Henry	3327
Robins, Eugene Frank	Brown, Redden	3328
Woolfley, Horace Louis Dufour	Flanders, Joseph	3329
Monsted, Charles Niels, Jr.	Dean, James Savage	3330
Carriere, Oliver Provosty, Jr.	Labatut, Jean Baptiste	3331
de la Houssaye, Joseph Kleber	de la Houssaye, Louis Alexandre le Pelletier	3332
Doherty, Lewis Stirling	Stirling, Lewis	3333
de la Houssaye, Arthur Joseph, Jr.	de la Houssaye, Louis Alexandre Le Pelletier	3334
Whiteford, Lingard Ignatius	Willingham, James	3335
Leber, Henry Hoke	Fuhrman, Philip	3336
Satterthwaite, Pennington	Duane, William	3337
Walsh, G. Lauriston, Jr.	Whitney, Abraham Johnson	3338
Draughn, Paul Vernon	Edmondson, Amos	3339
Sanders, Albert Covington	Moak, Andrew	3340
Horner, Thomas Marland	Horner, John	3341
Howard, Allen Rider	Howard, Oliver, Jr.	3342
Symington, Donald Leith	Glover, Charles	3343
de la Barre, Pierre Francois Volant, IV	Seghers, Dominque	3344
		3345 Void
Dinkins, Joseph Airey	Dinkins, James	3346
Cavaroc, John Peter	Lamothe, Jean-Baptiste	3347
Forsyth, Hewitt Laurie	Forsyth, Gideon Comstock	3348
Villere, Andre Louis	Villere, Jacques Philippe	3349
Sarpy, Robert Henry, Jr.	Fortier, Michel, II	3350
Lyons, Shirley Carlton	Lyons, Samuel	3351
Aldige, Hugh Dumas	Lepretre, Jean-Batiste	3352
de la Vergne, Jacques Perez	Villere, Jacques Phillipe	3353
Wolfe, Bernard Peter	Bernard, Onesiphore	3354
Wolfe, Frederick J., Jr.	Bernard, Onesiphore	3355
Sizemore, James Middleton	Middleton, Zachariah	3356
Sizemore, James Middleton Jr.	Middleton, Zachariah	3357
Clerc, Joseph Fred	Blouin, Charlesville	3358
Delery, Frank de la Souchere	Lanaux, Charles Julian	3359
Bres, Edward S., Jr.	Seghers, Dominique	3360
Hanks, Stedman Shumway	Shumway, Duty	3361
Clark, Robert Philbrick	Richardson, Gilman	3362
Aud, Edward Trujean	Aud, Asa	3363
Seaver, George Arthur, Jr.	Wyman, John	3364

MEMBER	ANCESTOR	GEN. SOC. NO.
Ehlinger, Marquez Pillot	Ducatel, Germain	3365
Clymer, William Branford Shubrick	Shubrick, William Branford	3366
Randall, Giles Deshon	Randall, William	3367
Kendrick, Marvin Hayne	Kendrick, Jones	3368
Roueche, Mossman	Christy, Andrew	3369
Soniat, Theordore Louis Lucien	Bermudez, Joaquin	3370
Colton, Edwin Thome	Colton, Edward Bond	3371
Maginnis, Gordon Hobson	Bush, Joseph Reuben	3372
Livaudais, Alfred Friedrichs	de Fazende, Sebastein Francois Morriere	3373
Arthur, John Stephen	Pearson, Isaac	3374
Baird, Bruce, Jr.	Baird, Thaddeus	3375
Carriere, James Dupress	Labatut, Jean Baptiste	3376
Harris, Lyttleton Tazwell	Elliott, John Lisle	3377
Derbes, Stephen Joseph	De Laronde, Pierre Denis, IV	3378
Martin, Joseph A.	Kleinpeter, Franz (Francis)	3379
Knight, John Thornton, Jr.	Knight, John Hughes	3380
Green, Arthur de la Houssaye	de la Houssaye, Louis Alexandre LeP.	3381
Breckinridge, Preston Marshall	Breckinridge, Robert	3382
Kirk, Pierre leMercier-duQuesnay	Des Forges, Louis Hus	3383
Eustis, John Douglas	Chotard, Henry	3384
Young, William Waller, Jr.	Millet, Peter Alexander Maximillian	3385
Moore, George Albert	Chambers, Joseph	3386
Lapeyre, Felix Henri, Jr.	Foucher, Pierre	3387
Street, Edward Parker	Borden, Francis	3388
Munnikhuysen, John Bryarly	Gover, Robert	3389
deLaureal, Henry Howard	Voorhies, Cornelius	3390
Manget, Daniel Thomas, Jr.	Dent, John Turner	3391
Young, Leonard Albert	Young, Daniel	3392
St. Paul, Hugh de la Vergne	deVillere, Jacques Philippe	3393
Eustis, Lawrence Bres, Jr.	Eustis, Abram	3394
Robertson, John McEnery	Sparks, Wright Brue	3395
Parham, Duncan de Puech	D'Aquin, Charles Louis	3396
Dunlap, John Bettes, Jr.	Carpenter, James	3397
Winslow, Caleb, Sr.	Leiper, George Gray	3398
Millholland, Geroge Harrison	Millholland, Robert Douglas	3399
Grove, James Mason	Brockenbrough, Austin	3400
Rountree, John Griffin R.	Farrow, William H.	3401
Finger, Allen Whelchel	Meadows, Barney	3402
Finger, John Martin	Meadows, Barney	3403

MEMBER	ANCESTOR	GEN. SOC. NO.
Sanford, James Terry	Larew, Joseph	3404
	Darst, Benjamin, Jr.	
Crane, Moses Woodruff, Jr.	Bragaw, Abraham	3405
Young, John Randolph, Jr.	Young, Daniel	3406
Fortier, Robert Eugene	Fortier, Jacques	3407
LeDoux, Marion John	LeDoux, Zenon	3408
Breckinridge, John Marshall	Breckinridge, Robert	3409
Labry, Robert Alexander	Durel, Jean-Baptiste Neuville	3410
Sarpy, Henry Leon	Fortier, Michel	3411
Sleet, Phillip Milton, Jr.	LePretre, Jean Baptiste	3412
Lapeyre, James Martial	Foucher, Pierre	3413
Rapier, Michael Joseph	Des Forges, Louis Hus	3414
Carriere, Pierre Francis	Fernandez y Mendoza, Jose Joaquin	3415
Dart, Henry Plauche, III	Plauche, Jacques Henri Urbain	3416
Charbonnet, Louis Sidney, III	Villere, Rene Gabriel	3417
Pilie, Joseph Maurice	Pilie, Louis Philippe	3418
Crawford, William Franklin	Woodyear, Joseph	3419
Ashbridge, Whitney	Nichols, Francis	3420
Charbonnet, Clayton Jos., Jr.	Rumsey, Stephen	3421
Diaz, Rafael Eduardo, II	Manning, Caleb	3422
Aubert, Edward McCormack	Aubert, Juan Batiste	3423
Villere, Plauche Francois, Jr.	Villere, Jacques Philippe	3424
DeLaureal, Wm. David, Sr.	Voorhies, Cornelius	3425
Schoenberger, Sidney Conrad	Duncan, Abner, Lawson	3426
Andry, Claude Dudley, Jr.	Andry, Manuel	3427
Curren, John G., Jr.	Seghers, Dominique	3428
Baker, John Pope, II	Todd, Robert S.	3429
Sharp, Roger Post, Jr.	Latil(le), Joseph Timecourt	3430
de la Houssaye, J. Larue	de la Houssaye, Louis Alexandre	3431
Delery, Gerald de la Souchere	Lanaux, Charles Julian	3432
McCandless, William Howard, III	Perkins, Hardin	3433
Soule, Robert Spencer, Jr.	Hogeboom, Peter	3434
Sharp, John Winfield	Latil(le), Joseph Timebourt	3435
Martin, Daniel Julian	Kleinpeter, Franz	3436
Bowman, Charles Harwood, Jr.	Bendall, Jesse	3437
Murphey, Walter B. W.	Smith, Thomas Jarratt	3438
Jaycox, Warren Cecil	Battle, James	3439
Birely, William Cramer	Horton, James	3440
Sultan, Arthur Phillips	Phillips, Manuel	3441
Williams, Charles Herman	Hauck, William	3442
Smith, Clifford Neal	Awalt, Michael, II	3443
Bryan, Leslie Aulls	Wheeler, Nathan	3444

108 The Roster

MEMBER	ANCESTOR	GEN. SOC. NO.
Moale, John Foster, Jr.	Moale, Samuel	3445
Pugh, William N. S., Jr.	Hopper, Daniel Cox	3446
Smith, D. Carlos, Jr.	Albright, John	3447
Wright, John Maxwell	Heinrich, Johan	3448
Pabst, Ralph Malcom	Marshall, John	3449
Alexander, George Louis	McCluney, William John	3450
Rice, Turner	Austill, Evan	3451
Vogtle, Jesse Stringer	Armstrong, Jesse	3452
Adams, David, III	Carter, Jarrett	3453
Pryor, William Brand	Baldwin, Justus	3454
Merrill, George Grenville	Leaycroft, Viner	3455
Carlton, Emory Linwood	Carlton, Ellis Watts	3456
Garretson, Oliver Kelleam	Garrettson, Mason	3457
Thurtle, Robert Glenn	Cornish, Benjamin	3458
Burgess, Howard Benjamin	Freeman, John	3459
Town, Edward Arthur	Town, Thomas	3460
Street, Phillips B.	Borden, Francis	3461
Blair, Thomas Ashton	Jenkins, Thomas	3462
Blair, William Richardson, Jr.	Jenkins, Thomas	3463
Ashburner, John La Cour	Bush, Joseph Reuben	3464
Bement, Russell, III	Worrell, Isaac	3465
Ridge, Bradley Bateman	Bateman, John Mills	3466
Tucker, Robert Gene	Boothe, James	3467
	Eaton, Richard, Sr.	
	Zenor, George, Sr.	
Ernst, Charles Augustus, IV	Duane, William	3468
Ernst, Christophr Gardner	Duane, William	3469
Scullin, John Gardner	Duane, William	3470
Baker, Calvin Shelton	Land, Nathaniel Drew	3471
Short, William	Nicholas, Robert Carter	3472
Howard, Sabin Gilardi	Howard, Maurice	3473
Dilks, Peter Durfor	Hyland, Stephen	3474
Bunker, John Cadwalader	Williams, Jonathan	3475
Bunker, Lambert Cadwalader	Williams, Jonathan	3476
McKinney, Harry Ellery	McKinney, Seth	3477
Marr, William Corbin	Barroll, James	3478
Allen, Robert Hugh	Cornish, Benjamin	3479
Metzger, Fred J.	Metzger, Jacob	3480
Whiteford, Lingard I., Jr.	Willingham, James	3481
Benson, Richard Steward	Smith, Sabritt	3482
Cameron, Donald Eugene A.	Eames, Joshua	3483
Henry, Francis Jenkins	Henry, John	3484
Smith, James Roy, Jr.	Little, John Everett	3485

MEMBER	ANCESTOR	GEN. SOC. NO.
Knight, Monte Hugh	Griffin, Hugh	3486
Cook, Robert Tayloe, III	Wood, John	3487
Short, Robert Carter N.	Nichols, Robert Carter	3488
Gordon, Robert Lee	Castephens, John	3489
Verlander, Henry Smith, Jr.	Toledano, Christopher	3490
Higgins, Jerry Lynn, Sr.	Blackman, Jeremiah	3491
Nash, Edward Francis	Adams, Nathaniel	3492
Parrish, Roy Thomas	Dalrymple, William	3493
Flowers, John Baston, III	Flowers, John	3494
Mason, Judson Philip	Kelsey, Francis Hollister	3495
Hughes, James Lewis, Jr.	Winston, Anthony	3496
Allen Matthew Brenden	Cornish, Benjamin	3497
Rives, Ralph Hardee	Bellamy, John F.	3498
Perret, Edmund James, II	Pascal, Francois	3499
Maginnis, Donald Ambrose, III	Bush, Joseph Reuben	3500
Charbonnet, Robert Henry	Rumsey, Stephen	3501
Pipes, William Fort, Jr.	Pipes, David	3502
Gresham, Charles Reed	Preston, Archibald	3503
Brady, William Conolly	de la Houssaye, Louis A.	3504
Brady, William Milner	de la Houssaye, Louis A.	3505
St. Paul, Townsley D.	Villere, Jacques Philippe	3506
Schoenberger, George C., Jr.	Duncan, Abner Lawson	3507
Brown, William Perry, III	Blanchard, Reuben K.	3508
Whitley, Andrew Thomas	Whitley, William	3509
Rapier, Edward Sebastian	Desforges, Louis Hus	3510
Baldwin, John Render	Terry, Nathaniel, Jr.	3511
Baugh, Eugene Bibb, Jr.	Keen, John	3512
Gordon, Lloyd Paul	Castephens, John	3513
Roxby, William C., Jr.	Horn, Abraham	3514
Roxby, William C.	Horn, Abraham	3515
Whealen, John Joseph, Jr.	Colby, Jonathon	3516
Groff, John Marshall	Colby, Jonathan	3517
Romig, Gerald Christian	Christian, John	3518
Baker, James Winsor, Jr.	Baker, Henry	3519
Willard, Craig Kenneth	Willier, Peter, Jr.	3520
Brown, Paul Kalck	Brown, Edmund, Sr.	3521
Ashburner, Charles B.	Bush, Joseph Reuben	3522
Bentley, Henri Farrar	Farrar, Bernard Gaines	3523
Kitchel, Robert S., Jr.	Sanborn, Jonathan C., Jr.	3524
Ordway, Albert James	Shannon, William	3525
Core, Jesse Rozell, III	Montague, Thomas C.	3526
Haight, Sherman Post, Jr.	Everest, Isaac	3527

MEMBER	ANCESTOR	GEN. SOC. NO.
Shields, Alexander M.	McMillan, Alexander	3528
Kepler, Christopher A.	Kepler, Israel	3529
Conway, Hewitt A.	Jones, George W.	3530
Wittenmeyer, Chares E.	Wittenmeyer, Jacob	3531
Crumley, David Shiffer	Shiffer, John	3532
Persell, Ralph Mountjoy	Buck, Charles, III	3533
Fowler, H. Waller, Jr.	Hicky, Philip	3534
Michinard, George S., Jr.	Dimitry, Andrea	3535
Rawle, William Morris	Rawle, Francis William	3536
Wilson, Craig Hawley	Miller, Abraham	3537
Wilson, Fried Ruger	Miller, Abraham	3538
Crowell, William Babcock	Babcock, Samuel	3539
Humes, James Calhoun	Graham, Robert Findley	3540
Bement, Russell, Jr.	Worrell, Isaac	3541
Matthew, William McGowan	Diller, Adam	3542
Van Gulick, Robert R.	Gulick, Peter	3543
Stevens, Lawrence L., Jr.	Johnson, Reverdy	3544
Cline, William Findley	Cline, Philip, Jr.	3545
Hires, John Bacon	Colby, Jonathan	3546
Usilton, William E.	Usilton, Robert	3547
Goldsborough, Richard H.	Goldsborough, Robert H.	3548
Jones, Edward Graham, Jr.	Smick, Peter	3549
Beetem, Donald Gilbert	Beetem, Abraham	3550
		3551 Void
Van Pelt, David W. S.	Van Pelt, Peter H.	3552
Aller, Harris Coles, 3rd.	Aller, Peter	3553
Aller, William Drew	Aller, Peter	3554
Angelo, Hunter Buchanan	Solliday, Jacob	3555
Johnston, Hugh Buckner	Thomas, Hilliard	3556
Davis, Edwin Bonner, Jr.	Davis, Micajah	3557
Luckie, Robert Ervin, Jr.	Carter, Jarrett	3558
Regester, Robert Thomas	Thomas, Sterling	3559
Abey, Joseph Samuel	Abey, Joseph	3560
Abell, Richard Bender	Eichelberger, Frederick	3561
Rice, Atwood Lumberd, Jr.	Burton, William Martin	3562
Kemmerly, Kenneth Wright	Beard, John	3563
Mysing, August W., Jr.	Foster, Isaac	3564
Everngam, G. Gregg	Beetem, Abraham	3565
Gieske, Edward T., Jr.	Webb, William	3566
Adams, Philip Reed	Wimberly, Ezekiel	3567
Diaz, Theodore Peter	Manning, Caleb	3568
Eustis, Charles Logan	Eustis, Abram	3569

The Roster 111

MEMBER	ANCESTOR	GEN. SOC. NO.
Blain, Daniel	Waller, Robert Page	3570
	Griffin, Samuel Stuart	
Schnebly, Keith G., Jr.	Schnebly, James	3571
Dwight, Charles H.	Schneider, Henry	3572
French, Robert Lewis	Nealey, Ebenezer	3573
McGuire, E. Thomas	Waldorf, Philip	3574
Borum, Wylie Griffin	Burton, John H.	3575
Crumley, David Oliver	Shiffer, John	3576
Moore, Howard Shackleford	Duncan, Charles	3577
Gallagher, Bernard J., Jr.	Duncan, Charles	3578
Duncan, Neal Holland	Ball, Horatio	3579
Southerland, Edwin W.	Lamb, John	3580
Harnett, Maurice A., III	Morris, John B.	3581
Van Antwerp, Lee Douglas	Simons, Levi	3582
Knight, William Chapman	Knight, John Hughes	3583
Dawkins, William Lee	Harry, John Bishop	3584
Robins, Robert Wayne	Thomas, William, Jr.	3585
Andrews, William Phillip	Reneau, John Fleming	3586
Brown, George M., Jr.	Wilson, James	3587
Page, Alfred F., Jr.	Lasere, Jaques	3588
Maxwell, Murvan Morris	Serpa, Antoine	3589
Grout, John Clifford, Jr.	Stirling, Lewis	3590
Ward, Nicholas Donnell	Woodman, Moses	3591
	Delamater, William	
McConnell, James Thomas	Hartsfield, Warren	3592
Cresson, Frederick L.	Bowman, Abraham	3593
Umhau, John Bernard	Beall, Basil	3594
Dale, John, Jr.	Inman, Richard	3595
Gleason, Frederick B., III	Brockway, Ezra	3596
Fellows, Lloyd Welker	Fellows, Levi	3597
Browne, Delbert Victor	Every, Andrew Perry	3598
Barrosse, Bertin O., Jr.	De Castera, Auguste G.	3599
Barrosse, Rushton Garic	De Castera, Auguste G.	3600
Bezou, Charles Henry	Delery, Jacques Monplaisir C.	3601
Glassie, Donelson Caffery	Caffery, John	3602
Fontana, Jules August, Jr.	deVillere, Jacques Philippe R.	3603
Reichner, Henry Harold, Jr.	Fraser, James P.	3604
Wiener, Clifford Cogshall	Anderson, Jennifer	3605
Jenner, William Trayton	Lines, Henry	3606
Woolever, Harry, Jr.	Logue, John	3607
Graham, James Brooks, Jr.	West, Lynn	3608
Umhau, John Bernard, Jr.	Beall, Basil	3609
Welsh, Donald Green	Beall, Basil	3610

112 The Roster

MEMBER	ANCESTOR	GEN. SOC. NO.
Chenery, James Hollis	Winston, William D.	3611
Wiener, Edward McIntosh, Jr.	Anderson, Jennifer	3612
Gerhart, George Henry	Blumer, Jacob	3613
Allen, Roscoe Jackson, Sr.	Sharp, George	3614
Stubblefield, John Seely	Stubblefield, Peter Beverley	3615
Schweppe, Palmer Dallis Thompson	Talmadge, Thomas	3616
Chapman, Ronald Bernard	Shivers, Thomas Wilson	3617
Avant, David Alonzo, Jr.	Avent, Ransome Davis	3618
Lowe, Bromley Wharton	Tompkins, Daniel D. Tomkins, Elijah	3619
		3620 Void
Partlow, Thomas E.	Partlow, Thomas	3621
Gray, Edward Morris, Jr.	Saucier, Severin Descoteaux	3622
Scrivener, Milton Emmons	Conant, Joseph	3623
Benson, Carville Dickinson	Linthicum, Abner	3624
Wilson, Massey Francis	Cocke, John Fleming, I	3625
Moore, Jerry Edward	Dance, William	3626
Koenig, John Lance	McLean, John, Jr.	3627
Dale, John, III	Inman, Richard	3628
Estes, Ernest Herwell, Jr.	Estes, John Bartlett	3629
Dale, Wilton Roger	Inman, Richard	3630
Dart, John Peacock	Plauche, Henry Urbain	3631
Eustis, David Leeds	Chotard, Henry	3632
Overington, John	Beatty, Henry	3633
Jamison, John Jay	Thomas, Benjamin	3634
Burt, William Charles	Dally, Charles S.	3635
Crook, Wilson Walter, Jr.	Stell, George Washington Yates, William	3636
Bockstruck, Lloyd DeWitt	Moody, Andrew	3637
Dingley, Edward Nelson, Jr.	Dingley, Jeremiah	3638
Atwood, Roswell Levi	Atwood, Solomon	3639
Metzger, Howard Allison	Metzger, Jacob	3640
Dunlap, Clarke	Dunlap, John	3641
Byers, Joshua Clarence	Byers, Michael	3642
Anderson, Richard Kerfoot	Childs, Thomas	3643
Wright, Leslie Stephen	Wright, Lewis	3644
Brown, Kennell Philip, Jr.	Moore, Lewis, IV	3645
Tritico, Frank Edward	Street, Joseph	3646
Brush, Robert Edward deBrus, Sr.	Brush, Elijah	3647
Tierney, Gordon Paul	Brown, Absalom	3648
Marshall, Chesley Brown	Crooks, Richard	3649
Horton, Clarence Alfred	Doran, Jeremiah	3650

MEMBER	ANCESTOR	GEN. SOC. NO.
Borgman, Theodore Joseph, Jr.	Herndon, James	3651
Fortier, Louis Renshaw	Fortier, Michel, II	3652
Kennedy, Russell Vance	Kennedy, William Doak	3653
Bumpas, Guy Hartwell, III	Lake, George	3654
Kennedy, Charles M.	Kennedy, William Doak	3655
Acuff, Alfred Marshall	Scheetz, Henry	3656
Pegram, Roger Miller	Bost, Daniel	3657
Worthing, Clifford Arthur	Doe, Jonathan	3658
Potts, Ewell Cardwell, Jr.	Garic, Francois	3659
Warfield, John Ogle, Jr.	Green, Grief	3660
Fincher, Myron Gustin	Fincher, Jesse	3661
Wilcoxen, Raymond J.	Willcockson, Elijah	3662
Henry, Elwin O.	Henry, Isaac	3663
Hamilton, Glenn Clark	Hoagland, Isaac	3664
Hamilton, Howard Laverne	Jayne, Benaiah	3665
Brumbaugh, Stiles Daniel	Hosmer, Henry	3666
Dean, Homer Franklin	Rigg, Thomas Dean, Joseph	3667
Darnall, Joseph Rogers	Darnall, Elias	3668
Baldwin, Charles H.	Streett, John	3669
Delery, Oliver Stanislaus	deLivaudais, Jean B. E. Lanaux, Charles Julien	3670
Benjamin, Alfred Henry	Benjamin, William	3671
Couturie, Louis Maurice, Jr.	Garidel, Louis Ambroise	3672
Elliott, Thomas Hugh, III	Bienvenu, Alexandre deVince, II	3673
Flores, Adolph Anthony, Jr.	Rambin, Francois Augustin	3674
Watrous, Philip Maish	Trowbridge, William Frasier	3675
Coltrin, Gerald Edward	Killion, Michael	3676
O'Bryant, Alan Melvin	O'Bryant, Joseph	3677
Moseley-Clarke, Thomas Stevenson	Clarke, John Salle	3678
Delhaye, Alcide Veeder	Verret, Godfroi	3679
deLaBarre, Francois Duffossard Volant	Seghers, Dominique	3680
Gray, Gordon	Gray, Samuel	3681
Whitten, Jerry E.	Brownlow, William	3682
Richardson, Francis Joseph, III	DeGruy, Dufochar	3683
Thomas, Noah Oscar, Jr.	Reneau, William T.	3684
Coulter, Joseph Stewart	Cress, George	3685
Carmichael, Jack Kemper	Sparks, Stephen	3686
Shields, Richard Barba	Acosta, Roque	3687
Bone, Robert Gehlmann, Sr.	Bone, Elihu	3688
Gieske, James Chapman	Webb, William	3689

MEMBER	ANCESTOR	GEN. SOC. NO.
Carroll, George Earl	Morgan, Elias	3690
Kloman, Antony Joseph Trapnell	Aisquith, Edward	3691
Reardon, Richard James	Tyrrell, Artemas	3692
Williams, Robert Wesley	Williams, Wesley	3693
Sparrow, Richard Stenley, Jr.	Sparrow, Seth, Sr.	3694
Walker, Paul Howard	Wear, George	3695
Blizzard, Dennis Craig	Arbaugh (Earbaugh), John	3696
Halbert, Virgil Allen	Halbert, William	3697
Felty, Harold G.	Martin, Clem	3698
Wiseman, Howard Willard	Shurrager, Conrad	3699
McLaughlin, Marcellus Hood, Jr.	Rogers, William Charles	3700
Hill, George H., 3rd.	Fraser, James P.	3701
Brown, Henry Brock, Jr.	Brown, Edmund, Sr.	3702
Brennan, Ronald Wesley	Herndon, Elijah	3703
Romig, Gerald Christian, Jr.	Christian, John	3704
Worthington, James Drewry	Worthington, Joab	3705
Weer, Winfield Scott	Weer, Joseph	3706
Burget, Dean Edwin, Jr.	Blackburn, William	3707
Blair, Thomas Ashton, Jr.	Jenkins, Thomas	3708
Blair, William Richardson, 3rd.	Jenkins, Thomas	3709
Gardner, Hilton Bowen, Jr.	Jenkins, Thomas	3710
Hill, Michael Webster	Jenkins, Thomas	3711
Amesbury, Walter Raleigh, Jr.	Drake, Lemuel	3712
Hocker, Douglass William	Keplinger, George	3713
Slaymaker, Samuel Cochran, III	Slaymaker, Henry Fleming	3714
Ernst, Timothy Walker	Duane, William	3715
Coonley, Howard, III	Duane, William	3716
Blain, Daniel Jr.	Waller, Robert Page	3717
Blain, Peter Travis	Waller, Robert Page	3718
Eshleman, Benjamin, 3rd.	Davis, John	3719
Boyd, William Paxton	Paxton, Robert	3720
Hinkle, Henry Louis	Hinkle, Peter	3721
VonDouris, John Wallace	Fife, William, Jr.	3722
Brooks, Clifton Rowland	Scott, John Morin	3723
Marshall, John McClellan	Smith, Byrd	3724
Arthaud, John Bradley	Head, William	3725
Averett, George Wesley	Furr, Paul	3726
Hinkle, John William	Hinkle, Peter	3727
Talte, Andrew Frank, Jr.	Tate, Jesse Overton	3728
Brooks, Clifton Rowland, Jr.	Scott, John Morin	3729
Edmondson, James Howard, III	Edmondson, Andrew Jackson	3730
Creekmore, Thomas Vannoy, Sr.	Rogers, John	3731

The Roster 115

MEMBER	ANCESTOR	GEN. SOC. NO.
Bartholomew, Earl F.	Livingston, John J.	3732
Ely, Duncan Cairnes	Newbold, William	3733
DeLee, Alva Augustus	Austin, John Jones	3734
Pease, Richards Kenneth	Keithly, William	3735
Prather, William Roy	Doherty, William	3736
McLaughlin, Marcellus Hood, 3rd.	Rogers, William Charles	3737
Fish, Steven Byers	Byers, Michael	3738
Wright, Zelma Hudson, Jr.	Jenkins, William	3739
	Steele, Samuel	
Shannon, Michael C.	Guseman, Godfrey	3740
	Insall, Thomas	
Brakebill, Clovis Hunter	Martin, Benjamin	3741
Jeter, Robert Mobley	Groves, Samuel	3742
Myrick, Victor Ray	Sanders, Malachi	3743
Frankenfield, Edgar Charles	Strunk, Peter	3744
Davis, Walter Ashley, Jr.	Bolen, Thomas	3745
Smith, Doyle Jackson, II	Smith, John	3746
Oxx, Wm. Garderner, III	Oxx, William, 3rd.	3747
Abey, Joseph Gregory	Abey, Joseph	3748
Williamson, Fletcher Phillips	Phillips, Benjamin	3749
Weimer, Douglas Reid	Philson, Robert	3750
		3751 Void
Denis, Alfred Cecil	Carmick, Daniel	3752
Legrand, Georges Marie	Pascal, Francois	3753
Buffington, Byrd Mayson	Yount, David	3754
de la Houssaye, Frank Julien, Jr.	de la Houssaye, Louis Le Pelletier	3755
de Verges, Philip Cajetan	de Chalmette, Ignace de Lino	3756
Hero, George Alfred, III	Forstall, Edmond John	3757
Landry, Arthur F.	Landry, Benjamin	3758
Lyons, George Dewey, III	Lyon, Asahel Dimick	3759
Lyons, Michael Bivens	Lyon, Asahel Dimick	3760
Stockton, Milton Anthony, III	Olivier, Jean Baptist	3761
Jack, Charles Harold, Jr.	Ostrander, James	3762
de Verges, Vincent Paul	de Chalmette, Ignace de Lino	3763
Lebeuf, George Louis	Fortier, Michel, II	3764
Schafer, Gordon Frank, Jr.	deChalmette, Ignace de Lino	3765
Mahool, John Blatter	Mahool, Thomas	3766
Thurtle, Robert Joseph Patrick	Cornish, Benjamin	3767
Ashbridge, Richard Downing	Nichols, Francis Boude	3768
Wilkinson, Hugh Miller, III	Wilkinson, James	3769
Mitchell, Frank Paull, Jr.	Paull, George	3770
Jones, Edward Graham, III	Smick, Peter	3771

MEMBER	ANCESTOR	GEN. SOC. NO.
		3772 Void
Sangston, Laurence Purdy	Adams, Minos	3773
Hollinger, Edwin Theodore	Diehl, John	3774
Jackson, William Benjamin, 3rd.	Bush, William S.	3775
Dorsey, Thomas Lee, Sr.	Hooper, James	3776
Taylor, George Dunham, Jr.	Gupton, Jacob	3777
Dart, Henry T.	Plauche, Jacques Henri Urbain	3778
Prados, Wilfred Olivier	de Vezin, Jean Baptiste Olivier	3779
Livingston, Darby Gary	Darby, George	3780
	White, Silas Hathaway	
Sparrow, Wendall Keats	Sparrow, Patrick (Parrie)	3781
Caldwell, Arthur Brann	Cornell, Archibald	3782
Hudson, William Romuald	Hudson, Henry O.	3783
Hyde, L. Kaye	Hyde, Eleazar	3784
Banks, Myron Carroll	Downs, Frederick	3785
	Rose, Harmon	
	Ives, Elijah	
Bills, Robert Wesley	Bill, Phineas	3786
Crowson, William Larry	Roberts, Abraham, II	3787
Morgan, Charles Boyd	Hawthorn, John Rogers	3788
Wright, Douglas Chandler	Searl, Jeriah	3789
Fortier, Robert Laird	Fortier, Jacques	3790
Franklin, Benjamin Robert, Jr.	Franklin, Bedney Abednego	3791
Hymel, Gene Joseph	Fernandez y Mendoza, Jose Joaquin	3792
Maxwell, James Edward	Serpa, Antoine	3793
O'Neil, James Francis, Jr.	Roy, Joseph	3794
Wood, Earl VanDorn	Brandon, Gerard C.	3795
Harrison, Robert Myron	Gilmore, Robert	3796
Ward, Fred Deryl	Ward, Francis Asbury	3797
Young, Robert John, Jr.	Godfrey, Benjamin	3798
Carriere, Dennis Howell	Lebatut, Jean Baptiste	3799
David, Jeff McHugh	McHugh, John	3800
McIntosh, William, III	Hynes, William Rose	3801
	Powers, Frederick	
Noble, Clyde E., Jr.	Showalter, David, Sr.	3802
Willhite, John Moore	Vinnedge, John	3803
Brower, Walter William	Brower, Abraham	3804
Clark, Robert Murel, Jr.	Vincent, Francis Alva	3805
Weidner, William Daniel, III	Arnoult, Pierre Gervais	3806
Weidner, David Eric	Arnoult, Pierre Gervais	3807
Grange, Cecil William	Hunt, James	3808
Bourne, Robert Gordon Bruce	Byerly, John	3809
Brown, Hugh Edmund	Brown, Edmund, Sr.	3810

MEMBER	ANCESTOR	GEN. SOC. NO.
Brown, Frank Clark	Brown, Edmund, Sr.	3811
Brown, Timothy Edward	Brown, Edmund, Sr.	3812
Wallace, James Nelson	Vananda, Jacob	3813
Pepper, Harris Laning Perry	Perry, Oliver Hazard	3814
de Montluzin, Adrian Davis	West, Lynn	3815
Altemus, Edward Lee	Altemus, Thomas	3816
Moore, Albert Wilson Luce, Jr.	McQuiddy, Benjamin	3817
Shirey, Clarence Ray	Shiry, John	3818
Tolson, Jay Henry	Leidich, Joseph	3819
Zearfoss, Herbert Keyser	Zearfoss, Joseph George	3820
Brown, Ryan Michael, Jr.	Brown, Edmund, Sr.	3821
McCone, Percy Vere	Haybarger, George	3822
Gradeless, Donald Eugene	Gradeless, Nathaniel	3823
Garic, Harold Nicholas, II	Garic, Francois	3824
DeSonier, James Patrick	de Chalmette, Ignace de Lino	3825
DeVerges, Paul Hanlon	de Chalmette, Ignace de Lino	3826
Gillespie, John Douglas	Lones, Henry	3827
Beadles, Glenn Harris, Sr.	Rowlett, Thomas	3828
Blizzard, Arthur Keith	Arbaugh (Earbaugh), John	3829
McCurley, James Bernard, Jr.	McCurley, Felix	3830
Bessent, Carl Francis	Mott, Benjamin	3831
Brooke, Brian Wesley	Bissell, Daniel Russell	3832
Rittenhouse, Samuel Albert	Burneston, William Reed	3833
O'Dell, Theron Jerome	Church, Peter	3834
Rome, Curtis Perrin, Jr.	Rome, Jean Andre	3835
Stoffle, Merton Wayne	Perrine, Stephen	3836
Kemmerly, Carl Edward, III	Beard, John	3837
Schoenfeld, Robert Morlas	Decuir, Godefroi	3838
Yockey, James Hewson	Bonaventura y Alpuente, Don Francisco	3839
Riley, Bernard Michael	Kretzer, John Jost	3840
Van Rensselaer, Bernard Sanders	Van Rensselaer, John Sanders	3841
Gentry, John Richard	Estes, William	3842
Fox, Falvey Jerome, Jr.	Coulon, Charles de Villiers Jumonville	3843
Villere, Marin Pierre	Villere, Jacques Philippe	3844
McQuilling, Andrew Thomas, III	Serpa, Antoine	3845
Brower, Walter Wilson	Brower, Abraham	3846
Legett, Thomas Riley, Jr.	Herring, Giles	3847
Eatman, George Lowe	Eatman, Irwin	3848
Bennett, Paul Warren	Bennett, Archibald Akright, Isaac Bridgewater, Isaac	3849

118 The Roster

MEMBER	ANCESTOR	GEN. SOC. NO.
Hicks, Louis Edward	Ensor, John of George	3850
Grange, Franklin Ernest, II	Hunt, James	3851
Johnston, John Walter	Seavey, Amos	3852
Kent, Lawrence	Horner, Isaac	3853
Parks, Lorne Clements	Fisher, George	3854
Osborne, Robert Vandervoort	Osborne, Thomas	3855
White, Albert Sidney Johnston, III	White, Maunsel	3856
Rapier, Edward Sebastian, Jr.	Desforges, Louis Hus	3857
Swigart, Frederic Robert, III	Duplessis, Francois, III	3858
Crawford, William Lusk	Crawford, James	3859
Brame, Arden Howell, Jr.	Hobbs, Benedict H.	3860
Burnett, Donald Mott	Gale, Charles	3861
Schwaner, William John	Flournoy, Samuel	3862
Tustin, Albert Weigand, III	Rivell, Adam	3863
Brown, Bennie Lewis	Campbell, Andrew	3864
Clark, Joe Burney, Jr.	Lashley, Amos Veach	3865
Labry, Lyman Martin	Durel, Jean-Baptiste Neuville	3866
Butler, Bruce Baird	Jones, Mathew	3867
Stouse, Malcolm Renshaw	de la Ronde, Pierre Denis	3868
Jones, Cereno St. Clair	Whipple, John	3869
Yeatts, Lynn Marshall	Dobbin, John	3870
McMullin, William Craig	McMullin, James	3871
Fritz, James Mason	Carman, Frederick Mark	3872
Ewing, Vernon Lee, Jr.	Stansbury, Charles	3873
Plauche, Edouard McCall	Plauche, Jean Baptiste	3874
de Boisblanc, Rene Louis	Forstall, Edmond John	3875
Phares, Marvin Olcott	Dillingham, John	3876
Melancon, Paul Mire	Melancon, Alexander	3877
McCarty, Stewart Boone, Jr.	Boone, Daniel Morgan	3878
Christian, Langdon Taylor, III	Christian, Gideon	3879
Chunn, Calvin Ellsworth	Farmer, Nathan	3880
Finch, Ronald Milton	Black, Noah	3881
Clark, Raymond B., Jr.	Seth, James	3882
Stearns, Parley Mark, II	Wyatt, Daniel	3883
Willie, Leroy Ellis	Bennett, Reuben	3884
Wilcoxen, Joseph Kelly	Willcockson, Elijah	3885
Cummins, James William	Lincoln, George	3886
Davis, Richard Lee	Field, John	3887
Milton, Walter Scott	McLaughlin, Daniel	3888
Weber, Donald Robert	McDonald, John	3889
Ferguson, Alfred Ludlow, III	Kinney, William Burnet	3890
Lovejoy, Charles Douglas	Cook, Phillip	3891

MEMBER	ANCESTOR	GEN. SOC. NO.
Eldredge, Pierce Schank	Eldredge, Aaron, II	3892
Whitley, David Lawrence	Whitley, William	3893
Brown, Thomas Moore	Moore, Lewis, IV	3894
Sutherlin, George Hawes, Jr.	McWillie, Adam	3895
Thomson, Jack Waddell	Morrison, John	3896
Buchanan, Theodore Stewart, Jr.	Buchanan, George	3897
Curtius, Jon Pelot	Pelot, John Francis	3898
Pipkin, Robert Worth	Wimberley, Ezekiel	3899
Halberstadt, James Franklin, Jr.	McKinney, James	3900
Dean, H. Clark	Orton, Timothy	3901
Gladwin, Robert	Jordan, Isaac	3902
Clark, Charles Cleveland, Jr.	Henderson, John Tole	3903
Reese, William Willis	Stevens, Ebenezer	3904
Clark, Lester Merritt	Toothaker, William Rodick	3905
Bolton, Robert Coles	Ford, Seth	3906
Prather, George Woodrow	Doherty, William	3907
MacLamroc, Brian Gwaltney Westwarren	Bell, Benjamin C.	3908
MacLamroc, Alan Gwaltney Westwarren	Bell, Benjamin C.	3909
Davis, Mark Jefferson	de la Ronde, Pierre Denis	3910
Villere, Maurice Francois	Villere, Jacques Philippe	3911
Pinac, Andre Louis, Jr.	Roche, Pierre Felix	3912
Willie, David L.	Bennett, Reuben	3913
Redmond, Bruns D'Aunoy	D'Aunoy, Etienne de Bore Favre	3914
Curren, Dennis Patrick	Seghers, Dominique	3915
Curren, Timothy Barlow	Seghers, Dominique	3916
Sanborn, Earl Boyce, Jr.	Boyce, William	3917
Hosier, Scott Foye	Woods, Andrew Washington	3918
Whitsitt, Dawson Bradford	Whitsett, William	3919
Baldwin, Oliver Hazard Perry, Jr.	Perry, Oliver Hazard	3920
Newman, George Frederick	Culbertson, John	3921
Hanson, Theodore George, Jr.	Patterson, Charles	3922
Altemus, Nicholas Ward	Altemus, Thomas	3923
Tobin, Mark Cleveland	Cleveland, Erastus	3924
Stick, Howard Edward Morgan	Waters, Richard Rawlings	3925
Stick, Alexander Wade	Waters, Richard Rawlings	3926
Wilson, Rowland Steele	Sommerville, John	3927
Loucks, Charles Ernest	Snell, James	3928
Swift, Lee Wilson, Jr.	Swift, Charles Logan, William	3929
Benefield, Joseph Turberville	Newcomb, Elisha	3930
Guidry, Douglas David	Dupuis, Hypolite	3931

120 The Roster

MEMBER	ANCESTOR	GEN. SOC. NO.
Salassi, Gerard Octave, III	Villere, Jacques Philippe	3932
Fluker, Denis McCammon	Fluker, Hardy	3933
Morris, Albert Tingley	Sutton, Tingley	3934
Stockham, Herbert Cannon	Sangster, James	3935
McCarthy, Matthew Wesley	Stoughton, James	3936
McCarthy, Harold LeRoy	Stoughton, James	3937
Schmitt, Roger M. L.	Jones, Walter	3938
Pettit, Absalom John	Deslonde, Andre	3939
Fontenot, Ozeme Dudley	Fontenot, Alexandre Charles Baptiste	3940
Barnes, Edward	Vanosdol, Robert	3941
Lynn, Henry Sharpe	Hansell, John Walker	3942
Harris, Raymond Cutler	Bell, William	3943
Jordon, Joseph Martin	Stanton, Malachi	3944
Stellwagon, Horace D., Jr.	Stillwaggon, William	3945
Walton, William Wyclif	Carter, Joshua	3946
Stick, David Fitchett	Waters, Richard Rawlings	3947
Clark, Charles Cleveland, III	Henderson, John Tole	3948
Cockrell, William Brewster	Gates, William	3949
Wheatley, Timothy Stephen	Hutton, John S.	3950
Sharrock, Charles Everett	Sharrock, Everard	3951
Simmons, Edwin James	Simmons, James, Sr.	3952
Foster, John Alexander, II	Bell, William	3953
Fraser, Peter	Labroquere, Bernard Keplinger, Michael	3954
King, Arthur Mansfield	Burns, Thomas	3955
Sutherland, Spurgeon	Utley, Alvin Satterfield, Archabald	3956
Utech, John Jacob, 3rd.	Tilley, Reuben Dodson Salmon, Benjamin Van Meter, John	3957
Tope, Boyce McBrier	Boyce, Isaac	3958
White, John Gordon	White, Joshua	3959
Finch, Albert Patric, Jr.	Vaughn, Manoah	3960
Sutton, Raymond Ellsworth	Sutton, Smith Fobes (Forbes), Porter Wolf, George Frederick Applegate, Hezekiah	3961
Roth, Frederic Hull	Hull, Elijah Gaylord	3962
Moore, Beverly Polk	Smick, Peter	3963
Martz, Ralph Fraley	Martz, George D.	3964
		3965 Void
Moore, Christopher Polk	Smick, Peter	3966
Brooke, Dandridge	Bissell, Daniel Russell	3967

MEMBER	ANCESTOR	GEN. SOC. NO.
Brooke, Randall Whitney	Bissell, Daniel Russell	3968
Erhardt, Clement Dumont, III	Reilly, Patrick	3969
Stirling, Thomas King Nelson	Taws, Kenny (McKenna)	3970
Dorsey, Vachel Paul	Hooper, James	3971
Deavers, Richard Lynn	Keown (Kown), Nathan Lusk	3972
Barris, William Henri	Norman, Robert	3973
Green, E. Ray	Haltom, William	3974
Ingram, Oscar Finis, Jr.	Edgar, Nicholas	3975
Johnson, Ross Byron	Johnson, Friend	3976
Merchant, Henry Preston	Green, Samuel	3977
Reed, Robert Duncan	Henderson, John Tole	3978
Crowley, Gary Edwin	Bonneval, Alexandre	3979
Wogan, Rene Steven	Labranche, Jacques Hermogene	3980
Judice, Robert Charles	Boutte, Antoine	3981
Golden, Robert Bleakley	Bernard, Elysee Leon	3982
Riggs, Robert Meldrum	Fitch, Jonathan	3983
Gurney, John Thomas, 3rd.	Gurney, Gridley	3984
Cailleteau, Edward Overton	King, George	3985
Schlenker, Richard Carl	Merwine, Jacob	3986
Berkeley, Merrill Duane	Richardson, William Hervey	3987
Freeland, Samuel Lyles	Cole, William	3988
Houser, Jack Kay	DeWitt (Witt), Willard	3989
Anderson, James Raymond	Kimball, Benjamin	3990
Charles, Michael Harrison	Martin, David	3991
Kearns, John Taylor Stark	Williams, James	3992
Pattison, Hal Cushman	Cabeen, Samuel	3993
Carroon, Robert Girard	Squire, Jonathan	3994
Hill, Robert C.	Gann, William	3995
Bresnehen, Thomas, Francis, Jr.	Mifflin, Thomas	3996
	Doner, John	
Lemmons, Thomas	Hufstedler, Jacob	3997
Church, Coleman Frederick	Church, Nathaniel	3998
Brown, James Barrow, Jr.	Richardson, Allen	3999
Love, Homer Townsend, Jr.	Noland, Smallwood Turner	4000
Hamff, James Edward	Prince, William	4001
Caples, Robert Martin	Caples, Jacob	4002
Clements, James Stanley	Clements, Thomas	4003
Kolb, Charles Edward Mealey	Kolb, John William	4004
		4005 Void
		4006 Void
Zirkle, Richard Lee	Hess, Peter, Jr.	4007
Rucker, Tinsley White, IV	Harris, Jeptha Vining	4008
O'Neal, Moncure Camper, Jr.	Coffee, John	4009

MEMBER	ANCESTOR	GEN. SOC. NO.
Davison, David Paul	Davidson (Divison), Bracket	4010
Roth, Frederic Hull, Jr.	Hull, Elijah Gaylord	4011
Sullivan, Chapman	Finks, Fielding	4012
Curtis, Thomas Pelham	Lewis, Morgan	4013
Osborne, Lucien Gianella	Osborn (Osburn), Thomas	4014
Jones, Bernard Gerald, Jr.	van Schaumburg, Bartholomew	4015
de Verges, George Louis	de Chalmette, Ignace deLino	4016
Winter, Ernst Hicklin	Hicklin, Thomas	4017
		4018 Void
Tingley, Charles Alvah	De Lavergne, Theodoras B.	4019
Adkins, Ralph Austin	Adkins, Levi	4020
McClanahan, James Frederick	McClanahan, Williams	4021
Clark, Joseph Mark	Stevens, Obediah	4022
Clark, Joseph Morris, Jr.	Stevens, Obediah	4023
Fisher, Wheeler Yule	Wheeler, Erastus	4024
Coulson, George Arley	Endicott, John A.	4025
Spurr, Jerome Lyon	Fessenden, William	4026
Howard, Stanley Lewis	McKean, James	4027
Beaumont, John Erwin, 2nd.	Allen, Isaac	4028
Ogden, Henry Duplessis, IV	Ogden, Peter Voorhees	4029
Roth, Jon Biddle	Wilkinson, James	4030
White, Maunsel	White, Maunsel	4031
Scutt, Charles William	Tipton, Luke	4032
Patterson, Denis W.	Holmes, Isaac	4033
Dallery, Edgar Laird	Cloninger, Adam, Jr.	4034
Reed, William Corwin, Jr.	Scott, Alexander	4035
	Ingle, James	
Osborne, Robert Vandervoort, Jr.	Osborne (Osburn), Thomas	4036
Ellis, Virgil Wiley	McCutchen, John	4037
Lynch, Charles Clifford, Sr.	Hall, Levi	4038
Lynch, Charles Clifford, Jr.	Hall, Levi	4039
Linthicum, Sweetser	Linthicum, Abner	4040
Eastwood, Ralph Allen, Sr.	Owings, Thomas of Richard	4041
Pardee, Ernest Lewis	Elliott, John	4042
Schempp, George Grant, II	Morse, Amasa	4043
	Glick, George	
Riggs, David Lynn	Reese, Charles	4044
Runells, David Charles	Newby, Elsey	4045
Farley, Myron Foster	Hamilton, Thomas, 3rd.	4046
Mounts, Dennis Eugene	Cox, Joseph	4047
Thorp, Crofton Elwyn, Jr.	Colby, Samuel S.	4048
London, Richard Carrol	London, James	4049
London, George Abraham	London, James	4050

The Roster 123

MEMBER	ANCESTOR	GEN. SOC. NO.
Carter, Edwin Royall, Jr.	Kennon, Erasmus	4051
Smith, Arthur M.	Rowles, David	4052
Smith, Michael K.	Rowles, David	4053
Smith, Frederick D.	Rowles, David	4054
Shaw, Lynn Jackson	Battle, William, III	4055
Ritchie, Robert Field	Caruthers, John	4056
Woodfield, Denis Buchanan	Johnson, Jeremiah	4057
Young, Buford Allen	McCullah, Alexander	4058
Firth, William Rutherford, Jr.	Foster, Jacob	4059
Dimick, Gregory Forrest	Pelton, Phineas	4060
Cowper, William Henry	Goodspeed, Zenas	4061
Schweitzer, Kenneth	Renninger, Jacob	4062
Hollinger, Ammon Lester	Hollinger, Jacob	4063
Harting, Robert Morgan	Morgan, John	4064
Schaeffer, Forrest Rickenbach	Schaeffer, Philip	4065
Aumock, George Harry	Antonides, Peter	4066
Lilley, John Thomas, Jr.	Koser (Keyser), Jonathan	4067
Firth, William Rutherford	Foster, Jacob	4068
Stroh, Oscar Henry	Stroh, Benjamin	4069
Robertson, James Stevens	Robertson, John	4070
Armitage, Jim Rodgers	Devane, Benjamin	4071
Dalton, Donald Henry	Hollister, George	4072
Tingley, George Frederick	De Lavergne, Theodoras B.	4073
Little, Melvin Weaver	Rice, George	4074
Arnold, Robert Burtram	Adams, William Ellis	4075
Jones, John Hallberg	Lincoln, Elijah	4076
York, James Arthur Gamble	Hailey, Edward Taylor	4077
Wolfe, Richard Peel	Lyon, Peter	4078
Newcomb, Fred Norman	Burneston, William Reed	4079
Tull, Willis Clayton, Jr.	Milbourne, James	4080
Brown, Herbert Thomas, Jr.	Chamberlain, Henry	4081
Williamson, Jeffrey Phillips	Phillips, Benjamin	4082
Finlay, Luke William	Carroll, William	4083
Andriano-Moore, Richard Norvel	Moore, Asa	4084
Kurth, Robert Lee	Caffee, John C.	4085
Wollard, Charles Rainwater	Lile, Malachi	4086
Scheetz, George Henry	Scheetz, Gerhard Henrich	4087
Zillman, Marcus Patrick	Patrick, Ralph	4088
Ramsey, Carl Allan	McCracken, Robert	4089
Sutherland, Frank Sheldon	Thrall, Walter	4090
Palmer, Harding	Palmer, Noyes	4091
Hubbard, William Jackson	Magee, Robert	4092

MEMBER	ANCESTOR	GEN. SOC. NO.
Harris, William Lloyd	Harris, Thompson	4093
Morris, Charles Edward	Bushnell, Sterling Graves	4094
Fawkes, Charles Elliott	Woodruff, Ephraim	4095
Needham, George Fisk, 3rd.	Reese, John	4096
Houston, Frank Matt	Houston, David	4097
Devoe, Thomas Elliott	Shibley, John, Jr.	4098
Wilder, K. Lee	Bartholomew, Joseph	4099
Coltrin, Lyle W.	Winters, Nathan	4100
Kruemcke, Max Randolph, Jr.	Taylor, Thomas	4101
Dougherty, Cary M., Jr.	Peirce, Joseph Hardy	4102
Costa, Jacob Louis	Chexnaidre, Andre	4103
Williams, James Albert, Jr.	Warren, Ebenezer	4104
Franklin, Benjamin Robert, 3rd.	Franklin, Bedney Abednego	4105
Gandolfo, Henri A.	Meunier, Etienne	4106
Pitts, James Patrick	Withington, John	4107
Richard, Euclid Leones	Bernard, Francois	4108
Jones, Alvin Edward	von Schaumburg, Bartholomew	4109
Slatten, William Anthony	Delery, Louis Chauvin	4110
Hill, Robert C., Jr.	Gann, William	4111
Carter, Clayton Cann	Roberts, Lydia Macdonough	4112
Jenkins, Eugene Augustine, Jr.	Jenkins, John J.	4113
Kolb, David William, VI	Kolb, John William	4114
Randall, John LeMoyne	Randall, Thomas	4115
Taft, Howland Guild	Fletcher, John Swift	4116
Starke, Bolling Powell, Jr.	Kennon, Erasmus	4117
Warterfield, John Robert	Warterfield, Peter	4118
Metz, Donald Leroy	Shively, Solomon	4119
Chadwick, Robert Lane	Dubbs, Jacob	4120
Roddis, William Henry	Leddell, William, II	4121
Dyer, Frank Merrill	Bell, John	4122
Weller, Richard Alan, Sr.	Weller, George	4123
Morris, Joseph Paul, Jr.	Wheeler, Jonathan Jones	4124
Metz, Craig Huseman	Worthington, Joab	4125
Patterson, Philip Cooper	Taylor, James, 5th.	4126
Groff, Clyde Lester	Swisher, Henry Woodrow	4127
Betelle, Milton	Kennedy, Robert	4128
Bird, Matthew David	Belote, Isaac	4129
Dodge, Richard Keller	Cochran, Richard Ellis	4130
Paris, Francklyn Wynne	Riter, Michael	4131
Walker, Forrest Sean	Schaeffer, Philip	4132
Lockwood, Randolph Scott Dewey	Dewey, Chauncey	4133
Gibbons, David Cartan Loker	Jenkins, Benedict Joseph	4134

MEMBER	ANCESTOR	GEN. SOC. NO.
Forstall, Paul Charles	Forstall, Nicholas Michel Edmond	4135
Forstall, Warren Anthony, Jr.	Forstall, Edmond John	4136
Flowers, John Robert, Jr.	deChalmette, Ignace deLino	4137
Harris, Ballard Eustis	Eustis, Abram	4138
Barrosse, Lionel Edward, Jr.	DeCastro, Auguste Genevieve Valentin D'Auezac	4139
Baer, Herbert Lou, Sr.	Baer, Jacob Shellman	4140
Galles, Duane LeRoy Charles Mealman	Kimball, Russell	4141
Morris, Benjamin Hume	Hastings, William	4142
Patrick, Lee Wellington	Patrick, Robert	4143
Stuck, Charles Albert, Jr.	McCullough, Samuel	4144
Davidson, Keith Wickwire	Wickwire, Isaac	4145
Finnell, Arthur Louis	Finnell, John	4146
Grover, Robert LaVern	Grover, Silas Grover, Zadock	4147
Smith, Marshall Mervin	Barber, Ebenezer	4148
Smith, George Floyd	Barber, Ebenezer	4149
Young, Roger Vincent	McCullah, Alexander	4150
Crosby, Caleb Pickens	Neilson, William Douglas	4151
Melching, Don A.	McKinney, James	4152
Meek, Louis Frank, III	Perry, Ransom	4153
Mason, Judson Philip, Jr.	Kelsey, Francis Hollister	4154
Oliver, Curtis John	Oliver, John	4155
Moore, Clifford Charles	Foster, John, 2nd.	4156
McCormack, Benny Hale	McCormack, James	4157
Chesnut, Nelson Robert	DeLong, John Francis	4158
Rolfe, Gerald Clifton	Lester, Lewis	4159
Petro, Kenneth Johnson	Petro, Michael	4160
Dunn, Leward Leon	Hartsfield, James	4161
Arnold, David Wayne	Adams, William Ellis	4162
Dahlene, Oscar, Jr.	McCurdy, Samuel	4163
Smith, Hester Moore	Hickman, Joseph	4164
Wolff, Paul Leigh	Robinson, Edward	4165
Halberstadt, Max Glenn	McKinney, James	4166
Trout, John Truman, Jr.	Wells, James	4167
Arnold, Ketron Elliott	Adams, William Ellis	4168
Pryor, John Gatwood	Adams, William Ellis	4169
Hogan, William Dudley	Harper, Wyatt	4170
Mitchell, Phillip Michael	Taylor, Lemuel Greenberry	4171
Robert, Edward Bane, Jr.	deBlanc, Pierre Georges Cesaire	4172
Wurz, Kenneth Franklin	Grover, Asa R.	4173

MEMBER	ANCESTOR	GEN. SOC. NO.
Quarles, Julian Minor, Jr.	Quarles, Peter	4174
Andruss, Harvey Adolphus, Jr.	Henry Robert	4175
Shaw, C. Battle, Jr.	Battle, William, III	4176
Ragland, Robert Allen	Butler, Bailey	4177
Bostick, Raymond Harrison	Witt, Silas	4178
Frank, Samuel Boone	Frank, Samuel Boone	4179
Decoursey, William Leslie	Decoursey, Isaac	4180
Metts, Albert Caswell, Jr.	Taylor, Elias	4181
Seaman, Lawrence McClean	Jones, David	4182
Adams, William Eugenius, Jr.	Crouch, Isaac Overstreet, James Adams, Andrew Morrison Nesbit, Alexander	4183
Walker, George Fuller	Maples, William Cordra Moon, Nathaniel	4184
Bledsoe, Jack Othel	Tuggle, William, Sr.	4185
Smith, David Carline	Williams, Ralph Cagle, Sampson	4186
Fraser, David	Sandidge, Garrett Longmire	4187
Echols, John L.	Lauderdale, Josiah	4188
Caldwell, William Walpole	Walpole, Horace	4189
Norris, Thomas Lloyd, Jr.	Norris, Silas C.	4190
Mason, David Pierce, Sr.	Mason, David	4191
Graham, James Kenneth	Graham, Gabriel	4192
Hume, William Haywood	Rawlins, Levi	4193
Wright, John MacNair, Jr.	Barr, James	4194
Edwards, James MacDonald	Hubbard, Joseph	4195
Thurber, Donald MacDonald Dickinson	Brady, Hugh	4196
Lewis, James Dean	Lewis, Jabish York	4197
Christhilf, Nicholas Dorsey	Christhilf, Henrich	4198
Schiaffino, George Evans	Aler, Thomas	4199
Christhilf, Philip Raab	Christhilf, Heinrich	4200
McFadden, A. Weems	Brice, Nicholas	4201
Reeder, Thomas Leonard, Jr.	Reeder, Charles	4202
Finch, Willard Robert	Black, Noah	4203
Sloan, Ralph Wiley	Wiley, John	4204
Ball, James Winston, Jr.	Ball, Lewis W.	4205
Prewitt, John Marshall	Marshall, William	4206
David, Salem Kalil, Jr.	de La Houssaye, Francois Balthasar	4207
Landry, Robert Broussard, Jr.	Plauche, Jean Baptiste	4208
Ruddock, Theodore Davis	Fortier, Michel, II	4209
Winslow, John Leiper, Jr.	Leiper, George Gray	4210

MEMBER	ANCESTOR	GEN. SOC. NO.
Spragins, Samuel Hamilton, Jr.	Green, Grief	4211
		4212 Void
Mackey, Harold Kenneth	McCauley, James	4213
Coats, J. Blood, Jr.	Knox, John	4214
Norris, Thomas Lloyd	Norris, Silas C.	4215
Gann, Thomas Huey	Gann, William	4216
Lemley, Kenneth McRae	Lemley, Jacob	4217
Fraser, James William	Sandidge, Garrett Longmire	4218
Stancil, Walter Dorsey	Young, Robert, Sr.	4219
Collins, John Wesley	Shelton, Crispin (Chrispian) Eli, Sr.	4220
Howell, Kenneth Lamar	Howell, Burwell	4221
Garner, Ervin Leon	Shaw, Thomas	4222
Crosby, William Dalton	Neilson, William Douglas	4223
Felt, Frederick Christian	Bunker, Ebenezer	4224
Johnson, Forrest Clark, III	Trowbridge, Abner	4225
Polk, George Johnston	Horney, Samuel	4226
Hartman, Thadeus Lee	Henthorn, Adam	4227
Orton, George Soliday	Cleveland, Erastus	4228
Printz, Charles Francis	Lucas, Simeon	4229
Printz, Charles Francis, Jr.	Lucas, Simeon	4230
Chesson, Wesley Earle, Jr.	Hudgins, Robert	4231
Orton, William Rutledge, II	Cleveland, Erastus	4232
Orton, Thomas Graves	Cleveland, Erastus	4233
Wall, Wendell Glen	DeFrance, Hawkins Boone	4234
Jordan, Horace Richard	Walker, Richard Henry	4235
Norris, Clayton	Clayton, Zephaniah	4236
Riley, David Leslie	Adams, David	4237
	Claggett, Thomas Wilson	
	Riley, Zachariah	
	McDarment, John	
	Meadows, Gabriel B.	
	Ransdall, Zachariah	
	Watts, John	
	Sebree, John	
	VanDeren, Stephen	
	McKee, John	
	Watts, John T.	
	Castleman, Lewis	
	Riley, James	
	Vallandingham, Richard	
	Riley, Ninian	
	Castleman, John H.	
	Watts, Julius	

MEMBER	ANCESTOR	GEN. SOC. NO.
	Poindexter, David	4237
	Castleman, Jacob	
	VanDeren, Godfrey	
	Castleman, David	
Whisenant, Herman Arthur, Jr.	Parsons, John	4238
Jones, David John	Lincoln, Elijah	4239
Kellogg, Thomas Richards	Kellogg, Samuel	4240
	Kellogg, Justin	
Baker, Louis Stannard	Baker, Ozi	4241
Snapp, Albert Bryan	Ashley, William J.	4242
Mead, James Russell, Jr.	Lutton, William	4243
Ming, William Lee	Allen, Hudson	4244
Mullen, Patrick Walter	Mullen, James	4245
Baker, Charles Estell	Stevenson, William	4246
Carter, Randolph Scott Eastham	Randolph, Charles Carter	4247
Parshall, Alfred Glen	Clemmens, Daniel	4248
Perry, Joseph Frank	Harrington, Charles	4249
Pitts, Alvin Lane	DeBellevue, Francois Barbin	4250
Hollyday, Thomas James	Hollyday, Henry	4251
Lipscomb, Thomas H., III	Gardner, Hiram	4252
Chanler, Sidney Ashley Astor	Armstrong, John A., Jr.	4253
Rayfield, James Horace, Jr.	Melvin, Daniel	4254
Schauffler, Frederick Allen	Reynolds, Samuel	4255
Winslow, Blaine Frederick	Sears, Alfred	4256
Windsor, Laurence Charles, Jr.	Hosmer, Jacob	4257
Swogger, Larry K.	Swogger, John, Jr.	4258
Echols, John Lynn, Jr.	Lauderdale, Josiah	4259
Abney, Joe L.	Abney, Elias	4260
Toso, Donald Richard	Boynton, John	4261
Mhoon, Robert Brinkley, III	Provost, Godfroy, Sr.	4262
Toso, Michael Joseph, Jr.	Boynton, John	4263
Gandolfo, Roger Joseph, Jr.	Meunier, Etienne	4264
Stadler, James Robert	Stadler, John	4265
Stokes, Lee Duncan	Duncan, George	4266
Knight, George Stephens	Dillon, Henry	4267
Rose, Dan W.	Kirk, Thomas	4268
Killian, Michael John	Simpkins, Darius	4269
McCoin, Donald Douglas	Price, Soloman	4270
Butler, William Bradley, III	Butler, Aaron W., Jr.	4271
Cowherd, Leonard Mallonee	Hill, Ambrose Powell	4272
Fail, Welton Ruel	Cowan, Thompson	4273
Pitts, Neal Chase	Allee, William	4274
Byrd, John Earl	Bird, John Wesley	4275

The Roster 129

MEMBER	ANCESTOR	GEN. SOC. NO.
Trout, Robert Rayle	Wells, James	4276
Twiggs, Albert J.	Twiggs, David E.	4277
McBee, Charles Douglas, Sr.	Ince, John	4278
Olivier, Henry John, Jr.	deVezin, Jean Baptiste Olivier	4279
Daly, John Michael	Daly, Lawrence	4280
de la Houssaye, Wayne Robert	de la Houssaye, Francois Chevalier	4281
Ernshaw, Daniel J.	Davie, Samuel	4282
Peden, Henry Clint, Jr.	Bagby, John	4283
Bradley, Melvin James	Gilles, George	4284
Halbert, James Warren	Halbert, William	4285
Slingluff, Robert Lee	Slingluff, Jesse	4286
Barber, Donald Franklyn	Barber, Ebenezer	4287
Fortier, Jacques Lanauze	Fortier, Michel, II	4288
Anderson, George Parker	Enochs, Isaac	4289
McCoin, Edgar Royce	Price, Solmon	4290
Mettee, Bradley T. J., Jr.	Mettee, Martin	4291
Richardson, Aubrey DeVaughn	Worley, Elijah	4292
Howell, Ronald Jay	Howell, Joshua	4293
Jackson, John Davies, Jr.	Spears, John	4294
Hendershot, Edgar Albert	Morgan, Ebenezer	4295
Powell, David Wayne	Knight, John	4296
Flint, Goerge William Treat	Risdon, David	4297
Caldwell, William Wallace, Sr.	Fewell, William	4298
Chandler, Glenn Edwin	Boyt, James	4299
Winslow, Albert Foster	Winslow, Kenslin	4300
Grohgan, Fred Alfred, Jr.	Ries (Reese), Christian	4301
Fraser, Carlos Enrique	Sandidge, Garrett Longmire	4302
Howell, David Neil	Howell, Burwell	4303
Binion, Terrance Robert	Binion, Robert Burton	4304
Pryor, Robert McBride, Jr.	Adams, William Ellis	4305
Pryor, William Adams, III	Adams, William Ellis	4306
Harrison, Patrick Morgan	Buchanan, John, I	4307
Williamson, Dalton	Pope, James	4308
Wilkinson, Roy Winston	Wilkinson, Stephen	4309
Wilkinson, Joel Winston	Wilkinson, Stephen	4310
Plaisance, Paul Joseph Avila, Jr.	Plascencia, Jean Juan Mathias	4311
Murray, Samuel Lynn	Bartlett, Joshua	4312
Smith, Alfred McLean	Anderson, Athel Smith, John Joseph	4313
Hyer, Stanley Earl	Jackson, Asa Finster, Jacob	4314
Dick, R. Elvin	Hurst, Elijah, Sr.	4315

MEMBER	ANCESTOR	GEN. SOC. NO.
Connelly, John E., IV	Guy, John	4316
Pilgrim, Curtis Merle	Rosenkrans, Benjamin	4317
Streets, David Henry	Miller, Abraham	4318
Sutton, Lynn Arden	Linkous, Adam	4319
Cullen, Charles A., Jr.	Waite, Oliver	4320
Lankford, David Skelton	Skelton, Zachariah	4321
Trowbridge, Michael Lynn	Trowbridge, Jacob	4322
Shull, Richard Bruce	Cole, Joseph	4323
Johnston, Otis C., Jr.	Spigner, Samuel Johnston, Nathan	4324
Martin, Reed Ammerman, Sr.	VanDeren, Stephen	4325
Martin, Reed Ammerman, Jr.	VanDeren, Stephen	4326
Kennison, Richard Adrian	Herkimer, John	4327
Ritchie, Lee Canfield	Caruthers, John	4328
Ritchie, Robert Allan	Caruthers, John	4329
Yeilding, Thomas David	Kellum, Edward	4330
Buffington, Byrd Mayson, Jr.	Yount, David	4331
Dupuy, Peter Hillyer	Dupuy, Aubry	4332
Woolverton, Dalton Leo	Percy, Ferdinand Bonaventure Francois	4333
Laird, James Douglas	Sutliff, Salmon	4334
Paris, William Francklyn Mercer, II	Riter, Michael	4335
Roy, Robert Garth Bingham	Bingham, Lemuel	4336
Lyons, James Thomas	Estes, Benjamin Hall	4337
Gradeless, Rex Lavern	Gradeless, Nathaniel	4338
Adkins, Howard Patrick	McComas, Elisha	4339
Howcott, Harley Butler, Jr.	Adair, John	4340
Stockton, Maurice, III	Fortier, Michel, II	4341
Jenkins, Jack Simmons	Jenkins (Jinkins), Lewis	4342
Swisher, Michael Scott	Tanner, Nathan	4343
Pennell, Donald James	Sanders, George	4344
Fontaine, Edgar Benjamin, Jr.	Sicard, Marcelin	4345
Sauner, Richard Garry	Lowther, Robert Roberts, James	4346
Dick, Kalvin Ryan	Hurst, Elijah, Sr.	4347
Dick, Winfred Elbert	Hurst, Elijah, Sr.	4348
de Butts, Daniel Heath	Ashby, Samuel	4349
Alford, Julius Mosby	Catching, Philip	4350
Davis, Donald Eugene	Holland, Charles Miller	4351
Bever, Paul Stewart	McGee, Robert	4352
Doliber, Donald Arthur	Tucker, Amos Dennis	4353
Bullard, Rickey H.	Billings, George	4354

The Roster 131

MEMBER	ANCESTOR	GEN. SOC. NO.
Dorsey, Brice Marden	Dorsey, John Worthington of Caleb	4355
Maglidt, Henry Wilson	Wilson, Nicholas	4356
Worthington, Thomas Carroll, Jr.	Kent, Robert Wheeler	4357
Marbury, Francis Cross	Slingluff, Jesse	4358
Young, Gary Edward	McCall, William	4359
Posey, Robert Michael	Posey, Joseph Harrison	4360
Ashley, Keith Drew	Holter, George, Jr.	4361
Howell, Douglas Lamar	Howell, Burwell	4362
Little, Augustine Patterson, III	Landrum, Thomas	4363
Colgin, George Larkin, Jr.	Colgin, John	4364
Pryor, William Adams, III	Adams, William Ellis	4365
Pryor, Robert Lee	Adams, William Ellis	4366
Carey, Richard Ellis	McCallister, Hugh	4367
Brodbeck, Thomas Raymond, Jr.	Korn, Charles	4368
Dutcher, Russell Kenneth, III	Brokaw, Cornelius	4369
Woolverton, David Michael	Percy, Ferdinand Bonaventure Francois	4370
Griffin, Leonard Gaines	Patton, Dorington "Dorn"	4371
Cleveland, Craig Webster	Cleveland, Joseph	4372
Tete, William Thomas	Tete, Auguste	4373
Young, Robert Joseph	Boynton, John	4374
McKendrick, Charles Stuart, III	Dumontier, Onesiphore Bernard	4375
Earhart, Valentine Adam, Jr.	Moore, Robert Burwell	4376
McArthur, Donald Joseph	Valere, Charles	4377
Paxton, Richard Gentry	Gentry, Richard	4378
Fell, John Corry	Green, John Williams	4379
Johnston, Otis C., III	Spigner, Samuel Johnston, Nathan, III	4380
Douglass, Edward Trent, Jr.	Cabarrus, Augustus, Jr.	4381
Garber, Alexander Christian, Jr.	Eubank, Robert	4382
Trigg, James Knox	Wilson, Hiram Isaac	4383
Butterfield, John Homer	Shepherd, John	4384
Lay, Kenneth Edward, Sr.	Fetter, Jacob	4385
Slingluff, Michael McCormick	Slingluff, Jesse	4386
Roper, Emmett Allan, Jr.	McCraw, Oliver B.	4387
Snyder, Frederick Russell, Jr.	Gorton, Rufus	4388
Dutcher, Russell Kenneth, Jr.	Brokaw, Cornelius	4389
Stewart, Averill Thatcher	Waterman, Barnabas	4390
Peterson, David Howard	Kuns (Kuntz), Daniel	4391
Ward, William Ray	Dixon, Jeremiah	4392
Lee, William Justice, Jr.	Rodney, Daniel	4393
Kurth, Robert Lee, Jr.	Caffee, John C.	4394

132 The Roster

MEMBER	ANCESTOR	GEN. SOC. NO.
Wetzel, Ronald Joseph	Kelso, John	4395
Barr, Dixon A.	Capron, Laban	4396
Loker, Lawrence Lorenzo	Carr, Caleb	4397
Weaver, James Albert, II	Triplett, William Harrison	4398
Viosca, Barry Francis	Percy, Ferdinand Bonaventure Francois	4399
Stakelum, William David	Percy, Ferdinand Bonaventure Francois	4400
Bush, Edward Church	Robertson, Cornelius	4401
Moore, John L.	Young, George, Jr.	4402
Bertram, Richard David	Percy, Ferdinand Bonaventure Francois	4403
Sublette, Donald Jackson	Baldwin, Joseph, IV	4404
Gist, William Claude, Jr.	Gist, John	4405
Pohl, Clifford Hugo, Jr.	Hall, Thomas Graves McCarty, Reuben	4406
Darby, Robert Davison	Darby, Barthelemy Francois St. Mark	4407
Thomas, Harold Ashton	Thomas, Philemon	4408
House, Nelson Charles	House, Allen	4409
Blackett, Larry Lee	Kimmis, Samuel	4410
Germond, George Frederick, III	Sherman, Solomon	4411
Kurth, Roy Collins	Caffee, John C.	4412
Steward, Morton Collins, Jr.	Waterman, Barnabas	4413
Powell, Harold Frederic	Crane, Samuel	4414
Forbes, William Albert	Forbes, Benjamin Gilbert	4415
Lloyd, Mark Frazier	Bell, James	4416
Rowntree, Gradie Raymond	Rowntree, Henry	4417
Nass, Walter Pool, Jr.	Reed, Michael Spencer, Benjamin	4418
Couch, Robert David	Douglass, Robert	4419
MacGunnigle, Bruce Campbell	Shaw, William Holder	4420
Jones, Felix Henley, Jr.	Jones, Thomas G.	4421
Carpenter, Donald Alfred	Carpenter, Daniel	4422
Field, Charles Kellogg, III	Webb, Adin	4423
Harrison, Keith Graham	Silver, Jacob	4424
Martin, Paul Edmond	Martin, Thomas	4425
Guice, Gerald Pipes	Guice, Jacob Pipes, David	4426
Maples, Glen	Maples, William Cordra	4427
Bernstorf, Philip W.	Downs, William	4428
Thomas, George Reber	Thomas, Elam	4429
Owen, James Jarratt	Brightwell, Jason	4430
Gordon, Paul Tulance, III	Charlton, James D.	4431

MEMBER	ANCESTOR	GEN. SOC. NO.
Jobson, Robert Clifford	Rightmyer, John	4432
Long, Frank McDowell, Jr.	Hord, Elias	4433
Smith, Robert T.	Current, John	4434
Girdley, Harry Watson	Girdley, Joseph	4435
Rush, Everett Neil	Gardner, John, Jr.	4436
Clements, Charles McCall, III	McGough, Robert	4437
Johnson, Hardwick Smith, Jr.	Lowe, Curtis	4438
Turpin, William Beverly	Lovett, Thomas Fens	4439
Kollock, David Hall, III	Kollock, James Patriot Wilson	4440
Chappell, Earl Stanley	Evans, Andrew J.	4441
Ruby, John Lindley	Depauw, John Ruby, Peter, III	4442
Shannon, James J., Jr.	Finnell, John	4443
Riley, Thomas Leslie	Riley, Ninian	4444
Smith, Sherrill Montrose, Sr.	Pattillo, Edward	4445
Rash, Wallace McDonald	Elkin, Robert	4446
Herrington, Kenneth Frank, III	Winn, James M.	4447
Hawkins, Leland Barnes, III	Gist, Benjamin, Jr.	4448
Calhoun, James Robert	Calhoun, Mark	4449
Truitt, Robert Ralph, Jr.	Hanks, Peter, IV	4450
Norrid, Henry Horatio	Norrid, Larkin	4451
Bush, Edward Milton	Henderson, John	4452
Boulter, Eldon Beau	Scarborough, Allen	4453
Rebillot, Todd James	Swift, Zebulon	4454
Mathis, Addis	Mathis, Gabriel Throckmorton	4455
Stevenson, James Thomson	Thomson, David	4456
McColley, Sutherland	Anderson, Jenifer	4457
Hilliard, John Mauk	Daniel, Jesse	4458
Lane, Garrison Fairfield	Lane, Loring, Sr.	4459
Snider, Ernest Lorin	Oliver, John	4460
Dennis, Kenneth Allen	Conner, Harrison	4461
Mack, Chester Floyd, Jr.	Bannon, Michael	4462
Roberts, William Wesley	Gardner, Jesse	4463
Crocker, Albert Rudolph	Crocker, Lemuel Grant	4464
Freeman, Reuben Byron, II	Freeman, Edmond (Edman)	4465
Prejean, Edward Joseph, Jr.	Bourgeois, Jean Baptiste	4466
Willis, Todd Bradford	Willis, William W.	4467
Klumb, Robert Michael	Austin, John Jones	4468
Zeitler, Vernon Arthur	Hickox, Reuben	4469
Wightman, Thomas Alan	Roberts, James	4470
Woelfel, Roger Harold	Murray, Thomas Clinton	4471
Morris, Benjamin Hume, II	Hastings, William	4472
Vick, James Andrew	Love, Edom C.	4473

MEMBER	ANCESTOR	GEN. SOC. NO.
Evetts, Livingston Spaulding	Reed, Michael	4474
		4475 Void
Whetstone, Martin Allen	Potter, Isaac	4476
	Gue, Joseph	
Vest, Stephen Matthew	Myers, Joseph, Sr.	4477
Young, Robert Kirkland	Girdler (Gridley), James	4478
Norrid, Henry Gail	Norrid, Larkin	4479
Higley, Wayne Earl, Jr.	Sherman, Jacob	4480
Wells, Charles Chauncey	Wells, Jonathan	4481
Wells, Charles Andrew	Wells, Jonathan	4482
Wells, Joseph Nathan	Wells, Jonathan	4483
Treppa, Allan Ralph	Mitchell, Aden	4484
Bernstorf, David James	Caldwell, William	4485
Cooper, Clarence Clyde	Cooper, Meredith	4486
Spaulding, George Edgar, Jr.	Gilbert, Abner	4487
Page, Henry, III	de la Roche, George Henri Frederick Franck	4488
Saunders, Willard Gerald, II	Lewman, Noah	4489
Barroll, Reginald Stewart	Barroll, James Edmondson	4490
Bond, Calhoun	Bond, Thomas Talbott	4491
Newell, John Davis	Swisher, John	4492
Winslow, Nathan John	Leiper, George Gray	4493
Massie, Cecil Miles, Sr.	Poindexter, Richard	4494
Holliday, William David	Holliday, Peter Alexander	4495
Corey, Roland Reece, Jr.	Nivin, David	4496
Middleton, Arthur Pierce	Dant, William	4497
Chambers, Lawrence Bailey	Elliott, Abraham James	4498
McCandless, Robert Boyd	Ralston, John	4499
Davies, Robert Wynter	Lockett, Samuel Locke	4500
Everngam, Douglas Howard	Beetem, Abraham	4501
Brown, Hugh Bennett	Goodrum, Sterling	4502
Showers, Burton LaVerne	Sypher, Jacob	4503
Simpson, Dennis William	Simpson, William	4504
	Adams, John	
Harden, Victor Richard	Reaves, James	4505
McDonald, Francis Goodall	McDonald, Allen	4506
Pope, Joe Delwin	Ellison, Lewis	4507
Hawkins, Frederick Barnes	Gist, Benjamin, Jr.	4508
Meroney, William Albert	Meroney, William	4509
Fortenberry, William Lowery	Magee, Jacob	4510
Murphy, Philip Julian	Mills, William	4511
Morse, Ruel Adel-Verne	Pond, Moses	4512
Woolverton, Nicholas Winnot	Woolverton, Jacob	4513

The Roster 135

MEMBER	ANCESTOR	GEN. SOC. NO.
David, Romeal Kalil	de la Houssaye, Francois Balthaser	4514
Dunlap, John Bettes, III	Carpenter, James	4515
McCandless, Stanley Kaar	Ralston, John	4516
Schwartz, John Bonicamp	Cox, Martin	4517
Howell, Hampton Person, Jr.	Saunders, Samuel Little	4518
diZerega, Augustus, V	Jacobs, Price	4519
Irvine, William Burriss, III	Moses, John Folsom	4520
Griffin, Lowell Miland	Tyler, David E.	4521
Groves, Fergus Coleman	Groves, Samuel	4522
Gray, James Hammer	Gray, James	4523
Brooks, Paul Robert Michael	Wright, James	4524
Bennett, John Henry Van Swearingen, Jr.	Bennett, Van	4525
Shepard, John Steadman, Jr.	Nixon, William	4526
Long, Harry Clarence	Dougherty, John	4527
Dye, David Allen	Dye, Luke	4528
Holt, Harry Ewell	Moore, Joseph	4529
Williams, Fred Arthur	Futhey, Robert K.	4530
Moore, Jasper Lewis	Pullen, Jenks	4531
Heiple, James Dee	Kyes, Laban	4532
McCandless, Tracy Conrad	Ralston, John	4533
Gooch, David Barr	Torrey, Nathan, Jr.	4534
Pilie, Joseph Maurice, Jr.	Pilie, Louis Philippe	4535
Warren, James Robert	Wade, James	4536
Lane, John Robert, Jr.	Millard, Bennett, Sr.	4537
Jordan, Colon Earl, Sr.	Gunn, Elisha	4538
Pinnell, Gary Ray	Day, Lewis	4539
Coon, John Elton	Coon, Jasper S. M.	4540
Erwin, Harry Louis	Bailey, Levi	4541
Guice Jeffrey Pipes	Pipes, David	4542
Hafter, Jerome Charles	Bickham, Thomas	4543
Duck, William Charles	Gee, James Hicks	4544
Smith, Richard Earnest	Adair, William	4545
Heiple, Jonathan James	Kyes, Laban	4546
Heiple, Jeremy Hans	Kyes, Laban	4547
Carney, Leonard Lawson	Willis, Daniel	4548
Kollock, David Peter	Kollock, James Patriot Wilson	4549
Kollock, George Tams	Kollock, James Patriot Wilson	4550
Mix, Richard Lawrence	Randall, Ornan	4551
Kilgore, Robert Annis	Merrill, Joseph Annis	4552
Meroney, Charles Murray	Meroney, William	4553
Salassi, Walter Lee	Luckett, James	4554

MEMBER	ANCESTOR	GEN. SOC. NO.
Thomas, Joseph Burghard	Cox, James	4555
Price, Paul Patrick	Price, Ralph	4556
Webb, William David	Thaxton, Thomas	4557
Williams, Howard Bailey	Bonner, William	4558
Kirkland, Leonard Wade	Massengill, George Washington	4559
Kirkland, David Lynn	Massengill, George Washington	4560
Reynolds, Alvin Parker, Jr.	Turner, Peter	4561
Burkey, Lee Melville	Kelley, Samuel	4562
Lincoln, Percy Marsh, Jr.	Anderson, Alexander	4563
Webb, Mark Stephen	Thaxton, Thomas	4564
Matheny, James Robert	Wilson, George P.	4565
Bishop, Lee Edward, Jr.	Robinson, George Rogers	4566
Kellum, Mervyn J., Sr.	Kellum, Edward, Sr.	4567
Hopkins, James Robert	Gettys, Joseph	4568
Moore, Allen Wendell	McKee, Henry	4569
Robbins, Gregory Lynn	Robbins, Thomas, Sr.	4570
Adams, Thomas Richard	Overstreet, James	4571
Parsly, Lewis Fuller	Montanye, Thomas B.	4572
Colgin, Harvey Lee	Colgin, John	4573
Stouse, Maurice de la Ronde	de la Ronde, Pierre Denis	4574
Parker, David Ozro	Easter, Lewis	4575
Bourke, Clyde Edwin, Jr.	Boone, Charles	4576
Hill, John Stell	Stell, George Washington	4577
Falkner, James Calton	Kellum, Edward, Sr.	4578
Limmer, Early Alva, Jr.	Higginbotham, Benjamin Graves	4579
Reed, Ralph C.	Teegarden, William	4580
Hartnett, Walter Falkner	Kellum, Edward, Sr.	4581
Hale, James Rayburn	Hembree, Benjamin Franklin	4582
Risley, Ronald David	Risley, Eli, Jr.	4583
Turpin, Thomas Jefferson	Butler, Thomas Langford	4584
Donan, William Page	Donan, David Cox	4585
Grim, Robert Elroy	Grim, Jonathan	4586
Kielman, L. E.	Rimmer, Thomas	4587
Wiley, William Richard, Jr.	Wiley, John	4588
Wood, Robert Spencer	Obenshain, William	4589
Mobley, Richard Isaiah	Guice, Jonathan	4590
Stephens, Hartzell Oscar	Hodges, Josiah	4591
Stephens, Carl Lynn	Jones, Branch	4592
Zell, Harold Johnston, Jr.	Vanderslice, Isaac	4593
Ming, Robert Sterling	Allen, Hudson	4594
Farnandis, W. Walter	Farnandis, Walter	4595
Melancon, Paul Mire, Jr.	Melancon, Alexandre	4596

The Roster 137

MEMBER	ANCESTOR	GEN. SOC. NO.
Lincoln, Thomas Albert	Anderson, Alexander	4597
Kellum, Mervyn J., Jr.	Edward Kellum, Sr.	4598
Manchester, Robert Grant	Calmes, Marquis, IV	4599
Bedwell, Wiles Kline	Whitman, Henry Nostrand	4600
Nicholson, Bruce Howland	Nicholson, George William	4601
Hill, James Joseph	McLemore, Moses	4602
Dickey, Gary Alan	Dickey, James	4603
Harris, Timothy Charles	Cowles, Alpheus	4604
Caldwell, James Allen	Caldwell, William	4605
Patterson, Donald Gene	Neal, Sherman M.	4606
Langworthy, John Alan	Langworthy, Benjamin	4607
Dent, William Eugene, Jr.	Campbell, Beasley	4608
Gonzales, John Malcolm	Gonzales, Joseph	4609
Spragins, Samuel Hamilton	Green, Grief	4610
Cupp, Frederick Franklin	Cupp, Frederick	4611
Schoen, Joseph Michael, IV	Bollinger, Moses	4612
Bond, Thomas Jefferson, Jr.	Chisam, John	4613
Dobbins, John William	Austin, William Skelton, Zedock	4614
McBee, Charles Douglas, Jr.	Ince, John	4615
Lynn, Henry Sharpe, Jr.	Hansell, John Walker	4616
Lynn, George Gambrill	Hansell, John Walker	4617
Bradford, James Philip	Robinson, Jabez	4618
Pennell, George Mather, II	Sanders, George	4619
Davis, Michael W. R.	Davis, Phanuel	4620
Holland, George Vincent	Garlick, Samuel	4621
Barnard, Ronald August	Keyser, Conrad	4622
Mallett, Robert Evans, Jr.	Smith, Jacob Sheafe	4623
Jones, James Thomas, Jr.	Rogers, Joseph	4624
Harris, Thomas Christopher	Dustin, Eliphalet	4625
Peak, Paul Reed, Jr.	Witherow, David	4626
Smith, Thomas Mayhew	Little, Luther	4627
Trebing, David Martin	Christie, Israel	4628
Davis, John Mattison	Davis, Phanuel	4629
Peak, Roger Worley	Witherow, David	4630
Gray, Harold	Richardson, Phinehas	4631
Morehouse, Elnathan Paul, Jr.	Osborn, Joseph	4632
Cooper, Edward Franklin	Cooper, Jacob	4633
Lyons, Robert Ellsworth	Watkins, John	4634
Faulkner, Nelson Franklin, Jr.	Pinkfield, Samuel	4635
Foust, Perry Elihu	Foust, Michael	4636
Edmiston, R. B.	Edmiston, Zebulon Brevard	4637
Watkins, Frank Raymond	Fry (Frye), Samuel	4638

MEMBER	ANCESTOR	GEN. SOC. NO.
MacPherson, Earl	*Wright, George W.*	4639
Cummings, James Whitnell	*Floyd, Nathaniel*	4640
Mossburg, George Washington	*Mossburg (Masberg), John*	4641
Pewett, Edwin Henkel, Jr.	*Caffery, John*	4642
Price, Donald Lee	*Currence, Samuel*	4643
Harding, Harry Joseph	*Mendenhall, John*	4644
Laughlin, Henry Prather	*Stover, Daniel*	4645
Stewart, Thomas William	*Stewart, John*	4646
Floyd, William N., Jr.	*Floyd, Nathaniel*	4647

CHRONICLES OF THE STATE SOCIETIES

ALABAMA

The Society of the War of 1812 in the State of Alabama is thirty years old. Its charter was delivered on the Chalmette Battlefield near New Orleans during the 30th Biennial Convention of the General Society, January 5, 1959. At the first meeting, Colonel William Thomas Carpenter was elected president emeritus. At the next meeting, John Miller Bradley was elected president emeritus in recognition of his hard work and dedication in forming the Alabama Society.

Initially the meetings were informal, attended only by members of the society. As time went on, meetings became more formal. In 1988 a dinner meeting was held at the Redstone Club on Lake Logan Martin.

Many events concerning the War of 1812 occurred within what in 1819 became the State of Alabama. Creek Indians, returning from Pensacola in Spanish West Florida where they had obtained arms and ammunition from the British, were met by local militia under Colonel James Caller at the Battle of Burnt Corn, July 27, 1813. After defeat at New Orleans the British fleet, not knowing of the Treaty of Ghent, captured Fort Bowyer at the entrance to Mobile Bay and did not withdraw until March 1815.

The Alabama Society erected a historical marker to commemorate the Battle of the Holy Ground which took place on the south bank of the Alabama River on December 23, 1813. Two muskets were presented to the Horseshoe Bend National Battlefield Park. The late Thomas Martin, president of the Alabama Power Company, was instrumental in getting Congress to dedicate the Horseshoe Bend Battlefield as a National Park on lands donated by the Alabama Power Company. Mr. Martin was made an honorary member of the Alabama Society.

The Alabama Society has given books about the 1812 era to the Birmingham Public Library, the Samford University Library, and the Emmet O'Neal Library.

When organized there were 26 members. Most charter members are now deceased. There are now 21 members.

CALIFORNIA

"The Petition of Dennis William Simpson, Lee Edward Bishop, Jr., J. Blood Coats, Jr., Gary Alan Dickey, John Corry Fell, George W. T. Flint, James Dean Lewis, Howard S. Moore, William Ray Ward, Roger Harold Woelfel and John Earl Byrd humbly show that the aforesaid gentlemen have been duly admitted to membership in the General Society of the War of 1812.

"That the aforesaid gentlemen are desirous of being admitted into the General Society of 1812 as a new state society under the style and title of the *Society of the War of 1812 in the State of California*.

"Given in the City of North Hollywood, County of Los Angeles, State of California, this 18th day of February in the Year of Our Lord One Thousand nine hundred eighty-nine and of the Independence of the United States of America, the Two hundred twelfth.

"Charter granted at the Annual Meeting of the Board of Directors of the General Society of the War of 1812, March 4, 1989 at Philadelphia, Pennsylvania."

DISTRICT OF COLUMBIA

Several members of the Pennsylvania Society, residing in Washington had felt that the General Society should be represented at the Nation's Capital, the seat of government, and the residence of many retired officers of the army and navy, eligible for membership in the Society. Dr. Marcus Benjamin, who undertook the details of organization, met with eight others at the residence of Gen. Greely, 1914 G Street, N.W., on the evening of the eighteenth of April, 1896, some two years after the organization of the General Society. Gen. Greely, who at the time was President of the Pennsylvania Society and had been in 1891 and 1892, President of the recently organized D.C. Society of the Sons of the American Revolution, explained that the object of the meeting was the formation of a Society of the War of 1812 in the District of Columbia. On motion of Dr. Benjamin, such an organization was effected, temporary officers elected, and the Executive Committee directed to send a delegate to the coming meeting of the General Society asking admission as one of its constituent members.

Those present at this first meeting were Gen. Adolphus Washington Greely, who was chosen President, Admiral Francis Asbury Roe, who was chosen First Vice President, Dr. Marcus Benjamin, who was chosen Second Vice President, Henry Randall Webb, who was chosen Secretary, Frank Birge Smith, who was chosen Registrar, James Malcolm Henry, Dr. James Aloysius Maloney, Alonzo Howard Clark, James Bowen Johnson, and John Elfreth Watkins, Jr. An Executive Committee, consisting of Comrades Greely, Webb, Clark and Watkins, was directed to elect a delegate to the meeting of the General Society, June 19, 1896. The annual dues were placed at one dollar, and the Constitution and Bylaws of the Pennsylvania Society were adopted temporarily.

FLORIDA

On 14, September 1977, a membership certificate was prepared and mailed to new member-at-large Joe Burney Clark, Jr. in Jacksonville, Florida. Early in 1978, Mr. Clark requested information from Ashby Canter, secretary for members-at-large, to form a Florida Society. Shortly thereafter, he was designated the organizing president in the state of Florida. Names of society members who lived in Florida were invited to join the new Florida Society. Mr. Clark also distributed membership applications to friends who were members of other hereditary societies such as the S.C.V. and S.A.R.

Compatriot Tinsley White Rucker, IV hosted the first organizational meeting at his home in Jacksonville during the summer of 1981. Seven compatriots were present and plans progressed. A picture of those present and an article about the meeting was printed in the "War Cry" by editor Dennis F. Blizzard. This was a definite morale booster for the Floridians. That year Michael H. Charles of St. Augustine became a champion recruiter. On February 23, 1982 a request was made to the General Society to create a Florida Society. This was granted at the board meeting in Philadelphia on March 13, 1982. Eighteen members were listed on the charter that was signed by President General Edward C. Beetem, II.

In July of 1982 the Florida Society held its first business and social meeting since being chartered at the home of Compatriot John G. R. Rountree in St. Augustine. A by-laws committee was appointed and officers were elected. They were Joe B. Clark, Jr., President; Charles A. Tingley, Vice-President; Lt. Col. Charles E. Morris, Secretary-Treasurer; Michael H. Charles, Registrar-Genealogist; and Harding Palmer, Chaplain. The new society recognized the invaluable aid and assistance given by the General Officers while the society was being organized.

The Florida Society holds an annual social meeting each winter. They have been held in Jacksonville, St. Augustine, and Ocala. In 1984 the society conducted a wreath laying ceremony at the graves of four War of 1812 veterans who are buried in the National Cemetery in St. Augustine. Three out of the four were killed in the Dade Massacre near Ocala, Florida. The society by itself paid to recondition the grave monuments to 1812 veteran Col. Joseph L. Smith and his wife, Frances Kirby, in St. Augustine. They are the parents of the famous Confederate General Edmond Kirby-Smith. The Florida Society is healthy and has a good growth potential with twelve million people living in Florida.

GEORGIA

The organizing meeting of the Georgia Society was held 18 June 1982, the 170th anniversary of the date on which President Madison signed the declaration of war in 1812. Ten members-at-large, residents of Georgia, met at the headquarters of the Atlanta Historical Society. It was unanimously agreed to petition the General Society for a state charter and to request the Georgia Society be chartered 12 September 1983, the anniversary of "Defenders' Day." Robert B. Arnold was elected organizing president.

The Charter Meeting was held 12 November 1983 in the rotunda of the Old State Capitol Building in Milledgeville, Georgia's capital city during the War of 1812. District Deputy President General M. Camper O'Neal presented the Charter to the organizing president and Georgia Society Membership Certificates to 19 charter members and eight founding members. Seventy-five members and guests attended the charter ceremony, which was designated an "Official Event" of the Georgia Semiquincentenary.

The 1984 Annual Meeting was held in Macon at historic Fort Benjamin Hawkins, a southern fort at the time of the War. The 1985 meeting was held in Milledgeville where the Society honored David Brydie Mitchell, who was Georgia's first governor during the War and the Society placed an 1812 marker on his grave. The 1986 meeting was held in Atlanta, the site of Fort Peachtree, a frontier fort of the period. The 1987 meeting was held in Greensboro where the Society honored Peter Early, the second of Georgia's governors during the War, and placed an 1812 marker on his grave. It was at this meeting that the Society initiated its annual Memorial Service, which honors veterans of all the United States' wars.

The highlights of the 1988 meeting, held in Athens were the visit to the Society by President General Slaymaker and Mrs. Slaymaker and a band concert by the Regimental Band, 37th Georgia Volunteer Infantry. Under the direction of Bandmaster (and Georgia Society member), Major Clyde E. Noble, the program's emphasis was on American and British music of the 1812 era. The Georgia Society has enjoyed steady growth during the past seven years and now has 50 members.

ILLINOIS

The Illinois Society of the War of 1812 was chartered on September 3, 1895, and its organizational meeting was held on September 19, 1895 at the University Club in Chicago. The Society's first president was Col. Charles Page Bryan, a former United States Minister to Belgium.

Prior to 1980, the Society held its Annual Meetings in Chicago each January to commemorate the Battle of New Orleans. The Society maintained an office in Chicago and employed a secretary.

For many of the early years, the Illinois Society served all 1812 Society compatriots of the central states, being the only Society west of Pennsyvlania. It often joined with the Daughters of 1812, the S.A.R., and other patriotic societies to jointly sponsor commemorations of the Fort Dearborn Massacre, Commodore Perry's Victory, the Battle of Tippecanoe, the Battle of New Orleans, and other patriotic observances.

Always a small group, the Illinois Society functioned quite well in patriotic activities up to the year 1918. From 1918 to 1937, the minute ledgers show very little activity. In 1938 a "renaissance" of sorts began with the presidency of Dr. Harold I. Meyer, who guided the Society both in growth and in prestige to prosper through the mid 1960's.

From the late 1960's into the 1980's, the Society was again relatively inactive as to implementing its major objectives to commemorate and to perpetuate the memories of the War of 1812 patriots and battles. Yearly meetings were routinely held, but in the 1980's the Society functioned with meetings held sporadically. A group of dedicated and conscientious compatriots are now devoting much time and effort to reorganizing the Society.

A new constitution has been written and is ready to go into effect in 1990: the first revision since the original 1895 constitution. The Society has increased its membership to 42, plans public meetings for all the members, and participates in patriotic activities.

The future appears promising as newer members are recruited, and a regularly issued newsletter, *The 1812 Messenger*, keeps the membership informed of all Society activities.

KENTUCKY

The Kentucky Society War of 1812 began its reorganization on July 1, 1986 when William C. Gist and Benjamin Hume Morris, both residents of Kentucky and members of the Minnesota Society, met to rekindle the Kentucky Society.

A reorganizational meeting was held at the Louisville Boat Club on September 6, 1986 with 20 members and prospects attending. At this meeting Benjamin Hume Morris was elected Vice President General for Kentucky; William C. Gist, Jr., President; Richard Zirkle, Secretary; Reed A. Martin, Jr., Treasurer; and Lee Duncan Stokes, Registrar. The Kentucky Society was especially grateful to B. Allen Young of the Minnesota Society for the invaluable aid he gave during the reorganization.

At the Triennial Convention of the General Society in New Orleans in January 1987, Compatriots Stokes, Gist and Morris represented the Kentucky Society.

On Saturday, August 29, 1987, the Kentucky Society held its Annual Meeting and dinner at the Louisville Boat Club. In appreciation for his contribution to our reorganization, B. Allen Young of the Minnesota Society was invited to attend and to present a program on historic Fort Snelling. He was given a commission as a *Kentucky Colonel* by Martha Layne Collins, Governor of Kentucky.

On Saturday, August 27, 1988, the Kentucky Society's Annual Meeting was highlighted by a visit of President General Samuel R. Slaymaker. The President General addressed the audience on genealogical societies in the 1980's. Also attending this meeting was Mary Normal Keissling, the National President of the United States Daughters of 1812. Both she and President General Slaymaker were granted commissions as *Kentucky Colonels* by Wallace G. Wilkinson, Governor of Kentucky. At this meeting Dr. Thomas Riley of Hopkinsville was elected president of the Kentucky Society.

The Kentucky Society continues to give aid in presenting ROTC awards within the *Bluegrass State.* Also, on November 24, 1988, Thanksgiving Day, the Society placed the first of the new bronze veteran markers on the tomb of President Zachary Taylor, a veteran of the War of 1812. The hero of the battle of Fort Harrison in the War of 1812, President Taylor's 204th birthday was an appropriate time for the marking of his mausoleum.

LOUISIANA

The Society of the War of 1812 in the State of Louisiana was initiated as a result of the question put to Mr. B. H. Richardson by 1812 President General William H. Pitcher as to why Louisiana had not become associated with the General Society. Mr. Richardson agreed that the New Orleans area was in every way appropriate for such an alliance and in 1951 his resolve was set to the task.

In the summer of 1951, the first meeting was held at the home of the founder, Beale Howard Richardson, IV, New Orleans, Louisiana. At this meeting thirty-four gentlemen, descendants of the many Louisianians who fought under General Andrew Jackson on the fields of Chalmette, signed the charter which was then forwarded to the National Society. The charter was formally endorsed at the National Convention in New Orleans, January 8, 1952: incorporation granted, February 11.

It was set forth that the purposes of the Louisiana Society were threefold: to honor and perpetuate the memory of those who fought and died in the War of 1812, and particularly at the Battle of New Orleans, to commemorate by appropriate ceremonies the anniversary of the Battle of New Orleans on each January 8th, and to foster and promote patriotic Americanism and the ideals of our forebears.

At a meeting in the opening year, Vice President Richmond Favrot presented himself as a "battle-scarred warrior" wearing the uniform of the 24th U.S. Infantry of the War of 1812. He was classified as "Exhibit A" and was examined with such successful results that everyone in attendance placed an order for a similar costume for the price of $25.00. The actual uniform ordered was that of the 7th Regiment of Regulars of the U.S. Army which were 1,000 strong at the Battle of New Orleans and was copied in detail from one in the collection of the Cabildo Museum.

Each year hence the Society has conducted a memorial exercise on January 8th. The programs have consisted of musical renditions by military bands, invocations by religious leaders, placing of wreaths by the governor, mayor, British consul, French consul and others, the firing of military salutes and principal addresses. The addresses have been delivered by flag officers of the military forces or distinguished historians who have provided historical insight from the period, as well as encouraged patriotism and love of country.

Other historical aspects of the Society have been the placing of bronze plaques on the graves of veterans of the War of 1812 and the fundraising and restoration of the tomb of Major Daniel Carmick, U.S.M.C. He was a Pennsylvania native who as a young officer served as Marine commander aboard the U.S.S. *Constitution* ("Old Ironsides") and later achieved the position of the second ranking officer of the Marine Corps. Wounded in action during the engagement of December 28, 1814, he died in 1816.

The members of the Society annually host a Grand Military Victory Ball which attempts to recreate the festive celebration that occurred following the decisive victory at Chalmette. The president of the Society portrays General Andrew Jackson while the role of Governor William C. C. Claiborne and Mayor Nicholas Girod are portrayed by other board members. Twenty-one "Belles of New Orleans" are presented to General Jackson. The young ladies are generally daughters or granddaughters of the members of the Society and are presented by their father or grandfather in his colorful uniform. *Les demoiselles* represent the City of New Orleans, the eighteen states which comprised the Union at that time and the goddesses of Justice and Liberty. After all of the young ladies have been presented and the colors retired, a waltz is played during which the young ladies and their uniformed escorts dance to complete the tableaux.

The Society has had the pleasure of hosting three Triennial Conventions of the National Society. The membership is limited to three hundred and officers of recognition have been: Beale Howard Richardson, IV, President Emeritus; Brigadier General Francis A. Woolfley, U.S.A. Retired; Malcolm L. de la Houssaye, Past President General, Past President; Charles J. Sinnott, Past President, Captain Emeritus.

MARYLAND

In response to a Baltimore newspaper notice, a group of veterans of the "War with Great Britain Declared 18 June of 1812" met on Friday, 14 May 1841 to consider forming their number into a society to aid indigent veterans, their widows and orphans. A year later the actual organization took place at an "encampment" held at Mount Clare where delegates from Pennsylvania, the District of Columbia, and Virginia were present. The "Old Defenders" were honored with the presence of President Tyler and General Winfield Scott.

A constitution was adopted in 1842 for "The Association of the Defenders of Baltimore" and subscriptions were made to a fund for funeral expenses and family aid when needed by veterans. By this year, Baltimoreans had noted every September 12 with most of the city's able-bodied men participating in the celebrations which originated at the time of the laying of Battle Monument's cornerstone in 1815.

The Association of Defenders, directed by veterans from 1841 to 1887, rejected a proposal to admit descendants "until such time when this Association shall be unable for want of numbers to continue its aims and purposes." When no veterans were able to participate in 1888, sons and grandsons took up the charge granted thirty years before with the name "Association of the Descendants of the Defenders of the War of 1812–1814." This group became incorporated 25 October 1893 as the "Society of the War of 1812 in Maryland of Baltimore City."

At the time of the 1914 Centennial, the Maryland Society had 128 hereditary members largely from the professional and financial callings, and state legislation had made September 12 a bank and government holiday.

By 1950 the 1812 Society in Maryland was foremost in efforts to perpetuate the historic and patriotic significance of the events of 1812–1814. The observance of Defenders' Day had continued unbroken, but public concern flagged as the remembrance of larger and more recent conflicts took precedence.

Great effort was exerted by the Society to keep alive the spirit of the War of 1812, and members adopted a broader format which included a Memorial Cavalcade to many of Baltimore's 1812 monuments and an enlarged program at Ft. McHenry with fireworks, U.S. Navy gunnery, and U.S. Marine Corps music. Attendance increased each year with nearly 10,000 spectators in 1988.

The 150th Anniversary Biennial Convention met in Baltimore in 1964 which marked Maryland's welcome to three of the last ten national assemblies. There are now 176 compatriots on the Society's roster and the endowment is able to contribute importantly to Flag House Foundation, Restoration Fund: U.S. Frigate "Constellation," Ft. McHenry Guards, Maryland Historical Library, and University of Baltimore History Prize.

MASSACHUSETTS

The Massachusetts Society was organized on April 3, 1894, following the interests of a previous Boston organization, the New England Association of Soldiers of the War of 1812. The Society was one of the four state groups which met in Philadelphia, Pennsylvania on April 14, 1894 to adopt a Constitution for a General Society which would become national in scope. The first meeting was on August 7, 1894, and the Society Certificate of Incorporation was filed with the Commonwealth on September 10, 1894.

The Society holds its Annual Meeting on January 8 in commemoration of the Battle of New Orleans. Existing records contain minutes from 1929, the Society being most active in the 1930's and 1940's. In 1935 a legislative Act directed the Governor of the Commonwealth to issue a Proclamation declaring January 8 to be observed as a day of remembrance, along with an artillery salute fired on Boston Common. The Proclamation is still issued on request, though the artillery fire ceased in 1969. The Society also published a Bulletin through these years.

In 1933 the Society began its presentation of an award to an outstanding graduating student engineer of the Massachusetts Maritime Academy and supported the restoration of the U.S. Frigate "Constellation."

In October, 1947, the Society participated in the 150th Anniversary celebration of the launching of the U.S. Frigate "Constitution" on September 27, 1797, now berthed in Boston.

The Society has consistently communicated with its sister organization, the United States Daughters of 1812 and supports the Constitution Museum on an annual basis. In 1978, under the direction of President Homer Dean, all member applications, previously folded and stored, were gathered into a newly obtained post binder, and for the first time in the Society's history, all obtainable original applications, plus copies available from the General Society were placed into a single book for safe keeping and easy reference. The Society is grateful to Past Registrars General Col. Whitney Ashbridge AUS Ret., Rear Admiral Frank P. R. Mitchell, Jr. and Past Assistant Registrar General Howard B. Burgess for their assistance in this project.

In 1980 the Society, under Dean, also printed a booklet, the only complete membership listing since 1894, along with an informational flyer for prospective members. The roster notes the last surviving veteran of the War and the Society was Hiram Cronk, Mass. #70, who joined, and died in 1905 at the age of 105.

The Massachusetts Society is enjoying a revival, receiving many new applicants, ensuring the success of new projects and the continuation of ideals and goals of the Society.

MICHIGAN

The Michigan Society was Chartered 4 May 1946 in Detroit, Michigan with 12 members. The Society never had a membership exceeding 20. With such a small base, and inevitable attrition, the Society began to shrink, with 1963 being the last year in which a member was added.

The Society has, thanks to one of the charter members, Harold M. Hastings, some records of activities during the "first Michigan period." Compatriot Hastings is 100 years old and attends an occasional meeting. He has fortunately retained a personal file of activities when he was president.

The meetings consisted of study of the War of 1812, with special emphasis of the War in the Michigan and Ontario areas. The Society gained approval to erect a large bronze Michigan Historical Marker in downtown Detroit to mark the place where over 300 soldiers were lost during the recapture of the city of Detroit from the British. The marker was dedicated on the 150th anniversary of this battle, 29 September 1963, and became a reality due to the efforts of Harold M. Hastings. The event took place with many city dignitaries taking part.

Michigan became reactivated under the leadership of Donald J. Pennell who became president. He was encouraged in this effort by General Society VPG B. Allen Young. The renewal meeting was held 2 July 1986 at the home of Donald M. D. Thurber. The reorganized Society had nine members: one reinstatement, four transfers, two dual members, and two from MAL status. Since then it has grown to a membership of 32 compatriots.

The Society participated in other events, including the reburial of soldiers from the 1813 cemetery that were unearthed in 1986 when the City of Detroit was excavating for foundations for its People Mover. It was active in the Symposium commemorating the 175th anniversary of The War of 1812.

At least one meeting per year is held with the Michigan U.S. Daughters of 1812. In 1987 and 1988, the two Societies had joint annual meetings. In 1987, the speakers were Mrs. Robert J. Moore, National President of the Daughters of 1812, who spoke on "War in the Chesapeake Bay," and the Re-enactment Association spoke on "Daily Lives of Soldiers Fighting in Michigan: Equipment and Uniforms."

President General Samuel R. Slaymaker II and Mrs. John K. Keisling, National President of the U.S. Daughters, visited the Society in 1988 and attended the rededication of the Michigan Historical Marker and the Second International Symposium in Windsor, Ontario.

MINNESOTA

The first meeting of the Society of the War of 1812 in the State of Minnesota was held on 10 September 1982 at Kozlaks Royal Oaks Restaurant in Saint Paul. It began with a dinner followed by a discussion of and a motion to establish the

Minnesota Society, which was approved unanimously. B. Allen Young, the founder and moving spirit, was nominated as president. Three other individuals participated in this event: John H. Jones, Duane L. C. M. Galles and Michael S. Swisher.

During the next four months the formal proceedings were initiated to charter the Minnesota Society. Meanwhile, on Saturday, 18 December 1982, the first commemorative event of the Society was held to mark the end of the War of 1812, the annual *Treaty of Ghent Remembrance*. This consisted of a ceremony at Oakland Cemetery where Nathaniel McLean, veteran of the War of 1812, is buried, followed by a luncheon and program during which an address was given by Arthur L. Finnell on the 1812 veterans buried in the state of Minnesota.

Three months later, on 12 March 1983, the Minnesota Society was formally chartered at a meeting of the General Society of the War of 1812 in Philadelphia, and enacting documents were presented to President Young who was in attendance. After two months, on 5 May 1983, the Society was incorporated as a nonprofit organization in the state of Minnesota.

Later that same month on 21 May 1983 at the Saint Paul Hotel, the first annual meeting opened with the presentation of the colors and dinner. A business session followed during which the formal organizational procedures were completed and the Society began its existence.

Six years after the inaugural meeting, the Society is a vital and growing organization of 33 active members with several applications awaiting approval. This remarkable growth is due to the cooperation and hard work of many people, who are currently engaged in completing our major project, the marking of the graves of all the veterans of the War of 1812 in Minnesota.

MISSISSIPPI

On Fort Rosalie Hill at Natchez, the Mississippi Society of the War of 1812 held its first meeting on the 9th of May, 1987, as a chartered society. The petition for the charter was presented on 10 January 1987, by Member At Large, Gerald Pipes Guice during the General Society's Triennial Meeting in New Orleans. The ambitions of 17 Members-At-Large were realized.

The first meeting of the Mississippi Society was an organizational exercise; however, a slate of officers was proposed. It was agreed that only one meeting a year be held until the number developed to a level where goals and programs could be defined. A sense of direction and a keen desire to build a membership across the state were indicated.

Official contact was established with the leading patriotic groups throughout Mississippi. The U.S. Daughters of 1812, The Order of the First Families of Mississippi, the Sons of the American Revolution and others were targeted as recruit areas. The officers began direct mailing programs and personal visits to various meetings. As rapport developed, there began a flow of applications for membership.

The second meeting took place on 27 June 1987, at the home of Compatriot Persell in Natchez. Agreement was reached for the by-laws. This meeting's attendance was twice that of the first, but still too few compatriots were present to do business. It was agreed that future meetings would start with a social period to include members, their ladies and prospective members and that no one member could have the floor for more than one minute. Again, a stronger feeling of direction and a semblance of organization was sensed.

The third meeting was held on 14 May 1988, with good attendance as the compatriots viewed for the first time the new charter framed and matted for all to enjoy. During this year, Mississippi 1812 became involved in the ROTC Awards Program and developed some ideas on grave markers. The Society of the War of 1812 in the State of Mississippi has attained a membership of 35 Compatriots.

NEW JERSEY

On January 25, 1898, Mr. Appleton Morgan of Westfield, New Jersey sent out a call for a meeting to be held at the hotel at Springfield on February 24, 1898 for the purpose of organizing the "Society of the War of 1812 in the State of New Jersey." There were seven present at this meeting but before the final organization five more members were admitted, making a total of 12 charter members. The society was admitted to the General Society June 21, 1898.

In 1925 the total membership had reached 56 compatriots with Samuel Drayton, Esq. as president and Dr. J. Albert Van Horn of Montclair as secretary. Under the presidency of John L. Merrill and secretary F. Starr Reynolds, the New Jersey roster stood at about 70 members in 1930.

The General Society's Conventions were hosted by the New Jersey Society in September 1934 at the Berkeley-Carteret Hotel, Asbury Park; in September 1942 at the Princeton Inn, Princeton; in September 1962 at the Claridge Hotel, Atlantic City and at the Holiday Plaza, Bordentown-Burlington in October 1981. The 1981 Triennial Convention was organized and directed by Howard W. Wiseman, President of the New Jersey Society of the War of 1812. It was held on conjunction with the U.S. Naval Academy Collegiate Conference on Naval History in Burlington, the home of Captain James Lawrence of War of 1812 fame.

Some General Society officers of note from New Jersey have included Robert MacCowan (Emeritus Vice President), Commodore W. W. Vanderhoff, Major Lawrence Stratton, William Y. Pryor, Ross K. Cook, Hon. Edgar Williamson, Jr., Dr. Harry L. Bowlby, Col. C. B. M. Gilman, Edgar Williamson, Jr., Crolian W. Edelen, Donald Townsend, George Meade Holden (President General), Richard A. Scudder, Howard W. Wiseman, James F. Villere and Charles H. Jack, Jr..

NEW YORK

The Society of the Second War with Great Britain
in the State of New York

Organized 3 July 1896
Admitted to the General Society 6 July 1896
Incorporated 6 July 1896
Chartered 12 February 1897
Corporate Name Changed by Order of the New York
Supreme Court 8 September 1900

NORTH CAROLINA

The Society of the War of 1812 in the State of North Carolina held its chartering ceremonies on September 18, 1971 at Tryon Palace in historic New Bern, North Carolina. The pomp and ceremony of the chartering event was highlighted by the attendance of special guests representing the General Society of the War of

1812 including President General Gordon Malvern Fair Stick and Past President General William H. Pitcher. Also in attendance was Edward C. Beetem of the Society of the War of 1812 in Maryland.

The initial officers of the new Society were Dr. Ralph H. Rives, President; Jerry L. Higgins and James G. W. MacLamroc, Vice Presidents; John B. Flowers, III, Secretary; Eugene B. Baugh, Jr., Treasurer; D. Carlos Smith, Genealogist; and Robert L. Gordon, Marshal.

The North Carolina Society has been involved in a number of projects over the years in support of Society goals and objectives. In 1972 a historical marker was dedicated in Roanoke Rapids, North Carolina to the memory of Lieutenant Colonel Andrew Joyner (1786–1856), an officer during the War of 1812. In 1981 an oil painting by Roger E. Kammerer, Jr. of the 1812 privateer, *The Snap Dragon*, was presented to the Wake Forest College Birthplace Society (formerly the Calvin Jones House Society). Calvin Jones was a Major General of the North Carolina Militia in the War of 1812. In 1982 an oil portrait of Captain Otway Burns was presented to the Hampton Mariner's Museum in Beaufort, North Carolina. Captain Burns was one of North Carolina's greatest naval heroes during the War of 1812. In 1983 a "Star Spangled Banner Flag" was presented to the Town of Swansboro during commemoration of the town's 200th anniversary celebration and the unveiling of a statue to Captain Burns. In 1984 a flag and flag stand were presented to the Greensboro Historical Museum on the occasion of the reopening of the Dolly Madison Room.

The North Carolina Society currently has 19 members scattered from the mountains to the coast.

OHIO

Very few records exist giving information on the Ohio Society. It was organized January 8, 1895, and admitted to the General Society on June 19, 1895. The original officers were: Orlando W. Aldrich, President; Gen. Roeliff Brinkerhoff, Vice-President; Gen. George Bohan Wright, Vice-President; Robert Mason Davidson, Vice-President; Bernard Van Horne Schultz, Secretary; Walter Nicholas Paine Darrow, Registrar; Daniel Hosmer Gard, Treasurer; Thomas Herbert Norton, Historian; Harry Parker Ward, Executive Committee; Hubert Herrick Ward, Executive Committee.

Serving from 1894–1896 in the General Society were Orlando Aldrick, Vice President General; Barnard Van Horne Schultz, Assistant Treasurer General; and Harry P. Ward, Executive Committee. Serving from 1906–1908 in the General Society were George Mitchell Wright, Vice President General and Daniel Hosmer Gard as Executive Committee.

The Ohio Society became dormant in 1915. At least one unsuccessful attempt was made to reactivate it in the ensuing 73 years. Finally, Keith Drew Ashley of Pomeroy, Ohio, reactivated the society with an organizational meeting at Columbus on October 8, 1988 with 11 members. At that meeting, three members attended to set up plans. Keith Ashley became president, Michael Trowbridge, secretary-treasurer; and Robert Grim, vice-president. The rest of the officers and the constitution and by-laws were finished at the December 3, 1988 meeting. The society has lost one member by death since organizing and gained several. The first annual conference of the society will be held March 18, 1989 at Canton, Ohio, in conjunction with the Ohio Daughters of 1812.

PENNSYLVANIA

The present Pennsylvania Society of The War of 1812 derived its existence from a national convention of the soldiers of the War of 1812, which convened at Independence Hall in Philadelphia on the 9th of January 1854. Twelve states, together with the District of Columbia, were represented and resolved that as veterans of the conflict, they will never overlook nor forget the aged, infirm and poor widows of their brave associates in arms.

On the 4th of July 1857, a constitution and bylaws were adopted, and on the same day an election was held for permanent officers.

On July 4, 1860, the constitution and bylaws were amended to admit the sons, or in default of sons, the grandsons of those who served their country in the War of 1812. In 1876 the first descendants of veterans were admitted to the organization.

The Pennsylvania Society of the War of 1812 was incorporated in 1892 as The Pennsylvania Society of The Soldiers of 1812. In 1894 the Maryland and Pennsylvania Societies met at Independence Hall, along with delegates from similar societies in Connecticut, Massachusetts and New York.

The Pennsylvania Society holds its Annual Meeting at The Union League of Philadelphia during the month of March. At that time, officers and members of the Board of Directors are elected, activities of the Board of Directors and the standing committees are reported, new members are welcomed, and a talk on a phase of the War of 1812 is heard. The Board of Directors meets three times each year to conduct the business of the Society.

Activities of The Pennsylvania Society include: welcoming new citizens each April at the Federal Court House with a reception and a brief program; a church service held in September in conjunction with The Maryland Society of Pennsylvania, The Society of the War of 1812 in Maryland and The Society of the War of 1812 in New Jersey, to commemorate the writing of the "Star Spangled Banner" by Francis Scott Key; and in cooperation with the General Society of the War of 1812, the awarding of a ribbon and a certificate to outstanding ROTC cadets at colleges and universities in Pennsylvania.

Commemorative treasures in the Pennsylvania Society's possession and on loan to the Pennsylvania Maritime Museum are: A silver presentation platter presented to Commodore Steven Decatur, Commander of the Frigate "United States" by the Citizens of Baltimore. The platter, with its elaborate chased border is the work of Baltimore silversmith, Andrew E. Warner. It descended in the Fotterall family who presented it to the Society in 1901. A silver presentation medal which commemorates the Battle of Lake Erie in 1813. The Congress of the United States presented such medals to the heroes of the War of 1812. The medal bears the picture of the battle leader, Commodore Perry and, on the reverse, a scene of the battle. This was given to the Society in 1979 by Captain Harris C. Aller in memory of George Bertram Regar, the first captain of the color guard of the Society.

TENNESSEE

On March 10, 1983, Lynn Jackson Shaw, Brownsville, Tennessee, with the idea in mind of starting a state society, wrote a letter to the Secretary General S. R. Slaymaker, II. A reply came on March 30 with some general information and some brochures for potential members. On April 8, 1983, a second letter was received from John Loose, Past President General. Quoting from Mr. Loose's letter, "I was Secretary General from 1956 until 1975, and I know there has never been a Tennessee Society." On the 15th of April, 1983, 25 letters were sent out to potential members to form a new society in Tennessee. Letters were also written to Richard Schlenker, V.P. and the Texas Society, War of 1812, soliciting names of possible Tennessee members. By the end of June, 1983, 11 members had qualified and had written letters of intent to join the new state society being formed in Tennessee. They were as follows: L. Jackson Shaw, C. Battle Shaw, Jr., Robert A. Ragland, Dr. James M. Edwards, Dr. B. H. Webster, Monte H. Knight, John L. Echols, Dawson B. Whitsitt, W. S. Milton, Richard L. Deavers, and Andrew Tate, Jr. With this accomplished, a petition for charter was drafted and sent to President General Edward C. Beetem II and other national officers.

At the January 7, 1984 Executive Meeting in Baltimore, Vice-President Schlenker advised that the required number of members had qualified and the Tennessee Society was notified on January 20, 1984 that a charter would be prepared.

On January 21, 1984, a letter from Mr. Shaw was sent to each new Tennessee Society member listing all members' names and asking that a president be chosen from that list and conveying the news of the charter. As a result of the election, L. Jackson Shaw was elected president.

It was decided to hold the official charter ceremony at the tomb of President Andrew Jackson on July 15, 1984. Six members were present, along with three ladies of the Tennessee Daughters of War of 1812 and guests. President Shaw read letters of congratulations from Tennessee Governor Lamar Alexander, U.S. Senator Howard Baker, and President-General Edward C. Beetem II. Since July, 1984, two charter members have died, two elections have been held, and new members have joined the ranks. A state newsletter, the *Old Hickory Report* has been started. Contact has been firmly established with the Tennessee Daughters of 1812. A Tennessee Society flag has been acquired. A long standing project of erecting a Tennessee monument for the War of 1812 will be realized in 1989.

TEXAS

The Texas Society was chartered on January 8, 1959. Tevis C. Smith, Jr. of Brownwood was the first member of the infant society. He was president in 1972, when the General Society published its *Register of Members*. Sixteen members were listed in the *Register*.

Alfred H. Benjamin of Dallas was president in 1976, when the *Bicentennial Supplement to the Register* was published. Thirty-one members were listed in the supplement.

By 1981, the society had grown to 47 members and Lorne C. Parks of Houston was president. He was succeeded by Thomas F. Bresnehen, Jr. of San Antonio in 1982. The society continued to grow during the next two years, and had 66 members at the end of 1984. Lloyd Bockstruck of Dallas was elected president at the 1984 annual meeting, and like his predecessors, served two years. He was succeeded by Joseph M. Clark, Jr. of Houston to serve two years.

Doctor Robert L. Kurth of Lufkin was elected president in 1988, and during his first year of office, two local chapters were instituted in Houston and Killeen-Temple. They are the Sam Houston chapter and the Edward J. Kellum chapter. The membership at the end of 1988 was 106. The growth of membership has been in part due to the formation of the Edward J. Kellum chapter. Vice President General Joseph M. Clark, Jr. and Dr. David Yeilding are the presidents of the Sam Houston chapter and the Edward J. Kellum chapter.

The society has had its annual meetings in March of each year in connection with the Sons of the American Revolution annual convention. This practice was instituted by President Clovis H. Brakebill during his term of office in 1979.

The society was a co-sponsor of the 175th anniversary of the Battle of Medina ceremonies in August, 1988, and was the host to President General Samuel R. Slaymaker and his wife in San Antonio at a dinner for its members.

VIRGINIA

During 1982 the planning for a Society of the War of 1812 in Virginia under the leadership of Judson P. Mason, Jr. who was a former District of Columbia officer, was concluded with the ceremonial chartering on March 13 at the General Society's session in Philadelphia.

Virginia residents had historically and regularly been members of the District of Columbia organization, but those who might qualify for membership and who resided at some distance from Washington had no convenient way to participate.

Since being organized the Society in Virginia has enjoyed substantial growth. It encourages the collection and preservation of Virginia rolls, records, books, and documents. The members also foster research and publications of historical and patriotic material.

Annually the Society joins in the General Society's program for recognition of outstanding achievement in the ROTC units of Virginia schools. The members have taken note of locations of War of 1812 engagements at Tangier Island and Windmill Point in the lower Chesapeake.

Plans were laid in 1988 to coordinate the June 1989 Annual Meeting with a Society of the War of 1812 commemoration at the grave of James Madison near Orange, Virginia at which time the membership anticipates the placement of a plaque to read *James Madison President of the United States of America and Commander in Chief of the Army and Navy 1809–1817*. A bronze Society of the War of 1812 Veteran Star is to be affixed to the tomb at the same occasion.

The Society of the War of 1812 in Virginia works closely with the Daughters of the War of 1812 in Virginia and it enjoys a special relationship with the District of Columbia Society as a result of the fact of dual membership held by many compatriots.

WISCONSIN

The Society of the War of 1812 in the State of Wisconsin
Chartered 13 March 1982

MEMBERS-AT-LARGE

With approval by the proper officers and the Board of Directors of the General Society, a candidate may be elected as a member-at-large providing there is no society functioning within the state of his residence. A member so elected is eligible to apply for membership upon approval of a state society. There are sixty-nine members so enrolled in the *Yearbook* of 1987.

ARCHIVAL SOURCES

Lancaster County Historical Society
Lancaster, Pennsylvania

GENERAL SOCIETY OF THE WAR OF 1812

ORIGINAL DOCUMENTS

No. 0001 to 1200	by 100's in folders.
No. 1201 to 1300	Bound Vol. 13
No. 1301 to 1400	Bound Vol. 14
No. 1401 to 1500	Bound Vol. 15
No. 1501 to 1600	Bound Vol. 16
No. 1601 to 1700	Bound Vol. 17
No. 1701 to 1800	Bound Vol. 18
No. 1801 to 1900	Bound Vol. 19
No. 1901 to 2000	Bound Vol. 20
No. 2001 to 2100	Bound Vol. 21
No. 2101 to 2200	Bound Vol. 22
No. 2201 to 2300	Bound Vol. 23
No. 2301 to 2400	Bound Vol. 24
No. 2401 to 2500	Bound Vol. 25
No. 2501 to 2600	Bound Vol. 26
No. 2601 to 2700	Bound Vol. 27
No. 2701 to 2800	Bound Vol. 28
No. 2801 to 2900	Bound Vol. 29
No. 2901 to 3000	Bound Vol. 30
No. 3001 to 3100	Bound Vol. 31
No. 3101 to 3200	Bound Vol. 32
No. 3201 to 3300	Bound Vol. 33
No. 3301 to 3400	Bound Vol. 34
No. 3401 to 3500	Bound Vol. 35
No. 3501 to 3600	Bound Vol. 36
No. 3601 to 3700	Bound Vol. 37
No. 3701 to 3800	Bound Vol. 38
No. 3801 to 4638	by 100's in folders.

MICROFILM

Reel 1	Years 1877–1892
Reel 2	G.S. #229 to 438
Reel 3	Years 1895–1897
Reel 4	Years 1896–1902
Reel 5	Years 1903–1908
Reel 6	Years 1908–1912
Reel 7	Years 1912–1925
Reel 8	Mixed
Reel 9	1524–1699
Reel 10	1700–1888
Reel 11	1889–2088
Reel 12	2089–2288
Reel 13	2287–2617
Reel 14	2406–2653
Reel 15	2654–2751
Reel 16	2752–2871
Reel 17	2872–2981
Reel 18	2982–3062
Reel 19	3063–3180

MICROFILM

Washington, D.C., Records of the General Society of the War of 1812, Applications for Memberships, Vol. 1, 1877–1892. Reel 1

Washington, D.C., Records of the General Society of the War of 1812, Applications for Memberships, Vol. 2, 1893–1894. Reel 2

Washington, D.C., Records of the General Society of the War of 1812, Applications for Memberships, Vol. 3, 1895–1897. Reel 3

Washington, D.C., Records of the General Society of the War of 1812, Applications for Memberships, Vol. 4, 1896–1902. Reel 4

Washington, D.C., Records of the General Society of the War of 1812, Applications for Memberships, Vols. 5–6, 1903–1908. Reel 5

Washington, D.C., Records of the General Society of the War of 1812, Applications for Memberships, Vols. 7–8, 1908–1912. Reel 6

Washington, D.C., Records of the General Society of the War of 1812, Applications for Memberships, Vol. 9, 1912–1925. Reel 7

Washington, D.C., Records of the General Society of the War of 1812, Applications for Memberships, Vols. 10–11, Mixed Dates and Numbers. Reel 8

Washington, D.C., Records of the General Society of the War of 1812, Gen. Soc. No.'s 1524–1699. Reel 9

Washington, D.C., Records of the General Society of the War of 1812, Gen. Soc. No.'s 1700–1888. Reel 10

Washington, D.C., Records of the General Society of the War of 1812, No.'s 1889–2088. Reel 11

Washington, D.C., Records of the General Society of the War of 1812, No.'s 2089–2288. Reel 12

Washington, D.C., Records of the General Society of the War of 1812, No.'s 2287–2617. Reel 13

General Society of War of 1812, Applications for Membership, 2406–2653, Pt. 1. Reel 14

General Society of War of 1812, Applications for Membership, 2654–2751, Pt. 2. Reel 15

General Society of War of 1812, Applications for Membership, 2752–2871, Pt. 1. Reel 16

General Society of War of 1812, Applications for Membership, 2872–2981, Pt. 2. Reel 17

General Society of War of 1812, Applications for Membership, 2982–3062, Pt. 1. Reel 18

General Society of War of 1812, Applications for Membership, 3063–3180, Pt. 2. Reel 19

(Microfilming Current With The 1989 Roster Is In Process.)

BOOKS

The Charter, Constitution and Rules of the General Society of the War of 1812 with the Register of Membership, February 1, 1893. Philadelphia, 1893. 69 pages, softbound.

The Charter, Constitution and Rules of the General Society of the War of 1812 with the Register of Membership, March 1, 1894. Philadelphia, 1894. 92 pages, hardbound.

General Society of the War of 1812, Proceedings. 1910 68 pages, softbound.

General Society of the War of 1812, Proceedings. 1912 83 pages, softbound.

General Society of the War of 1812, Proceedings. 1914 62 pages, softbound.

Archival Sources 155

General Society of the War of 1812, Proceedings. 1916-1920 121 pages, softbound.
General Society of the War of 1812, Proceedings. 1922-1925 110 pages, softbound.

Genealogical Society of Utah
Salt Lake City, Utah

SOCIETY OF THE WAR OF 1812
Applications for membership with card index.—Salt Lake City: Filmed by the *Genealogical Society of Utah*, 1953.— 14 microfilm reels; 35 and 16 mm.

Microreproduction of original ms. and typescript.

Card index	0002069
Applications v. 1 1877-1892	0002070
Applications v. 2 1893-1894	0002071
Applications v. 3 1895-1897	0002072
Applications v. 4 1896-1902	0002073
Applications v. 5-6 1903-1908	0002074
Applications v. 7-8 1908-1912	0002075
Applications v. 9 1912-1925	0002076
Mixed dates v. 10-11	0002077
General Society's numbers 1524-1699	0002078
General Society's numbers 1700-1888	0002079
General Society's numbers 1889-2088	0002080
Loose blanks and numbers 2089-2288	0002081
Loose blanks and numbers 2287-2617	0002082
Applications 1951-1954	0330236
Applications 1954-1955	0330237
Applications 1955-1957	0330238
Applications 1957-1958	0330239
Applications 1958-1960	0330240
Applications 1960-1963	0330241

1. United States—Military records. 2. United States—Societies.
RN:0382081

SOCIETY OF THE WAR OF 1812
Proceedings (Society of the War of 1812.—1st biennial meeting-   .—[S.L.: s.n., 1898].—v.

Biennial.
Description based on: 15th biennial meeting.

1. United States—Societies—Periodicals. I. Society of the War of 1812.

RN:0330519   973 C4sp

SOCIETY OF THE WAR OF 1812
The constitution and register of membership of the General Society of the War of 1812 to October 1, 1899.—
Philadelphia: The Society, 1899.—iii, 231 n

Includes a register of membership.
1. United States—Societies.
RN:0448399   973 C4con

SOCIETY OF THE WAR OF 1812. *Maryland.*
Applications for membership.—Salt Lake City: Filmed by
the Genealogical Society of Utah, *1948.*—2 microfilm
reels; 35 mm.

Microfilm copy of original records at Maryland Historical
Society, Baltimore.
Includes indexes. One for applicants and one for ancestors.

Indexes 0013146
   v. 1–2 Applications 1892–1909
   v. 3–4 Applications 1909–1928 0013147

Member Index

Abbott, Charles Wheaton, Jr., 0059
Abell, Richard Bender, 3561
Abert, William Stone, 0978
Abey, Joseph Gregory, 3748
Abey, Joseph Samuel, 3560
Abney, Joe L., 4260
Ackley, Charles Saxton, 1398
Acuff, Alfred Marshall, 3656
Adams, Arthur, 1436
Adams, David, III, 3453
Adams, Francis T., Jr., 2366
Adams, Harrington, 3206
Adams, Herbert Luther, 1781
Adams, James Frederick, IV, 2734
Adams, Jeremy Yvon M. du Q., 2774
Adams, Leon, 2842
Adams, Lionel, 2410
Adams, Lionel, Jr., 2460
Adams, Lloyd, 2462
Adams, Orr, 2461
Adams, Philip Reed, 3567
Adams, Robert, Jr., 0146
Adams, Thomas Richard, 4571
Adams, Washington Irving Lincoln, 0943
Adams, William Eugenius, Jr., 4183
Adams, William Porter, 0486
Adams, William Waugh, 1574
Adare, Charles Henry, Jr., 1939
Addison, Joseph, Jr., 3137
Addison, Taylor, 0282
Adkins, Howard Patrick, 4339
Adkins, Ralph Austin, 4020
Agens, Sylvester Halsey Moore, 1377
Ainsworth, Danforth Emmit, 0896
Akin, Henry Charles Robeson, 0939
Albaugh, Jacob, 0285
Albee, David Dempster, 2783
Alden, Charles Henry, 0221
Alden, Charles Henry Jr., 0110
Aldige, Hugh Dumas, 3352
Aldige, James George, 2509
Aldige, James George, III, 3323
Aldige, James George, Jr., 2415
Aldrich, Orlando Wesley, 0497
Aldrich, Richard Stoddard, 1633
Alexander, George Louis, 3450
Alexander, John S., 0061
Alford, Albert Gallatin, 0944

Alford, George Willaim, 0683
Alford, Julius Mosby, 4350
Alford, Newell Gilder, 1010
Alford, Reuben Gilder, 0729
Allen Matthew Brenden, 3497
Allen, Covington K., Jr., 2120
Allen, Crawford Carter, 0605
Allen, Edward Gray, 0077
Allen, Francis Burke, 1188
Allen, John Vincent, 0652
Allen, John Vincent, Jr., 1333
Allen, Joseph Aloysius, 1241
Allen, Louis Joseph, 0028
Allen, Philip M., 2175
Allen, Robert Hugh, 3479
Allen, Robert Webster, 2099
Allen, Roscoe Jackson, Sr., 3614
Allen, Theodore Lathrop, 0048
Allen, Thomas Eldridge, 2899
Allen, Thomas Lamb, 1515
Aller, Harris Coles, 1873
Aller, Harris Coles, 3rd., 3553
Aller, Harris Coles, Jr., 2689
Aller, William Drew, 3554
Allison, Albert Crawford Green, 1810
Altaffer, Maurice Willard, 1955
Altemus, Edward Lee, 3816
Altemus, Nicholas Ward, 3923
Ambler, Charles M., 2372
Ambler, Frank R., 2328
Ambler, Henry S., 2329
Ambrose, Paul, 0149
Ambrose, Thomas, 1897
Amee, Albert Francis, 0736
Amee, John, 1097
Amesbury, Walter Raleigh, Jr., 3712
Amick, Jacob William, 1319
Anderson, Charles Henry, 0894
Anderson, Edward Lane, 2610
Anderson, George Parker, 4289
Anderson, James Blythe, 0850
Anderson, James Raymond, 3990
Anderson, John Sherburne, 3152
Anderson, Nils, Jr., 2029
Anderson, Richard Kerfoot, 3643
Anderson, Thomas McArthur, 0219
Andrews, Charles Allen, 1294
Andrews, William Phillip, 3586
Andrews, William Taylor, 0359

158 *Member Index*

Andriano-Moore, Richard Norvel, 4084
Andruss, Harvey Adolphus, Jr., 4175
Andry, Allain Charles, III, 2885
Andry, Allain Charles, Jr., 2872
Andry, Charles Gilbert, 2432
Andry, Claude Dudley, Jr., 3427
Andry, George Ricau, 2499
Andry, William Louis, 2871
Angelo, Hunter Buchanan, 3555
Ansart, Louis Loomis, 1990
Anson, Edward Hiram, 2351
Appleton, Charles Brooks, 1093
Appleton, Daniel Fuller, 0127
Appleton, Floyd, 1482
Archinard, John Joseph, 2573
Archinard, Pierre Andre, 2572
Armant, Henry Joseph, 2602
Armistead, Lewis Addison, 1252
Armitage, Jim Rodgers, 4071
Armstrong, Harold Rodney, 1069
Arnold, Allen, 0606
Arnold, David Wayne, 4162
Arnold, Harvey Wilson, 2972
Arnold, Ketron Elliott, 4168
Arnold, Robert Burtram, 4075
Arnoult, Mandeville P., Jr., 2831
Arthaud, John Bradley, 3725
Arthur, John Stephen, 3374
Arthurs, Edward Ferguson, 0688
Ashbridge, Richard Downing, 3768
Ashbridge, Whitney, 1580
Ashbridge, Whitney, 3420
Ashburner, Charles B., 3522
Ashburner, John La Cour, 3464
Ashby, Bernard, 1531
Ashenhurst, James G., 3079
Ashenhurst, John W., 3080
Ashley, Keith Drew, 4361
Ashley, Lawrence I., 2340
Ashmead, William Harris, 0763
Athey, Charles Burch, 2577
Atkinson, Alan Watt, 3172
Atkinson, Benjamin Walker, 0115
Atkinson, Benjamin Walker, Jr., 1520
Atkinson, Guy, 3044
Atwood, Henry Estes, 2636
Atwood, Lee Brown, 2993
Atwood, Roswell Levi, 3639
Aubert, Edward McCormack, 3423

Aud, Edward Trujean, 3363
Aumock, George Harry, 4066
Aunkst, Straub B., 2236
Austin, Richard L., 2162
Avant, David Alonzo, Jr., 3618
Averett, George Wesley, 3726
Averill, Charles Sidle, 0833
Averill, Henry Ketchum, Jr., 0041
Avery, Frank Montgomery, 0452
Babbitt, Byron Fenner, 1559
Babcock, William Henry, 0971
Babson, John Capron, 2010
Backus, Brady Electur, 0226
Badgley, William Walton, 1863
Baer, Herbert Lou, Sr., 4140
Bailey, Joseph Trowbridge, 0259
Baird, Bruce, Jr., 3375
Baird, Henry Carey, 0120
Baird, James Mercer, 0586
Baird, William Mercer, 0700
Baker, Calvin Shelton, 3471
Baker, Charles Chaney, 1337
Baker, Charles Estell, 4246
Baker, George Comstock, 0589
Baker, George Fales, 0728
Baker, George Livingston, 0298
Baker, George Livingston, Jr., 0265
Baker, George T., 0101
Baker, Hamilton Wallace, 1505
Baker, Henry Gardner, 1043
Baker, James Winsor, Jr., 3519
Baker, John Mitchell, 1506
Baker, John Pope, II, 3429
Baker, Laurence Clark, 0626
Baker, Louis Stannard, 4241
Baker, Roy Ball, 0883
Baker, William Spohn, 0563
Baldridge, Joseph Evans, 1793
Baldwin, Albert Sr., 3322
Baldwin, Charles E., 2341
Baldwin, Charles Gambrill, 1632
Baldwin, Charles H., 3669
Baldwin, David Gilmore, Jr., 2591
Baldwin, Frederick J., 2178
Baldwin, Gustave B., Jr., 2474
Baldwin, John Ashby, 1695
Baldwin, John Render, 3511
Baldwin, Lawrence Jacob, 2508
Baldwin, Oliver Hazard Perry, Jr., 3920
Baldwin, Summerfield, Jr., 1651

Member Index 159

Baldwin, Willard Augustine, 1650
Baldwin, William M., 3142
Ball, Alfred J., 2294
Ball, Flamen, Jr., 0678
Ball, Harold Curtis, 2545
Ball, James Winston, Jr., 4205
Ball, Thomas Hand, 1367
Ball, Walter Vancion, 3141
Balthis, William Leonard, 1661
Banks, Clayton F., Jr., 2232
Banks, Clayton French, 1519
Banks, George Washington, 0926
Banks, Myron Carroll, 3785
Banning, Kendall, 1087
Banning, Pierson Worrall, 1408
Barber, Donald Franklyn, 4287
Barbour, Charles Justin, 0133
Barbour, Lucius Barnes, 1155
Barcus, Joseph Garland, 2799
Barker, James Higbie, 3002
Barker, Stanley Cline, 3017
Barnard, Ronald August, 4622
Barnes, Charles M., Jr., 3155
Barnes, Edward, 3941
Barnes, Norman, 2718
Barnes, Robert M., 3082
Barnes, Walter J., 2383
Barnes, William Calvin, 2983
Barnes, William Edgar, 0851
Barnes, Wilson K., Jr., 3092
Barnes, Wilson King, 3164
Barr, Dixon A., 4396
Barranger, Garic Kenneth, 2525
Barratt, Norris S., 2369
Barratt, Norris Stanley, 1000
Barratt, Norris Stanley, III, 2776
Barratt, Thomas Levering, 1480
Barrell, Harry Ferdinand, 0665
Barrell, Joseph E. M., 0698
Barrett, John L., 0229
Barrett, John Minot, 1461
Barris, William Henri, 3973
Barroll, Reginald Stewart, 4490
Barrosse, Bertin O., 3122
Barrosse, Bertin O., Jr., 3599
Barrosse, Lionel Edward, Jr., 4139
Barrosse, Rushton Garic, 3600
Barrow, Mercer, 2533
Barry, John Neilson, 1466
Barter, Forest Hermon, 2109
Bartholomew, Earl F., 3732

Bartlett, John Albert, 1428
Bartlett, Walter Manny, 2484
Barton, Lyman Guy, 1762
Barton, Wm. Eleazer, 1268
Bascombe, Western Radford, 0650
Baskette, Alvin K., 1807
Bates, Theodore Cornelius, 0735
Bates, William Graves, 0759
Battis, Edward Clarence, 0986
Bauer, Charles H., 2289
Bauer, Charles Humphrey, 1507
Bauer, Frederic Gilbert, 0941
Bauer, Louis Hopewell, 1491
Bauer, Richard Wingate, 2077
Bauer, Richard Wingate, 2765
Baugh, Eugene Bibb, Jr., 3512
Baughman, Charles Christian, 0961
Baughman, Emilius Allen, 0962
Baughman, Greer Harry, 0960
Bay, Charles Andrew, 1410
Bayles, Generes D., 2394
Beadles, Glenn Harris, Sr., 3828
Beal, Francis Leavett, 1100
Beale, Charles Frederick Tiffany, 0703
Beall, Clarkson J., 3125
Beall, William Marbury, 0898
Beall, Wilson Wylie, 3214
Bealmear, James Irving, Jr., 2980
Beals, Donald Marcy, 1735
Beals, John David, Jr., 1802
Beardsley, Harry Judson, 1953
Beatty, Frank Edmund, 0817
Beatty, Franklin Thomason, 0343
Beatty, John Edwin, 0997
Beatty, John Wood, 0822
Beaumont, John Erwin, 2nd., 4028
Becker, John Austin, 1665
Beckford, Walter Harry, 1291
Beckwith, Brainard K., 2106
Beckwith, George Henry, 0593
Bedwell, Wiles Kline, 4600
Beers, Walter Whitney, 1624
Beetem, Donald Gilbert, 3550
Beetem, Edward Charles, 2nd., 2793
Behm, Henry Godley, 1716
Behm, John William, 0930
Beitler, Lewis Eugene, 0853
Bell, Ola Walter, 0969
Bell, William Hemphill, 1034
Bellas, Henry Hobart, 0035

Member Index

Belsterling, Charles Starne, 1798
Beluche-Mora, Isidro, 2443
Bement, Russell, III, 3465
Bement, Russell, Jr., 3541
Bender, Addison F., Jr., 2185
Benedict, Charles Emerson, 1746
Benedict, Purdy Faitoute, 2787
Benefield, Joseph Turberville, 3930
Benham, Henry Hill, 0108
Benjamin, Alfred Henry, 3671
Benjamin, James L., 2307
Benjamin, Marcus, 0529
Bennett, Edgar Harrison, 2733
Bennett, John Henry Van Swearingen, Jr., 4525
Bennett, Paul Warren, 3849
Benson, Carville Dickinson, 3624
Benson, John Oregon, 2763
Benson, Oscar Suter, 1474
Benson, Richard Steward, 3482
Bentley, Henri Farrar, 3523
Berkeley, Merrill Duane, 3987
Berl, Charles Waggaman, 2492
Berl, Eugene Ennalls, II, 2736
Bernard, Alfred Duncan, 0627
Bernard, Guy Francis, 3149
Bernard, Joseph Grima, 2423
Bernard, Richard Constable, 1424
Bernard, Thomas Norton, 3324
Bernstorf, David James, 4485
Bernstorf, Philip W., 4428
Berry, Clarence Augustus, 2661
Berry, Clarence Melvin, 2659
Berry, Thomas Lansdale, 1176
Bertram, Richard David, 4403
Bessent, Carl Francis, 3831
Betelle, Milton, 4128
Betts, Philander Hammer, III, 1835
Betts, Philander, III, 1819
Bever, Paul Stewart, 4352
Bezou, Charles Henry, 3601
Bezou, George Marc, 2847
Bezou, Henry Charles, 2950
Bezou, James F., 2380
Bezou, Sidney L., 3158
Biays, James Phillip, 1437
Biays, Tolley Alexander, 1157
Bickford, Robert Sloane, 0868
Bickley, Ervin F., Jr., 2540
Biddle, Clement, 1325
Biddle, John, 0136

Biddle, Wm. Shepard, Jr., 0240
Bielaski, Frank Brooks, 2031
Bierbower, James Culver, 1192
Bigelow, William M., 2101
Bills, Robert Wesley, 3786
Binion, Terrance Robert, 4304
Binney, Amos, 0345
Binney, Arthur, 0472
Binney, William Greene, 0483
Birckhead, Lennox, 0695
Bird, Matthew David, 4129
Birely, William Cramer, 3440
Birkhaeuser, Theodore Kelso, 0584
Bishop, John Lester, 2805
Bishop, Lee Edward, Jr., 4566
Bispham, Harrison A., 2144
Bissell, Benjamin, 1177
Bissell, Charles M., 0900
Bissell, Thomas Teed, 0905
Bixler, Wm. Henry Harrison, 1303
Blackett, Larry Lee, 4410
Blacklock, Aubrey H., Jr., 3030
Blackwood, Norman Jerome, 1024
Blain, Daniel, 3570
Blain, Daniel Jr., 3717
Blain, Peter Travis, 3718
Blair, Frank Perrin, 1363
Blair, Irving James, 0942
Blair, Thomas Ashton, 3462
Blair, Thomas Ashton, Jr., 3708
Blair, William Richardson, 3312
Blair, William Richardson, 3rd., 3709
Blair, William Richardson, Jr., 3463
Blaisdell, Frank Moses, 0485
Blatchford, Charles Lord, 1787
Blauvelt, Louis L., 2772
Bledsoe, Jack.Othel, 4185
Blessing, Alexander Francis, 1717
Blinn, Charles P., Jr., 2250
Blinn, William Cady, 1279
Bliss, Charles J., 2247
Bliss, Maurice H., 2248
Blizzard, Arthur Keith, 3829
Blizzard, Dennis Craig, 3696
Blizzard, Dennis Frizzell, 2969
Blue, Rupert, 0938
Blue, Victor, 0937
Blunt, Stanhope English, 0235
Blythe, Donald Forbes, 2496
Bobart, Charles Carroll, 0403
Bockstruck, Lloyd DeWitt, 3637

Member Index 161

Boddie, John Bennett, 1334
Boden, Harry Clark, 1978
Boehringer, Karl Jay, 2690
Boggs, Francis Henry, 0388
Boggs, John Lawrence, 1968
Boggs, Thomas Hale, 2938
Boisfontaine, Curtis Rich, 2561
Boling, Eugene H., 1370
Bolles, Charles Harrington, 0555
Bolton, Robert Coles, 3906
Bond, Calhoun, 4491
Bond, John Russell, 2898
Bond, Thomas Jefferson, Jr., 4613
Bone, Robert Gehlmann, Sr., 3688
Bonelli, Louis Henry, Jr., 2044
Bonnaffon, Ashton Clagett, 1753
Bonnaffon, Charles A., 3073
Bonnaffon, Ferdinard Victor, 0272
Bonnaffon, Sylvester, III, 0638
Bonnaffon, Sylvester, Jr., 0273
Bonnell, Russell, 1161
Bonnet, Eldon Bernard, 3033
Bonniwell, Alfred E., 2087
Bonniwell, Bernard, 2088
Bonniwell, Charles Anthony, 1287
Bonniwell, Donald Raymond, 3211
Bonniwell, Eugene C., 2089
Bonniwell, Eugene Cahill, Jr., 1477
Bonniwell, Eugene Cleophas, 1208
Bonniwell, John Green, 2090
Bonniwell, Robert Budd, 2091
Bonniwell, Thomas John, 1286
Booth, Charles Maclay, 1127A
Borch, Fred G., 2199
Bordley, John Lawson, 2553
Borgman, Theodore Joseph, Jr., 3651
Borum, Wylie Griffin, 3575
Bosson, Frederick Needham, 1321
Bostick, Raymond Harrison, 4178
Boston, Leonard Napoleon, 0912
Boswell, Frederick Page, 1767
Botsford, Stephen Jason, 0977
Bottomley, Henry Stone, 1907
Boucher, Charles, 0646
Boughter, Francis, 0263
Boulden, Charles Newton, 1429
Bouldin, Augustus, 0288
Boulter, Eldon Beau, 4453
Bourke, Clyde Edwin, Jr., 4576
Bourne, Robert Gordon Bruce, 3809
Bowe, Dudley Pleasant, 2939

Bowen, Hessa Emery, 0350
Bowen, James Barton, 0431
Bowers, William, 0992
Bowley, Raymond F., 2240
Bowman, Charles Harwood, Jr., 3437
Bowman, Norwood David, 2694
Boyce, Albert Page, 0889
Boyce, Hayward Easter, 1150
Boyd, David Preston, III, 3225
Boyd, James Knox Polk, 0899
Boyd, William Paxton, 3720
Boyer, George Washington, 1582
Bradford, James Philip, 4618
Bradford, John, 0970
Bradford, Samuel Webster, 1025
Bradley, Cyrus Sherwood, 0339
Bradley, John Miller, 2866
Bradley, Melvin James, 4284
Brady, Thomas P., 3153
Brady, William Conolly, 3504
Brady, William Milner, 3505
Brakebill, Clovis Hunter, 3741
Brame, Arden Howell, Jr., 3860
Branch, Charles Henry Hardin, 0724
Branch, Henry, 0723
Brandel, Littleton Chandler, 0764
Bransby, John C., 0362
Brathwaite, Peter Lloyd, 3276
Brautigam, Edward, Jr., 2215
Breckinridge, John Marshall, 3409
Breckinridge, Preston Marshall, 3382
Breisacher, Karl Gustave, III, 2947
Brennan, Ronald Wesley, 3703
Brent, Julius H., 2245
Bres, Edward S., Jr., 3360
Bres, Edward Sedley, 2493
Bresee, Wilmer Edgar, 3020
Bresnehen, Thomas, Francis, Jr., 3996
Brevoort, Charles P., 1222
Brewster, Henry Colvin, 0528
Brice, Carroll Allyn, 2857
Brice, Philip Howard, 0406
Brierre, Roland Theodore, 2652
Briggs, Frank Harrison, 0243
Briggs, Herbert, 1122
Brinkerhoff, Roecliff, 0499
Brinkerhoof, Roeliff, 0444
Brinley, Henry DeNyse, 2662
Brinton, Edward Harvey, 2911
Brinton, Howard Futhey, 1089

Brinton, John Willard, 1366
Bristol, Henry Brevoort, 0072
Bristor, Joseph Whiteridge, 1156
Bristor, William Beverly, Jr., 3279
Bristor, Wm. Beverly, 1426
Bristow, Frank Henry, 0157
Britigan, Herbert Dana, 1789
Britigan, William Henry, 1788
Brittin, Lewis Hitchcock, 2050
Broad, William H. Jr., 3031
Brock, John William, 1654
Brodbeck, Thomas Raymond, Jr., 4368
Brodhead, Frank Chaplain, 3313
Brodhead, George Milton, 3311
Brodhead, Robert Packer, 0848
Brodhead, Truxtun Read, 3234
Brodnax, Marion Jack, 2954
Brokaw, Roberts Wyckoff, 2996
Bromley, John Lewis, 0711
Bronaugh, Frederick Louis, 1775
Brooke, Benjamin, 0071
Brooke, Brian Wesley, 3832
Brooke, Dandridge, 3967
Brooke, Edward, 2249
Brooke, Francis Mark, 1719
Brooke, John, 0070
Brooke, John Rutter, 0049
Brooke, Randall Whitney, 3968
Brooke, William Hill, 3223
Brookes, George Deshield, 0918
Brooks, Clifton Rowland, 3723
Brooks, Clifton Rowland, Jr., 3729
Brooks, Francis Mark, 0244
Brooks, Harold C., 2197
Brooks, James Taylor, 2943
Brooks, Paul Robert Michael, 4524
Brousseau, Andre Ringgold, 2548
Brousseau, Andre Ringgold, III, 2781
Brower, Ogden, 1890
Brower, Walter Jordon, 2948
Brower, Walter Scott, 2878
Brower, Walter William, 3804
Brower, Walter Wilson, 3846
Brown, Alexander Paul, 1794
Brown, Bache Hamilton, 1372
Brown, Bennie Lewis, 3864
Brown, Dudley Parrish, 0336
Brown, Francis S., III, 2293
Brown, Francis Shunk, Jr., 2069
Brown, Frank Clark, 3811

Brown, Friend Abner, 0864
Brown, George Edward, 0773
Brown, George Hollister, 1779
Brown, George Levi, 0863
Brown, George M., Jr., 3587
Brown, George McGehee, 3180
Brown, Gilbert Patten, 1396
Brown, Harold Atherton, 0531
Brown, Harry C., Jr., 3200
Brown, Harry Charles, 1836
Brown, Harry Webster, 1124
Brown, Harvey Newton, 2082
Brown, Henry Brock, Jr., 3702
Brown, Henry Kirk Bush, 0795
Brown, Henry Paul, III, 2067
Brown, Herbert Thomas, Jr., 4081
Brown, Hugh Bennett, 4502
Brown, Hugh Edmund, 3810
Brown, James Barrow, Jr., 3999
Brown, James Edgar, 0914
Brown, James Henry, 3151
Brown, James Newton, 1562
Brown, Kennell Philip, 2804
Brown, Kennell Philip, Jr., 3645
Brown, Paul Kalck, 3521
Brown, Russell, 3087
Brown, Ryan Michael, Jr., 3821
Brown, Thomas Moore, 3894
Brown, Timothy Edward, 3812
Brown, Walter Scott, 0601
Brown, William Findlay, 1754
Brown, William Findlay, Jr., 1755
Brown, William Perry, III, 3508
Brown, William Perry, Jr., 2846
Brown, William Samuel, Jr., 2016
Brown, Willis, 0509
Browne, Delbert Victor, 3598
Brownfield, Lee B.,II, 2137
Bruce, Oliver Herman, 1179
Bruce, Pearl Willard, 1603
Brumbaugh, John Daniel, 2728
Brumbaugh, Stiles Daniel, 3666
Brumfield, Jerome Edgar, 1074
Brush, Herbert S., III, 3098
Brush, Herbert S., Jr., 3097
Brush, Robert Edward deBrus, Sr., 3647
Bryan, Charles Page, 0095
Bryan, Frederic A., 3023
Bryan, Leslie Aulls, 3444
Bryant, Frederick Stewart, 1381

Buchanan, Theodore Stewart, Jr., 3897
Buchanan, William Insco, 0562
Buck, George Hickman, 0662
Buck, James Marshall, 3216
Buck, James Marshall, II, 3217
Buckenham, John Edgar Burnett, 0787
Buckey, Mervyn Chandos, 0825
Buckey, Thomas William, 0874
Buckingham, Charles Wesley, 0188
Buckland, Samuel Aldrich, 1563
Buckles, Frank W., 2244
Buffington, Byrd Mayson, 3754
Buffington, Byrd Mayson, Jr., 4331
Buffum, Wm. Mansfield, 0139
Buker, Horace Edward, 1217
Bulkeley, Houghton, 1776
Bulkeley, Morgan Gardner, 0381
Bull, Robert Berry, 0608
Bullard, Rickey H., 4354
Bulloch, Joseph G., 0227
Bullus, Wm. Ellison, 0069
Bumpas, Guy Hartwell, III, 3654
Bunker, John Cadwalader, 3475
Bunker, Lambert Cadwalader, 3476
Burbank, Abram Lincoln, 1448
Burbank, Charles Decker, 0755
Burbank, Clayton Sullivan, 0037
Burdett, Charles Lewis, 0099
Burgess, Howard Benjamin, 3459
Burget, Dean Edwin, Jr., 3707
Burgin, George Horace, 0236
Burgin, Herman, 0320
Burgner, Walter C., III, 3003
Burgoon, Norman Aaron, Jr., 3208
Burke, Michael Whittington, 2951
Burkey, Lee Melville, 4562
Burnett, Donald Mott, 3861
Burnett, Willard Elmer, 0753
Burpee, David, 2136
Burpee, Jonathan, 3198
Burpee, Washington A., III, 2019
Burpee, Washington A., Jr., 1940
Burroughs, Charles Frederick, 1168
Burroughs, James DeForris, 0648
Burt, Andrew Sheridan, 0539
Burt, Clarence Edward, 1451
Burt, Frank Hunt, 1851
Burt, William Charles, 3635
Burtnett, Bertrand Garrison, 1625

Burton, Chester Warren, 0233
Burton, LeGrand Stirling, 0794
Busch, Clarence Marshall, 1462
Busch, Henry Paul, 1516
Busch, Miers, 1211
Bush, Arthur Egbert, 2975
Bush, Edward Church, 4401
Bush, Edward Milton, 4452
Bushey, Arthur C., Jr., 3186
Butler, Bruce Baird, 3867
Butler, Gurdon Montague, 1829
Butler, James Barnard, 2713
Butler, Thomas Richard, 2709
Butler, William Bradley, III, 4271
Butterfield, John Homer, 4384
Byers, Joshua Clarence, 3642
Byrd, James Edward, 1044
Byrd, John Earl, 4275
Byrne, James de Buys, 2836
Cadle, Henry, 0382
Cadmus, Eugene Leroy, 1397
Cadwalader, Charles Evert, 0324
Cadwalader, Gouverneur, Jr., 2897
Cadwalader, John, 0015
Cadwalader, John, 0805
Cadwalader, John, III, 1756
Cadwalader, Lambert, 2640
Cady, Hiram Walworth, 0594
Cailleteau, Edward Overton, 3985
Cairns, Douglas Walker, 1883
Calder, Charles Grant, 0581
Calder, Philip Raymond, 1827
Calder, Philip Raymond, Jr., 1994
Calder, Robert M., 2110
Caldwalader, Thomas Francis, 1227
Caldwell, Arthur Brann, 3782
Caldwell, Francis Gustavus, 1088
Caldwell, James Allen, 4605
Caldwell, Newton W., 0706
Caldwell, William Wallace, Sr., 4298
Caldwell, William Walpole, 4189
Calhoun, James Robert, 4449
Calhoun, John Franklin, 0446
Calvert, George Chambers, 1682
Camden, Horace P., Jr., 2220
Cameron, Donald Eugene A., 3483
Cameron, Edward Madison, 0801
Cameron, Frederick Ward, 0895
Cameron, George Edward, 3289
Camp, Charles David, 1019
Camp, George A., 1313

164 Member Index

Camp, John Frederick, Jr., 3011
Campbell, John Deveny, 1224
Campbell, Lloyd Miles, 2949
Candler, Clarence L., 2179
Canedy, Albert W., 3091
Cann, Frank William, 1458
Canter, Ashby Hawkins, 3093
Capdevielle, Paul Maine, 2413
Caples, Robert Martin, 4002
Capp, Seth Bunker, 1194
Carey, Lee Cummins, 1984
Carey, Richard Ellis, 4367
Carleton, Horace Morrison, 0564
Carlton, Emory Linwood, 3456
Carman, Travers Denton, 1738
Carmeron, Arnold Guyot, Jr., 2818
Carmichael, Jack Kemper, 3686
Carney, Leonard Lawson, 4548
Carnrick, Millard, 2015
Carpenter, Donald Alfred, 4422
Carpenter, William T., Jr.,, 2828
Carpenter, William Thomas, 2821
Carr, Alfred Jarrett, 0181
Carr, Camillo Casatti Cadmus, 0045
Carr, Henry Lovell, 1348
Carr, James Edward Jr., 0174
Carr, Lovell Henry, 1072
Carr, William Edwin, 0508
Carriere, Dennis Howell, 3799
Carriere, James Dupress, 3376
Carriere, Lyle Francis, 3326
Carriere, Marion F., 3188
Carriere, Oliver Provosty, Jr., 3331
Carriere, Olivier P., 2494
Carriere, Pierre Francis, 3415
Carroll, George Earl, 3690
Carroon, Robert Girard, 3994
Carswell, Robert M., 2267
Carter, Clayton Cann, 4112
Carter, Edwin Royall, Jr., 4051
Carter, Randolph Scott Eastham, 4247
Carter, Woodward L., 2279
Cartier, Roy Anthony, 2773
Carty, Alton Burnside, 1868
Carty, Roy Franklin, 1869
Carver, Eugene P., Jr., 2042
Carver, Ransom Fuller, 2288
Case, David Brainard, 0212
Casebolt, Edwards T., 2716
Cass, Kingman Packard, 1783

Cassard, Jesse L., 0297
Cassard, John, 1009
Cassard, John Ernest, 2593
Cassard, William L., 0289
Cathcart, Asbury Roszel, 1023
Cauffman, Stanley Hart, 1483
Cavaroc, John Peter, 3347
Cavaroc, Roger Antoine, 2867
Cavaroc, Victor Viosca, 2882
Cavaroc, Victor Viosca, Jr., 2934
Cecil, Arthur Bond, 2274
Chadwick, Robert Lane, 4120
Chadwick, Winslow J., 3157
Chaffe, David Blackshear, Jr., 2566
Chambers, Charles Houghtaling, 0552
Chambers, Elias Hullfish, 0585
Chambers, George Brown, 0846
Chambers, Lawrence Bailey, 4498
Chambers, Robert Marion, 0179
Chambers, Walter Lee, 0553
Chambers, William Ely, 2990
Chandler, Frederick Emerson, 0607
Chandler, Glenn Edwin, 4299
Chaney, James Eugene, 2722
Chanler, Sidney Ashley Astor, 4253
Chapman, Arthur Stetson, 3120
Chapman, Paul Goddard, 0316
Chapman, Ronald Bernard, 3617
Chapman, Samuel Vannort, 3280
Chappell, Earl Stanley, 4441
Charbonnet, Clayton Jos., Jr., 3421
Charbonnet, Clayton Joseph, 3325
Charbonnet, Emmet Joseph, 2408
Charbonnet, Gilbert H., 2500
Charbonnet, Louis Sidney, 2407
Charbonnet, Louis Sidney, III, 3417
Charbonnet, Robert Henry, 3501
Charles, Michael Harrison, 3991
Chase, Ferdinand Walker, 1250
Chase, Thomas, 0003
Chauncey, Harry David, 0332
Chenery, James Hollis, 3611
Chenoweth, Alexander Crawford, 0254
Cherbonnier, Andrew Victor, 1057
Chesnut, Nelson Robert, 4158
Chesson, Wesley Earle, Jr., 4231
Chewning, Wm. Jeffries Jr., 1772
Chittenden, Leslie W., 2344
Christhilf, Edward, 0172

Christhilf, Nicholas Dorsey, 4198
Christhilf, Philip Raab, 4200
Christhilf, Stuart M., Sr., 2342
Christhilf, Stuart, Jr., 2306
Christian, Langdon Taylor, III, 3879
Chunn, Calvin Ellsworth, 3880
Church, Coleman Frederick, 3998
Church, William Conant, 0047
Claflin, Leander Chapin, 1963
Claflin, Leander Chapin, 2702
Claghorn, Charles E., 3rd., 2035
Claghorn, Wm. Crumby, 1071
Claiborne, Walter Herbert, 2430
Clark, Alonzo Howard, 0543
Clark, Alonzo Howard, 0567
Clark, Arthur Wellington, 0054
Clark, Augustus Taylor, 0694
Clark, Byron Nathaniel, 1094
Clark, Charles Cleveland, III, 3948
Clark, Charles Cleveland, Jr., 3903
Clark, Dwight, 1840
Clark, Elmer Sayre, 1728
Clark, Ephraim Stuart, 3114
Clark, Ivor Bach, 2047
Clark, Joe Burney, Jr., 3865
Clark, Joseph Mark, 4022
Clark, Joseph Morris, Jr., 4023
Clark, Lester Merritt, 3905
Clark, Raymond B., Jr., 3882
Clark, Robert Murel, Jr., 3805
Clark, Robert Philbrick, 3362
Clark, Samuel, 0904
Clarke, Francis Mann, Jr., 3227
Clarke, Francis Mann, Sr., 3221
Clarke, George Sharp, 1640
Clarkson, John Van Boskerck, 0761
Clay, William Rogers, Jr., 2098
Clearwaters, James Donald, 1680
Clearwaters, John Frederick, 1671
Clearwaters, John Harold, 1683
Clemens, Charles Eldon, 2784
Clement, Alfred Henry, 2590
Clement, Charles F., Jr., 2224
Clement, Charles Francis, 1440
Clement, Charles Francis, III, 2705
Clement, Charles Maxwell, 0164
Clement, Frederick T. J., 2957
Clement, Harrison H., 2132
Clement, Harrison H., Jr., 2684
Clement, Henry L., 2225
Clement, Henry Rawle, 2706
Clement, James H., 2131
Clement, James Higbie, 2942
Clement, James Higbie, Jr., 2686
Clement, John Browning, Jr., 2710
Clement, John Kay, Jr., 2707
Clement, Martin W., II, 2685
Clement, Martin Withington, 1481
Clement, Peter Withington, 2708
Clement, Theron B., 1439
Clement, William Edwards, 2448
Clements, Charles McCall, III, 4437
Clements, James Stanley, 4003
Clerc, Joseph Fred, 3358
Cleveland, Craig Webster, 4372
Clift, Garrett Glenn, 2712
Cline, William Findley, 3545
Clinton, Charles Kenneth, 2822
Clothier, Birchard T., 3245
Clothier, George B., 3230
Clothier, Isaac H., IV, 2865
Clothier, Isaac H., Jr., 2370
Clothier, William J., 2nd., 3248
Clymer, William Branford Shubrick, 3366
Coats, J. Blood, Jr., 4214
Cobb, Charles H., 0396
Cobb, Elliot, 2353
Cobb, John Devine, Jr., 2345
Cochran, Joseph A., 2169
Cochran, Joseph H., 2092
Cochran, Samuel Payntz, 1720
Cockrell, William Brewster, 3949
Coe, Charles Pierson, 0083
Coe, Henry Clark, 0546
Coffman, Joseph (*Veteran*), 0323
Colbert, Edwin Abbott, 1130
Colbert, Philip Maulsby, 1602
Colby, Archie R., 2183
Colby, Lafayette, 2040
Colcock, William Ferguson, 2531
Cole, John Carroll LeGrand, 0442
Cole, Robert Clinton, 0401
Coleman, Bertram D., 2331
Coleman, E. Richard, 2792
Coleman, Leighton, 0588
Colgin, George Larkin, Jr., 4364
Colgin, Harvey Lee, 4573
Collamore, John Hoffman, 0346
Collenberg, Henry T., Jr., 2164
Collenberg, Stewart Neale, 2420
Colles, Christopher John, 0057

Member Index

Collier, Arthur Luke, 3119
Collier, Dudley Foster, 3118
Collins, Charles F., 2051
Collins, Charles Lee, 0230
Collins, Charles, Jr., 3034
Collins, Edwin Barnes, 0951
Collins, George Gordon, 1454
Collins, Holdridge Ozro, 0078
Collins, John Wesley, 4220
Collins, Ralph Harry, 2880
Collmus, Charles Carroll, Sr., 1129
Colman, Paul Fessenden, 1770
Colomb, Charles L., Jr., 3160
Colton, Edwin Thorne, 3371
Coltrin, Gerald Edward, 3676
Coltrin, Lyle W., 4100
Colvin, Harold Riley, 1986
Comegys, Benjamin Bartis, 0536
Comegys, Edward Tiffin, 0743
Comegys, Wm. Henry, 0093
Condit, Oscar Halsted, 0696
Conkey, Maurice C., 3012
Conkling, Wm. Johnson, 1486
Connelly, John E., IV, 4316
Conover, Arthur Van Derveer, 0758
Conrad, James Madison Monroe, 0389
Conrad, Townsend Nelson, 0463
Constant, Robert F., 2297
Contee, Richard, 0217
Conway, Hewitt A., 3530
Cook, Joseph Tottenham, 0637
Cook, Robert Tayloe, III, 3487
Cook, Ross K., 2269
Cooke, William Dewey, 0965
Cool, Joseph Gilbert, 1125
Coon, John Elton, 4540
Coonley, Howard, III, 3716
Cooper, Clarence Clyde, 4486
Cooper, Edward Franklin, 4633
Cope, Jacob Erdman, 2541
Cope, William C., 2825
Coppage, John W., 1791
Corbusier, William Henry, 0023
Core, Jesse Rozell, III, 3526
Corey, Roland Reece, Jr., 4496
Corliss, Augustus Whittemore, 0062
Cornelius, Thomas Reese, 1494
Cornell, George Augustus, 0923
Cornett, Robert F., Jr., 3139
Cornman, Frank W., Jr., 2123

Cornog, David W. L., 2171
Cornwell, Ralph T. K., 2611
Corson, Alan, 1160
Corson, Alan, 3rd., 3298
Corson, Alan, Jr., 1830
Corson, Burton Francis, 1831
Corwin, David Rittenhouse Porter, 0744
Costa, Jacob Louis, 4103
Couch, Robert David, 4419
Coulson, George Arley, 4025
Coulter, Joseph Stewart, 3685
Couturie, Henry W., Jr., 3054
Couturie, Louis Maurice, Jr., 3672
Couturie, Maurice Louis, 2929
Cowen, Benjamin Rush, 0661
Cowherd, Leonard Mallonee, 4272
Cowper, William Henry, 4061
Cox, Edwin Birchard, 0573
Cox, Frederick Joseph, 0802
Cox, James William, 0625
Cox, James William, Jr., 1390
Cox, Thomas Riggs, 1391
Cox, William Emerson, 0574
Craddick, Joseph N., 0364
Craiger, Sherman Montrose, 0793
Cramer, Kenneth Frank, 2000
Crane, Moses Woodruff, Jr., 3405
Crane, Wm. Herbert, 1488
Cranford, Edward Beamer, 1435
Cranford, James Reed, 2205
Cranford, James William, 1404
Crawford, Henry Victor, 0993
Crawford, James Merrill, 2741
Crawford, William Franklin, 3419
Crawford, William Lusk, 3859
Creamer, Raymond Kemble, 2704
Creamer, William H., 2174
Creekmore, Thomas Vannoy, Sr., 3731
Creesy, George B., 2310
Cresson, Frederick L., 3593
Crisler, Lewis Allen, 1422
Crocker, Albert Rudolph, 4464
Crolius, Allen Potter, 1446
Cromwell, Andrew Grant, 1499
Cromwell, Benjamin Franklin, 1315
Cromwell, Charles, 0409
Cromwell, Oliver Colbert, 1818
Cronk, Hiram (*Veteran*), 0771
Crook, Wilson Walter, Jr., 3636

Member Index 167

Crosby, Caleb Pickens, 4151
Crosby, William Dalton, 4223
Crowell, James Gardner, 0731
Crowell, John Head, 1543
Crowell, John Head, 2973
Crowell, Robert, 2778
Crowell, Samuel B., III, 2330
Crowell, Samuel Babcock, 0671
Crowell, Samuel Babcock, Jr., 1542
Crowell, William Babcock, 3539
Crowell, William Sloan, 1352
Crowley, Gary Edwin, 3979
Crowninshield, Bowdoin Bradlee, 1146
Crowson, William Larry, 3787
Crozat, Edwin Paul, 3110
Crumley, David Oliver, 3576
Crumley, David Shiffer, 3532
Cullen, Charles A., Jr., 4320
Culver, Charles Mortimer, 0664
Culver, Francis Barnum, 0426
Cummings, James Whitnell, 4640
Cummins, James William, 3886
Cummins, Wm. Jennings, III, 1745
Cunningham, Carleton Brown, 1842
Cupp, Frederick Franklin, 4611
Curl, Jarrott (*Veteran*), 0307
Curren, Dennis Patrick, 3915
Curren, John G., Jr., 3428
Curren, Timothy Barlow, 3916
Currie, Edward A., Jr., 2359
Currie, Ulysses B., 2361
Currie, William Roberts, 3253
Currie, William Thomas, 1645
Currier, Charles Otis, 0982
Currier, Ross Hamilton, 2635
Curtis, Hanford Lorenzo, 0774
Curtis, Thomas Pelham, 4013
Curtius, Jon Pelot, 3898
Cushman, Norman F., 2256
Cushman, Seth Wilson, 1951
de Boisblanc, Rene Louis, 3875
de Butts, Daniel Heath, 4349
de Kernion, Paul S., 2392
de Mont, Edgar Rollins, 2405
de Montluzin, Adrian Davis, 3815
de Verges, Edward J., 2583
de Verges, Edward J., Jr., 2584
de Verges, George Louis, 4016
de Verges, Philip Cajetan, 3756
de Verges, Vincent Paul, 3763
de la Barre, Pierre Francois Volant, IV, 3344
de la Houssaye, Arthur Alexander, 3317
de la Houssaye, Arthur Joseph, Jr., 3334
de la Houssaye, Edward A., III, 2588
de la Houssaye, Frank Julien, Jr., 3755
de la Houssaye, J. Larue, 3431
de la Houssaye, Joseph Kleber, 3332
de la Houssaye, Louis P., 2470
de la Houssaye, Malcolm L., 2565
de la Houssaye, Roy Edward, 2485
de la Houssaye, Wayne Robert, 4281
de la Vergne, Charles E., 2384
de la Vergne, Hugues J., II, 2385
de la Vergne, Jacque P., 2544
de la Vergne, Jacques Perez, 3353
de la Vergne, Juillac H., 2569
de la Vergne, Jules Kristian, 2427
deColigny, Guerric Gaspard, 2429
deLaBarre, Francois Duffossard Volant, 3680
deLassus, Louis St. John, 2629
deLaureal, Henry Howard, 3390
deLavergne, Jacques DeB., 2674
diZerega, Augustus, V, 4519
du Fossat, Sidney Louis, 2582
du Mont, John Sanderson, 3318
D'Enbo, Francis J., 1903
Dabney, Thomas Ewing, 2676
Dahlene, Oscar, Jr., 4163
Dailey, Harry, 1083
Daingerfield, Foxhall Alexander, 1473
Dale, John, III, 3628
Dale, John, Jr., 3595
Dale, Wilton Roger, 3630
Dallam, Harry Gough, 1020
Dallas, Alexander J., 0039
Dallery, Edgar Laird, 4034
Dalton, Donald Henry, 4072
Daly, John Michael, 4280
Daly, Martin Ordway, 0658
Damon, Albert Forster, 0475
Damon, Edwin Adams, 0476
Dana, Edward, 1958
Dana, Harold Ward, 1966
Dana, Richard Hardy, 2041
Danaker, Edwin Thomas, 0363

168 Member Index

Daneker, William H., 0156
Danenhower, Edward Bushell, 1092
Danenhower, Edward Bushell, 1641
Daniels, Joseph, 1046
Danker, Albert, 0849
Danker, Frederick Harrison, 1324
Danker, Walton Stoutenburgh, 0897
Darby, Robert Davison, 4407
Darling, Carlos Parsons, 1350
Darnall, Joseph Rogers, 3668
Darrach, Edgar, 0672
Darrach, Henry, 0888
Darrow, Walter Nicholas Paine, 0502
Dart, Albert Laplace, 2817
Dart, Henry Plauche, III, 3416
Dart, Henry Plauche, Jr., 2521
Dart, Henry T., 3778
Dart, John, 2409
Dart, John Peacock, 3631
Dartt, John Gregg Lieb, 1242
Dashiell, Nicholas Leeke, 0854
Davenport, Richard Graham, 0030
David, Jeff McHugh, 3800
David, Romeal Kalil, 4514
David, Salem Kalil, Jr., 4207
Davidson, Arthur Cleveland, 2727
Davidson, Keith Wickwire, 4145
Davidson, Robert Mason, 0459
Davidson, Robert Mason, 0496
Davies, Robert Wynter, 4500
Davies, Wallace Evan, 3251
Davis, Arthur Christy, 1362
Davis, Augustus Plummer, 0087
Davis, Charles Luken, 0286
Davis, Charles Ross, 1336
Davis, Chester Wyman, 0873
Davis, Conner, Sanders, 2622
Davis, Curtis Carroll, 2764
Davis, Donald Eugene, 4351
Davis, Edward Lawrence, 3242
Davis, Edwin Bonner, Jr., 3557
Davis, Harry Alexander, 1555
Davis, James Madison, 1606
Davis, James William, 1285
Davis, John Mattison, 4629
Davis, Laurence R., 2184
Davis, Mark Jefferson, 3910
Davis, Michael W. R., 4620
Davis, Milton Wickers, Jr., 2858
Davis, Richard Lee, 3887
Davis, Robert Hare, 3291

Davis, Sussex Delaware, 1326
Davis, Walter Ashley, Jr., 3745
Davis, William McCay, 1834
Davison, David Paul, 4010
Dawkins, William Lee, 3584
Day, James Westbay, 1983
Dayton, Ralph, 1465
De Buys, Rathbone Emile, 2491
De La Vergne, Charles E., Jr., 2820
De Russy, Charles Nolte, 2532
DeForest, Louis Effingham, 1327
DeLaureal, Wm. David, Sr., 3425
DeLee, Alva Augustus, 3734
DeRussy, Charles Nolte, Jr., 2868
DeSonier, James Patrick, 3825
DeVerges, Paul Hanlon, 3826
DeWeese, Walter Earl, 1741
DeYoung, Arthur, 1090
DeYoung, Bertram Isaac, 0887
DeYoung, Charles Zadoc, 0294
Deadman, William Fiske, 0779
Deal, John Thomas Jr., 0175
Dean, H. Clark, 3901
Dean, Homer Franklin, 3667
Deatrick, Ambrose Winston, 1959
Deavers, Richard Lynn, 3972
Decoursey, William Leslie, 4180
Deffenbaugh, Goerge S., 2202
Delafield, Augustus Floyd, 0338
Delery, Baldwin Hunter, 3053
Delery, Frank Benjamin, 2530
Delery, Frank de la Souchere, 3359
Delery, Gerald de la Souchere, 3432
Delery, Joseph Charles, Jr., 2596
Delery, Lucien Carlisle, 2623
Delery, Oliver Stanislaus, 3670
Delgado, Manuel Odelon, Jr., 2837
Delhaye, Alcide Veeder, 3679
Dell, Albert Hampson, 1730
Dell, Charles Squires, 1711
Dell, Charles Squires, Jr., 2607
Dell, Samuel Mills, 1712
Dell, Thomas Medairy, 1076
Dell, Thomas Medairy, Jr., 1713
Demaree, Joseph Paul, 3010
Denis, Alfred Cecil, 3752
Denis, Augustus Henry, 0304
Denis, George Jules, 0866
Denis, Wilfred D., Jr., 3111
Denman, Abram C., Jr., 0717
Dennis, James Teackle, 0417

Member Index 169

Dennis, Kenneth Allen, 4461
Dennison, Herbert Elmer, 1463
Densmore, George Ellis, 2062
Dent, Daniel DuVal, 3300
Dent, William Eugene, Jr., 4608
Derbes, Charles J., Jr., 3009
Derbes, Clause Joseph, 2886
Derbes, Edward J., Jr., 3052
Derbes, Stephen Joseph, 3378
Derbes, Vincent Joseph, 2673
Derr, Andrew Fein, 0373
Deshon, George Durfee, 0922
Deshon, Percy, 1322
Desobry, Louis Edward, Sr., 2870
Detwiler, David Roy, 1961
Devenport, Joseph F., 3037
Devoe, Thomas Elliott, 4098
Dewey, George, 0710
Dewey, George Eugene, 0423
Dewey, Hiram Stapleford, 0424
Dewey, Hiram Todd, 0422
Dexter, Charles Asa, 1568
Dexter, Henry Clinton, 1532
Dexter, Theodore Everett, 1534
Deynoodt, Donald A., 3159
Deynoodt, Joseph F., 2386
Deynoodt, Joseph F., Jr., 2889
Diaz, Abram Henry, 3103
Diaz, Joseph Aurelio, 3105
Diaz, Rafael Eduardo, II, 3422
Diaz, Ralph Edouardo, 3102
Diaz, Theodore Peter, 3568
Diaz, Walter Palmer, 3104
Dick, Kalvin Ryan, 4347
Dick, R. Elvin, 4315
Dick, Winfred Elbert, 4348
Dickerman, Frank Elliott, 1077
Dickey, Charles Herman, 0377
Dickey, Edmund Sadtler, 1646
Dickey, Francis George, 2731
Dickey, Gary Alan, 4603
Dickey, John Lincoln, 0542
Dickey, Philip Sadtler, 0360
Dickie, Robert Burns, II, 3019
Dickinson, John, 2271
Dickson, Helion, Jr., 2840
Diggs, Charles Francis, 1620
Diggs, Ross Miles, 0934
Dilks, Charles Day, 3308
Dilks, John Hyland, 1656
Dilks, Peter Durfor, 3474

Dilks, Walter Howard, 0879
Dilks, Walter Howard, Jr., 1517
Dillenbeck, Clark, 1795
Dillon, Arthur Orison, 1389
Dimick, Gregory Forrest, 4060
Dingley, Edward Nelson, Jr., 3638
Dinkins, Joseph Airey, 3346
Dinkins, Ladd Augustine, 2615
Dinkins, Ladd Augustine, Jr., 3319
Dixon, Fitz-Eugene, Jr., 2368
Dobbins, John William, 4614
Dodd, Milton C., 2270
Dodge, Richard Keller, 4130
Doherty, Lewis Stirling, 3333
Dold, Douglas Meriwether, 1569
Dold, William Elliot, 1017
Dold, Wm. Elliott, Jr., 1570
Doliber, Donald Arthur, 4353
Dolliver, Alan Kemp, 3185
Donaldson, Francis Adams, Jr., 1612
Donan, William Page, 4585
Dorcy, Benjamin Holladay, 0385
Dorman, John Frederick, 2977
Dorney, Charles Polk, 1512
Dorrance, Charles Samuel, 1511
Dorsey, Brice Marden, 4355
Dorsey, Thomas Lee, Sr., 3776
Dorsey, Vachel Paul, 3971
Dougherty, Cary M., Jr., 4102
Dougherty, Clifford L., 3005
Douglas, Archer Wall, 0624
Douglas, Archer Wall, 1560
Douglass, Benjamin Dun, 0742
Douglass, Edward Trent, Jr., 4381
Douglass, George L., 1112
Douglass, Hiram Kennedy, 2917
Douglass, Robert Dunn, 0740
Douglass, Robert Graham Dunn, 0741
Douglass, Rudolph A.A., 2071
Dowling, Wilfrid S., 2204
Downs, Samuel Addison, 0012
Drapier, William Henry, 1264
Draughn, Paul Vernon, 3339
Drayton, Joseph William, 1547
Drayton, Samuel, 1235
Drayton, Samuel, Jr., 1501
Dresser, Frank Estervan, 1693
Drouilhet, Adrien Francois, 2978
Drown, Charles Lincoln, 1731
Drown, John Wilson, 0870

Member Index

DuBarry, Joseph N., III, 3029
DuBarry, Joseph N., IV, 3132
DuBarry, Joseph N., V, 3133
DuBarry, William Hagan, 2678
Duane, Russell, 0369
Duck, William Charles, 4544
Dudley, Augustus Palmer, 0275
Dudley, Edgar Swartout, 0073
Dukehart, Morton McIlvain, 1822
Dukehart, Thomas V., 2356
Dukes, Alexander Thompson, 1135
Dulany, John Highenbotham, 0397
Dulany, John Mason, 0248
Dulany, William Mason, 0249
Dulany, Wm. James Clarke, 0399
Dunbar, Walter Durke, 2579
Duncan, Charles Yarbrough, Sr., 2746
Duncan, Daniel Lewis, 1578
Duncan, Neal Holland, 3579
Dunkel, Joel Ambrose, 1183
Dunlap, Clarke, 3641
Dunlap, John Bettes, III, 4515
Dunlap, John Bettes, Jr., 3397
Dunlap, Sallows, 0745
Dunlap, Walter Eugene Briggs, 1364
Dunn, Leward Leon, 4161
Dupray, Frederick Hervey, 1922
Dupuy, Homer Joseph, 3286
Dupuy, Peter Hillyer, 4332
Durel, Homer Joseph, 3068
Durst, Ross Compton, 2981
Dutcher, Henry Redman, 1911
Dutcher, Russell Kenneth, III, 4369
Dutcher, Russell Kenneth, Jr., 4389
Dutton, Thomas Waltham, 0190
Duvall, Richard Mareen, 1037
Dwier, W. Kirkland, 2231
Dwight, Charles H., 3572
Dye, David Allen, 4528
Dyer, Frank Merrill, 4122
Earhart, Valentine Adam, Jr., 4376
Early, Clarence Fielding, 2796
Easby, May Stevenson, 2094
Easter, Arthur Miller, 0208
Easter, James Miller, 1070
Eastwick, Charles Henry, 0739
Eastwood, Ralph Allen, Sr., 4041
Eatman, George Lowe, 3848
Echols, John L., 4188
Echols, John Lynn, Jr., 4259
Eddy, Samuel Schuyler, 1369
Edelen, Crolian William, 2859
Edge, Nelson James Harrison, 0657
Edmiston, R. B., 4637
Edmondson, James Howard, III, 3730
Edmundson, Frank Busha, 1811
Edwards, James MacDonald, 4195
Edwards, Ray O., Sr., 2198
Egle, William Henry, 0264
Ehlinger, Marquez Pillot, 3365
Eiler, Homer, 1575
Eisenhower, Dwight David, 2630
Eld, Peter Fuller, 3040
Eld, Terry J., 3045
Elder, William Henry, 0629
Eldredge, Edward H., 0076
Eldredge, Pierce Schank, 3892
Elkins, George W., Jr., 2334
Ellington, Charles Townley, 1335
Elliott, John Stadden, 0820
Elliott, Thomas Hugh, III, 3673
Elliott, Thomas Ireland, 0507
Ellis, Albert Washington, 1261
Ellis, Edward Dimick, 0420
Ellis, Norman Stanley, 1452
Ellis, Virgil Wiley, 4037
Ellis, William, 0829
Elmendorf, Ten Eyck, 2160
Elmendorf, Wm. Ten E., Jr., 2854
Ely, Duncan Cairnes, 3733
Emerson, George Douglas, 1229
England, Charles, 0936
Englar, David F., Jr., 2080
Engle, Kline d'A., 3175
Erdman, George Brown, 2612
Erhardt, Clement Dumont, III, 3969
Erhardt, Clement Dumont, Jr., 3273
Erichson, Samuel C., 2608
Ernshaw, Daniel J., 4282
Ernst, Charles Augustus, IV, 3468
Ernst, Christophr Gardner, 3469
Ernst, Timothy Walker, 3715
Erwin, Harry Louis, 4541
Erwin, James J., 0600
Eshleman, Benjamin, 2007
Eshleman, Benjamin Franklin, 2564
Eshleman, Benjamin, 3rd., 3719
Eshleman, Benjamin, Jr., 3062
Eshleman, Sidney St. John, Jr., 2563
Esler, Charles Vansant, 3197
Esler, Lewis H., 2186

Member Index 171

Este, Charles, 0456
Estes, Ernest Herwell, Jr., 3629
Estes, Frederick Anson, 0680
Estes, John W. J., 3127
Estes, Webster Cummings, 0954
Etter, Thomas C., Jr., 3134
Etter, Thomas Clifton, 3243
Eustis, Charles Logan, 3569
Eustis, David Leeds, 3632
Eustis, Ernest Lewis, Jr., 2719
Eustis, Henry Chotard, 2518
Eustis, Henry Chotard, III, 3327
Eustis, John Douglas, 3384
Eustis, Joseph Bres, 2516
Eustis, Lawrence Bres, 2520
Eustis, Lawrence Bres, Jr., 3394
Evans, Clarence Richard, 1244
Evans, Daniel Goode, 3058
Evans, Ellwood Waller, 0245
Evans, Frank Barton, Jr., 2968
Evans, Frank Brooke, 0762
Evans, George Webster, 2959
Everhart, Lay Hampton, 1243
Everngam, Douglas Howard, 4501
Everngam, G. Gregg, 3565
Evetts, Livingston Spaulding, 4474
Ewing, Leslie Hand, 2724
Ewing, Vernon Lee, Jr., 3873
Faber, Willis Henry, 0491
Fackenthal, Benjamin Franklin, Jr., 1240
Fackenthal, Frank Diehl, 1530
Faget, William Edward, 3036
Faidley, Harvey Franklin, 1567
Fail, Welton Ruel, 4273
Fairbank, Leigh Cole, 1882
Fairbank, Leigh Cole, Jr., 1972
Fairbanks, Warren Evans, 3303
Fairchild, Benjamin Clyde, 0800
Falkner, James Calton, 4578
Farley, Myron Foster, 4046
Farmer, Zelah Rice, 1971
Farnandis, W. Walter, 4595
Farrington, Charles Lincoln, 0335
Farrington, Douglas F., 3090
Farwell, Charles A., 2535
Farwell, Frank Evans, 2534
Faulkner, Nelson Franklin, Jr., 4635
Favrot, Clifford F., 2395
Favrot, Gervais Freret, 2505
Favrot, Henri M., 2378

Favrot, Henri Mortimer, Jr., 2404
Favrot, Henry Richmond, 2401
Favrot, Joseph St. Clair, 1402
Favrot, Joseph St. Clair, Jr., 2422
Favrot, Laurence H., 2483
Favrot, Richmond G., 3176
Fawkes, Charles Elliott, 4095
Faxon, Charles Henry, 1877
Fell, Charles Woodford, 2032
Fell, John Corry, 4379
Fellows, Leon Wallace, 3173
Fellows, Lloyd Welker, 3597
Felt, Frederick Christian, 4224
Felton, Samuel M., 2273
Felton, Samuel M., Jr., 2336
Felty, Harold G., 3698
Fender, James Wade, 2801
Fender, Robert, Worthel, 2802
Ferguson, Alfred Ludlow, III, 3890
Fernley, George A., 2229
Fernley, Thomas A., Jr., 2230
Ferree, Sheridan, 1460
Ferris, David Brainard, Jr., 0824
Field, Charles Kellogg, III, 4423
Field, Thomas Yardley, Jr., 0917
Filkins, Daniel G., 1750
Filkins, Douglas C., 1749
Finch, Albert Patric, Jr., 3960
Finch, Ronald Milton, 3881
Finch, Willard Robert, 4203
Fincher, Myron Gustin, 3661
Finger, Allen Whelchel, 3402
Finger, John Martin, 3403
Finger, John Whelchel, 2642
Fink, Charles E., 2163
Finlay, Luke William, 4083
Finley, Mark Florus, 1535
Finley, Mark Florus, Jr., 1536
Finnell, Arthur Louis, 4146
Firth, William Rutherford, 4068
Firth, William Rutherford, Jr., 4059
Fischer, Frederick Hall, 2893
Fischer, Frederick Waters, 2895
Fischer, John Sargent, 2894
Fish, Erland Frederick, 1892
Fish, Roswell Oliver, 1740
Fish, Steven Byers, 3738
Fisher, James Henry, 1001
Fisher, Wheeler Yule, 4024
Fisk, Arthur Aylmer, 1082
Fisk, Charles William, 0756

Fissell, William H., 2634
Fitch, Edward Sherman, 0331
Fitchet, Seth Marshall, 1856
Fitler, Dale B., 2114
Fitler, Nathan M., 2159
Fitzhugh, Howard S., II, 2641
Fitzpatrick, Wm. Claude, 0948
Fleming, Allison Sweeney, 0972
Flint, Daniel Waldo Boone, 3309
Flint, Goerge William Treat, 4297
Flint, Wyman Kneeland, 0487
Flores, Adolph Anthony, Jr., 3674
Flower, John Sebastian, 1041
Flowers, John Baston, III, 3494
Flowers, John R., Jr., 2397
Flowers, John Robert, Jr., 4137
Floyd, William N., Jr., 4647
Fluker, Denis McCammon, 3933
Focke, Ferdinand Brauns, 1375
Focke, Harry Smull, 1537
Focke, Walter David, 1376
Fogg, Arthur Lloyd, 0630
Follett, Edgar Austin, 0540
Folsom, Wendell Burt, 1733
Fontaine, Edgar Benjamin, Jr., 4345
Fontana, Jules August, Jr., 3603
Fontenot, Ozeme Dudley, 3940
Forbes, Charles W., 2149
Forbes, Francis C., 2134
Forbes, William Albert, 4415
Forbes, William I., Jr., 2133
Forbes, William Innes, 1708
Forbush, Wm. Curtis, 0411
Ford, Henry Jones, 0996
Ford, John Donaldson, 0135
Ford, Thomas G., 0218
Foreman, Albert Watson, 1773
Forman, William Harper, 2737
Forman, Wm. Harper, Jr., 2735
Forstall, Allen Henry, 2452
Forstall, Earl Louis, 2456
Forstall, Frederick Joseph, 2455
Forstall, Frederick K., 2442
Forstall, Lawrence Peter, 2453
Forstall, Paul Charles, 4135
Forstall, Warren Anthony, 2454
Forstall, Warren Anthony, Jr., 4136
Forster, Andrew J., 3048
Forsyth, Hewitt Laurie, 3348
Fortenberry, William Lowery, 4510
Fortier, Jacques Lanauze, 4288
Fortier, Louis Joseph, 2845
Fortier, Louis Renshaw, 3652
Fortier, Robert Eugene, 3407
Fortier, Robert Laird, 3790
Fossier, Albert S., 2891
Fossier, Horace L., Jr., 3032
Foster, Clarence Dulany, 1064
Foster, Dulany, 2305
Foster, John Alexander, II, 3953
Foster, Richard Rushton, 2424
Foster, Romulus Adam, 1170
Foster, Volney William, 0651
Fotterall, Stephen Blakely, 0760
Fotterall, Wm. Foster, 1091
Foust, Perry Elihu, 4636
Fowler, Edward Sydney, 0126
Fowler, H. Waller, Jr., 3534
Fowler, Samuel Robert, Jr., 2551
Fowler, William Eric, 1453
Fox, Falvey Jerome, Jr., 3843
Fox, Wm. Carlton, 0875
Francis, Charles Spencer, 0844
Frank, Samuel Boone, 4179
Frankenfield, Edgar Charles, 3744
Franklin, Andrew McKee (*Veteran*), 0353
Franklin, Benjamin Robert, 3rd., 4105
Franklin, Benjamin Robert, Jr., 3791
Franklin, Robert Scott, 0501
Fraser, Carlos Enrique, 4302
Fraser, David, 4187
Fraser, James William, 4218
Fraser, Peter, 3954
Frazee, John Henry, 2753
Frazer, Goerge Augustine, 1629
Frazer, James Patriot Wilson, 0526
Frazer, John, 1195
Frazer, Persifor, 0150
Frazer, Reah, 0527
Frazier, Griffin Guy, 3210
Freeburger, Alexander Cooper, 0008
Freed, Willard Musselman, 2691
Freeland, Samuel Lyles, 3988
Freeman, Reuben Byron, II, 4465
Freeman, William, 0791
French, Bruce Hartung, 1995
French, Chester Lee, 1021
French, Louis Mardenbrough, 0337
French, Robert Lewis, 3573
French, Wm. Freeman, 0103

Freret, Adolphe Schreiber, 2653
Freret, Frederick George, 2664
Freret, Rene Alexis, 2471
Fretz, John Edgar, 0554
Frick, Albert W., 0152
Friebely, Howard Eugene, 2589
Frisbee, Franklin Senter, 0349
Fritz, James Mason, 3872
Frost, Timothy Prescott, 0038
Frye, Leslie Alva, 1734
Fuller, Burdett S., 2151
Fuller, Byron J., 2152
Fuller, Edward R., 2371
Gage, Seth Newton, 0473
Gagnet, John Lawson, 2875
Gaither, Alfred, 0689
Galibraith, Wm. Ayres, 1190
Gallagher, Bernard J., Jr., 3578
Galles, Duane LeRoy Charles Mealman, 4141
Galloney, Frank Hutchinson, 0738
Galloupe, Charles Wm., 0344
Galloupe, George Augustus, 0351
Galvin, Michael J., Jr., 3226
Gamble, Richard Whitaker, 2567
Gandolfo, Henri A., 4106
Gandolfo, Roger Joseph, Jr., 4264
Gann, Thomas Huey, 4216
Gans, Arthur D., 2165
Garber, Alexander Christian, Jr., 4382
Gard, Daniel Hosmer, 0457
Gard, Wordsworth, 0705
Gardiner, Edward Carey, 1925
Gardiner, William Howard, 1920
Gardner, Asa Bird, 0148
Gardner, Charles Frederic, 1154
Gardner, George Clinton, 0663
Gardner, Hilton Bowen, Jr., 3710
Gardner, Laurence Russell, 1954
Gardner, Lester Durand, 1771
Garic, Charles Anthony, 2417
Garic, Harold Nicholas, II, 3824
Garlington, Ernest Albert, 0142
Garner, Ervin Leon, 4222
Garnsey, John Henderson, 0836
Garrard, Joseph, 0025
Garretson, Oliver Kelleam, 3457
Garvin, Howard Madison, 1874
Gaumer, Daniel H., 0470
Gause, Francis Gregory, Jr., 3252

Geary, Cyril Paul, Jr., 2892
Geer, Herbert W., 2265
Gehring, John George, 0415
Gelpi, Chester Philip, 2446
Gelpi, Herman Kahle, 2445
Gentry, Franklin Marion, II, 2769
Gentry, John Richard, 3842
Gentry, William Richard, 1558
George, Thomas S., 2339
George, Thomas Stevens, Jr., 3163
Gerard, James Watson, II, 2815
Gerhart, George Henry, 3613
Germond, George Frederick, III, 4411
Getelman, Ralph, 1447
Gibble, Isaac O., 2130
Gibbons, David Cartan Loker, 4134
Gibbons, John Francis, III, 2537
Gibbs, Benjamin, 2173
Gibbs, Frederick Roccofort, 2011
Gibbs, Richard DeArmond, 2628
Gibbs, Robert Frederick, 3123
Gibbs, William Frank, 2063
Gibson, John McCullough, 3108
Gieske, Edward T., Jr., 3566
Gieske, James Chapman, 3689
Gilbert, Leon Jacques, 2928
Gill, Nicholas Rufus, 0439
Gill, Robert Lee, 0440
Gill, Roger Taney, 0441
Gill, Wm. Harrison, 0274
Gillespie, John Douglas, 3827
Gilman, Charles M., Jr., 3046
Gilman, Charles Malcolm B., 2760
Gilmore, Tiffin, 0466
Girdley, Harry Watson, 4435
Gist, William Claude, Jr., 4405
Gladwin, Robert, 3902
Glass, James Gamewell, 0635
Glassie, Donelson Caffery, 3602
Gleason, Frederick B., III, 3596
Glentworth, James, 0053
Glentworth, Theodore, 3rd., 1136
Glover, Charles Carroll, III, 1980
Glover, Charles Carroll, Jr., 1694
Goddard, Calvin H., 2180
Goddard, Leroy A., 1270
Godley, Walter, 1442
Goff, Sudduth, 2800
Gold, William B., Jr., 2373
Golden, Robert Bleakley, 3982
Goldsborough, Richard H., 3548

Goldsby, Joseph Hugh, Jr., 2810
Goltz, Carlos Washington, 1786
Gonzales, John Malcolm, 4609
Gooch, David Barr, 4534
Goodrich, Everett B., 2313
Goodrich, William, 1011
Goodridge, Edwin Tyson, 2020
Goodsell, Percy Hamilton, Jr., 2823
Goodson, Henry Grady, Jr., 2918
Goodspeed, Aloysius Berchmans, 2874
Goodspeed, Lawrence Archibald, 2873
Goodwin-Perkins, Charles A., 2211
Goodwin, Charles Ridgely, 0246
Goodwin, William G., 2258
Gordon, Lloyd Paul, 3513
Gordon, Paul Tulance, III, 4431
Gordon, Ray Tompkins, 0125
Gordon, Robert Lee, 3489
Gordon, William R., 2157
Gould, Lyttleton Bowen Purnell, 1885
Gowen, James Emmet, 2281
Gradeless, Donald Eugene, 3823
Gradeless, Rex Lavern, 4338
Graham, Arthur Butler, 1967
Graham, James Brooks, Jr., 3608
Graham, James Kenneth, 4192
Grange, Cecil William, 3808
Grange, Franklin Ernest, II, 3851
Grannis, George Washington, 0432
Graves, Henry Duncan, 0590
Gray, Edward Morris, Jr., 3622
Gray, Gordon, 3681
Gray, Harold, 4631
Gray, James Hammer, 4523
Gray, John Daniel, 1427
Greely, Adolphus W., 0036
Greely, John Nesmith, 1879
Green, Arthur de la Houssaye, 3381
Green, E. Ray, 3974
Green, Edwin Bernard, 2302
Green, Edwin Bernard, Jr., 2766
Green, Frank Delaplaine, 0515
Green, James Oscar, 0315
Green, Joseph E., Jr., 2300
Green, Richard Ellwood, 3025
Green, Richard Henry, 0051
Green, Robert McCay, 0976
Green, Robert McCay, III, 1796

Green, Samuel Alexander, Jr., 2907
Green, Seymour Ledyard, 2944
Green, Thomas Edward, 1309
Green, Thomas Neving, 0250
Green, William Webb, 0052
Greene, Norman Joy, 3059
Greene, Samuel Edward, III, 1430
Gregg, Levi Laertes, 0215
Gresham, Charles Reed, 3503
Gresham, John Chowning, 0276
Greve, Charles Theodore, 0655
Gridley, Edward Mead, 1433
Griffin, Leonard Gaines, 4371
Griffin, Lowell Miland, 4521
Griffith, Louis Philip, 0009
Griffith, Wm. Herrick, 0612
Grim, Robert Elroy, 4586
Grimes, George R., 2187
Grimke, Frederic Drayton, 1572
Grindall, Charles Sylvester, 1028
Groff, Clyde Lester, 4127
Groff, John Marshall, 3517
Grohgan, Fred Alfred, Jr., 4301
Grout, John Clifford, Jr., 3590
Grove, James Mason, 3400
Grover, Robert LaVern, 4147
Groves, Fergus Coleman, 4522
Grubert, Reese Thompson, 1952
Guernsey, Raimund Thomas, 1974
Guice Jeffrey Pipes, 4542
Guice, Gerald Pipes, 4426
Guidry, Douglas David, 3931
Gurley, George Poulin, 1378
Gurley, William Frank Eugene, 1371
Gurney, John Thomas, 3rd., 3984
Guthrie, Harry Jones, 1137
Guttery, John McQueen, Sr., 2860
Guy, William Burton, Jr., 2732
Gwynne, Abram Evan, 2759
Haas, William Henry, Jr., 1809
Hadden, Callender F., 2466
Hadden, Callender F., Jr., 2467
Hadden, Richard I., 2468
Hadden, Robert W., 2469
Haddock, Stanley Brickett, 0492
Hadel, Albert Kimberly, 0011
Hafter, Jerome Charles, 4543
Haight, Frederick Everest, 0141
Haight, Sherman Post, Jr., 3527
Haines, Burton C., 1305
Hains, John Power, 0260

Member Index 175

Halberstadt, George Howell, 0518
Halberstadt, James Franklin, Jr., 3900
Halberstadt, Max Glenn, 4166
Halberstadt, Robert LeConte, 3247
Halbert, James Warren, 4285
Halbert, Virgil Allen, 3697
Halbertstadt, Baird, 0261
Hale, Horace Charles, 1245
Hale, James Rayburn, 4582
Hale, Lawrence Herbert, 2497
Hale, Ledyard Park, 1171
Haley, Whitney Watson, 2084
Hall, Bordman, 0511
Hall, Clayton Colman, 1199
Hall, DeLou Perrin, 2747
Hall, Francis Compton, 2498
Hall, George A., 2319
Hall, Harrison, 0769
Hall, John William, 0721
Hall, Joseph Cotton, 0191
Hall, Reynold Thomas, 1338
Hall, Ross, 1113
Hall, Summerfield Davis, 1134
Hall, William Anderson, 1105
Hall, Wm. Hunt, Jr., 1820
Hambleton, Richard Nicolai, 2852
Hamff, James Edward, 4001
Hamilton, Alexander, 0340
Hamilton, George H., 2002
Hamilton, Glenn Clark, 3664
Hamilton, Howard Laverne, 3665
Hamley, Arthur J., 1432
Hammond, Andrew Goodrich, 0104
Hammond, Edward, 1496
Hampton, Vernon Boyce, 1962
Hampton, Wm. Judson, Jr., 1987
Hancock, James Etchberger, 1065
Hand, Augustus Noble, 0841
Hand, Billings Learned, 0639
Handy, John Curtis, 1002
Hanks, Stedman Shumway, 3361
Hanna, Meredith, 1653
Hansell, Charles Richardson, 2953
Hanson, Theodore George, Jr., 3922
Harden, Victor Richard, 4505
Hardesty, Marion N., 2242
Hardin Bayless E., 2743
Hardin, Harry S., Jr., 2398
Hardin, Sidney, L., 2399
Harding, Charles Trott, 1780

Harding, Harry Joseph, 4644
Hargett, Douglass Henry, 0734
Harnett, Maurice A., III, 3581
Harper, Marshall L., 3076
Harrah, Eric, 2814
Harrington Harrison Loring, 1184
Harrington, Arthur Clark, 1174
Harris, Ballard Eustis, 4138
Harris, Joseph N., 2263
Harris, Lyttleton Tazwell, 3377
Harris, Raymond Cutler, 3943
Harris, Thomas Cadwalader, 0931
Harris, Thomas Christopher, 4625
Harris, Timothy Charles, 4604
Harris, Walter St. George, 0869
Harris, William Barney, Jr., 1526
Harris, William Hall, 1148
Harris, William Hall, Jr., 1385
Harris, William Lloyd, 4093
Harris, Wm. Barney, 1490
Harrison, Carter, 0752
Harrison, George, 1729
Harrison, Henry Christopher, Jr., 2658
Harrison, John S., 4th., 2223
Harrison, Keith Graham, 4424
Harrison, Patrick Morgan, 4307
Harrison, Robert Myron, 3796
Harrison, Thomas, 0690
Harrison, Wm. Preston, 1470
Harsh, George Jr., 2624
Hart, Albert Bushnell, 1469
Hart, Byerly, 0374
Hart, Thomas, 1373
Harting, Robert Morgan, 4064
Hartman, Ralph William, 1715
Hartman, Thadeus Lee, 4227
Hartnett, Walter Falkner, 4581
Hartson, Maurcie John, Jr., 2841
Hartson, Maurice John, III, 2843
Harvey, Aylmer O., 1449
Haskins, George Lee, 3233
Hastings, Arthur Chapin, 0855
Hastings, Arthur Chapin, Jr., 1080
Hastings, Harold M., 2177
Hastings, Henry, 0436
Hastings, Morris Chase, 1697
Hastings, Orlando Burr, 1081
Hastings, Walcott Brown, 1231
Hatcher, Robert Stockwell, 0413
Hatfield, Henry Reed, 0478

176 Member Index

Hathaway, Harry St.Clair, 1718
Haverstick, George Henry, 0311
Hawkins, Elijah, 0750
Hawkins, Frederick Barnes, 4508
Hawkins, Leland Barnes, III, 4448
Hay, Maldom, 0007
Hay, Peter Stuart, 0001
Hay, Randall Groves, 1948
Hay, Southard, 0928
Hay, William Henry Odenheimer, 0006
Hayden, Charles Leslie, 0609
Hayden, Horace Edwin, 0134
Hayes, George Charles, 0681
Hayes, Philip Cornelius, 1254
Hays, Reese Henry, Jr., 2916
Head, Glenn Lloyd, 3096
Healy, Francis Augustine Alphonsus, 1843
Heaton, Guilford A., 1302
Heaton, John Edward, 0330
Hebert, Warren Harang, 2570
Heckler, Charles Edwin, 1109
Heckscher, Ledyard Hart, 2956
Hedges, Job Elmer, 0788
Heflin, James Lester, 2739
Heiple, James Dee, 4532
Heiple, Jeremy Hans, 4547
Heiple, Jonathan James, 4546
Helick, Reuben Harold, 1942
Helick, Reuben Martin, 2861
Hellick, Chauncey Graham, 0911
Hellick, George Franklin, 2058
Hellick, George Franklin, Jr., 2059
Helms, Paul Edward, 3169
Hendershot, Edgar Albert, 4295
Henderson, Branton H., Jr., 3171
Henderson, Branton Holstein, 1901
Henderson, Charles Franklin, 1042
Henderson, Charles Griffith, 1455
Henderson, Frank Clarence, 1613
Henderson, George Washington, 1504
Henderson, Gerald Van S., 3249
Hendrick, John Buford, Jr., 1166
Henkels, Joseph Felix, 1403
Henrici, Max, 1866
Henry, Elwin O., 3663
Henry, Francis Jenkins, 3484
Henry, James Malcolm, 0106
Henry, John Francis, Jr., 0223

Henry, John William, 0080
Henry, John William, 0569
Henry, Reginald Buchanan, 0913
Henry, William Louis, 0776
Henshaw, Alonzo Norton, 1220
Hepburn, Barry H., 2218
Hepburn, W. Horace, Jr., 2219
Herman, Walter F., 2222
Herndon, Dale L., 2122
Herndon, John Goodwin, Jr., 1312
Herndon, Richard M., 2096
Hero, Alvin Anthony, 2473
Hero, George Alfred, III, 3757
Herrick, Clinton Bradford, 0832
Herrick, Robert Webster, 1591
Herrick, Samuel, 1413
Herrington, Kenneth Frank, III, 4447
Hess, Frank Judson, 0659
Hester, Jacob, 0632
Heyl, Charles Heath, 0102
Heyl, Edward Miles, 0096
Hickey, Maunsel White, 2726
Hicks, Louis Edward, 3850
Higgins, Jerry Lynn, Sr., 3491
Higgins, Samuel C. (*Veteran*), 0352
Higley, Wayne Earl, Jr., 4480
Hildt, John C., 1055
Hildt, Thomas, 1056
Hill, Benjamin Jr., 3086
Hill, George H., 3rd., 3701
Hill, James Joseph, 4602
Hill, John Phillip, 1724
Hill, John Stell, 4577
Hill, Michael Webster, 3711
Hill, Nicholas Sluby, 0394
Hill, Norman Alan, 2070
Hill, Robert C., 3995
Hill, Robert C., Jr., 4111
Hill, Samuel Emory, 0379
Hill, Thomas, 0378
Hillery, Andrew F., 2543
Hilliard, John Mauk, 4458
Hills, Elbridge Romeyn, 0910
Hinds, Charles Franklin, 3161
Hinds, Ernest, 0733
Hinkle, Henry Louis, 3721
Hinkle, John William, 3727
Hinkson, J. T. Ward, 2021
Hires, Charles Edgar, 2613
Hires, Charles Edgar, Jr., 3294

Member Index

Hires, John Bacon, 3546
Hires, William L., 2121
Hisky, John Guido, 1509
Hisky, Thomas Foley, 1104
Hisky, William George, 1510
Hiss, Fielder Israel, Jr., 1487
Hitch, David Marshall, 1584
Hitch, Marshall D., 2095
Hitch, Marshall D., 2150
Hite, Drayton Meade, 1022
Hobart, David McKnight, 0065
Hobart, Robert Enoch, 1399
Hobart, Thomas Duncan, 1158
Hocker, Douglass William, 3713
Hodges, Fletcher, 1684
Hodgkins, Joseph Wilson, 0144
Hoefer, Frederick W., 3112
Hoefer, Richard Allan, 3113
Hoff, Arthur Bainbridge, 0067
Hoff, Arthur Bainbridge, Jr., 1926
Hoff, William B., 3145
Hoff, Wm. Bainbridge, 0066
Hoffman, Alexander Wm., 0130
Hoffman, Alfred Ayers, 1395
Hoffman, Benjamin Rose, 1893
Hoffman, Charles Wheeler, 0166
Hoffman, Eugene Baker, 0165
Hoffnagle, Harry Herbert, 1634
Hoffnagle, Herbert Daniel, 1524
Hogan, William Dudley, 4170
Hogeboom, Francklyn, 1878
Hogg, William Stetson, 1332
Holcombe, John Marshall, 0616
Holden, Edward Packard, 0780
Holden, Edward Packard, Jr., 0981
Holden, Edwin Roy, 1619
Holden, George Meads, 1346
Holden, Horace, 0994
Holden, Irvin, 2657
Holden, James Austin, 1233
Holden, James Cotton, 0707
Holden, James F., 2167
Holifield, Marvin Bertrie, 2745
Holland, George Vincent, 4621
Holland, Joseph, 0796
Hollander, Elmer Rand, 0086
Holliday, William David, 4495
Hollinger, Ammon Lester, 4063
Hollinger, Edwin Theodore, 3774
Hollis, Charles William, 1857
Hollis, Minot Everett, 1817

Holloway, Charles Thomas, II, 1365
Holloway, Reuben Ross, 0428
Hollyday, Thomas James, 4251
Hollyday, Thomas Worthington, 1739
Holmes, George James, 0617
Holmes, William Henry E., 2786
Holstein, Otto, 1159
Holt, Harry Ewell, 4529
Hooker, Bryan Edward, 1849
Hooker, Roland Mather, 1838
Hooker, Thomas Bedell, 1848
Hooper, James (Veteran), 0290
Hooper, James Mason, 1609
Hooper, Oliver Furbish, 1669
Hooper, Stuart Cator, 1889
Hopkins, Alfred Francis, 0940
Hopkins, Carroll Creswell, 2323
Hopkins, Henry P., 2354
Hopkins, Henry P., Jr., 2355
Hopkins, James Robert, 4568
Hopkins, John Cook, 1290
Hopkins, Joseph Carroll, 2487
Hopkins, Joseph Vincent, Jr., 3321
Hopkins, Robert Hiram, 1289
Hopkinson, Edward, Jr., 2054
Hopkinson, Francis, 3194
Hopkinson, Francis, Jr., 3240
Hopkinson, James P., 3246
Hopkinson, John Joseph, 3237
Hopkinson, Mark, 3315
Hord, Arnold Harris, 0611
Horn, Tiemann Newell, 0281
Hornblower, Josiah, 1521
Hornblower, William, 1523
Horner, Thomas Marland, 3341
Horton, Clarence Alfred, 3650
Horton, William Edward, 0114
Hosier, Scott Foye, 3918
Hotchkin, Walter Bryant, 0999
Houck, George Wesley, 1553
Houck, Harry Elijah, 1554
Hough, John Edward, 0185
Hough, Pliny Miles, 0645
Houghton, Ira Holden, 1027
House, Nelson Charles, 4409
Houser, Jack Kay, 3989
Houston, Frank Matt, 4097
Houston, Harold A., 2360
Houston, Henry Howard, 0371
Houston, Samuel Frederic, 0372

178 Member Index

Howard, Allen Rider, 3342
Howard, Ernest, 0183
Howard, Ezra Elkanah, 1441
Howard, George S., 2139
Howard, Harrison Sabin, 2688
Howard, Joshua Harrison, 3310
Howard, Morton, 2066
Howard, Morton, III, 2687
Howard, Robert Morton, 3170
Howard, Sabin Gilardi, 3473
Howard, Stanley Lewis, 4027
Howard, William Hanson, 0571
Howcott, Harley Butler, Jr., 4340
Howe, Henry Smith, 0026
Howell, David Neil, 4303
Howell, Douglas Lamar, 4362
Howell, Hampton Person, Jr., 4518
Howell, Kenneth Lamar, 4221
Howell, Ronald Jay, 4293
Hoyt, Henry Martyn, 0058
Hubbard, William Jackson, 4092
Huckel, William Gulager, 1205
Huddleson, James Howard, 1142
Hudson, Carlton Lee, 2627
Hudson, William Romuald, 3783
Huey, Malcolm S., 2147
Huffmaster, H. Taylor, 0892
Huffmaster, Isaiah Hayman, 0891
Huffmaster, James Taylor, 0804
Hughes, Adrian, 1513
Hughes, Carroll W., Jr., 2275
Hughes, Harry A. D., 2028
Hughes, Henry Douglas, 0132
Hughes, James Lewis, Jr., 3496
Hughes, John Francis, II, 2027
Hughes, Pierre Auguste, 2809
Hull, William, 0702
Hulse, John Innerarity, III, 2594
Hulse, William Brinkett, 0427
Hume, Edgar Erskine, 1128
Hume, Edgar Erskine, Jr., 1870
Hume, William Haywood, 4193
Humes, James Calhoun, 3540
Humrichouse, Christopher Peter, 3305
Humrichouse, James Walker, 3301
Humrichouse, Richard Huse, 3304
Hunt, Adelbert Bancroft, 0697
Hunt, Brandon Noble, 1551
Huntington, Frederick W., 2812
Hurd, Joy Seth, 1898

Hurd, Rukard, 0319
Huson, Hobart, 1349
Huson, Hobart, II, 1985
Hutchins, Arthur Briley, 0813
Hutchins, Charles Lewis, 0816
Hutchins, Daniel Voshell, 0819
Hutchins, James Anderson, 0818
Hutchins, Nathan Harrington, 0808
Hutchins, William Voshell, 0821
Hutchinson, William Brown, 2556
Hutchison, Joseph P., 1411
Hutchison, Rollo Ewing, 2645
Hyams, Robert Portis, Jr., 2834
Hyde, Edward Duncan, 2078
Hyde, Frank Charles, 0619
Hyde, James Clarence, 0521
Hyde, L. Kaye, 3784
Hyde, Raymond Newton, 0522
Hyer, Stanley Earl, 4314
Hyland, James, 0014
Hymel, Gene Joseph, 3792
Hynes, Lee Powers, 3228
Iglehart, James Davidson, 0395
Ijams, George E., Jr., 2291
Ijams, George Edwin, 1887
Ingram, Finis S., 1111
Ingram, Oscar Finis, Jr., 3975
Inloes, Joseph Howard, 3272
Irion, Valentine, 2519
Irvine, William Burriss, III, 4520
Irwin, Charles Megee, 1478
Isaacson, H. Harding, 3207
Ives, Francis Joseph, 0405
Ivy, Robert Eugene, 2869
Jack, Charles Harold, Jr., 3762
Jackson, Alfred Baury, 0317
Jackson, Charles B., 0116
Jackson, John Collins, 1561
Jackson, John Davies, Jr., 4294
Jackson, William B., Jr., 2312
Jackson, William Benjamin, 3rd., 3775
Jackson, Wm. Benjamin, Sr., 1593
Jacob, Julian H., 2188
Jacobs, Charles Robinson, Jr., 3264
James, Carlton, 1328
James, George Frank, 0348
James, John Faraday, 0479
Jamison, John Jay, 3634
Janeway, Augustine S., 3131
Janney, Mahlon Hopkins, 1841

Member Index 179

Jarves, Deming, 0538
Jaycox, Warren Cecil, 3439
Jayne, John Kennon, 2542
Jelke, John Faris, Jr., 1388
Jenkins, Arthur Darwin, 2879
Jenkins, Benjamin Wheeler, 1198
Jenkins, Edward Austin, 0614
Jenkins, Edward Felix, 2965
Jenkins, Eugene Augustine, Jr., 4113
Jenkins, Francis deSales, 0613
Jenkins, Jack Simmons, 4342
Jenkins, Michael, 1164
Jenner, William Trayton, 3606
Jenness, Herbert Leon, 1867
Jeter, Robert Mobley, 3742
Jett, Robert Samuel, Jr., 3274
Jewett, Charles Timothy, 1296
Jobson, Robert Clifford, 4432
Johness, Allen Henry, Jr., 3106
Johnson, Alfred B., 0050
Johnson, Andrew M., 3038
Johnson, Andrew R., Jr., 2375
Johnson, Boone Van Horn, 1541
Johnson, Charles Owen, 2447
Johnson, Forrest Clark, III, 4225
Johnson, Hardwick Smith, Jr., 4438
Johnson, Harvey, 0232
Johnson, James Bowen, 0547
Johnson, James Bowen, 0559
Johnson, John C., 0004
Johnson, Joseph Taber, 0704
Johnson, Lucius Warren, 1005
Johnson, Robert L., 3126
Johnson, Ross Byron, 3976
Johnston, Charles Calvin, 0461
Johnston, Henry Poellnitz, 2881
Johnston, Hugh Buckner, 3556
Johnston, John Alexander, 0654
Johnston, John Walter, 3852
Johnston, Lee Ralston, 0460
Johnston, Otis C., III, 4380
Johnston, Otis C., Jr., 4324
Jones, Albert Sydney, 0720
Jones, Alvin Edward, 4109
Jones, Bartlett Braxton, 3275
Jones, Bernard Gerald, Jr., 4015
Jones, Cereno St. Clair, 3869
Jones, Charles M., 2117
Jones, Constant Eakin, 0831
Jones, David John, 4239
Jones, Edward Graham, III, 3771

Jones, Edward Graham, Jr., 3549
Jones, Felix Henley, Jr., 4421
Jones, Hugh Burgess, 0402
Jones, J. Davis, 2116
Jones, James Thomas, Jr., 4624
Jones, John Hallberg, 4076
Jones, Joseph Merrick, 2586
Jones, Nathan Henry, 0592
Jones, Richmond Legh, 0257
Jones, Robert Copeland, 1702
Jones, Robert Copeland, Jr., 2643
Jones, Robert Randolph, 2909
Jones, Stockton White, 0451
Jones, Stockton White, 1425
Jones, W. H., 0708
Jones, William, 1722
Jordan, Colon Earl, Sr., 4538
Jordan, Horace Richard, 4235
Jordan, Scott, 0412
Jordon, Charles Philander, 0964
Jordon, Joseph Martin, 3944
Jordon, William Meserve, 0512
Joseph, Rupert Laurens, 1663
Joy, Leslie Wells, 1330
Joy, William Francis, 0604
Judice, Robert Charles, 3981
Judson, William Pierson, 0798
Kaufman, John Williams, 0947
Kay, Wm. DeYoung, 1193
Kaylor, Adrian Roy, 1068
Kearns, John Taylor Stark, 3992
Keen, George Benson, 2651
Keen, Gregory Bernard, 0280
Kehew, Nox McCain, 1927
Keim, Beverley Randolph, 0201
Keim, DeBenneville Randolph, 0679
Keim, George deBenneville, 0957
Keith, Arthur Leslie, 1471
Keith, Solomon Lorin, 0749
Keller, George Troxell, 1812
Kellogg, George Casper, 1007
Kellogg, Thomas Richards, 4240
Kellum, Mervyn J., Jr., 4598
Kellum, Mervyn J., Sr., 4567
Kelly, Irving Washington, 1251
Kelly, John Alexander, 1813
Kelly, Luther Sage, 0653
Kelly, William Dunham, 0636
Kemmerly, Carl Edward, III, 3837
Kemmerly, Kenneth Wright, 3563
Kemp, Edwin Faxon, 1066

Member Index

Kemp, George Washington, 1859
Kemp, Isaac, 1073
Kemp, Theodore Halsey, 1858
Kendall, Messmore, 1899
Kendrick, Marvin Hayne, 3368
Kenly, William Watkins, 0924
Kennedy, Charles M., 3655
Kennedy, Francis Sudlow, 0782
Kennedy, Russell Vance, 3653
Kennison, Richard Adrian, 4327
Kent, Lawrence, 3853
Kenyon, Howard N., Jr., 2358
Kenyon, Howard Nathaniel, 1778
Kenyon, Nathaniel C., 2357
Keogh, Chester Henry, 1386
Keogh, Lawrence Knapp, 2779
Kephart, Calvin Ira, 2958
Kepler, Christopher A., 3529
Keplinger, John Bernard, 0489
Kern, Charles Everett, 1282
Kern, Ralph Donald, 1803
Ketcham, John Lewis, 1900
Keys, Alexander Brooks, 0107
Kidder, George Sherman, 1014
Kielman, L. E., 4587
Kiersted, Andrew Jackson, 0684
Kileski, Frederic G., 2001
Kilgore, Robert Annis, 4552
Killian, Michael John, 4269
King, Arthur Mansfield, 3955
King, Charles Alfred Ely, 0596
King, Charles Daly, 2717
King, Clifford Alonzo, III, 2463
King, Frederic D., III, 3008
King, John Walden, 1234
King, Joseph Choate, 2052
Kinsey, John Ingham, 1705
Kirk, Charles Gilbert, 2049
Kirk, Pierre leMercier-duQuesnay, 3383
Kirkland, David Lynn, 4560
Kirkland, Leonard Wade, 4559
Kirkman, George Wyckerly, 0725
Kitchel, Robert S., Jr., 3524
Klinefelter, Arthur, 2982
Klinefelter, George Young, 2558
Klock, George Ferdinand, 0915
Kloman, Antony Joseph Trapnell, 3691
Klugh, Paul Brown, 1853
Klumb, Robert Michael, 4468
Klunk, Louis William, 1368
Knadler, Robert Warren, 2979
Knapp, Alfred Averill, 3094
Kneass, Carl Magee, 1579
Knight, Franklin Comly, 0880
Knight, Frederick H., 2272
Knight, Frederick H., 3rd., 2648
Knight, George Stephens, 4267
Knight, John Thornton, Jr., 3380
Knight, Monte Hugh, 3486
Knight, William Chapman, 3583
Knott, Aloysius Leo, 0649
Knowlton, Clarence Hinckley, 1253
Knox, John, 2251
Kock, Edouard James, 2428
Kock, Edouard James, Jr., 2472
Koenig, John Lance, 3627
Kohler, Frederic Dudley, 1943
Kolb, Charles Edward Mealey, 4004
Kolb, David W., 2346
Kolb, David William, VI, 4114
Kolb, Stanley D., Jr., 2343
Kolb, Stanley Denmead, 2208
Kollock, David Hall, III, 4440
Kollock, David Peter, 4549
Kollock, George Tams, 4550
Koontz, Amos R., 2669
Koontz, James W., II, 2729
Kopp, Heber C., 2261
Krais, Frederick Vernon, Jr., 3209
Kramer, Albert Ludlow, Jr., 1709
Kramer, Leighton, 1662
Kraner, Albert Ludlow, 1127
Kratovil, Cortlandt Otto, 2902
Kress, Claude Washington, 1658
Kress, Palmer John, 1659
Kruemcke, Max Randolph, Jr., 4101
Kuper, William Henry, 1744
Kurth, Robert Lee, 4085
Kurth, Robert Lee, Jr., 4394
Kurth, Roy Collins, 4412
Kyle, Walter James, Jr., 2940
LaBarre, Pierre Francois, 2526
LaCour, Arthur Burton, Jr., 2502
LaCour, Charles Maginnis, 2515
LaMont, Harvey Murray, 0872
Labry, Lyman Martin, 3866
Labry, Robert Alexander, 3410
Labry, Robert Stone, 2932
Lafargue, Fleury L. E., 2839
Lafaye, Albert Emory, 2512

Member Index 181

Lafaye, Albert Emory, Jr., 2762
Lafaye, Edward Emory, II, 2513
Laird, James Douglas, 4334
Lake, James Hammond, 2595
Lake, Richard Pinkney, 0792
Lakee, Eugene, 0541
Lallande, Joseph, 2411
Lallande, Sumter Louis, 2830
Lamb, Scott Grisell, 1944
Lamping, William, 0333
Lanahan, William Wallace, 1594
Landon, Herman Robert, 1799
Landry, Arthur F., 3758
Landry, Robert Broussard, Jr., 4208
Landry, Stuart Omer, 2890
Landstreet, John, 0950
Lane, Charles H., 3147
Lane, Garrison Fairfield, 4459
Lane, John Robert, Jr., 4537
Langhorne, Charles McIndoe, 0963
Langworthy, John Alan, 4607
Lankford, David Skelton, 4321
Lapeyre, Andre Charles, 2489
Lapeyre, Felix Henri, 2490
Lapeyre, Felix Henri, Jr., 3387
Lapeyre, Fernand Stephen, 2616
Lapeyre, James Martial, 3413
Lapeyre, Paul Martial, 3320
Lardner, James Lawrence, 0699
Larkin, Hanford William, 1763
Larkin, Orrell Town, 0595
Larue, Ferdinand deVesine, 2930
Lastrapes, Edwin P., 2393
Lattimer, John Kingsley, 3270
Laubenstein, Ezekias, 0493
Lauck, Gerold McKee, 3284
Laughlin, Henry Prather, 4645
Laughter, William Hunt, 0293
Lawrence, Frederick Kendall, 0834
Lay, Kenneth Edward, Sr., 4385
Lay, William, 1226
Le Gardeur, Rene Joseph, 2488
LeBlanc, Clyde Joseph, 2999
LeCorgne, Robert Edgar, Jr., 2449
LeDoux, Marion John, 3408
LeMar, Harold Diehl, 1979
LeMar, William B., 2233
Leary, Peter, Jr., 0685
Leary, Rudolph Williams, 1538
Leber, Henry Hoke, 3336
Lebeuf, George Louis, 3764

Lee, Edward Clinton, 0267
Lee, Howard Hall Macy, 0430
Lee, Leander R., 2260
Lee, William Justice, Jr., 4393
Leeming, Leonard B., 2348
Leete, Frederick Deland, 1685
Legett, Thomas Riley, Jr., 3847
Legier, John Robert, 2419
Legrand, Edmond G. J., 2675
Legrand, Georges Marie, 3753
Legrand, Paul Marie, 2832
Lehde, Pendleton Emile, 2742
Lehmann, Brent Dawson, 3026
Lehmann, Leslie Sexton, 2790
Lehmann, Wallace Kemp, 2851
Leidy, Philip, 0153
Leland, Amory, 1126
Leland, Charles Thurman, 1485
Leland, Edmund Francis, 1108
Lemley, Kenneth McRae, 4217
Lemmons, Thomas, 3997
Lenore, Clifford, 0991
Leonard, Laurence, 1800
Lescure, William J., 3rd., 3099
Lessig, Brooke Montgomery, 3236
Letford, William, 2906
Levis, Frederick Hemsley, 3193
Levy, Jefferson Monroe, 1050
Lewis, Albert Nelson, 0112
Lewis, Clifford, 3rd., 2777
Lewis, Edward McElhiney, 1565
Lewis, George Harlan, 1409
Lewis, James Dean, 4197
Lewis, Richard Brainard, 1604
Libby, Henry Mortimer, 1626
Liebmann, August George, 1751
Ligget, Robert Charles, 1929
Lillard, Gerald F., 2280
Lilley, John Thomas, Jr., 4067
Lilly, John, 0893
Limmer, Early Alva, Jr., 4579
Lincoln, Percy Marsh, Jr., 4563
Lincoln, Thomas Albert, 4597
Lindesmith, Eli Eashington, 0214
Linfield, Robert Paine, 2507
Linnard, George Brown, 0958
Linthicum, George E., III, 3088
Linthicum, George Milton, 1808
Linthicum, John Charles, 1765
Linthicum, Sweetser, 4040
Linville, Charles Hardesty, 1180

182 Member Index

Lipscomb, Thomas H., III, 4252
Litchfield, Wilbur Jacob, 1099
Little, Augustine Patterson, III, 4363
Little, Melvin Weaver, 4074
Litts, Raymond N. J., 2030
Livaudais, Alfred Friedrichs, 3373
Livaudais, Herbert S., 3189
Livaudais, Jacques A., 3069
Livingston, Darby Gary, 3780
Lloyd, James P., 2141
Lloyd, Malcolm, Jr., 2217
Lloyd, Mark Frazier, 4416
Lloyd, William Henry, 1960
Lobdell, Edward John, 1508
Lockhart, Jacob Trumbull, 0620
Lockwood, Randolph Scott Dewey, 4133
Logan, Harry Craig, 1970
Loker, David Cartan, Jr., 2536
Loker, Lawrence Lorenzo, 4397
London, George Abraham, 4050
London, Richard Carrol, 4049
Long, Charles Colfax, 1752
Long, Charles R., 2003
Long, Edgar Hall, 2476
Long, Frank McDowell, Jr., 4433
Long, Harry Clarence, 4527
Long, James Hall, 1774
Long, Oscar Fitzalan, 0033
Long, Samuel Burkett, 0184
Long, Wm. Frederick, 0180
Longfellow, James Griffith, 0809
Loose, John Ward Willson, 2619
Lord, Calvin, 0907
Lord, Frank Howard, 1576
Lord, William Adgate, 1790
Lord, Wm. Adgate, Jr., 1837
Lorton, Alfred Hathaway, 0902
Lott, James Filmore, 1119
Loucks, Charles Ernest, 3928
Loucks, Frank Horace, 1283
Love, Homer Townsend, Jr., 4000
Lovejoy, Charles Douglas, 3891
Lowe, Bromley Wharton, 3619
Lowe, John Williamson, 1048
Lowell, James Russell, 2991
Lowry, Nathan Parks, 0204
Lowry, Robert Kelly, 0210
Luckett, Robert L., 3085
Luckie, Robert Ervin, Jr., 3558

Ludington, Marshall Independence Day, 0005
Lumberson, John (Veteran), 0513
Lunt, William Wallace, 0737
Lutz, Parke H., 2140
Lyman, Charles Burt, 1269
Lyman, Silas Brownson, 0842
Lynch, Charles Clifford, Jr., 4039
Lynch, Charles Clifford, Sr., 4038
Lynch, Cleveland Michel, 2960
Lynde, Francis Engle Patterson, 0867
Lynn, George Gambrill, 4617
Lynn, Henry Sharpe, 3942
Lynn, Henry Sharpe, Jr., 4616
Lyon, John Augustus, 1949
Lyons, George Dewey, Jr., 2666
Lyons, George Dewey, III, 3759
Lyons, James Thomas, 4337
Lyons, Michael Bivens, 3760
Lyons, Robert Ellsworth, 4634
Lyons, Shirley Carlton, 3351
MacArthur, Arthur, 0858
MacArthur, Douglas, 2808
MacCarthy, Howard, Jr., 2670
MacChesney, Nathan Wm., 1018
MacClamroch, James G. W., 2325
MacDonald, John Stuart, 0966
MacDonald, Malcolm, 0143
MacDonough, Rodney, 0530
MacGunnigle, Bruce Campbell, 4420
MacKinley, William E. W., 0197
MacLamroc, Alan Gwaltney Westwarren, 3909
MacLamroc, Brian Gwaltney Westwarren, 3908
Mace, Clarence Eugene, 3148
Macgowan, Bates, Jr., 3101
Machold, Roland Morris, 3196
Machold, William Deas, 3316
Mack, Chester Floyd, Jr., 4462
Mackenzie, George Norbury, 0203
Mackenzie, George Norbury, IV, 1726
Mackenzie, John Moores Maynadier, 1699
Mackey, Harold Kenneth, 4213
MacPherson, Earl, 4639
Macy, Edward Warren, 1622
Magee, John Alexander, 3203.
Magee, Robert Towles, 2510

Maginnis, Donald Ambrose, III, 3500
Maginnis, Donald Ambrose, Jr., 2514
Maginnis, Gordon Hobson, 3372
Maglidt, Henry Wilson, 4356
Magruder, Caleb Clark, Jr., 1218
Mahool, John Barry, 0980
Mahool, John Blatter, 3766
Major, Ralph H., Jr., 2103
Mallary, Nelson Dagg, Jr., 2587
Mallett, Robert Evans, Jr., 4623
Malone, Edwin Scott, III, 2795
Maloney, James Aloysius, 0392
Maltbie, William Henry, 1062
Manchester, Robert Grant, 4599
Manget, Daniel Thomas, Jr., 3391
Manigault, Gabriel E., 0414
Mann, Eugene Turner, Sr., 3258
Mann, Robert Neville, 2955
Manning, Richard Charles, III, 2639
Manrose, Ernest Fitch, 1101
Maples, Glen, 4427
Maraspin, Davis G., 2241
Marbury, Francis Cross, 4358
Marbury, William Henry, 1405
Marine, Madison, 0921
Marine, Richard Elliott, 0920
Marine, William Matthew, 0558
Markle, Augustus Robert, 1674
Markle, Richard Theodore, 1696
Markley, Harvey Curtis, 3205
Markley, Russell Kindig, 2945
Marquez, Edward Leonhard, Jr., 2971
Marr, Robert E. L., 0195
Marr, William Corbin, 3478
Marr, William G., 0194
Marshall, Chesley Brown, 3649
Marshall, John McClellan, 3724
Marston, James Graham, 2730
Marston, John, 0387
Martin Thomas Wesley, 3014
Martin, Christian Hess, 2214
Martin, Daniel Julian, 3436
Martin, Edwin Hulshizer, 1586
Martin, George Kip, 1585
Martin, Harry Culver, 0535
Martin, Joseph A., 3379
Martin, Joseph P., 2299
Martin, Ora Alexander, 2033
Martin, Paul Edmond, 4425
Martin, Reed Ammerman, Jr., 4326

Martin, Reed Ammerman, Sr., 4325
Martin, Richard Massie, 2848
Martin, Wm. Arthur, Jr., 1550
Martz, Ralph Fraley, 3964
Mason, David Pierce, Sr., 4191
Mason, Judson Philip, 3495
Mason, Judson Philip, Jr., 4154
Mason, Theodorus Bailey Myers, 0123
Mason, Theodorus Bailey Myers, 0675
Massey, Edgar Wilson, 2703
Massey, Edward M., 3078
Massey, Frank Hogan, 0465
Massey, Frank Horgan, II, 1757
Massey, Henry Vogdes, 0454
Massey, Jay Richardson, 1758
Massey, Jay Richardson, Jr., 3195
Massey, Maurice Richardson, 1329
Massey, Maurice Richardson, Jr., 1759
Massie, Cecil Miles, Sr., 4494
Matheny, James Robert, 4565
Matheny, Willard Reynolds, 1981
Mathews, William E., 2074
Mathis, Addis, 4455
Matlack, John Rugan, Jr., 0453
Mattern, Edwin Lafayette, 1792
Matthew, William McGowan, 3542
Matthews, Harry Z., 3222
Matthews, James Alonzo, 1564
Maught, Adrien Andrew, 2426
Maxwell, James Edward, 3793
Maxwell, Murvan Morris, 3589
Maynadier, Thomas Murray, 1054
McAlpin, Charles Walter, 1679
McAlpin, Milo Frederick, 1678
McAlpine, Roderick K., 2195
McAlpine, Roderick K., Jr., 2196
McArthur, Donald Joseph, 4377
McBee, Charles Douglas, Jr., 4615
McBee, Charles Douglas, Sr., 4278
McBride, Robert Martin, 3130
McCain, Donald Rockefeller, 1033
McCain, Donald Rockefeller, Jr., 1928
McCain, George Nox, 0537
McCandless, Robert Boyd, 4499
McCandless, Stanley Kaar, 4516
McCandless, Tracy Conrad, 4533

184 Member Index

McCandless, William Howard, III, 3433
McCarthy, Harold LeRoy, 3937
McCarthy, Matthew Wesley, 3936
McCarty, Stewart Boone, Jr., 3878
McCauley, Bishop, 3039
McCauley, Edwin Douglas, 2631
McCaw, John Todd, 3255
McClain, Frank M., Jr., 3146
McClanahan, James Frederick, 4021
McClellan, John, 0163
McClinton, James Selby, Jr., 3165
McCloskey, Patrick John, 2699
McCloskey, Walter Stauffer, 2819
McCluer, Paul B., 3006
McCoin, Donald Douglas, 4270
McCoin, Edgar Royce, 4290
McColgan, Edward, 1595
McColley, Sutherland, 4457
McComas, Henry Angle, 1075
McComas, Henry Clay, 2209
McComas, Joseph Patton, 1393
McCone, Percy Vere, 3822
McConnell, James Thomas, 3592
McCord, James Hamilton, 0727
McCormack, Benny Hale, 4157
McCormick, Robert Laird, 0449
McCormick, W. Laird, 0726
McCowan, Robert Joseph Foster, 1258
McCracken, Robert T., 2327
McCreery, Samuel, 2005
McCreery, Samuel, Jr., 2022
McCulloch, Champe Carter, Jr., 0525
McCulloch, Robert Lemmon, 0565
McCullough, Robert A., 0673
McCurdy, Irwin Pounds, 0633
McCurley, Felix, 0251
McCurley, James Bernard, Jr., 3830
McCurley, James Wallace, 0252
McCurley, William Stran, 1766
McDonald, Francis Goodall, 4506
McDonald, Isaiah Heylin, 0828
McDonald, Kenneth Madison, 2829
McDonald, Walter Smith, 3259
McDonald, William Bartholow, 0946
McDonnell, Austin McCarthy, 1132
McDowell, Ralph Walker, 1029
McDowell, William Osborne, 0031
McFadden, A. Weems, 4201
McGarry, Wm. Rutledge, 1764

McGaw, George Keen, 1107
McGuire, E. Thomas, 3574
McIntire, Alexander R., 2170
McIntire, Allyn Brewster, 2201
McIntire, Edward Harding, 1996
McIntosh, William, III, 3801
McIntyre, Allan Fellows, 1196
McKelvey, William James, 0642
McKendrick, Charles Stuart, III, 4375
McKinley, Gerald A., 2235
McKinnell, William Wendell Bollman, 1607
McKinney, Harry Ellery, 3477
McLaughlin, Marcellus Hood, 3rd., 3737
McLaughlin, Marcellus Hood, Jr., 3700
McLellan, Hugh, 1061
McLellan, Malcolm Nye, 1262
McLeod, Kenneth, Jr., 3075
McMaster, Fitzhugh, 2920
McMaster, George Hunter, 0576
McMaster, Richard K., 3083
McMichael, Cyrus, 2036
McMullin, Nelson VanBuskirk, 1359
McMullin, William Craig, 3871
McNair, Hugh, 1785
McNair, James Birtley, 1577
McNair, Thomas Speer, 0237
McNamee, Charles, 1207
McNeal, Joshua Vansant, 0693
McQuilling, Andrew Thomas, III, 3845
McShea, Walter Ross, 1356
Mead, James Russell, Jr., 4243
Meade, Thomas W., 2228
Means, Edward Barnwell, 2465
Means, Walker Wilson, 3100
Mears, Adelbert Warren, 1636
Mears, Christian Emmerich, 1637
Medairy, Bernard J., Jr., 3162
Medairy, Bernard John, 3204
Medairy, George Roberts, 0239
Medairy, Jacob Henry, 0247
Meek, Louis Frank, III, 4153
Megaw, Fred Holmes, 0784
Meigs, Henry Benjamin, 0877
Melancon, Paul Mire, 3877
Melancon, Paul Mire, Jr., 4596
Melching, Don A., 4152

Mellen, William Henshaw, 2824
Melvin, Frank W., 2189
Merchant, Henry Preston, 3977
Mercur, James Watts, 0447
Mercur, James Watts, Jr., 1941
Mercur, Rodney Augustus, 0287
Meroney, Charles Murray, 4553
Meroney, William Albert, 4509
Merrell, Richard I., 1318
Merrikin, David Welles, 0177
Merrill, Charles Warren, 0909
Merrill, George Grenville, 3455
Merrill, John Lenord, 1204
Merritt, James Black, III, 0925
Merritt, James Miller, 3278
Merseles, Frank H., Jr., 2295
Merseles, Frank Hornblower, 1522
Merwin, Walter Lee, 0309
Merwin, William Walters, 1947
Messick, Andrew Stewart, 2438
Metcalf, Charles Henry, 1343
Metcalf, Willis Charles, 1004
Metcalfe, Clinton James, 0881
Metcalfe, John Elias, 0852
Mettee, Bradley T. J., Jr., 4291
Metts, Albert Caswell, Jr., 4181
Metz, Craig Huseman, 4125
Metz, Donald Leroy, 4119
Metz, Robert E. L., 2061
Metzger, Fred J., 3480
Metzger, Howard Allison, 3640
Meyer, Harold Irving, 1784
Meyer, Paul Rogers, 3081
Meyer, Robert Brooks, 3213
Mhoon, Robert Brinkley, III, 4262
Michel, Edouard Jules, 2876
Michel, Robert Emory, 3138
Michinard, George S., 2528
Michinard, George S., Jr., 3535
Middendorf, John William, Jr., 2554
Middlebrook, Louis Frank, 0988
Middleton, Arthur Pierce, 4497
Miffling, James, 0490
Miles, Benjamin Cottman, 1614
Miles, Joseph Starne, 1615
Miles, Rowland, 1379
Miller, Burke Hammond, 1919
Miller, Charles Robert, 1539
Miller, Clair LeMoine, 1689
Miller, Elmer Pliny, 0984
Miller, Harry E., 2243

Miller, James Francis, 3115
Miller, John Henry, 1095
Miller, Lewis H., 0010
Miller, Philip Schuyler, 1358
Miller, Sylvester Barton, 0591
Millholland, Geroge Harrison, 3399
Millholland, James H., 2158
Mills, Ezekiel Jr., 0182
Mills, George Albert, 0192
Mills, Rowland Yearley, 1341
Mills, Stephen Crosby, 0147
Milton, Walter Scott, 3888
Miner, Sidney Roby, 0407
Ming, Robert Sterling, 4594
Ming, William Lee, 4244
Minge, Jackson C., Jr., 3055
Mitchell, Frank Paull, Jr., 3770
Mitchell, Phillip Michael, 4171
Mitchell, Robert Levis, 1456
Mitchell, William A., 2213
Mix, Richard Lawrence, 4551
Moale, John Foster, Jr., 3445
Moale, John Gray Foster, 2791
Mobley, Richard Isaiah, 4590
Mohler, Isaac Wimbert, Jr., 1178
Monnette, Orra Eugene, 1117
Monroe, Francis Adair, 2437
Monroe, Malcolm Logan, 2568
Monsted, Charles Niels, Jr., 3330
Montgomery, Eugene Miller, 1197
Montgomery, Hugh E., 2064
Montgomery, Shelley Hoskins, 1306
Montgomery, Thomas Lynch, 1660
Montgomery, William J., III, 2576
Moody, Alfred Alric, 1988
Moore, Albert Wilson Luce, Jr., 3817
Moore, Allen Wendell, 4569
Moore, Arthur Allison, 1212
Moore, Beverly Polk, 3963
Moore, Christopher Polk, 3966
Moore, Clifford Charles, 4156
Moore, Daniel McFarlan, 1255
Moore, Gardere Francis, 2931
Moore, George Albert, 3386
Moore, Harry Thornton, 0092
Moore, Harry Thornton, 1340
Moore, Henderson A., Jr., 2362
Moore, Henry Virginius, 1825
Moore, Howard Shackleford, 3577
Moore, Jasper Lewis, 4531
Moore, Jerry Edward, 3626

186 Member Index

Moore, John L., 4402
Moore, John W., 0079
Moore, Malcolm, 1237
Moore, Myron Foster, 1300
Moore, Pierre Albert, 2326
Moorhead, Robert G., 2268
Moorhead, Robert L., 2193
Morehouse, Elnathan Paul, Jr., 4632
Morgan, Appleton, 0060
Morgan, Charles Boyd, 3788
Morgan, Charles Lemon, 1912
Morgan, Daniel Taylor, 1016
Morgan, George Edward, 1686
Morgan, James Henry, 0105
Morgan, John Hurst, 0425
Morgan, Philip Sidney, 1826
Moriarty, George Andrews, Jr., 1747
Morley, Charles Sheriff, 1457
Morling, Frank L., 0176
Morrell, Edward deVeaux, 0419
Morris, Albert Tingley, 3934
Morris, Benjamin Hume, 4142
Morris, Benjamin Hume, II, 4472
Morris, Charles Edward, 4094
Morris, Elliston Joseph, Jr., 1894
Morris, Galloway Cheston, 0303
Morris, John Delashmutt, 2864
Morris, Joseph Paul, Jr., 4124
Morris, Lawrence Johnson, 1832
Morrison, Benjamin Olivier, 2908
Morrison, DeLesseps Story, 2937
Morrow, James William, 1278
Morse, Richard C., 2264
Morse, Richard C., Jr., 2335
Morse, Ruel Adel-Verne, 4512
Moseley-Clarke, Thomas Stevenson, 3678
Moss, Clive Arthur, 3116
Mossburg, George Washington, 4641
Mott, George H., 2677
Moulton, George Mayhew, 1374
Mountain, William, 0916
Mounts, Dennis Eugene, 4047
Moyer, Nevin Wilberforce, 0953
Moyer, R. Kirk, 2527
Moylan, Chalres E., Jr., 3128
Muhlenberg, Francis Benjamin, 0138
Muhlenberg, Frank Peter, 1248
Mulholland, Roye Artice, 2912
Mullen, Patrick Walter, 4245
Munnikhuysen, John Bryarly, 3389

Munson, Marvin Morgan, 0462
Murphey, Elijah Warriner, 0647
Murphey, Walter B. W., 3438
Murphy, Herschel Stratton, 2788
Murphy, Philip Julian, 4511
Murray, Charles Henry, 0055
Murray, James Anderson, V, 3219
Murray, Samuel Lynn, 4312
Musser, Earl Beachy, 1973
Myers, Joseph A., 0305
Myers, Philip, 1886
Myers, Philip, III, 2298
Myrick, Victor Ray, 3743
Mysing, August W., Jr., 3564
Napier, John H., III, 3121
Nash, Charles Wesley, 0216
Nash, Edward Francis, 3492
Nass, Walter Pool, Jr., 4418
Naylor, Emmett Hay, 1106
Needham, Charles Willis, 0884
Needham, George Fisk, 3rd., 4096
Neeper, Creed Arbuthnott, 3202
Neilson, George Peabody, 0772
Neilson, Robert Musgrave, 0692
Nellis, William Jacob, 0845
Nelson, Richard Douglas, 1844
Nelson, William Jones, Jr., 2921
Nelson, William Wallace, 0468
Nesbit, Harry Van Tyle, 1301
Nevers, Edward, 0623
Nevin, Edwin Channing, 1357
Nevius, Arthur Seymour, 1272
Newcomb, Fred Norman, 4079
Newell, Edward Harvey, 1013
Newell, John Davis, 4492
Newell, Louis Henry Field, 1401
Newell, William Clayton, 0830
Newkirk, Eugene, 1587
Newman, George Frederick, 3921
Newman, Harry Wright, 2626
Newton, Sanford Hamilton, 1249
Nicaud, Frederick Harvey, 2900
Nicholls, Thomas C., Jr., 2400
Nichols, George Frederick, 0242
Nichols, Henry Kuhl, 0241
Nichols, James Allen, 0786
Nichols, Marvin Curtis, 2807
Nichols, Maury, 0029
Nichols, Thomas Brainerd, 0597
Nichols, Willard Atherton, 0885
Nicholson, Bruce Howland, 4601

Nicoll, Benjamin Brevard, 0189
Noble, Clyde E., Jr., 3802
Noble, Henry Harmon, 0520
Noble, John Harmon, 1059
Noel, Jacob Edmond, 0560
Nolte, Lawrence W., 3271
Norrid, Henry Gail, 4479
Norrid, Henry Horatio, 4451
Norris, Abell A., Jr., 3071
Norris, Alex Wilson, 0367
Norris, Clayton, 4236
Norris, James Biscoe, II, 2604
Norris, Thomas Lloyd, 4215
Norris, Thomas Lloyd, Jr., 4190
Norton, Richard Pearson, 1805
Norton, Thomas Herbert, 0504
Norwood, Randolph, 0302
Nott, George W., 2396
Noyes, Charles Phelps, 0326
Noyes, James Atkins, 0325
Nye, Bartlett, 1060
Nye, Cornelius (Veteran), 0354
O'Bryant, Alan Melvin, 3677
O'Dell, Theron Jerome, 3834
O'Hara, V. Winthrop, 2668
O'Neal, Moncure Camper, 2862
O'Neal, Moncure Camper, Jr., 4009
O'Neil, James Francis, Jr., 3794
O'Neill, Charles Frank, 0450
O'Neill, Hugh Lewis, 0410
O'Neill, James Busick, 0386
O'Neill, James Wilkes, 0089
Obertenffer, Herman Freytag, 0767
Obertenffer, Reece Marriner, 0766
Offutt, Thomas Worthington, 1700
Ogden, Henry D., 2377
Ogden, Henry Duplessis, IV, 4029
Oliver, Charles Augustus, 0318
Oliver, Curtis John, 4155
Oliver, Henry Addison, 1881
Oliver, Norris Schermerhorn, 2994
Olivier, Felix LaRue, 2433
Olivier, Henry John, Jr., 4279
Olivier, Pierre De V., Jr., 2538
Omer, Lewis, 1298
Orcutt, Harry P., 2227
Orcutt, Husdon Earl, 1417
Ord, Edward. O. C., 0196
Ordway, Albert James, 3525
Ordway, Frederick Ira, III, 3124
Ordway, Frederick Ira, Jr., 2904
Ordway, Richard Shannon, 2754
Orebaugh, David Alvin, 1472
Orem, John Henry, Jr., 1086
Orrick, Metcalf, 2901
Orton, George Soliday, 4228
Orton, Thomas Graves, 4233
Orton, William Rutledge, II, 4232
Orvis, Arthur Emerton, 1917
Orvis, Edwin Waitstill, 1914
Orvis, Homer Waitstill, 1915
Orvis, Schuyler Adams, 1936
Orvis, Schuyler Adams, Jr., 1937
Orvis, Warner Dayton, 1916
Osborn, Stuart Rae, 1189
Osborne, Horace Bond, 1202
Osborne, Horace Sherman, 1257
Osborne, Lucien Gianella, 4014
Osborne, Robert Vandervoort, 3855
Osborne, Robert Vandervoort, Jr., 4036
Osgood, Everett, 1084
Osterhoudt, Harvey Jay, 1415
Otis, Walter Joseph, 2387
Ottey, Abram Carter Farr, 1760
Otto, John, 0090
Ouellette, Arthur Russell, 2877
Ovenshine, Samuel, 1120
Overington, John, 3633
Overington, Robert Bruce, 2072
Owen, Franklin Buchanan, 1492
Owen, James Jarratt, 4430
Owens, Edward Burneston, 0687
Owens, Edward Burneston, Jr., 1588
Owens, William C., 2290
Oxx, Wm. Garderner, III, 3747
Pabst, Ralph Malcom, 3449
Packard, Ambrose, 0510
Packard, Kent, 1964
Packer, Frank Marcus, 1621
Paddock, Edwin Loveland, 1861
Page, Alfred F., Jr., 3588
Page, Carroll Smalley, 1380
Page, Henry, III, 4488
Page, Proctor Hull, 1384
Page, Thomas Neilson, 2026
Palfrey, Campbell, 2414
Palmer, Frederic Courtland, 2118
Palmer, Harding, 4091
Palmer, Robert Ellis, 2813
Palmer, William Morgan, 1317
Pardee, Ernest Lewis, 4042

188 Member Index

Parham, Duncan de Puech, 3396
Paris, Francklyn Wynne, 4131
Paris, William Francklyn Mercer, II, 4335
Parker, Albert, 2083
Parker, Alvin Mercer, 1214
Parker, Arthur Caswell, 1172
Parker, David Ozro, 4575
Parker, Edward Hegeman, 1006
Parker, Francis Hubert, 1051
Parker, George Turner, 1557
Parker, Herbert C., 2391
Parker, Herbert C., Jr., 2390
Parker, Joseph Brooks Bloodgood, 1215
Parker, Montgomery Davis, 0131
Parker, William Alderman, 2752
Parkhurst, Charles Dyer, 0718
Parkhurst, George Comfort, 1459
Parks, Lorne Clements, 3854
Parlange, Walter Charles, Jr., 2501
Parmenter, Elmer Ellsworth, 1721
Parr, Guy Hudson, 2303
Parr, Guy Hudson, Jr., 2552
Parr, Lee S., 2317
Parrish, James Hagerty, 0383
Parrish, Roy Thomas, 3493
Parrish, William F., 3129
Parrish, William Tippett, 0384
Parry, Richard, 3060
Parshall, Alfred Glen, 4248
Parsly, Elmer G., 3049
Parsly, Lewis Fuller, 4572
Parsons, Charles Sumner, 0677
Partlow, Thomas E., 3621
Parvis, William Thomas, 0815
Pascal, Gabriel Louis, 2887
Patchett, Henry Powell, 2692
Patrick, Lee Wellington, 4143
Patterson, Denis W., 4033
Patterson, Donald Gene, 4606
Patterson, James Otey, 1965
Patterson, Philip Cooper, 4126
Patterson, Robert, 0523
Patterson, Wm. Houston, 0495
Pattison, Hal Cushman, 3993
Paulding, Charles Henry, 0064
Paulding, Tattnall, 0256
Paxton, Richard Gentry, 4378
Payne, Charles Rockwell, 0803
Payne, Daniel Safford French, 0640

Payne, Harry Francis, 1260
Peak, Cassius S., 2076
Peak, Paul Reed, Jr., 4626
Peak, Roger Worley, 4630
Peale, Augustin Runyon, Jr., 0886
Pear, Albert Marston, 0790
Pearson, Arthur Emmons, 1098
Pearson, Joseph Hiram Starr, 0437
Pearson, Robert Humphreys, 1546
Pease, Richards Kenneth, 3735
Peck, Carlos Erbine, 2756
Peck, John Ama, 0615
Peck, Paul Noble, 1052
Peck, Robert McCracken, 2811
Peck, Theodore Safford,, 1058
Peck, William Noble, 0641
Peden, Henry Clint, Jr., 4283
Pegram, Roger Miller, 3657
Peice, George, 1667
Peirce, George Fales, 1850
Pendergast, James Lynch, 0781
Pendleton, Edmund, 0445
Pendleton, Neal F., Jr., 2888
Pendleton, Neal Francis, 2738
Pendleton, Reuben Allen, III, 2910
Pendleton, Reuben Allen, Jr., 2933
Pennell, Donald James, 4344
Pennell, George Mather, II, 4619
Pennington, Josias, 1096
Pennypacker, Bevan A., 2057
Pennypacker, Samuel Whitaker, 0255
Penrose, Charles Wilkinson, 0097
Penrose, George Hoffman, 0022
Pentz, Benjamin H., 2081
Pentz, Franklin Eldridge, 0826
Pentz, Harry G., 2079
Pentz, John Angelo, 1884
Pentz, Wm. Fletcher, 0827
Pepper, Edward, 0524
Pepper, Harris Laning Perry, 3814
Peregoy, Frederick C., Jr., 2237
Perkins, Constantine Marrast, 1737
Perkins, George Henry, Jr., 1133
Perkins, Mahlon Fay, 1871
Perret, Edmund James, II, 3499
Perrilliat, Howard A. K., 2457
Perrilliat, William C., 2435
Perry, Herbert J., 2093
Perry, James DeWolf, 1191
Perry, James Dewold, Jr., 1238

Perry, Joseph Frank, 4249
Persell, Ralph Mountjoy, 3533
Petefish, Russell H., 3302
Peters, Winfield, 0404
Peterson, David Howard, 4391
Peterson, Robert C., 2316
Peterson, Robert Karl, 2770
Petro, Kenneth Johnson, 4160
Pettingell, Frank Hervey, 0985
Pettit, Absalom John, 3939
Pewett, Edwin Henkel, Jr., 4642
Phares, Marvin Olcott, 3876
Pharr, Eugene A., Jr., 3043
Phebus, Joseph Scott, 0987
Phifer, Robert Smith, Jr., 0945
Philbrook, Alfred S., 0355
Philbrook, Charles Calhoun, 0347
Philbrook, Charles Frederick Bacon, 0117
Phillips, Charles Alan, 2715
Phillips, George Thomas, 1152
Phillips, George Thomas, 1361
Phillips, Levi Benjamin, 1497
Pickens, Henry, 1904
Pierce, Arthur Johnson, 1769
Pierce, Charles Carroll, 1652
Pierce, George Francis, 0656
Pierce, Richard Donald, 3022
Pierce, Samuel, Jr., 3013
Pierce, William Greene, 1992
Pilgrim, Curtis Merle, 4317
Pilie, Joseph Maurice, 3418
Pilie, Joseph Maurice, Jr., 4535
Pilie, Louis Andrieu, 2529
Pilie, Louis Henry, 2524
Pilie, Martin Arnaud, 3056
Pinac, Andre Louis, Jr., 3912
Pinkerton, Paul Price, 1921
Pinkerton, Samuel Stanhope Smith, 0310
Pinkney, Townsend, 0974
Pinnell, Gary Ray, 4539
Pipes, William Fort, 2486
Pipes, William Fort, Jr., 3502
Pipkin, Robert Worth, 3899
Pirkle, Charles Gaston, 2863
Pitcher, Griffith Fontaine, 2767
Pitcher, William Henry, Jr., 1768
Pitts, Alvin Lane, 4250
Pitts, James Patrick, 4107
Pitts, Neal Chase, 4274

Plaisance, Paul Joseph Avila, Jr., 4311
Plauche, Edouard McCall, 3874
Plauche, Henry, 2406
Plauche, Henry Hester, 2816
Plauche, Henry Hester, Jr., 2935
Plauche, James Joseph, Jr., 2418
Plauche, Paul Sidney, 2936
Plauche, Walter Flower, 2425
Pleasanton, Frank Rodney, 1038
Plummer, Thomas Parran, 1918
Pohl, Clifford Hugo, Jr., 4406
Polk, George Johnston, 4226
Pollock, William Franklin, 2806
Pond, Ashley, 0861
Pond, Levi Sheldon, 0862
Pond, Thomas Temple, 2637
Pond, Walter Hinckley, 1723
Pool, Wellington, 0296
Poore, Benjamin Andrew, 0161
Poorman, S. Sturgis, 3238
Poorman, S. Sturgis, Jr., 3239
Pope, James Worden, 0091
Pope, Joe Delwin, 4507
Porter, Augustus Drum, 0768
Porter, David Dixon, 1821
Porter, John Biddle, 0109
Porter, Robert Lee, Jr., 1666
Posey, Henry Tharp, 2441
Posey, Robert Michael, 4360
Potter, Thomas, Jr., 0225
Potter, William, 0198
Potts, Ewell Cardwell, Jr., 3659
Potts, Thomas Alva, 2693
Povenmire, Harlo Monroe, 1814
Powell, David Wayne, 4296
Powell, Harold Frederic, 4414
Powell, Washington Bleddyn, 1031
Power, John Leonard, 1503
Power, Martin John, 1307
Powers, Robert Benjamin, 3143
Prados, Wilfred Olivier, 3779
Prather, George Woodrow, 3907
Prather, William Roy, 3736
Pratt, Gerald O'Connor, 2412
Pratt, Robert Armstrong, 3290
Pratt, Walter Merriam, 1630
Prejean, Edward Joseph, Jr., 4466
Prentiss, William, 1103
Prewitt, John Marshall, 4206
Price, Donald Lee, 4643

Member Index

Price, Paul Patrick, 4556
Primrose, Samuel Fletcher, 0178
Prince, Levi Bradford, 0871
Printz, Charles Francis, 4229
Printz, Charles Francis, Jr., 4230
Pritchard, Arthur John, 1049
Privett, William K., 3061
Provosty, Michel Becnel, 2480
Provosty, Michel Olivier, 2458
Pryor, John Gatwood, 4169
Pryor, Robert Lee, 4366
Pryor, Robert McBride, Jr., 4305
Pryor, William Adams, III, 4306
Pryor, William Adams, III, 4365
Pryor, William Brand, 3454
Pryor, William Young, 2671
Pugh, Alexander Lefever, Jr., 1549
Pugh, Henry Donne, 1854
Pugh, William N. S., Jr., 3446
Pugh, William Nussear S., 2997
Puig, Felix Joseph, 2495
Purdy, Thomas L., Jr., 2989
Purkhiser, Edward Grant, 1115
Quackenbos, Henry Forest, 1210
Quackenbush, Claire Courtney, 0959
Quarles, Julian Minor, Jr., 4174
Querens, Allan Eustis, 2987
Querens, Percy Lennard, 2970
Quin, Everett Michael, 2974
Raborg, Edward Livingston, II, 1221
Radford, Harry Vincent, 0859
Ragland, Robert Allen, 4177
Rambo, Bertram Pierre, 1977
Rambo, Ormond, Jr., 1815
Ramond, Charles Knight, 3191
Ramsey, Carl Allan, 4089
Rand, Waldron Holmes, Jr., 1852
Randall, Giles Deshon, 3367
Randall, John LeMoyne, 4115
Randall, Watson Beale, 0398
Rankin, John Hall, 0481
Ransom, Porter Virgil, 0785
Rapier, Edward Desforges, 2523
Rapier, Edward Sebastian, 3510
Rapier, Edward Sebastian, Jr., 3857
Rapier, George E., 3066
Rapier, George Senac, 2522
Rapier, Michael Joseph, 3414
Rareshide, Clarence, 2780
Rash, Wallace McDonald, 4446
Raub, George R., Jr., 2672

Raub, George R., Sr., 2654
Raub, William Henry, 2700
Rawle, James, 2nd., 3136
Rawle, William Brooke, 0231
Rawle, William Morris, 3536
Rawlings, James Madison, 1725
Rayfield, James Horace, Jr., 4254
Rea, Henry Robinson, 1265
Rea, Samuel, 0266
Read, Charles Favrot, 2450
Read, Charles French, 1003
Read, Harold Comer, 1638
Read, John Joseph, 0211
Reardon, Richard James, 3692
Reasoner, Mark Howard, 1676
Rebillot, Todd James, 4454
Redding, George Hyde, 2315
Reddish, Craig Leslie, 1935
Redman, John Lyne, 0783
Redmond, Bruns D'Aunoy, 3914
Reed, John Ludovicus, 0416
Reed, Ralph C., 4580
Reed, Robert Duncan, 3978
Reed, Thomas, 0837
Reed, William B., 2278
Reed, William Corwin, Jr., 4035
Reed, William Edgar, 3293
Reed, Willis McCook, 3229
Reed, Worth, 1288
Reeder, Amos Alphonse, 1647
Reeder, Charles Howard, 1596
Reeder, Charles Leonard, 1597
Reeder, Charles Merrick, 1589
Reeder, Charles Merrick, 1670
Reeder, Clarence, 1628
Reeder, James Dawson, 1598
Reeder, Leonard Ben, 1599
Reeder, Maurice Lanahan, 1600
Reeder, Oliver H., 2324
Reeder, Thomas Leonard, 1648
Reeder, Thomas Leonard, Jr., 4202
Reese, Howard Hopkins, 1053
Reese, William Willis, 3904
Reeves, Howard Gendell, 1875
Reeves, John Woolson, II, 1707
Regan, James, III, 1902
Regar, Clayton, 2129
Regar, George Bertram, 1895
Regar, Gordon R., 2102
Regar, Henry, 2127
Regar, Howard S., 2126

Regar, Isaac C., 2146
Regar, Jason W., 2142
Regar, Newton K., 2128
Regar, Philip W., 2115
Regar, Ralph E., 2145
Regester, Robert Thomas, 3559
Reichner, Henry Harold, Jr., 3604
Reichner, Louis Irving, 1331
Reichner, Morgan S. A., 2060
Reichstein, Arthur F., 3004
Reid, Henry Nelson, 0477
Reid, James Thompson, 1573
Reid, Robert Joseph, 1274
Reid, Samuel Chester, 0435
Reid, William Magraw, 0835
Reifsnider, John Milton, 1147
Reilly, Andrew Jackson, 0002
Reilly, George Francis, 0016
Reilly, Paul, 0017
Reip, Alfred H., 0167
Reip, Thomas Henry, 0169
Remington, Cyrus Kingsbury, 0040
Reno, Jesse Wilford, 1213
Rex, Daniel Ferrell, 1993
Reynaud, Clarence Sidney, 2477
Reynolds, Alvin Parker, Jr., 4561
Reynolds, Charles Ambrose, 0322
Reynolds, Frank Starr, 1608
Reynolds, William Butler, 0238
Reynolds, Wm. Butler, 0583
Rhinelander, Philip, 0578
Rhoades, Lyman, 0258
Rhoads, Samuel Creadick, 2620
Rice, Atwood Lumberd, Jr., 3562
Rice, Edmund, 0032
Rice, Joseph Clarence, 3018
Rice, Lewis, 0514
Rice, Turner, 3451
Rice, William E., Jr., 2364
Rice, William Elmer, 2009
Rich, John Allen, 1913
Rich, William L., Jr., 2262
Richard, Albert Earl, 2985
Richard, Euclid Leones, 4108
Richards, Charles Spielmann, 0715
Richards, Earl Morgan, 3167
Richards, Frederick Barnard, 1079
Richards, George Herbert, 0757
Richards, Jeremiah, 0714
Richards, John Bion, 1845
Richards, Williams Stiger, 0860

Richardson, Aubrey DeVaughn, 4292
Richardson, Baury Bradford, 1592
Richardson, Beale H., IV, 2321
Richardson, Francis Joseph, III, 3683
Richardson, Frank Byron, Jr., 2844
Richardson, George Eliot, 0713
Richardson, George Lynde, 1169
Richardson, George Lynde, 1467
Richardson, Hervey Bigelow, 1687
Richardson, Horace Kimball, 2603
Richardson, James Barbour, 1230
Richardson, Julius Gray, 2884
Richardson, Royall Roller, 1420
Richardson, William Miller, 2748
Rider, Charles J., 2203
Ridgate, Thomas Howe, 0603
Ridge, Bradley Bateman, 3466
Rieck, Chester E., Jr., 2276
Rieman, Charles E., 2322
Riggs, Clinton Levering, 1149
Riggs, David Lynn, 4044
Riggs, Manfred Moses, 0751
Riggs, Richard Cromwell, 1714
Riggs, Robert Meldrum, 3983
Riley, Bernard Michael, 3840
Riley, David Leslie, 4237
Riley, Thomas Leslie, 4444
Rinehart, Evan Urner, 0968
Rinehart, Thomas Warden, 0967
Ripley, Winfield Scott, Jr., 0301
Risley, Ronald David, 4583
Ristine, Harley Thompson, 1690
Ristine, Theodore Harmon, 1691
Ristine, Warren Henry, 1692
Ritchie, Lee Canfield, 4328
Ritchie, Robert Allan, 4329
Ritchie, Robert Field, 4056
Rittenhouse, Samuel Albert, 3833
Rives, Ralph Hardee, 3498
Roak, Christopher Dale, 3299
Roane, Samuel Bertrand, 1342
Robb, Eugene Willard K., 3296
Robbins, Gregory Lynn, 4570
Robbins, Howard Sumner, 0482
Robe, Charles Franklin, 0162
Robe, Lucien Stevens, 0270
Robert, Edward Bane, Jr., 4172
Roberts, Charles Bailey, 0488
Roberts, Graham, 1710
Roberts, Harry, 2105
Roberts, Robert L., Jr., 2221

192 Member Index

Roberts, Robert Leonard, 2212
Roberts, Thomas Owen, 2988
Roberts, William Wesley, 4463
Robertson, George Sadtler, 1151
Robertson, Haywood Lawrence, 3201
Robertson, James Stevens, 4070
Robertson, John McEnery, 3395
Robertson, William C., III, 3051
Robertson, William C., IV, 3150
Robeson, Fielding Tecumsch, 0670
Robeson, John Terrell, 0566
Robinett, Clifton Harvey, 2711
Robinett, Frank Appleby, 2714
Robinett, Paul McDonald, 2597
Robins, Eugene Frank, 3328
Robins, Irvine Ashton,, 3190
Robins, Reginald Starr, 3109
Robins, Robert Wayne, 3585
Robinson, Bradford,, 3184
Robinson, Edward Augustus, 0686
Robinson, Erdis Geroska, 1556
Robinson, Herbert Fulwiler, 0676
Rockenbach, Samuel Dickerson, 0220
Rockwell, Paul Ayres, 1865
Roddis, William Henry, 4121
Roe, Fayette Washington, 0018
Roe, Francis Asbury, 0019
Roe, George, 0042
Rogers, Archibald, 0516
Rogers, Edward Sidney, 0532
Rogers, John Philip, 2660
Roggenburger, Adolphus, 1400
Rolfe, Gerald Clifton, 4159
Rolston, Lyon, 2039
Rome, Curtis Perrin, Jr., 3835
Romig, Gerald Christian, 3518
Romig, Gerald Christian, Jr., 3704
Roosevelt, Julian K., 3000
Roosevelt, Ralph Moross, 1736
Roper, Emmett Allan, Jr., 4387
Rose, Dan W., 4268
Roseboom, Jesse Garretson, 1431
Rosebrock, Alden Ivan, 0901
Rossmann, Edward Albert, 2614
Roth, Edward, Jr., 2638
Roth, Frederic Hull, 3962
Roth, Frederic Hull, Jr., 4011
Roth, Jon Biddle, 2946
Roth, Jon Biddle, 4030
Rothermel, John Jacob, 0610
Roueche, Mossman, 3369

Rountree, John Griffin R., 3401
Rouse, Francis Willis, Jr., 0956
Roush, Lyman Plummer, 1644
Rowan, Robert Livingston, 1416
Rowntree, Gradie Raymond, 4417
Roxby, William C., 3515
Roxby, William C., Jr., 3514
Roy, John Overton, Jr., 2838
Roy, Joseph Folse, 3035
Roy, Robert Garth Bingham, 4336
Royer, John Whittier, 1138
Royse, Samuel Durham, 1308
Royse, William Coates, 1131
Ruby, John Lindley, 4442
Rucker, Henry Cowles, III, 3107
Rucker, Tinsley White, IV, 4008
Ruddock, Theodore Davis, 4209
Rue, Howard S., 2153
Rue, Howard S., Jr., 2154
Rue, John R., 4th., 2156
Rue, William H., 2155
Runells, David Charles, 4045
Runk, John Ten Broeck, 1930
Runk, Louis Barcroft, 1931
Runyan, Forrest Mitchell, 0666
Rupley, George, 1445
Rupp, Henry G., 0376
Rupp, Henry Wilson, 0268
Rush, Everett Neil, 4436
Rusk, Jacob Krebs, Jr., 0712
Russell, Charles Jacob, 1797
Russell, Lyman Brightman, 1643
Rutherford, Milton D., 2304
Rutter, Wm. Ives, Jr., 0878
Ryan, Franklin Winton, 1743
Rymers, George Henry, 1232
Sadler, Lucien MacDowell, 1909
Sadtler, Charles Edward, 0765
Sadtler, Charles Herbert, 0207
Sadtler, Christopher Columbus, 0306
Sadtler, Howard Plitt, 0186
Sadtler, John Philip Benjamin, 0334
Saffarrans, George Coolidge, 0464
Safford, Ralph Kirkham, 1225
Sage, William H., 1649
Sahm, William Knopp Tridel, 1216
Salassi, Gerard Octave, III, 3932
Salassi, Walter Lee, 4554
Salmon, Clarke, 2835
Salmon, Clarke, Jr., 3050
Salmon, Harvey Wallis, III, 1618

Salmon, Stephen Decatur, 1292
Salter, John L., Jr., 2320
Sample, Mathias William, 1514
Sanborn, Earl Boyce, Jr., 3917
Sander, George Francis, Jr., 2560
Sanders, Albert Covington, 3340
Sanders, Robert Stuart, 2744
Sands, James Thomas, 0368
Sanford, George Bliss, 0113
Sanford, James Terry, 3404
Sanford, John Lowry, 1407
Sanford, William Lanahan, 2048
Sangston, Laurence Purdy, 3773
Sanno, James Madison Johnston, 0082
Sapp, E. S., 1277
Sapp, Frank M., 1276
Sappington, Thomas Jonas, 2559
Sargent, Compton, 2023
Sargent, Edward Rotan, 1975
Sargent, Fitzwilliam, 2190
Sargent, Fitzwilliam, 3rd., 2004
Sargent, Gorham P., Jr., 2216
Sargent, Samuel Worcester, 1998
Sargent, Samuel Worcester, 2697
Sargent, Winthrop, 2964
Sargent, Winthrop, 3rd., 1997
Sargent, Winthrop, IV, 2696
Sargent, Winthrop, Jr., 1976
Sarpy, Henry Leon, 3411
Sarpy, Robert Henry, 2434
Sarpy, Robert Henry, Jr., 3350
Satterlee, Herbert Livingston, 0701
Satterthwaite, Pennington, 3337
Saunders, Willard Gerald, II, 4489
Sauner, Richard Garry, 4346
Saxton, Henry Dearborn, 0628
Saylor, Harold Durston, II, 3295
Saylor, Henry Durston, II, 2695
Saylor, Henry Durston, III, 3314
Sayre, Lansing Glen Lytle, 1571
Sayres, Edward Stalker, 0474
Schaal, Frederick G., 2111
Schaeffer, Forrest Rickenbach, 4065
Schafer, Gordon Frank, Jr., 3765
Schaff, David S., Jr., 2068
Schall, John Hubley, IV, 3241
Schauffler, Frederick Allen, 4255
Schauffler, Wm. Gray, 0719
Scheetz, George Henry, 4087
Schempp, George Grant, II, 4043

Scherck, Henry Joseph, 0952
Schermerhorn, Frank Earl, 0682
Schiaffino, George Evans, 4199
Schlenker, Richard Carl, 3986
Schmidt, Manfield, 1872
Schminke, Frederick William, 0170
Schmitt, Roger M. L., 3938
Schnebly, Keith G., Jr., 3571
Schoen, Joseph Michael, IV, 4612
Schoenberger, George C., Jr., 3507
Schoenberger, Sidney Conrad, 3426
Schoenfeld, Robert Morlas, 3838
Schrum, John Luther, 1673
Schrum, Otto David, 1681
Schryver, Floyd Wade, 1782
Schultz, Bernard Van Horne, 0494
Schwaner, William John, 3862
Schwartz, John Bonicamp, 4517
Schweitzer, Kenneth, 4062
Schweppe, Palmer Dallis Thompson, 3616
Scott, David J., 2125
Scott, Frank Bertram, 3089
Scott, George Addison, 2014
Scott, George Eyster, 1206
Scott, James K., 2181
Scott, John Fulton Reynolds, 1121
Scott, John Morin, 1012
Scott, John, Jr., 1209
Scott, Leon Lake, Sr., 3224
Scott, Peter D., 2191
Scranton, Lewis Bruce, 2549
Scrivener, Milton Emmons, 3623
Scudder, Richard Alan, 3182
Scullin, John Gardner, 3470
Scully, Charles Alison, 2018
Scutt, Charles William, 4032
Seaman, John T., 2112
Seaman, Lawrence McClean, 4182
Seaman, Wayne DeWitt, 3267
Sears, Francis Richmond, 1824
Seaver, George Arthur, Jr., 3364
Seavey, Fred Hannibal, 0775
Seghers, Guy Joseph, 2459
Seghers, Guy Joseph, Jr., 2803
Seghers, Paul D'Otrenge, 2617
Sellers, Edwin Foote, 1067
Sellers, John Harrison, 3288
Sellers, Nicholas, 3074
Sells, John Davis, 1479
Semple, Frank, Jr., 1118

194 Member Index

Sener, Samuel Miller, 0284
Seymour, Origen Storrs, 0434
Shane, Edward Melburn, 1880
Shank, Charles Abram, 1382
Shannon, Irwin Vick, 2581
Shannon, James J., Jr., 4443
Shannon, Michael C., 3740
Sharp, Alfred Elliott, 1175
Sharp, Alfred Elliott, 1727
Sharp, John Winfield, 3435
Sharp, Roger Post, Jr., 3430
Sharpe, Alfred Clarence, 0020
Sharrock, Charles Everett, 3951
Shattuck, Levi Hubbard, 1908
Shattuck, Marquis E., 3187
Shaw, C. Battle, Jr., 4176
Shaw, Lynn Jackson, 4055
Shaw, Morgan Langford, 2547
Shehan, Daniel Edward, 2301
Shehan, J. Brooke, 2598
Shehan, Robert Joseph, 2967
Shehan, William Henry, 2599
Shehan, William Henry, Jr., 2625
Sheib, Samuel Henry, 0949
Sheldon, Henry Luther, 0598
Shelly, Howard Merrell, 1444
Shepard, Benjamin, 1182
Shepard, John Steadman, Jr., 4526
Shepherd, William E., 2363
Sherman, Franklin Chapman, 1847
Sherman, Fred Henry, 0857
Sherman, Roy H., 2376
Sherman, William Edgar, 1698
Sherron, James Fenton, Jr., 1945
Shields, Alexander M., 3528
Shields, Richard Barba, 3687
Shirey, Clarence Ray, 3818
Shirley, Rufus George, 0556
Shober, Reginald K., 1655
Shoemaker, Harvey, 0667
Shoemaker, Henry Wharton, 1266
Shoemaker, James Duncan, 0660
Shoemaker, Joshua Lippincott, 0668
Shoemaker, Michael Myers, 0429
Shoemaker, Owen, 0669
Shope, Edward Pierce Lentz,, 1616
Shope, Samuel Zimmerman, 1617
Short, Robert Carter N., 3488
Short, William, 3472
Shotts, James Edgar, Sr., 2922
Showers, Burton LaVerne, 4503

Shreffler, Benjamin Franklin, 1040
Shreve, Milton William, 1140
Shriner, Edward Derr, Jr., 2794
Shriver, Alfred Jenkins, 1187
Shubrick, Edward Rutledge, 0118
Shufeldt, William Techumseh, 1354
Shull, Richard Bruce, 4323
Shute, George Cameron, 2100
Sicussatt, St. George Charles
   Leakin, 1223
Sill, Harold Montgomery, 0577
Sillcocks, Henry, 2257
Simmons, Edwin James, 3952
Simmons, James M., 2309
Simmons, Manfred Elliston, 1846
Simmons, Wellington Gerowe, 0814
Simonds, Frederic Pond, 1392
Simpson, Dennis William, 4504
Simpson, Jay Maxwell, 1339
Sinnott, Charles J., 3178
Sinnott, James Butterfield, III, 2511
Sizemore, James Middleton, 3356
Sizemore, James Middleton Jr., 3357
Skiddy, Wm Wheelwright, 0370
Skillern, Ross P., 2374
Skinner, Henry Whipple, 0716
Skinner, Maurice Edward, 1828
Slatten, William Anthony, 4110
Slavens, Thomas Horace, 1923
Slaymaker, Samuel C., II, 3041
Slaymaker, Samuel Cochran, III,
   3714
Slaymaker, Samuel R., II, 3042
Slayton, William Taft, 1419
Sledge, Joseph W., Jr., 3015
Sleet, Phillip Milton, Jr., 3412
Slingluff, Jesse, Jr., 2107
Slingluff, Michael McCormick, 4386
Slingluff, Robert Lee, 4286
Sloan, Charles Wortham, 1236
Sloan, John Hope, 0929
Sloan, Ralph Wiley, 4204
Slocum, James Edward, 0621
Slothower, Henry, 1527
Smallwood, Grahame Thomas, Jr.,
   2927
Smart, Edward (Veteran), 0356
Smartt, Ephraim Herbert, 2976
Smith, Alfred McLean, 4313
Smith, Arthur M., 4052
Smith, Asa H., 0193

Member Index 195

Smith, Carlisle F., 3212
Smith, Clifford Neal, 3443
Smith, D. Carlos, Jr., 3447
Smith, David Carline, 4186
Smith, Doyle Jackson, II, 3746
Smith, Edward Levi, 0906
Smith, Eleazer (*Veteran*), 0357
Smith, Elizur Yale, 1989
Smith, Erwin Weir, Jr., 2665
Smith, Francis Scott Key, 1540
Smith, Frank Birge, 0568
Smith, Frank Edmond, 1200
Smith, Frederick D., 4054
Smith, George Floyd, 4149
Smith, George Louge, 1165
Smith, Guy J., 1275
Smith, Harold Raphael, 3047
Smith, Harry Pattison, 1185
Smith, Hester Moore, 4164
Smith, James Roy, Jr., 3485
Smith, Jesse Marion, 1544
Smith, John Augustine, 2504
Smith, L. Bertrand, 0983
Smith, Len Young, 2775
Smith, Leroy, 2113
Smith, Lloyd D., 2161
Smith, Marshall Mervin, 4148
Smith, Michael K., 4053
Smith, Ormond Gerald, 0548
Smith, Richard Earnest, 4545
Smith, Robert Palmer, 1855
Smith, Robert T., 0013
Smith, Robert T., 4434
Smith, Sherrill Montrose, Sr., 4445
Smith, Stephen DeWitt, 2075
Smith, Tevis Clyde, Jr., 2721
Smith, Thomas Mayhew, 4627
Smith, Walter Frank, 1186
Smith, Winfield Ross, 2984
Smith, Wm. Poultney, 1876
Smull, George Warner, 1906
Snapp, Albert Bryan, 4242
Snider, Ernest Lorin, 4460
Snow, Henry, 1635
Snyder, Charles E., 0919
Snyder, Frederic Antes, 0269
Snyder, Frederick Russell, Jr., 4388
Snyder, George Duncan, 0200
Snyder, John Avery, 3292
Snyder, Leo Harter, 1311
Snyder, Martin P., 2482

Snyder, Russell William, 1344
Somervell, William Howe, 0903
Somervell, Woodruff Marbury, 1063
Soniat, Disney, L., Jr., 3285
Soniat, Theordore Louis Lucien, 3370
Soule, Evan Ragland, 2479
Soule, Frederick William, 0438
Soule, George, 2478
Soule, Robert Spencer, Jr., 3434
Southard, Lawrence, 1732
Southard, Louis Carver, 1259
Southerland, Edwin W., 3580
Southerland, Henry deLeon, Jr., 3254
Spahr, Boyd Lee, 2647
Spangler, Tileston Fracker, 0480
Sparhawk, Charles Wurts, 0137
Sparhawk, John, Jr., 0145
Sparks, John F., 1284
Sparrow, Richard Stenley, Jr., 3694
Sparrow, Wendall Keats, 3781
Spaulding, George Edgar, Jr., 4487
Spear, Harry William, 0955
Spencer, William Gardner, 0024
Spencer, Wm. Chetwood, 0271
Spragins, Samuel Hamilton, 4610
Spragins, Samuel Hamilton, Jr., 4211
Springer, Robert G., 2194
Sproat, Harris Elric, 0206
Spurr, Jerome Lyon, 4026
Spurrier, Oliver Walter, 2856
St. Paul, Hugh de la Vergne, 3393
St. Paul, John, Jr., 2382
St. Paul, Townsley D., 3506
Stacey, Edward Porter, 0807
Stadler, James Robert, 4265
Staehle, Jack Carl, 3095
Stafford, Donald Bernard, 2421
Stafford, Morgan Hewett, 1590
Stafford, Russell Henry, 1639
Stahl, Elias Brinton, 1273
Stahl, John Henry, Jr., 1085
Stahl, Resler Meloy, 1271
Stakelum, William David, 4400
Stamford, Llewellyn M., 0519
Stancil, Walter Dorsey, 4219
Stansbury, James E., 2318
Stansfield, George J., 2200
Stanton, Herbert Charles, 1706
Stark, Lloyd Rider, 1351
Starke, Aubrey Harrison, 2667

Starke, Bolling Powell, Jr., 4117
Starling, Guy W., Jr., 2234
Stearns, Parley Mark, II, 3883
Steele, Frank Bartlett, 1864
Steelman, Hiram, 1434
Steely, Harlin Melville, 1412
Steers, Francis F., 2259
Stein, Charles F., Jr., 2239
Stein, Charles Francis, III, 2555
Stellwagon, Horace D., Jr., 3945
Stephens, Carl Lynn, 4592
Stephens, Hartzell Oscar, 4591
Stephens, Uel, Jr., 2798
Sterling, Montaigu M., 2138
Sternbergh, Van R., Jr., 3140
Stetson, Francis Lynde, 1201
Stevens, George Beckwith, 1141
Stevens, John Conynham, 0329
Stevens, Lawrence L., Jr., 3544
Stevens, William Coppee, 0328
Stevens, William Kerper, 1032
Stevenson, James Madison, 0408
Stevenson, James Thomson, 4456
Stevenson, John McAllister, 2797
Steward, Morton Collins, Jr., 4413
Stewart, Ambler Jones, 0973
Stewart, Andrew, 1228
Stewart, Averill Thatcher, 4390
Stewart, Carl Hoak, Jr., 2966
Stewart, Donald Franklin, 3260
Stewart, Earl Ruthven, 1443
Stewart, Francis Edward, 1581
Stewart, Frank Ross, 2915
Stewart, Henry Christopher Hand, 1484
Stewart, James Edmundson, 0582
Stewart, John Trusedale, 1387
Stewart, Thomas William, 4646
Stibbs, John Henry, 2506
Stick, Alexander Wade, 3926
Stick, David Fitchett, 3947
Stick, Gordon M. F., Sr., 3063
Stick, Gordon, M. F., Jr., 3067
Stick, Howard Edward Morgan, 3925
Stick, Thomas H. F., 3065
Stickney, George Henry, 0366
Stiff, Ashby G., 2308
Stiff, Ashby Gordon, Jr., 2575
Stiness, Edward Clinton Bessom, 1533
Stirling, Thomas King Nelson, 3970
Stockham, Herbert Cannon, 3935
Stockton, Jack Potter, III, 2771
Stockton, Maurice, III, 4341
Stockton, Milton A., Jr., 3177
Stockton, Milton Anthony, III, 3761
Stockton, Richard, 6th., 1203
Stockwell, David Hunt, 2097
Stockwell, Herbert Grant, 1610
Stockwell, John Wesley, Jr., 1583
Stockwell, Joseph Francis, 1611
Stoddard, Henry H., Jr., 2252
Stoffle, Merton Wayne, 3836
Stokes, Lee Duncan, 4266
Story, Henry Clement, 2592
Stoughton, Oscar B., Jr., 2350
Stouse, Malcolm Renshaw, 3868
Stouse, Maurice de la Ronde, 4574
Stowe, Benjamin Levi, 1293
Stowell, Wm. VanNess, 1219
Straight, Charles Tillinghast, 0990
Stratton, M. Lawrence, 2761
Street, Edward Parker, 3388
Street, Phillips B., 3461
Streets, David Henry, 4318
Strobel, Albert Perigo, 0380
Strobel, James William, 1045
Stroh, Oscar Henry, 4069
Strother, Charles Jackson, 2850
Strother, James Herschel, 2849
Stroud, Howard D., 2365
Stuart, Charles J., 2226
Stuart, Harold L., 2182
Stuart, Russell Allen, 2903
Stubblefield, John Seely, 3615
Stuck, Charles Albert, Jr., 4144
Stull, Adam Arbuckle, 0129
Stull, Raymond, 1545
Sturgis, Samuel B., 2006
Subers, Albert R., 3250
Subers, Christopher V., 2539
Sublette, Donald Jackson, 4404
Sullivan, Chapman, 4012
Sultan, Arthur Phillips, 3441
Summers, Walter Penrose, 1026
Sumner, William Henry, 0856
Sumwalt, John Wesley Richardson, 1566
Sustendal, George F., 3156
Sutcliffe, Richard E., 2104
Sutherland, Charles, 0122
Sutherland, Frank Sheldon, 4090

Member Index 197

Sutherland, Spurgeon, 3956
Sutherlin, George Hawes, Jr., 3895
Sutter, William Henry, 1833
Sutton, Fredus Edmund, 2656
Sutton, James P., 2282
Sutton, Lynn Arden, 4319
Sutton, Raymond Ellsworth, 3961
Swan, Kenneth F., 2255
Swartwout, Egerton, 0074
Swartwout, John Henry, 0341
Swartwout, Satterlee, 0075
Swayer, James Estcourt, 0094
Swearer, Herbert Dayne, 1247
Swearingen, Thomas Townsley Van, 0471
Sweeney, Henry W. S., 3183
Swift, James Marcus, 2043
Swift, Lee Wilson, Jr., 3929
Swigart, Frederic Robert, 2451
Swigart, Frederic Robert, III, 3858
Swing, Albert Holmes, 1896
Swing, Edward C. K., 2037
Swing, James Truman, 1932
Swing, Robert H. D., Jr., 2038
Swing, Robert Hamill D., 1933
Swisher, Charles H., 2352
Swisher, Michael Scott, 4343
Swogger, Larry K., 4258
Swords, Robert Stanard, 1414
Sykes, A. McKnight, 2065
Symington, Donald Leith, 3343
Symmes, Samuel Dunn, 1688
Synder, Martin Avery, 3244
Taft, Howland Guild, 4116
Talbot, Archie Lee, 1145
Talbott, Hattersly Worthington, 0691
Talbott, Hattersly Worthington, Jr., 0839
Talbott, Otho Holland Williams, 0838
Talte, Andrew Frank, Jr., 3728
Tarr, Frederick Crey, 0979
Taylor, Arthur Rodney, 1668
Taylor, Benjamin Franklin, 0935
Taylor, Blair, 1672
Taylor, Clarence Wills, 0291
Taylor, Clement Newbold, 3028
Taylor, Clifford, 0173
Taylor, George Dunham, Jr., 3777
Taylor, Harold, 1674A
Taylor, Howard Richards, 2600

Taylor, Ira Thomas, 2046
Taylor, James L., Jr., 2332
Taylor, James Lookerman, 0085
Taylor, Thad Talmage, 1323
Teale, Charles Edward, 0747
TenEyck, Peter Gansevoort, 1703
Terrell, Daniel Skidmore, 2757
Terrell, John Edward, 2758
Tete, William Thomas, 4373
Thacker, Henry Heston, 1675
Thayer, Corwin Moffat, 1525
Thomas, Belton Earp, Jr., 2905
Thomas, David, 2nd., 2053
Thomas, Frank Warner, 0797
Thomas, George Reber, 4429
Thomas, Guy Alfred, 1956
Thomas, Harold Ashton, 4408
Thomas, Harry George, 1701
Thomas, Joseph Burghard, 4555
Thomas, Noah Oscar, Jr., 3684
Thomas, Warner Roberts, 1518
Thompson, Gilbert, 0810
Thompson, Henry Oliver, 1394
Thompson, Marshall Putnam, 1143
Thompson, Porter Lindsley, 1304
Thompson, Raymond Webb, 1263
Thompson, Robert Wilkins, 2618
Thompson, Robert Wilkins, 2941
Thompson, Willard M., 2571
Thompson, William Norton, Jr., 2431
Thomsen, Rossel Cathcart, 1498
Thomson, Jack Waddell, 3896
Thorne, Albert George, 1605
Thorne, Samuel, Jr., 2992
Thornell, Lewis Taylor, 1345
Thornton, James Brown, 0722
Thorp, Crofton Elwyn, Jr., 4048
Thorp, Wakeman Blanchard, 2952
Throckmorton, Charles Woodson, 0998
Thurber, Donald MacDonald Dickinson, 4196
Thurtle, Robert Glenn, 3458
Thurtle, Robert Joseph Patrick, 3767
Tiblier, Sidney L., Jr., 3070
Tiblier, Thomas Joseph, 3057
Tierney, Gordon Paul, 3648
Tifft, John Alden, 1761
Tilden, Albert Colburn, 0770
Tilton, Francis Theodore, 1353
Tinges, Charles H., 2238

198 Member Index

Tingley, Charles Alvah, 4019
Tingley, George Frederick, 4073
Tobin, Mark Cleveland, 3924
Toca, Roland Garic, 2883
Todd, Galbraith Hall, 2605
Todd, James Mulherrin, 2833
Tollerton, Robert Wm., 1823
Tolson, Jay Henry, 3819
Tompkins, Daniel D., 1320
Tootle, Milton, Jr., 0622
Tope, Boyce McBrier, 3958
Toso, Donald Richard, 4261
Toso, Michael Joseph, Jr., 4263
Tower, Charlemagne, 2024
Tower, Lawrence Phelps, 3277
Towle, George Francis, 0021
Town, Charles M., 2621
Town, Edward Arthur, 3460
Towne, John William, 1924
Towne, Phineas, 1862
Townsend, Arthur Liston, 2826
Townsend, David, 2254
Townsend, Donald, 2644
Townsend, James Hill, 0140
Townsend, Rufus M., 0205
Townsend, Thomas Gerry, 0455
Townsend, Thomas Gerry, 0631
Townsend, Thomas Gerry, 0843
Tracy, Robert C., 2108
Trebing, David Martin, 4628
Trenchard, Edward, 0027
Treppa, Allan Ralph, 4484
Trigg, James Knox, 4383
Tritico, Frank Edward, 3646
Trout, John Truman, Jr., 4167
Trout, Robert Rayle, 4276
Trowbridge, Charles Reuben, 1657
Trowbridge, Michael Lynn, 4322
Trueheart, Herbert L., 2347
Truitt, Robert Ralph, Jr., 4450
Truman, Henry Hertel, 1035
Tschudi, Samuel Werner, 1468
Tschudy, Harold T., 1502
Tucker, Brison C., 2266
Tucker, James Armstrong Owens, 0400
Tucker, Robert Gene, 3467
Tuckerman, Alfred, 1173
Tudbury, Warren Chamberlain, 1153
Tufford, Walter H., 0253
Tull, Willis Clayton, Jr., 4080

Tullis, Charles Owen, 2751
Tupper, Tullius C., 0063
Turner, Arthur Campbell, 1495
Turner, Ellwood J., Jr., 2683
Turner, Everett Pendleton, 1078
Turner, Frederick Fairthorne, 2681
Turner, George Henry Brown, 1438
Turner, Huntley Sigourney, 1450
Turner, James Varnum Peter, 0084
Turner, John Clock, 0358
Turner, John Henry, 1552
Turner, Molyneaux Lawrence, 1806
Turner, Will Sidney, 1310
Turner, William Howard, 2682
Turney, Omer Asa, 0469
Turpin, Morley Bebee, 0313
Turpin, Thomas Jefferson, 4584
Turpin, William Beverly, 4439
Tustin, Albert Weigand, III, 3863
Tuttle John William, 2750
Twiggs, Albert J., 4277
Twining, Robert Barber, 2995
Umhau, John Bernard, 3594
Umhau, John Bernard, Jr., 3609
Urquhart, Kenneth Trist, 2416
Usilton, William E., 3547
Utech, John Jacob, 3rd., 3957
Van Antwerp, Lee Douglas, 3582
Van Dine, Warren L., 2782
Van Duersen, Wm. Walter, 0100
Van Dyke, Edward James, 2785
Van Gilder, William C., 1110
Van Gulick, Robert R., 3543
Van Horn, Arthur, 1167
Van Horn, John Albert, 1181
Van Pelt, David W. S., 3552
Van Rensselaer, Bernard Sanders, 3841
VanDeventer, Horace, 1999
VanDuersen, Wm. Walter, 0467
VanDyke, Harry Weaton, 0544
VanDyke, Harry Weston, 0587
Vanderhoof, William W., Jr., 2723
Vanderslice, Franklin F., 2609
Vanuxem, Louis Clark, 0222
Vaughan, Edwin Steuart, 3084
Verlander, Henry Smith, Jr., 3490
Vest, Stephen Matthew, 4477
Vick, James Andrew, 4473
Vickers, Wm. Handy Collins, 0674
Viele, Sheldon Thompson, 0068

Villere, Andre Louis, 3349
Villere, Ernest C., 2388
Villere, Henri Francois, 2403
Villere, James F., 2381
Villere, Marin Pierre, 3844
Villere, Maurice Francois, 3911
Villere, Pierre, 2517
Villere, Plauche Francois, 2578
Villere, Plauche Francois, Jr., 3424
Villere, Sidney L., 2379
Villere, Walter Peter, 2440
Vincent, Charles R., 2284
Vincent, Charles R., Jr., 2285
Vincent, Patrick T., 2286
Viosca, Barry Francis, 4399
Viven, John Ludlow, 0199
Vogtle, Alvin Ward, Jr., 3256
Vogtle, Jesse Stringer, 3452
Vollmer, Earl S., 3231
Vollmer, Earl S., Jr., 3232
Vollmer, John Frederick, 3168
Von Schrader, Frederick, 0111
Von der Poel, Peter G., 2349
VonDouris, John Wallace, 3722
Voorhees, George Van Wickle, 1256
Voorhies, Gordon, 0098
Wade, Samuel Henry, 0393
Wadhams, Albion James, 0799
Wadhams, Albion James, 3235
Wadhams, Albion Varet, 0644
Wadhams, Frederick Eugene, 0602
Wadleigh, Albert P., 2311
Wadsworth, Charles, Jr., 0730
Wager, John Philip, 2013
Wakeman, Jessup, 0299
Walker, Forrest Sean, 4132
Walker, George Fuller, 4184
Walker, Isaac Henry, 2017
Walker, John Mort, Jr., 2896
Walker, Paul Howard, 3695
Walker, Robert C., 2367
Walker, William Samuel Crittenden, 1267
Wall, Alfred Clements, 0754
Wall, Wendell Glen, 4234
Wallace, Hamilton Stone, 0908
Wallace, Herbert Fairfax, 0119
Wallace, James Nelson, 3813
Wallace, Wyndham Stokes, 1423
Walling, Arthur Patrick, 3281
Walling, Arthur William, 3269

Walling, Stephen Patrick, 3282
Walls, John Abbet, 2574
Walmsley, Hughes Philip, 2475
Walmsley, James Armineous, 1139
Walsh, G. Lauriston, Jr., 3338
Walton, George Edward Cooper, 0732
Walton, H. Harrison, 0561
Walton, John M., Jr., 3154
Walton, William Wyclif, 3946
Walworth, Arthur Clarence, 1144
Walworth, Hiram, 0043
Ward, Aaron, 0300
Ward, Frank Anthony, II, 3287
Ward, Fred Deryl, 3797
Ward, Harry Parker, 0498
Ward, Hurbert Herrick, 0458
Ward, Hurbert Herrick, 0500
Ward, John W., Jr., 2246
Ward, Nicholas Donnell, 3591
Ward, Swan Sullivan, 2580
Ward, William Ray, 4392
Warder, Walter, 1280
Warder, William H., 1281
Warfield, Edwin, 0390
Warfield, Edwin, III, 2314
Warfield, John Ogle, Jr., 3660
Waring, Benjamin Harrison, 0933
Waring, William Emory, Jr., 0932
Waring, William Hunter, 3257
Warne, Edward Paul Broy, 0927
Warne, William Budd, Jr., 1246
Warner, Culbreth Hopewell, 0321
Warner, George E., 0209
Warner, John Edwin, 0171
Warren, Albert Marshall, 0643
Warren, George Copp, 1464
Warren, George Rodney, Jr., 2650
Warren, Henry Dexter, 0155
Warren, Henry Joseph, 0433
Warren, James Robert, 4536
Warren, Lawrence Seymour, 1946
Warren, Ulysses Grant, Jr., 2124
Warterfield, John Robert, 4118
Washburn, Lester Allison, 1938
Waters, Samuel Kyle, 2998
Watkins, Frank Raymond, 4638
Watkins, John Elfroth, 0550
Watkins, John Elfreth, 0570
Watkins, John Elfreth, Jr., 0579
Watkins, Oscar Leon, 1677
Watmough, James Horatic, 0224

Member Index

Watrous, Philip Maish, 3675
Watson, David Coleman, 3064
Watson, William A., 3199
Watson, William Anthony, 3307
Watts, Benjamin, 0187
Watts, David Miller, 2025
Wayne, William, 0314
Weakley, Raymond DeCamp, 2012
Weaver, Ethan Allan, 1239
Weaver, James Albert, II, 4398
Weaverling, Charles Clair, 1891
Webb, DeWitt, 0278
Webb, Edward Joseph, Jr., 1500
Webb, Haywood Hutchinson, 1406
Webb, Henry Randall, 0549
Webb, John Sidney, 0847
Webb, Mark Stephen, 4564
Webb, William David, 4557
Webb, William Rollins, 1601
Webb, Wm. Rollins, Jr., 1860
Weber, Donald Robert, 3889
Webster, Burnice Hoyle, 3117
Webster, Edmund Kirby, 0121
Webster, Frank Daniel, 0283
Webster, Leroy Charles, 0034
Weed, George Standish, 0599
Weeks, George W., III, 2045
Weeks, John Wingate, 0484
Weeks, Sinclair, 1623
Weeks, Wm. Raymond, 0709
Weer, Winfield Scott, 3706
Wehrle, Clarence Sebastian, 2913
Weidner, David Eric, 3807
Weidner, William D., Jr., 3077
Weidner, William Daniel, III, 3806
Weimer, Douglas Reid, 3750
Weinmann, John Giffen, 2444
Weisheit, Joseph Elmer, Sr., 2557
Weitzel, Eben Boyd, 0865
Welch, Elwood Stuart, 1360
Welch, Robert N., 2768
Weld, John Gardner, 1969
Weller, Richard Alan, Sr., 4123
Wells, Charles Andrew, 4482
Wells, Charles Chauncey, 4481
Wells, Frederick Howard, 1015
Wells, Guy Everett, 0806
Wells, Joseph Nathan, 4483
Wells, William John, Jr., 3283
Welsh, Donald Green, 3610
Welsh, William (*Veteran*), 0361

Wenrich, Risdon Keeler, 2649
Wentz, Christopher Wildner, 2963
Wentz, Theodore Hillsley, 2827
Wentz, Theodore Hillsley, Jr., 2961
Wentz, Timothy Frazer, 2962
Werst, Harry K., 2740
Wessells, Charles H., 0151
Wessells, Henry Walton, 0279
Wesson, James Leonard, 0840
West, Edward N., 2119
Westbrook, Frederick Edward, 0056
Westfall, John Henry, 1008
Weston, Clement Walker, 2725
Wetherbee, Winthrop, 0124
Wetherill, Alexander Macomb, 0202
Wetmore, Wm. Boerum, 0234
Wetter, John King, 1316
Wetzel, Ronald Joseph, 4395
Whealen, John Joseph, Jr., 3516
Wheatley, Timothy Stephen, 3950
Wheeler, Arthur D., 1114
Wheeler, Harry M., 2283
Wheeler, Walter Raymond, 1476
Whelan, Thomas A., 2253
Whelden, Ford H., 2176
Whelden, Gilbert Hart, 2206
Whelden, Gilbert Hart, Jr., 2207
Whetstone, Martin Allen, 4476
Whipple, Charles Henry, 0292
Whipple, Charles Henry, 1704
Whisenant, Herman Arthur, Jr., 4238
Whish, John David, 0882
White, Albert Sidney Johnston, III, 3856
White, Frank S., III, 3016
White, Geoffrey Roberts, 2923
White, Glenn William, 1801
White, John Gordon, 3959
White, John Tobin, 2402
White, Maunsel, 4031
White, Richard David, 2919
White, Richard Kerr, 2055
White, Thomas Roberts, Jr., 2056
White, William Warner, 3144
White, William Zebulon, 2853
Whiteford, Daniel Francis X., 3215
Whiteford, Lingard I., Jr., 3481
Whiteford, Lingard Ignatius, 3335
Whiteford, Roger Streett, Jr., 2789
Whitesides, Lawson Ewing, 2749

Member Index

Whitley, Andrew Rieger, 2986
Whitley, Andrew Thomas, 3509
Whitley, David Lawrence, 3893
Whitlock, Bache McEvers, 2720
Whitney, Allan Joseph, 1991
Whitney, Edson Leone, 1804
Whitney, Eli, 0618
Whitney, Eugene Walcott, 0746
Whitney, William R., 2073
Whitsitt, Dawson Bradford, 3919
Whitten, Jerry E., 3682
Whittinghill, George David, 1839
Whyte, Isaac Hezekiah, 0975
Whyte, Wm. Pinkney, Jr., 0228
Wickersham, Robert O'Neill, 0327
Widener, George D., 2192
Widener, Peter A. B., III, 2333
Wiederseim, Theordore E., 2143
Wiederseim, William C., 2135
Wiegand, William E., 1489
Wiegand, William Green, 1528
Wiener, Alexander L., 2679
Wiener, Alexander Loder, Jr., 2924
Wiener, Clifford Cogshall, 3605
Wiener, Edward, 2646
Wiener, Edward McIntosh, 2925
Wiener, Edward McIntosh, Jr., 3612
Wiener, Edward, 3rd., 2680
Wier, Herbert W., 2287
Wiggin, Burton Howe, 1664
Wight, Oliver Birckhead, 2655
Wightman, Thomas Alan, 4470
Wilbar, Waldo Morton, 1957
Wilcox, Edwin Howard, 1383
Wilcox, Reynold Webb, 0044
Wilcoxen, Joseph Kelly, 3885
Wilcoxen, Raymond J., 3662
Wilder, K. Lee, 4099
Wilder, William Murtha, 1888
Wiley, William Richard, Jr., 4588
Wilkinson, Charles Marion, 1493
Wilkinson, Hugh M., Sr., 2389
Wilkinson, Hugh Miller, III, 3769
Wilkinson, Hugh Miller, Jr., 2503
Wilkinson, James III, 2585
Wilkinson, Joel Winston, 4310
Wilkinson, Ogden Dungan, 0448
Wilkinson, Roy Winston, 4309
Wilkinson, William Scott, 2464
Willard, Craig Kenneth, 3520
Willard, James LeBarron, 0748

Willcox, Robert Irving, 2926
Willey, Wm. Lithgow, 0081
Willhite, John Moore, 3803
Williams, Arthur, 0890
Williams, Charles, 0128
Williams, Charles Collier, 0789
Williams, Charles Herman, 3442
Williams, Charles Roper, 2085
Williams, Fred Arthur, 4530
Williams, George B., 2086
Williams, George Washington, 1529
Williams, Herman Warner, Jr., 1742
Williams, Howard Bailey, 4558
Williams, James Albert, Jr., 4104
Williams, John Kennedy, III, 3268
Williams, Leonard D., 3174
Williams, Lester James, 1816
Williams, Robert Wesley, 3693
Williamson, Dalton, 4308
Williamson, Edgar, Jr., 2663
Williamson, Fletcher Phillips, 3749
Williamson, Jeffrey Phillips, 4082
Williamson, Thomas Wilson, 0995
Willie, David L., 3913
Willie, Leroy Ellis, 3884
Willis, Conover English, 1934
Willis, John Edward, 1777
Willis, Todd Bradford, 4467
Willis, Urban George, 1982
Willis, William Clifford, 1910
Willis, William Nicholas, 0876
Wilson, Charles Maurice, 2606
Wilson, Clifford William, 2914
Wilson, Craig Hawley, 3537
Wilson, Francis Vaux, III, 3220
Wilson, Frank Stedman, 0572
Wilson, Fried Ruger, 3538
Wilson, Goerge Fried, Jr., 3135
Wilson, John Appleton, 0308
Wilson, John James, 0391
Wilson, John Sanford, 0557
Wilson, Massey Francis, 3625
Wilson, Rowland Steele, 3927
Wiltbank, George E., 2296
Winans, Carlton George, 1347
Winans, James Dusenberry, 1548
Windsor, Laurence Charles, Jr., 4257
Wing, William Arthur, 1631
Winlock, William Cranford, 0575
Winlock, Wm. Crawford, 0580
Winne, Robert L., 0088

Winslow, Albert Foster, 4300
Winslow, Blaine Frederick, 4256
Winslow, Caleb, Sr., 3398
Winslow, John Leiper, Jr., 4210
Winslow, Lorenzo Simmons, 1642
Winslow, Nathan John, 4493
Winter, Ernst Hicklin, 4017
Winters, George Edward, 1950
Wintringer, George C., 2148
Wisdom, Norton Labatt, 2439
Wisdom, William Bell, 2436
Wiseman, Howard Willard, 3699
Wittenmeyer, Chares E., 3531
Woelfel, Roger Harold, 4471
Wogan, Philip Bernard, 2632
Wogan, Rene Steven, 3980
Wogan, Victor Louis, Jr., 2633
Wolcott, John Dorsey, 2008
Wolfe, Bernard Peter, 3354
Wolfe, Frederick J., Jr., 3355
Wolfe, Richard Peel, 4078
Wolff, Paul Leigh, 4165
Wolford, Charles A. P., 2755
Wolford, Lionel Thomas, Jr., 2601
Wolford, Thomas Lionel, 2562
Wollard, Charles Rainwater, 4086
Woltz, James Mitchell, 0503
Wood, Benjamin Franklin, 0046
Wood, Charles Ogden, 0154
Wood, Charles P., 3021
Wood, Earl VanDorn, 3795
Wood, Edward Allen, 1102
Wood, Marshall William, 0213
Wood, Philip Bryson, 0418
Wood, Robert Spencer, 4589
Wood, Walter Aaron, 1163
Woodard, Theron Royal, 0533
Wooden, Ernest E., 2277
Woodfield, Denis Buchanan, 4057
Woodman, Andrew Jackson, 0823
Woodman, Clarence Eugene, 0421
Woodman, Walter Irving, 1748
Woodruff, Cadwell, 1314
Woodruff, Leslie Rae, 3181
Woods, Joseph Wheeler, 3027
Woodward, Edwin Tully, 0262
Woodward, M. Stevens, 0778
Woolever, Harry, Jr., 3607
Woolfley, Francis A., 3179
Woolfley, Horace Louis Dufour, 3329
Woolverton, Dalton Leo, 4333

Woolverton, David Michael, 4370
Woolverton, Nicholas Winnot, 4513
Worth, William Scott, 0277
Worthing, Clifford Arthur, 3658
Worthington, James Drewry, 3705
Worthington, Miltenberger, Jr., 2855
Worthington, Richard Walker, 1421
Worthington, Thomas Carroll, Jr., 4357
Worthington, Thomas Chew, 1418
Worthington, Thomas Chew, III, 1475
Wortman, Glen R., 1116
Wright, Douglas Chandler, 3789
Wright, George Bohan, 0443
Wright, George Mitchell, 0506
Wright, George Riddle, 0375
Wright, Howard P., 2292
Wright, Jacob Ridgway, 0312
Wright, John MacNair, Jr., 4194
Wright, John Maxwell, 3448
Wright, John Randolph, 0168
Wright, Leslie Stephen, 3644
Wright, Zelma Hudson, Jr., 3739
Wurts, John Sparhawk, 2034
Wurz, Kenneth Franklin, 4173
Wyeth, Huston, 0777
Yardley, John L. M., Jr., 3297
Yardley, Ralph B., 3306
Yates, Emmet Quintard, 2546
Yeager, Frederick Musser, 0517
Yeager, James Gernerd, 3001
Yeager, James Martin, 0634
Yeager, Wayne Evans, 3072
Yeakle, Joseph W., 2172
Yeakle, Walter Atwood, 1355
Yeatts, Lynn Marshall, 3870
Yeilding, Thomas David, 4330
Yockey, James Hewson, 3839
Yockey, Ross Paul, 3192
Yokum, Jules DeFazende, 3007
York, James Arthur Gamble, 4077
Young, Andrew Brodbeck, 2701
Young, Benjamin Loring, 2550
Young, Buford Allen, 4058
Young, Charles D., 2338
Young, E. Weldon, 0534
Young, Edward E., 2337
Young, Gary Edward, 4359
Young, Howard Edward, 1627
Young, Jared Wilson, 1047

Young, John Randolph, 2481
Young, John Randolph, Jr., 3406
Young, Leonard Albert, 3392
Young, Robert John, Jr., 3798
Young, Robert Joseph, 4374
Young, Robert Kirkland, 4478
Young, Roger Vincent, 4150
Young, William Waller, Jr., 3385
Zearfoss, Herbert Keyser, 3820
Zeitler, Vernon Arthur, 4469
Zell, Harold Johnston, Jr., 4593
Zieber, Eugene, 0295
Ziegler, Jacob Stanley, 1039
Ziegler, Walter Macon Lowrie, 1030
Zillman, Marcus Patrick, 4088
Zimmerman, Charles Ballard, 1123
Zirkle, Richard Lee, 4007
Zoll, Allen A., III, 2166
Zoll, Allen Alderson, 1905
Zoll, Allen Alderson, II, 2698
Zoll, George C., 2168
Zook, Erle Will, 1162

Ancestor Index

Abbott, Joel, 0059
Abernathy, Charles Clayton, 3253
Abert, John James, 0978
Abey, Joseph, 3560, 3748
Abney, Elias, 4260
Acheson, Thomas, 2180
Ackley, Oliver, 1398
Acosta, Roque, 3687
Adair, John, 2437, 2568, 2744, 4340
Adair, William, 4545
Adam, Dennis, 1240
Adams, Alexander, 1178
Adams, Andrew Morrison, 4183
Adams, Daniel, 1436
Adams, David, 4237
Adams, John, 4504
Adams, Minos, 3773
Adams, Nathaniel, 3492
Adams, William Ellis, 4075, 4162, 4168, 4169, 4305, 4306, 4365, 4366
Adkins, Levi, 4020
Agens, James, 1377
Ahl, Peter, 3229, 3293
Ainsworth, Danforth, 0896
Aisquith, Edward, 3691
Akin, Abraham, Jr., 1762
Akin, Martin James, 1762
Akright, Isaac, 3849
Albaugh, William, 0285
Albee, Samuel, 2783
Albright, John, 3447
Alden, Charles Henry, 0110, 0221
Alden, Ebenezer, 1773
Aldrich, Thomas Canby, 0694
Aler, Thomas, 4199
Alexander, Hugh, 0061
Alexander, James, 1996, 2170, 2201
Alford, Ami, 0944
Allee, William, 4274
Allen, Howard, 0605
Allen, Hudson, 4244, 4594
Allen, Isaac, 4028
Allen, James, 2284, 2285, 2286
Allen, John, 0652, 1241, 1333
Allen, Jonathan, 3233
Allen, Moses, 0048
Allen, Robert, 0393
Allen, Shubael, 2332
Allen, William Henry, 1515

Aller, Peter, 1873, 2689, 3553, 3554
Allison, Hugh, 1564
Allison, Uriah, 2076
Allison, William, 2092, 2169
Alliston, Dennis, 1938
Alpuente, Don Francisco, 3192
Altaffer, John, 1955
Altemus, Thomas, 3816, 3923
Altman, William, 2672, 2700
Ambrose, Mordecai, 1897
Amee, Jacob, 0736, 1097
Amick, Jacob, 1319
Anderson, Alexander, 4563, 4597
Anderson, Athel, 4313
Anderson, Bolitha, 2680
Anderson, Isaac, 2610
Anderson, James, 0894
Anderson, Jenifer, 4457
Anderson, Jennifer, 2679, 2924, 2925, 3605, 3612
Anderson, John William, 2204
Anderson, Oliver, 0850
Anderson, Reuben, 2646
Andrews, Thomas, Jr., 1294
Andry, Manuel, 2499, 2871, 2872, 2885, 3427
Andry, Michel, 2432
Ansart, Felix, 1990
Anson, Brinton Payne, 2351
Anthony, Joseph, 0065, 0878
Anthony, Joseph, Jr., 0035
Anthony, Thomas, 0035
Antonides, Peter, 4066
Appleby, John, 0426
Applegate, Hezekiah, 3961
Appleton, Benjamin Barnard, 1093
Appleton, James, 0060, 0127, 1482, 3027
Appold, George, 2607, 2734
Arbaugh (Earbaugh), John, 2969, 3696, 3829
Armistead, George, 0265, 0970
Armistead, Walker Keith, 1252
Armstrong, Jesse, 3256, 3452
Armstrong, John, 0611
Armstrong, John A., Jr., 4253
Armstrong, John Adams, 1416
Armstrong, Peter, 0282
Armstrong, Robert, 0611

Armstrong, Samuel, 0584
Armstrong, Thomas, 1028, 1353
Arnold, Seth Shaler, 0473
Arnoult, Cyril Honore, 2411, 2830
Arnoult, Pierre G., 3077
Arnoult, Pierre Gervais, 3806, 3807
Arthur, Ambrose, 3116
Ashby, Nimrod, 1531
Ashby, Samuel, 4349
Ashenhurst, Oliver, 3079, 3080
Ashley, William J., 4242
Ashley, Wilson, 2906
Ashmead, Isaac, 1940, 2019, 2136, 3198
Atherton, Abel Willard, 0885
Atkins, Quintus Flaminius, 1557
Atkinson, Henry, 0115, 1520
Atlee, William Pitt, 2136
Atwood, Solomon, 2993, 3639
Aubert, Juan Batiste, 3423
Aud, Asa, 3363
Aultman, William, 2654
Aungst, Daniel, 2236
Austill, Evan, 3451
Austin, Alexander, 2162
Austin, John Jones, 3734, 4468
Austin, William, 4614
Avent, Ransome Davis, 3618
Averill, Henry Ketchum, Sr., 0041, 1007
Averill, Stephen Noble, 0833
Avery, Ebenezer, 3rd., 0452
Avery, Elisha, 0990
Awalt, Michael, II, 3443
Ayer, Herbert, 1051
Babbitt, Amos, 1559
Babcock, Lodowick Stanton, 0971
Babcock, Samuel, 1352, 2330, 2778, 2973, 3539
Babcock, Samuel, Jr., 0671, 0731, 1542, 1543
Babcock, Samuel, Sr., 0671, 0731
Backus, Electur Malloy, 0226
Bacon, Jonathan, 0117
Bacon, Septimus, 0912
Badger, Bela, 1483
Badgley, Aaron, 1863
Baer, Jacob Shellman, 4140
Bagby, John, 4283
Bailey, ——, 0259
Bailey, Levi, 4541

Bailty, Jacob G., 1954
Bainbridge, William, 0066, 0067, 1926, 3145
Baird, Thaddeus, 3375
Baird, Thomas J., 0261
Baird, Thomas James, 0120, 0518, 1920, 1925, 3247
Baker, Conrad, Jr., 2959
Baker, David, 0883
Baker, George Nice, 0563
Baker, Henry, 3519
Baker, John, 3201
Baker, Joshua, 2901
Baker, Ozi, 4241
Baldwin, Charles North, 0086
Baldwin, David, 1865
Baldwin, Joseph, IV, 4404
Baldwin, Justus, 2671, 3454
Baldwin, Stephen, 1934
Baldwin, Sylvester, 2178
Baldwin, William Henry, 1632, 1650, 1651, 1695, 2341
Ball, Cyrus, 0756, 1082
Ball, Horatio, 3579
Ball, Israel R., 2294
Ball, Lewis W., 4205
Ball, Samson Edward, 2545
Balthis, George, 1661
Bancroft, John, III, 1707, 1875
Bankston, John, 2383, 2898
Banning, Calvin, 1087
Bannon, Michael, 4462
Barber, Ebenezer, 4148, 4149, 4287
Barber, Noah, 1189
Barbour, John, Jr., 1155
Barclay, John Mortimer, 0027
Barcroft, Stacy Brown, 1931
Barnes, Asa, 3155
Barnes, Elijah, 1877
Barnes, James, 1680, 1683
Barnes, Joseph Goff, 0851
Barnet (Brandt), Michael, 2373
Barney, Joshua, 1490, 1526, 3023
Barnum, Daniel, 3094
Baron, Noel Auguste, 2512, 2513, 2762
Barr, James, 4194
Barrett, John, 0470
Barrett, John M., 0229
Barrett, John Miller, 1461
Barroll, James, 3478

Barroll, James Edmondson, 4490
Bartholomew, Deming, 1476
Bartholomew, Joseph, 4099
Bartholomew, Sherman, 3005
Bartlett, Ebenezer, 1428
Bartlett, Joshua, 4312
Bartlett, Josiah, 2484
Barton, Benjamin, 0068
Barton, Eleazer, 1268
Barton, William, 1356
Bateman, Benjamin, 1811
Bateman, John Mills, 3466
Bates, Levi, 0759
Bates, Obadiah, 0735
Battis, John, 0986
Battle, James, 3439
Battle, William, III, 4055, 4176
Baury, Frederick, 0317
Baxter, William, 1162, 1445
Bay, Andrew, 1083, 1410
Bay, Thomas, 0973
Bayless, Benjamin, 1720
Beach, Peter, 0519
Beach, Samuel Jr., 0103, 0337
Beal, Caleb, 1100
Beale, Chester, 0703
Beale, George N., 3234
Beall, Basil, 3594, 3609, 3610
Beall, John Hilleary, 3125
Beall, John of L., 3071
Beall, Lloyd, 0898, 3214
Beall, Reazin, 2506
Beall, Walter, Jr., 2977
Beall, William Dent, 2567
Bealmear, Francis, 2980
Beals, Henry, 0298
Beard, John, 0933, 3563, 3837
Beatty, George, 2786
Beatty, Hamilton, 1793
Beatty, Henry, 2072, 3633
Beatty, James, 0343, 0817, 0822
Bebee, James C., 0313
Beckwith, Elisha, 0869
Beebe, Ebenezer, 1067
Beers, Abel, 1624
Beetem, Abraham, 2793, 3550, 3565, 4501
Belknap, Chaundey, 0126
Bell, Benjamin, 2325
Bell, Benjamin C., 3908, 3909
Bell, Cecelius, 3186

Ancestor Index 207

Bell, Holly, 1005
Bell, James, 4416
Bell, John, 4122
Bell, William, 3943, 3953
Bellamy, John F., 3498
Belote, Charles, 1636, 1637
Belote, Isaac, 4129
Beluche, Renato, 2443
Bendall, Jesse, 3437
Bender, Jacob A., 2185
Benedict, Isaac, 1746
Benedict, Joseph, 2787
Benjamin, Elias, 1386
Benjamin, Jesse, 1098
Benjamin, Samuel, 1591
Benjamin, William, 3671
Bennett, Abijah, 3038
Bennett, Archibald, 3849
Bennett, Reuben, 3884, 3913
Bennett, Van, 4525
Bentley, James, 2909
Bentley, John, 0148
Benton, John, 1866
Benton, Samuel, 0682
Berlin, Philip, 2061
Bermudez, Joaquin, 2582, 3285, 3370
Bernard, Elysee Leon, 3982
Bernard, Francois, 4108
Bernard, Onesiphore, 3354, 3355
Berrell, Jeremiah, 0762
Berry, John, 0263, 0425, 0608, 1826, 1885
Betts, James, 1819, 1835
Betz, George, 1993
Beverly, John, 1373
Biays, James, 0980, 1437
Biays, James, Jr., 1157
Bickham, Thomas, 4543
Biddle, Clement Cornell, 1325
Biddle, John, 0109, 0136, 0240
Bienvenu, Alexandre de Vince, II, 2841, 2843, 3673
Bienvenu, Pierre Terville, 2601, 2755, 2562
Bill, Phineas, 3786
Billings, Andrew, 0055
Billings, George, 4354
Bingham, Lemuel, 4336
Binion, Robert Burton, 4304
Binney, Amos, III, 0345, 0472, 0483
Binney, John, 0346, 0472, 0483

Birckhead, Hugh, 0695
Bird, John Wesley, 4275
Birge, Cyrus, 0568
Bisbee, Daniel, 2603
Biscoe, James, 2604
Bishop, Isaac, 2805
Bishop, Zepheniah (Phannel), Jr., 2182, 2226
Bissel, Daniel, 0111
Bissell, Daniel, 0900, 0905
Bissell, Daniel Russell, 3832, 3967, 3968
Bixler, David, 1303
Bize, Daniel, 3259
Black, Noah, 3881, 4203
Blackburn, William, 3707
Blacklock, Nicholas F., II, 3030
Blackman, Jeremiah, 3491
Bladisdell, Moses, 0485
Blair, Alexander, 1118
Blair, Ezekiel, 0942
Blair, Francis, 2531
Blair, James, 1363
Blake, William, 0941
Blanchard, Reuben K., 3508
Blanchard, Reuben Kimball, 2809, 2846
Blauvelt, Jacob I., 2772
Blevins, John, 3061
Blin, Theodore, 1279
Blish, Daniel, 0592
Bliss, Francis, 2247, 2248
Blizzard, William of W., 2969
Bloodgood, Aaron, 1214, 1215
Bloomer, Daniel, 1175, 2717
Bloomfield, Joseph, 2414
Blouin, Charlesville, 3358
Blue, John, 0937, 0938
Blumer, Jacob, 3613
Blunt, Francis, 2317, 2552
Blunt, Mark S., 0235
Blythe, James, 0850
Boardman, James, 2179
Bobart, Charles Carroll, 0403
Bobenmoyer, John, 1814
Boden, John, 1978
Boerstler, Charles G., 1048
Boerstler, Jacob, 1048
Boerum, William, 0234
Bogardus, Robert, 1883
Boggs, Alexander Lowry, 0388

Bolen, Thomas, 3745
Bolles, Frederick D., 0555
Bollinger, Moses, 4612
Bollman, Thomas (Gottlieb), 1607
Bonaventura y Alpuente, Don, 2960
Bonaventura y Alpuente, Don Francisco, 2876, 3839
Bond, Elial, 1335
Bond, Thomas E., 1054
Bond, Thomas Talbott, 4491
Bone, Elihu, 3688
Bonnaffon, Anthony, 0272, 0273, 0638, 1753, 3073
Bonner, William, 4558
Bonneval, Alexandre, 3979
Boomer, Daniel, 1727
Boone, Charles, 4576
Boone, Daniel Morgan, 3878
Boone, Mordecai, 1717
Boothe, James, 3467
Borden, Francis, 1960, 3276, 3388, 3461
Borzorth, William, 3167
Bosson, Jonathan Davis, 1321
Bost, Daniel, 3657
Boswell, Henry, 1767
Boucher, Henry, 0646
Boulden, Nathaniel L., 1429
Bouldin, Jehu, 2339, 3163
Bouldin, John, 0288
Bouligny, Charles J. D., 2380
Bouligny, Charles Joseph, 2591
Bouligny, Charles Joseph D., 2474, 2570
Boulingny, Joseph Dominque, 2508
Boulingy, Charles Dominique, 3322
Bourgeois, Jean Baptiste, 4466
Boutte, Antoine, 3981
Bowe, Nathaniel, 2939
Bower, Jacob, 0198, 0225
Bowers, Henry, 0992
Bowie, Eversfield, 1702, 2643
Bowie, Rezin Pleasants, 2931
Bowman, Abraham, 3593
Bowman, Andrew, 1243
Boxley, George, 1337
Boyce, Isaac, 3958
Boyce, William, 3917
Boyd, George, 0205
Boyd, John, 1779
Boyd, William, 1307

Boyer, William, 1582
Boyle, Philip, 1211, 1516
Boynton, John, 4261, 4263, 4374
Boyt, James, 4299
Bradford, John, 0970
Brady, Hugh, 2350, 4196
Bragaw, Abraham, 3405
Brandeberry, Philip, 2984
Brandel, William, 0764
Brandon, Gerard C., 3795
Brankston, John, 2622
Branner, John, 2694
Brannon, Thomas, 1493
Breckinridge, Robert, 3382, 3409
Breed, Aaron, 2044
Breed, Holton Johnson, 1153, 1392
Breidenthal, Henry, 1961
Brent, John, 2245
Bresee, Harmon, 3020
Brevoort, Henry B., 0072
Brewer, John, 2782
Brewster, Elisha Belcher, 0528
Brice, Nicholas, 0406, 2857, 4201
Bridgewater, Isaac, 3849
Briggs, Edward D., 0043
Briggs, Griffin, 2447
Briggs, Thomas Otis, 0243
Brigham, Nathaniel, 0514
Brightman, George Cleaver, 1643
Brightwell, Jason, 4430
Bringier, Michel Douradou, 2819
Brinkerhoff, George R., 0444, 0499
Brinley, Henry, 2662
Briscoe, Thomas, 2798
Bristor, George, 1156, 1426, 3279
Brittin, William, 0788, 2050
Brock, John, Jr., 1654
Brockenbrough, Austin, 3400
Brockway, Ezra, 3596
Brodhead, Garrett, Jr., 0848
Brodhead, Richard, 3311, 3313
Brodnax, Edward Brooking, 2954
Brohawn, John, 1889
Brokaw, Cornelius, 4369, 4389
Brokaw, Isaac C., 2996
Bromley, Lewis, 0711
Bronaugh, William, 1775
Brooke, Jesse, 0070, 0071
Brooke, Nathan, 0244, 1719
Brooke, William, 0049, 0119, 0908, 1423, 1505, 1506, 1761

Brookes, John, 0918
Brooks, Alexander Scammell, 0107
Brooks, Charles, 1093
Brooks, John, 0107
Brower, Abraham, 2878, 2948, 3804, 3846
Brower, John Lefoy, 1890
Brown, Absalom, 3648
Brown, Aloysius Lewis, 2913
Brown, Amasa, 0773
Brown, David, 1387, 1789, 1853
Brown, Edmund, Sr., 3521, 3702, 3810, 3811, 3812, 3821
Brown, George, 2082
Brown, Gustavus, 3223
Brown, Ira, 3087
Brown, Jacob, 0097
Brown, Joseph, 2304
Brown, Levi, 0601, 0863, 0864, 0906
Brown, Redden, 3190, 3328
Brown, Samuel Byrne, 0914
Brown, Stewart, 2016, 3200
Brown, Stewart (Stuart), 1836
Brown, Thomas, 0624, 1560
Browne, Hugh, 3289
Brownlow, William, 3682
Bruce, Robert, 1179
Brumfield, William, 1074
Bruner, Solomon, 1323
Brush, Elijah, 3097, 3098, 3647
Bryan, William, 0095
Bryant, Daniel Chandler, 1381
Bryant, Hiram, 1128
Bryant, Levi, Jr., 3184
Bubier, John, 0144
Buchanan, George, 0562, 3897
Buchanan, James, 0913
Buchanan, John, I, 4307
Buck, Benjamin, 0662, 0687, 1588, 1666, 2237, 2347
Buck, Charles, III, 3533
Buck, William Richardson, 2911
Buckingham, Levi, 0188
Buckland, Frank, 1563
Buffum, James R., 0139
Buker, Jonah, 1217
Bulkeley, Joshua, 1989
Bullus, John, 0069
Bunker, Ebenezer, 4224
Bunting, John, 0507
Burbank, Peter, 0755, 1448

Burbank, Sullivan, 0037
Burch, Richard, 1170
Burgin, John, 0236
Burgoon, Jacob, 3208
Burham, James, 0315
Burk, Thomas, 3017
Burke, Francis, 1188
Burks, Daniel, 3121
Burks, Rowland Peartree, 1874
Burlew, Cornelius, 2949
Burneston, William Reed, 3833, 4079
Burnett, Stephen Grover, 1122
Burnham, George W., 0270
Burns, James, 0734
Burns, Thomas, 3955
Burr, Timothy, 0855, 1080, 1081, 1231, 1697
Burroughs, Enoch, 1168
Burroughs, James, 1139
Burt, Franklin, 1851
Burtnett, Daniel, 1625, 1626
Burton, Hiram, 0233
Burton, John H., 3575
Burton, Salmon, 0233
Burton, Simon, 0233
Burton, Simon, Jr., 0233
Burton, William, 0233
Burton, William Martin, 3562
Busch, John Francis, 1462
Bush, Henry C., 2671, 2975
Bush, Joseph Reuben, 2502, 2514, 2515, 3372, 3464, 3500, 3522
Bush, Oliver, 2927
Bush, William S., 1593, 2312, 3775
Bushnell, Sterling Graves, 4094
Bushnell, William, 1469
Busick, John, 0386, 0410, 0450
Butler, Aaron W., Jr., 4271
Butler, Bailey, 4177
Butler, George Pollard, 2713
Butler, Lemuel G., 1829
Butler, Thomas Langford, 4584
Butterfield, Joseph, 0349
Butterworth, Buckley, 3141
Buvinger, Leonard, Jr., 2261
Byerly, John, 0374, 2956, 3809
Byers, Michael, 3642, 3738
Cabarrus, Augustus, Jr., 4381
Cabeen, Samuel, 3993
Cadle, John, 0382
Cadmus, Thomas, 1397

Cadwalader, Thomas, 0015, 0324, 0805, 1756
Caffee, John C., 4085, 4394, 4412
Caffery, John, 3602, 4642
Cagle, Sampson, 4186
Cahoon (Calhoun), Caleb, 3147
Cain, Mathew, 3283
Calder, William, 1827, 1994, 2110
Caldwalader, Thomas, 1227
Caldwell, James, 3074
Caldwell, James St. Clair, 1088
Caldwell, Thomas, 2021
Caldwell, William, 4485, 4605
Calhoun, Daniel (David), 0446
Calhoun, Mark, 4449
Calliham, David, 2421
Calliham, John, Jr., 2580
Calmes, Marquis, IV, 4599
Cameron, James, 0801, 0895, 2818
Camp, Cyrus Talmage, 1019
Campbell, Andrew, 3864
Campbell, Beasley, 4608
Campbell, George Washington, 1495
Campbell, James, 2547
Campbell, John, 3268
Campbell, Thomas, 1224
Campbell, Walter, 1310
Candee, Enos, 2823
Candler, John, Jr., 2353
Canedy, Zebulon L., 3091
Cann, John, 1458
Cannon, William, 1168
Canter, Henry, 3093
Cantrelle, Michel B., Jr., 3075
Capes, William, 1208, 1286, 1287, 1477, 2087, 2088, 2089, 2090, 2091, 3211
Caples, Jacob, 4002
Capron, Laban, 4396
Carey, William, 1192
Carlock, Abraham, 2276
Carlton, Ellis Watts, 3456
Carman, Frederick Mark, 3872
Carman, Richard, 1738
Carmick, Daniel, 0304, 0866, 3111, 3752
Carnes, John, 0543, 0567
Carpenter, Daniel, 4422
Carpenter, Francis, 1642
Carpenter, James, 3397, 4515
Carr, Caleb, 4397

Carroll, William, 4083
Carswell, Robert, 2267
Carter, Benjamin, 1250
Carter, Curtis, 2279
Carter, Daniel, 1608
Carter, Ephriam, Jr., 0708
Carter, Jarrett, 3453, 3558
Carter, Joshua, 2826, 3946
Carter, Parsons, 2447
Caruthers, John, 4056, 4328, 4329
Cary, Robert James, 2031
Cassard, Gilbert, 0289, 0297, 1009, 1053, 1588
Cassin, John, 2482, 3244, 3292
Castephens, John, 3489, 3513
Castleman, David, 4237
Castleman, Jacob, 4237
Castleman, John H., 4237
Castleman, Lewis, 4237
Catching, Philip, 4350
Cathcart, Robert, 1023, 1498
Causten, James H., 2609
Cave, Thomas, 0524, 1195
Cave, Thomas, Jr., 0150
Chadwick, James, 3157
Chamberlain, Henry, 4081
Chambers, James, 1682, 1715
Chambers, John McLaughlin, 0179
Chambers, Joseph, 3386
Chambers, Perdue, 0846
Chambers, Ralph, 0552, 0553, 0585
Champion, Henry, 1802
Champion, Roswell, Jr., 1740
Champion, Sylvester, 1735
Chaney, Thomas, 2722
Chapman, Asa, 0420
Chapman, Ebenezer, 0316
Chappell, Miles, 2860
Charlton, James D., 4431
Chase, Thomas C., 0003
Chattle, Thomas, 2354, 2355
Chaytor, Daniel, 2730
Chenet, Eugene, 3106
Cherbonnier, Pierre, 1057
Cheston, James, 0303, 1832, 1894
Chewning, Reuben, 1772
Chexnaidre, Andre, 4103
Chiem, Richard Henry, 0724
Childs, Thomas, 3643
Chinn, Thomas Withers, 2870
Chipman, Timothy Fuller, 2797

Chisam, John, 4613
Chotard, Henry, 2518, 3327, 3384, 3632
Chretien, Hyppolite, 3156
Christhilf, Harry, 0172
Christhilf, Heinrich, 2306, 2342, 4200, 4198
Christian, Gideon, 3879
Christian, John, 3518, 3704
Christie, Israel, 2801, 2802, 4628
Christy, Andrew, 3369
Church, Nathaniel, 3998
Church, Peter, 3834
Churchill, Shepard, 2240
Clagett, Elie, 1527
Claggett, Thomas Wilson, 4237
Claghorn, John William, 1071, 2035
Claiborne, Ferdinand Leigh, 2430, 2435, 2815
Claiborne, William C. C., 2457
Clark, Christopher, 1166
Clark, David, 0904
Clark, John R., 0054
Clark, Lathrop, 1260
Clark, Norman, 0521, 0522
Clark, Norman, Jr., 0619
Clark, Ralph, 2000
Clark, Samuel, 1728, 2927, 3114
Clarke, John Salle, 3678
Clarke, Thomas, 0791
Clarke, William, 0114
Clary, Ethan Allen, 0628
Clay, Green, 2098
Clayton, Philip, 1724
Clayton, Zephaniah, 4236
Clement, Evan C., 0164
Clement, Evan Collins, 1439, 1440, 1481, 2131, 2132, 2224, 2225, 2542, 2684, 2685, 2686, 2705, 2706, 2707, 2708, 2710, 2957, 3299, 3300
Clement, Henry, 2448, 2590
Clements, Reuben, 0754
Clements, Thomas, 4003
Clemmens, Daniel, 4248
Cleveland, Erastus, 3924, 4228, 4232, 4233
Cleveland, Joseph, 4372
Clift, Newton, 2712
Cline, Philip, Jr., 3545
Clingman, George Washington, 3213

Clinton, Alexander, 1372, 2822
Cloninger, Adam, Jr., 4034
Cobb, Josiah, 0396
Cobb, Samuel, 0036
Coburn, James W., 2806
Cochran, Richard Ellis, 4130
Cocke, John, 1011, 3028
Cocke, John Fleming, I, 3625
Cockrill, Thomas, 2983, 3092
Coe, Adam Simmons, 0546
Coe, Darius, 0083
Coffee, John, 2862, 4009
Coffin, Robert Stevenson, 0230
Colby, Jonathan, 2613, 3294, 3517, 3546, 3516
Colby, Samuel S., 4048
Colby, Thomas W., 2040, 2183
Coldwell, John Campbell, 2534, 2535
Cole, Barnet, 1844
Cole, James Alexander, 0997
Cole, Joseph, 4323
Cole, Royal, 1908
Cole, Samuel, 0602, 0644
Cole, William, 0401, 3988
Coleman, Henry Embry, 2085, 2086
Coleman, John, 0588
Coleman, Richard, 3064
Coleman, Robert L., 2367
Coles, James, 2039
Colgin, John, 4364, 4573
Colles, James, 0057
Collins, Eben Hall, 0951
Collins, John, 2880
Collins, John Alexander, 1454, 1561
Collmus, Levi, 1129, 1244
Colton, Edward Bond, 3371
Comegys, Cornelius Parsons, 0093, 0536, 0743
Comstock, Peter, 0589, 0626
Conant, Airs (Ayres), 3202
Conant, John, 0047
Conant, Joseph, 3623
Condit, Ezekiel, 2668
Condit, Jothan, 0696
Condit, Stephen, 1202
Conkey, Thomas Hamilton, 3012
Conkling, John Johnson, 1486
Conner, Andrew, 1422
Conner, Harrison, 4461
Conrad, David, 0389, 0463
Constant, John, 2297, 2316

Contee, John, 0217
Cook (Cooke), Adam, 2269
Cook, Bernard Henry, 2766, 3025
Cook, Bernard Henry, Sr., 2302
Cook, Joel, 0141
Cook, Phillip, 3891
Cook, Richard Fielding, 1565
Cooley, Henry, 3205
Coombs, George, 2099
Coon, Jasper S. M., 4540
Cooper, Francis, 0586, 0700, 0732
Cooper, Jacob, 4633
Cooper, Meredith, 4486
Cooper, Robert, 0008
Corliss, Ebeneza, 0062
Cornell, Archibald, 3782
Cornell, Henry, 0923
Cornish, Benjamin, 3458, 3479, 3497, 3767
Cornwell, William, 2008
Corwin, David, Jr., 0744
Cory, William, 1825
Cotting, William, 1840
Couch, Philip, 1901, 3171, 3249
Coulon, Charles, 3843
Cowan, Thompson, 4273
Cowen, Benjamin Sprague, 0661
Cowles, Alpheus, 4604
Cox, Caleb, 2181
Cox, James, 4555
Cox, Joseph, 4047
Cox, Martin, 4517
Cox, Matthew, 0573, 0574
Cox, Thomas, 0625, 0802, 1390, 1391
Coy, Alvin, 0873
Craddick, Joseph, 0364
Crain, John, 3085
Crain, Richard More, 0291
Crane, Aaron T., 2549
Crane, Elias, 1910, 1934
Crane, Elias B., 1488
Crane, John, 1910, 1934
Crane, Samuel, 4414
Cranford, James, 1404, 1435, 2205
Cranston, James, 1722
Crawford, James, 3859
Crawford, Moses, 0993
Crawford, William Bradford, 0254
Cress, George, 3685
Crey, Frederick, 0979
Crist, Jacob, 1128

Crittenden, William Gatewood, 1226, 1267
Crocker, Lemuel Grant, 4464
Crockett, Samuel, 1338
Cromwell, Nathan, 0409
Cromwell, Oliver, 1315, 1499, 1818
Crooks William, 1986
Crooks, Richard, 3649
Crosby, Stephen, 0147
Crouch, Isaac, 4183
Crowninshield, Benjamin W., 1146
Culbertson, John, 3921
Cumming, Robert, 2266
Cummins, David, 2175
Cummins, John, 1745, 1984
Cunningham, John, 1842
Cupp, Frederick, 4611
Curley, Isham, Jr., 2866
Currence, Samuel, 4643
Current, John, 4434
Currie, Ezekiel, 1645
Curtis, Ebenezer, 0774
Curtis, George, 1969
Curtis, Lebbeus, 0737
Curtis, Moses, 2101
Cushman, Don Alonzo, 2256
Cushman, Seth, 1951
Cutter, Fitch, 2429
Cutter, Joshua, 1409
d'Herbigny, Charles Zenon, 2875
de Buys, Pierre Gaspard, 2836
de Chalmette, Ignace de Lino, 2397, 2583, 2584, 3756, 3763, 3825, 3826, 4016
de Fazende, Sebastein Francois Morriere, 3373
de Kernion, Crispin Charles, 2392
de La Houssaye, Francois Balthasar, 4207
de Vezin, Jean Baptiste Olivier, 3779
de Villiers Jumonville, 3843
de la Garciniere, Charles Fagot, 2410
de la Houssaye, Francois Balthaser, 4514, 4281
de la Houssaye, Louis A., 2382, 2470, 2485, 2565, 2588, 3504, 3505
de la Houssaye, Louis Alexander, LePelletier, 3317
de la Houssaye, Louis Alexandre, 3431

de la Houssaye, Louis Alexandre Le Pelletier, 3334
de la Houssaye, Louis Alexandre LeP., 3381
de la Houssaye, Louis Alexandre le Pelletier, 3332
de la Houssaye, Louis Le Pelletier, 3755
de la Roche, George Henri Frederick Franck, 4488
de la Ronde, Pierre Denis, 3868, 3910, 4574
de la Ronde, Pierre Denis, II, 2445, 2446
de la Vergne, Hugues, 2569
deBlanc, Pierre Georges Cesaire, 4172
deChalmette, Ignace de Lino, 3765, 4137
deLivaudais, Jean B. E., 3670
deVezin, Jean Baptiste Olivier, 4279
deVillere, Jacques Philippe, 3393
deVillere, Jacques Philippe R., 3603
delaGarciniere, Charles Fagot, 2460, 2461, 2462
duBois, Jeremiah Greenman, 2117
D'Aquin, Charles Louis, 3396
D'Aunoy, Etienne de Bore Favre, 3914
D'Avezac, Auguste G., 3122
Dagg, John Leadley, 2587
Daingerfield, Leroy Parker, 1473
Dale, Adam, 1312
Dallas, Alexander James, 0039
Dalliba, James, 0618
Dally, Charles S., 3635
Dalrymple, William, 3493
Daly, James, 0658
Daly, Lawrence, 4280
Dames, Augustus, 2301, 2598, 2599, 2625, 2967
Damon, Joseph, 0475, 0476
Dana, Francis, 1605
Dana, George, 1966
Danaker, John Jacob, 0363
Dance, William, 3626
Daneker, John Jacob, 0156, 1494
Daniel, Chisolm, 2955
Daniel, Jesse, 4458
Daniels, Joseph, 1046, 1108, 1126
Danker, John J., 1566
Dant, William, 4497

214 Ancestor Index

Darby, Barthelemy Francois St.
  Mark, 4407
Darby, George, 3780
Darling, James, 0218
Darlington, Meredith, 0494
Darlington, William, 2366
Darnall, Elias, 3668
Darrach, Thomas Bradford, 0672
Darrow, Leavitt, 0502
Darst, Benjamin, Jr., 3404
Dart, Reuben, 0133
Dashiell, Henry, 0854
Daugherty, Daniel, 1430
Davenport, Isaiah, 0030
Davenport, William, 1190
Davey, Hugh, 0216
Davidson (Divison), Bracket, 4010
Davidson, James, 0395
Davidson, Lewis, 2235
Davidson, Robert, 0459, 0496
Davie, Samuel, 4282
Davis, Amasa, 0131
Davis, Eliphalet, 0486
Davis, Isaac, 0286, 1285
Davis, Jacob, 0087
Davis, James, 0393
Davis, John, 0287, 0447, 1479, 1941, 2007, 3062, 3719
Davis, Lothrop, 2241
Davis, Micajah, 3557
Davis, Phanuel, 4620, 4629
Davis, Samuel Boyer, 1326, 1405, 1423, 3291
Davis, William, 1555, 1606, 2028
Dawson, Thomas, 2321
Day, James, 2252
Day, Lewis, 4539
Day, Morgan, 1983
De Alpuente, Francisco B., 2572
De Buys, Pierre Gaspard, 2491
De Castera, Auguste G., 3599, 3600
De Chemilly, Germain D., 3070
De Fazende, Sebastien F., 3069
De La Garciniere, Charles Fagot, 2842
De La Ronde, Pierre Denis, II, 2548
De La Vergne, Hugues, 2674
De Laronde, Pierre Denis, IV, 3378
De Lavergne, Theodoras B., 4019, 4073
De Peyster, William, 2405

De Russy, Lewis Gustavus, 2532
DeBellevue, Francois Barbin, 4250
DeCastro, Auguste Genevieve
  Valentin D'Auezac, 4139
DeChemilly, Germain D., 3057
DeFazende, Sebastien, 3007
DeFlaugeac, Antoine P., 3035
DeForest, Philip, 0660
DeFrance, Hawkins Boone, 4234
DeFriese, Hiram Abiff, 2863
DeGruy, Dufochar, 3683
DeLaronde, Pierre Denis, IV, 2886, 2947, 2999
DeLong, John Francis, 4158
DePeyster, William S., 2677
DeRussy, Lewis Gustavus, 2868
DeWitt (Witt), Willard, 3989
DeYoung, Isaac, 0294, 0887, 1090, 1193
Deadman, William, 0779
Dean, James Savage, 3330
Dean, Joseph, 3667
Dean, Joseph, II, 1029
Deane, Ambrose, 1791
Decatur, Ann Pine, 3196, 3316
Decker, Andrew D., 3048
Decoursey, Isaac, 4180
Decuir, Godefroi, 3838
Delafield, Edward, 0338
Delamater, William, 3591
Deland, Levi, 1685
Delaney, Jacob, 0129, 1945
Delano, Jesse, 1163
Delery, Jacques M. C., 3158
Delery, Jacques Monplaisir C., 3601
Delery, Jacques Monplaisir Chauvin, 2831, 2847, 2950
Delery, Louis Chauvin, 4110
Delery, Nicolas Chauvin, 3053
Demaree, Samuel, 3010
Denbo, Joseph, 1903
Dennis, Adam, 1530
Dennison, Isaac, 1463
Dent, John Turner, 3391
Depauw, John, 4442
Derr, Michael, 0373
Des Forges, Louis H., 3066
Des Forges, Louis Hus, 2522, 2523, 2774, 3383, 3414
Desforges, Louis Hus, 3510, 3857
Deshon, Daniel, Jr., 1322

Deslonde, Andre, 3939
Despeaux, John, 1065
Devane, Benjamin, 4071
Devenport, Jean, Jr., 3037
Dewey, Chauncey, 4133
Dewey, Jeremiah, 0422, 0423, 0424
Dewey, Simeon, 0710
Dewing, Timothy, 1622
Dewing, Warren, 1622
Dickey, James, 4603
Dickinson, David, 2571
Dickinson, Solomon, 2271
Dickson, John, 1131, 1308, 2099
Diehl, John, 3774
Dietrich, Jacob, 2630
Diggs, Beverly, 0934, 1620
Dill, Robert, 1000, 1480, 2369
Diller, Adam, 3542
Dilley (Dillie), Lewis, 2668
Dillingham, John, 3876
Dillon, Henry, 4267
Dimitry, Andrea, 2528, 3535
Dingley, Jeremiah, 3638
Dinkins, James, 2615, 3319, 3346
Dixon, Jeremiah, 4392
Dobbin, John, 3870
Dodge, Robert, 1204
Doe, Jonathan, 3658
Doherty, William, 3736, 3907
Dold, Samuel Miller, 1017, 1569, 1570
Donaldson, James Lowry, 3260
Donaldson, William, 2264, 2335
Donan, David Cox, 4585
Doner, John, 3996
Donnell, John, 1390, 1391
Doran, Jeremiah, 3650
Dorrance, George, 1511
Dorsey, John Worthington of Caleb, 4355
Dorsey, Jonathan, 2864
Doty, Nathaniel, 0633
Dougherty, John, 4527
Douglass, George, 0740, 0741, 0742
Douglass, Robert, 4419
Dove, William Geoghegan, 1512
Dowd (Doud), Samuel, 1364
Downe, Nathaniel H., 0385
Downing, Howell, 0203, 1699
Downs, Frederick, 3785
Downs, William, 4428

Doyns, Chichester, 2627
Drake, Aaron, 2760, 3046
Drake, Lemuel, 3712
Draper, Gideon, 1264
Dresser, Thomas, 1693
Drummer, Stephen, 0516
Du Bourg, Pierre F. S. C., 2699
DuMontier, Onesiphore B., 3149
Duane, William, 0369, 2678, 3029, 3132, 3133, 3337, 3468, 3469, 3470, 3715, 3716
Dubbs, Jacob, 4120
Ducatel, Germain, 2900, 3365
Ducros, Rodolphe Joseph, 2496
Dudley, Patrick, 0275
Dudley, Peter, 0073, 1549, 1854
Dudley, William, 0336, 2775
Dukehart, Henri Van Arden, 2356
Dukehart, Henry V., 1822
Dulany, Samuel, 0248, 0249, 0397, 0399, 1064, 2305
Dumontier, Onesiphore Bernard, 4375
Dunaway, Rawleigh, 0276
Dunbar, George Towers, Sr., 2813
Dunbar, Hosea, 1742
Duncan, Abner Lawson, 3507, 3426
Duncan, Alexander, 0319
Duncan, Charles, 3577, 3578
Duncan, George, 4266
Duncan, Wesley Leland, 1578
Dunham, Shubael, 1196
Dunkel, John, 1183
Dunlap, John, 3641
Dunlap, Josiah, 1364
Dunlap, Sallows, 0577, 0745, 0830, 1013, 1401, 2141
Dunn, Nathaniel A., 1688
Dunsmoor, Phineas, 0457, 0705
Duplessis, Francois, III, 2424, 3858
Duplessis, Francois, Jr., 2451, 2471
Dupre, Jacques, 3207
Duprey (Dupray), Thomas, 1922
Dupuis, Hypolite, 3931
Dupuy, Aubry, 3286, 4332
Durel, Jean-Baptiste Neuville, 3410, 3866, 2932
Durel, Michel, V., 3068
Durfee, Daniel, Jr., 0922
Durst, John, 2981
Dustin, Eliphalet, 4625

Dutton, John, 0190, 0204, 0210
Duvall, Barton, 1037, 2979
Dye, Luke, 4528
Dyer, William Hay, 2332
Eakin, Samuel Hunter, 0451, 0831, 1425
Eames, Joshua, 3483
Easter, Lewis, 4575
Eastwick, Thomas, 0739
Eatman, Irwin, 3848
Eaton, Richard, Sr., 3467
Ebur, John Francis, 3222
Eby, Jacob, 2690
Eckert, Jacob, 2282
Edgar, Nicholas, 3975
Edge, Isaac, II, 0657
Edie, David, 1016
Edmiston, Zebulon Brevard, 4637
Edmondson, Amos, 3339
Edmondson, Andrew Jackson, 3730
Edson, Joseph, 0544, 0587
Edward Kellum, Sr., 4598
Edwards, Daniel, Sr., 2810
Eichelberger, Frederick, 3561
Eichelberger, William, 2655
Elbert, Samuel, 0949, 2790, 2851, 3026
Elder, Basil Spalding, 0629
Eldredge, Aaron, II, 3892
Eldredge, Oliver, 0076
Elfreth, John, 0550, 0570, 0579
Elkin, Robert, 4446
Elkins (Elkens), George W., 2192
Elkins, George W., 2334, 2368
Elliott, Abraham James, 4498
Elliott, John, 4042
Elliott, John Lisle, 3377
Ellis, Aaron, 2761
Ellison, Lewis, 4507
Elmendorf, Martin, 2160, 2854
Ely (Eli), George, 0596
Ely, Epaphras Cook, 2990
Emerson, Nathaniel, 1229
Emery, John, 0655
Emmet, Thomas Addis, 2720
Emory, John King Beck, 1176
Endicott, John A., 4025
Enochs, Isaac, 4289
Ensor, John of George, 3850
Erichson, Christian, 2608
Esselstyn, John Brodhead, 2197

Estes, Benjamin Hall, 0954, 4337
Estes, John Bartlett, 3629
Estes, Triplett Thorp, 3127
Estes, William, 3842
Etchberger, William, 1065
Etter, Philip, 3134, 3243
Eubank, Robert, 4382
Eustis, Abram, 2520, 2719, 3394, 3569, 4138
Evans, Andrew J., 4441
Evans, James, 0762, 2968
Everest, Isaac, 3527
Everett, Joseph, 1813
Every, Andrew Perry, 3598
Ewing, Jeremiah, Jr., 2724
Ewing, Robert, 2676
Faber, Samuel, 0491
Faget, Jean-Baptiste, 3036
Faidley, John, 1567
Fair, Peter, 3063, 3067
Fairbank, George, 1882, 1972
Fairbanks, David, 3303
Fairchild, Benjamin Smith, 0800
Farmer, John, 1971
Farmer, Nathan, 3880
Farnandis, Walter, 4595
Farrar, Bernard Gaines, 3523
Farrington, Elijah, 0335, 1963, 2702
Farrow, William H., 3401
Favort, Louis Estevan, 2401, 2378, 2395, 2404, 2450, 2477, 2483, 2505
Favrot, Luis Estevan, 3176
Favrot, Philogene, 1402, 2422
Faxon, Walter Stiles, 1877
Fell, Robert W., 3008
Fellows, Levi, 3597
Felter, John P., 1073
Felter, John Polhemus, 1858, 1859
Felton, Cornelius Conway, 2273, 2336, 2709
Felton, John, 2540
Ferguson, William, 0688
Ferlot, Antoine, 2970, 2987
Fernald, Josiah, 0775
Fernandez y Mendoza, Jose Joaquin, 3188, 3326, 3415, 3792
Ferree, Joel, 1460
Ferrell, Lewis Wells, 1993
Ferris, Jacob, Jr., 0824
Fessenden, Thomas, 1770
Fessenden, William, 4026

Fetter, Jacob, 4385
Fewell, William, 4298
Fick, Adolph Christian, 0284, 0610
Field, John, 0727, 3887
Fife, William, Jr., 3722
Fillmore, Comfort Day, 2177
Finch, Jonathan, 3225
Fincher, Jesse, 3661
Finks, Fielding, 4012
Finley, William, 1535, 1536
Finnell, John, 4146, 4443
Finster, Jacob, 4314
Fish, Lemuel, 1261, 1452
Fish, Simeon, Jr., 1892
Fish, Simeon, Sr., 1892
Fisher, George, 3854
Fisher, Messenger, 0532
Fiske, Mark, 2877
Fissell, Henry, Jr., 2634
Fitch, Jonathan, 3983
Fitch, Joseph Pratt, 0331
Fitchet, James N., 1856
Fite, Caspar, 2187
Fitler, William, 2114, 2159
Fitzhugh, Philip, 2641
Fitzpatrick, Rene, 0948
Flanders, Joseph, 3179, 3329
Flansburg, Jacob, 2073
Flansburgh, Jacob, 1991
Fletcher, John Swift, 4116
Fletcher, Phineas Parker, 2001
Fletcher, Thomas, Sr., 2770
Fletcher, William, 0532
Flint, Daniel, 3309
Flournoy, Samuel, 3862
Flower, Gustavus, 1041
Flowers, John, 3494
Floyd, Nathaniel, 4640, 4647
Fluker, Hardy, 3933
Fobes (Forbes), Porter, 3961
Fobes, Joshua, 2nd., 1957, 2765
Fogg, Nathan, 0630
Follett, Martin Dewey, 0458, 0498, 0500, 0540
Follett, Oran, 0678
Folsom, Josiah, 1733
Fontenot, Alexandre Charles Baptiste, 3940
Forbes, Benjamin Gilbert, 4415
Forbes, Murray, 1708, 2133, 2134, 2149

Forbush, Asa, 0411
Ford, George W., 0430
Ford, Isaac, 0784
Ford, John, 0135
Ford, Seth, 3906
Forstall, Edmond John, 2442, 2452, 2453, 2454, 2455, 2456, 2473, 2653, 2664, 3757, 3875, 4136
Forstall, Nicholas Michel Edmond, 4135
Forster, John, III, 2338, 2481
Forsyth, Gideon Comstock, 3348
Fortier, Jacques, 3407, 3790
Fortier, Jean Michel, 3142
Fortier, Michel, 3411
Fortier, Michel, II, 2434, 2845, 3350, 3652, 3764, 4209, 4288, 4341
Foster, Adams, 1170
Foster, Isaac, 3564
Foster, Jacob, 4059, 4068
Foster, John C., 0651
Foster, John, 2nd., 4156
Fotterall, Stephen Egan, 0760, 1091
Foucher, Pierre, 2449, 2489, 2490, 2616, 3320, 3387, 3413
Foucher, Pierre Edmond, 2930
Fountain (Fontain), Henry, 2767
Fountain, Andrew, 1909
Fountain, Henry, 1768
Foust, Michael, 4636
Fowble, William, 0252
Fowler, Gilbert Ogden, 0126
Fowler, John, 1453
Fox, Augustus Carlton, 0875
Francis, John, 1838
Frank, Samuel Boone, 4179
Franklin, Bedney Abednego, 3791, 4105
Fraser, James P., 1331, 2060, 3604, 3701
Frazee, John, 2753
Frazer, James, 1629
Frazier, Thomas, 1388
Freeman, Edmond (Edman), 4465
Freeman, John, 3459
Freeman, Samuel, 0977
French, Ebenezer, 3173
French, Ephraim, 1451
French, Grovey, 1995
French, Joel, 0640, 0803, 0857, 1059
French, William, 1021

Frick, Jacob, 0152
Frisbie, Levi, 1185, 1186
Fritz, Michael, 0493
Frost, Timothy Moore, 0038
Frowert, John, 1367
Frushour (Freshour), George, 2251
Fry (Frye), Samuel, 4638
Fuhrman, Philip, 3336
Fuller, Asaph, 2151, 2152
Fuller, Calvin Perry, 3040, 3045
Fuller, Daniel, 0790
Fuller, Moses, 1749, 1750
Fuller, Nathaniel, 2371
Fuller, Simeon, 3005
Fulmer, John, 1518
Furlong, William, 0404
Furr, Paul, 3726
Futhey, Robert, 1089, 1366
Futhey, Robert K., 4530
Gaillard, Pierre, 2573
Gaither, Henry, 0689
Gale, Charles, 0753, 3861
Gale, Peter, 0223
Gallop, Isaac, 0344, 0351
Gann, William, 3995, 4111, 4216
Gano, John S., 0539
Gardner, Charles Kitchell, 0663
Gardner, David, 2313
Gardner, Edward, 1154
Gardner, Hiram, 4252
Gardner, Jesse, 4463
Gardner, John, Jr., 4436
Garic, Francois, 3659, 3824
Garic, Jean Francois, 2417, 2525, 2883
Garidel, Louis A., 3054
Garidel, Louis Ambroise, 2929, 3160, 3672
Garlick, Samuel, 4621
Garlington, Christopher, 0142
Garr, Benjamin, 3212
Garrard, Daniel, 0025
Garrard, James, 1192
Garrettson, Mason, 3457
Garsuch, Thomas, 1474
Gates, William, 3949
Gaulden, Zachariah, 3152
Gault, James, 1212, 1237
Gaumer, Daniel, 0470
Gautier, John Sinclair, 0556
Gautier, Samuel John Sinclair, 0974

Gee, James Hicks, 4544
Geer, Harris, 2265
Generelly, Fleury Theotime, 2839
Gentry, Richard, 1558, 4378
Gentry, Richard, II, 2769
George, William, Jr., 1689
Gerard, James Watson, 2815
Germain, Stephen, 0794
Gettys, Joseph, 4568
Gibbs, George, 1173
Gibbs, Isaac, 2173
Gibbs, Jacob, 2011, 2063, 3123
Gibbs, Jacobs, 2628
Gibson, Jacob, II, 3108
Gibson, John, 0197
Giddings, Hiram, 2176, 2206, 2207
Gifford, William, 3086
Gilbert, Abner, 4487
Gilbert, Judson, 0810
Gilberthorp, William, 2263
Gilbreath, Benjamin, 2049
Gilder, Reuben, 0683, 0729, 1010
Gilkyson, Andrew, 2784
Gill, Stephen, 0439, 0440, 0441
Gill, William Lowry, 0274
Gilles, George, 4284
Gillette, Jonathan, 3219
Gilman, Nathaniel, III, 1159
Gilmore, Robert, 3796
Gilmore, William Young, 0466
Girdler (Gridley), James, 4478
Girdley, Joseph, 4435
Gist, Benjamin, Jr., 4448, 4508
Gist, John, 4405
Glass, John, 0635
Gleim, Christian, 0565
Glentworth, James, 0053
Glick, George, 4043
Glover, Charles, 1694, 1980, 3343
Glover, John, 1128
Gobrecht, Christian, 0888
Godfrey, Benjamin, 3798
Godman, Samuel, 1092
Goff, Elisha, 2800
Goldsberry, Thomas, 0477
Goldsborough, Robert, 2163
Goldsborough, Robert H., 3548
Goldthwaite, Oren, 3270
Gonzales, Joseph, 4609
Goodard, Charles, 0305
Goodard, James, 1270

Goodhue, Joseph, 1899
Goodman, Samuel, 1641
Goodrich, Silas, 0648
Goodridge, Ira, 2020
Goodrum, Sterling, 4502
Goodspeed, Levi, 2873, 2874
Goodspeed, Zenas, 4061
Goodwin, James, 2258
Goodwin, John, Sr., 2211
Goodwin, Robert Norris, 0246
Goodwin, Tristam, 0680
Goodwin, Tristram, 2636
Gookins, William, Jr., 1671
Gordon, Samuel, 2193, 2268
Gore, George, 0627, 1424
Gorham, Barna (Barnabas), 1652
Gorman, David, 2988
Gorsuch, George W., 3128
Gorton, Rufus, 4388
Gotham, John, 0901
Goucher, Robert, 1603
Gough, Harry Dorsey, 1020
Gould, James, 0252
Gould, John, 0841
Gove, Enos Sanborn, 1094
Gover, Robert, 3389
Gradeless, Nathaniel, 3823, 4338
Grady, Anthony, 0392
Graham, Gabriel, 4192
Graham, George, 0030, 1710
Graham, Henry, 1967
Graham, Robert Findley, 3540
Graham, Thomas, 0763
Graham, William, 0251, 0252
Grandy, William, 2348
Grannis, Alva, 0432
Grant, William, 1555
Grasty, George, 3216
Graves, Eliphalet W., 2202
Graves, Jacob, 2669, 2729, 2732
Graves, Jeremiah, 0590
Graves, Lucius, 1678, 1679, 2075, 2195, 2196, 3019
Graves, Luther, 0906
Gray, Alexander, 2884
Gray, Isaac, 2768
Gray, James, 4523
Gray, John, 1066
Gray, Samuel, 3681
Gray, William Fairfax, 2665
Greely, John Balch, 0036, 1879

Green, Alanson, 3059
Green, Charles Bosley, 0995, 026
Green, Grief, 3660, 4211, 4610
Green, Isaac, 0515, 0976, 1796
Green, Jesse, 2003
Green, John Williams, 4379
Green, Richard, 0051, 0052
Green, Samuel, 2300, 3977
Green, Thomas, 1309
Greer, George, 0960, 0961, 0962
Gregg, William, 0487
Gregory, Francis Hoyt, 3252
Gregory, John, 2104
Gridley, Sylvester, 2083
Griffin, Hugh, 3486
Griffin, Samuel Stuart, 3570
Griffin, Stephen, 1125
Griffith, Howard, Jr., 0009
Griffith, Joshua, 0612
Griffith, Lyde, 2858
Griffith, Thomas, 2239, 2555, 2767
Grim, Jonathan, 4586
Grima, Barthelemy, 2423
Grindall, John Gibson, 1028
Grinnell, Moses, 0581
Grover, Asa R., 4173
Grover, Silas, 4147
Grover, Zadock, 4147
Groves, Samuel, 3742, 4522
Gue, Joseph, 4476
Guffin, Andrew, 2391
Guice, Jacob, 4426
Guice, Jonathan, 4590
Gulick, John, 2974
Gulick, Peter, 3543
Gunn, Elisha, 4538
Gunn, John, 1823
Gupton, Jacob, 3777
Gurney, Gridley, 3984
Guseman, Godfrey, 3740
Guth, Henry, 2715
Guy, John, 4316
Gwinn, James, 1478
Gwynne, David, 2363, 2759, 2814
Haas, Samuel, 1809
Hackstaff, William Greene, 0530
Hagler, Benjamin James, 2157
Huil, John, 2749
Hailey, Edward Taylor, 4077
Halbert, William, 3697, 4285
Hale, Benjamin, 1171, 1245

Haley, Noah, 2084
Hall, Bainbridge, 2747
Hall, Edward Pearsall, 1820
Hall, Frye, 0511
Hall, Giles, 1371
Hall, James, 0769, 1105
Hall, Joseph, 0191
Hall, Levi, 4038, 4039
Hall, Martin, 2319
Hall, Richard Wilmot, 2498
Hall, Thomas Graves, 4406
Hall, Thomas William, 1199
Hall, William, 2624
Halliburton, Martin, 2807
Hallowell, Isaac, 2370, 2865, 3230, 3245, 3248
Halsey, Jacob B., 0717
Haltom, William, 3974
Hamilton, John Chruch, 0340
Hamilton, Thomas, 2727
Hamilton, Thomas 3rd., 4046
Hamilton, William, 2002, 2566
Hammond, Elisha, 2595
Hammond, Lloyd Thomas, 1496
Hammond, Thomas, 2825
Hampton, Thomas, 1165
Hand, Samuel, 0639, 0841
Hanks, Peter, IV, 4450
Hanna, John, 1653, 2153, 2154, 2155, 2156
Hannah, William, 0220
Hansell, John Walker, 3942, 4616, 4617
Hansell, William, 2953
Haraden, Nathaniel, 2010
Hardesty, Edward, 2242
Harl, Baldwin, 3199, 3307
Harper, Wyatt, 4170
Harriman, James, 0532
Harrington, Charles, 4249
Harrington, Seth, 3206
Harrington, Simon, 1184
Harris, Benjamin James, 0723, 0724
Harris, Benton, 0854
Harris, David, 1148
Harris, Davis, 1385
Harris, Jeptha Vining, 4008
Harris, Jonathan, 0869
Harris, Oliver, 1077
Harris, Robert Lacey, 1584, 2095, 2150

Harris, Thomas, 0931
Harris, Thompson, 4093
Harris, William, 3060
Harrison, Frederick, 0849, 0897, 1324
Harrison, Gustavus, 0690
Harrison, Joel, 2684, 2942, 2943, 3002
Harrison, Stephen, 2658, 2670
Harrison, Thomas Edward, 1729
Harrison, William Henry, 2223, 3055
Harry, John Bishop, 3584
Harsen, Cornelius, 0258
Hart, Bernard, 1663
Hart, William H., 0146
Hart, William Watts, 1810, 2121
Hartley, Michael, 2589
Hartsfield, James, 4161
Hartsfield, Warren, 3592
Hartzel, Jacob, 2541
Hascall, Ralph, 1201
Hastings, Walter, 0436
Hastings, William, 4142, 4472
Hatcher, Archibald, 0413
Hatfield, Adam, 0478
Hauck, William, 3442
Hawes (House), John, 0134
Hawkins, Elijah, 0750
Haws, Joel, 0092, 1340
Hawthorn, John Rogers, 3788
Hay, Daniel, 1106
Hay, Peter, 0001, 0006, 0007, 0928, 1948, 2539, 3250
Haybarger, George, 3822
Hayden, Horace H., 0134, 0609
Hayes, Gaylor, 1254
Hayes, Joseph, 0681
Hayes, Patrick, 2218, 2219
Hayes, Walter Cody, 0442, 1130, 1602
Haynes (Hanes, Haines), John, 2068
Head, William, 3725
Hebrard, Antoine, 2433, 2501, 2538, 2652
Hegeman, Daniel, 1006
Heinrich, Johan, 3448
Helfmeier, Herman, 1484
Helick, Jacob, 2861
Hellick (Helick), Jacob, 1942
Hellick (Hellic), Jacob, 2058, 2059
Hellick, Jacob, 0911
Helmbold, George, 0930
Helmbold, George, Jr., 1442

Helmbold, Goerge, 1716
Helms, Cadwalader M., 3169
Hembree, Benjamin Franklin, 4582
Henderson, Daniel, 0607
Henderson, Daniel C., 0836
Henderson, John, 1359, 1613, 4452
Henderson, John Tole, 3903, 3948, 3978
Henderson, Peter, 1042, 1455
Henderson, Peter H., 1504
Henry Robert, 4175
Henry, Isaac, 3663
Henry, John, 3484
Henry, Stephen Chambers, 0776
Henshaw, William Slaughter, 2326, 2412, 2579
Henthorn, Adam, 4227
Herkimer, John, 4327
Herman, John Caner, 0320
Herndon, Elijah, 3703
Herndon, James, 3651
Herrick, Edward, 1413
Herrick, Samuel, 1413
Herring, Giles, 3847
Hess, Denis, 0659
Hess, Peter, Jr., 4007
Hester, John Dipolt, 0632, 0667, 0668, 0669
Heyl, Philip, 0096, 0102
Hicklin, Thomas, 4017
Hickman, Joseph, 4164
Hickox, Reuben, 4469
Hicky, Philip, 3534
Higginbotham, Benjamin Graves, 4579
Hildt, John, 1055, 1056
Hill, Ambrose Powell, 4272
Hill, David Bailey, 3082
Hill, Joseph, Jr., 1684
Hill, Thomas Gardner, 0378, 0379, 0394, 0400, 2070
Hills, Elijah, 0910
Hillyer, Simon, 1235, 1501, 1547
Hilton, John, 2015
Hilton, Morrill, 2250
Hinckley, Nathaniel, 0862, 1723
Hind, William, 3161
Hinds, Byram, 0733
Hine, Tamerlane, 1330
Hinkle, Peter, 3721, 3727
Hiser, William, 1412

Hiss, Philip, 1487
Hitch, Hardy Elgit, 3251
Hite, James, 0874
Hite, James Madison, 1022
Hoagland, Isaac, 3664
Hobart, Enoch, 1138
Hobart, Nathaniel Potts, 0065
Hobart, Robert Enoch, 1158, 1399
Hobbs, Benedict H., 3860
Hobensack, George, 2620
Hobert, Robert Enoch, 0878
Hobson, Matthew, 3015
Hoddy, John, 0503
Hoddy, Richard, 0503
Hoddy, Robert, 0503
Hodges, George Washington, 1573
Hodges, Josiah, 4591
Hodges, Wilson Blount, 3221, 3227
Hodsdon, Isaac, 1174
Hoffman, Jacob, 1893
Hoffman, John, 1734
Hoffman, Julius, 1395
Hoffman, Peter, 2527
Hoffman, William, 0022, 0097, 0130, 0165, 0166
Hoffnagle, John, 1524, 1634
Hogeboom, Peter, 2478, 2479, 3434
Hogeboom, Peter L., 1878
Hogg, Samuel, 1332
Holden, Abel, 1346, 1556, 1619, 2167
Holden, Horace, 0707, 0780, 0981, 0994
Holden, Moses, 0124, 1233
Holifield, William, 2745
Holland, Charles Miller, 4351
Holland, Jonah, 0796
Holliday, Peter Alexander, 4495
Hollinger, Jacob, 4063
Hollis, Jonathan, 1817, 1857
Hollister, George, 4072
Hollyday, Henry, 4251
Holmes, Bartlett, 0617
Holmes, Isaac, 4033
Holmes, Israel, 1207
Holmes, Nathaniel, Jr., 1852
Holter, George, Jr., 4361
Hooper, James, 3776, 3971
Hoover, John, 1574
Hope, Robert, 0929
Hopkins, Charles B., 1960
Hopkins, Elias, 2692

Hopkins, Hiram, 1289, 1290
Hopler, Conrad, 2723
Hopper, Daniel Cox, 2997, 3446
Hord, Elias, 0611, 4433
Horn, Abraham, 3514, 3515
Horn, Joseph, 0281
Horn, Otis Baker, 2765
Hornblower, Josiah, 1465, 1521, 1522, 1523, 2215, 2295
Horner, Isaac, 3853
Horner, John, 3341
Horney, Samuel, 4226
Horsford, Jedaiah, 0504
Horton, James, 3440
Horton, Simeon, 1451
Hoshall, Jesse, II, 3089
Hosmer, Henry, 3666
Hosmer, Jacob, 4257
Hotchkin, Eliphalet, 0999
Houck, John, 1553, 1554
Hough, Ezra, 0529
Hough, Thomas, 2203
Houghton, Ralph, 0054
House, Allen, 4409
Houston, David, 4097
Houston, Samuel Nelson, 0371, 0372, 2067
Howard, James Powell, 1441
Howard, Maurice, 2066, 2687, 2688, 3170, 3310, 3473
Howard, Oliver, Jr., 3342
Howell, Burwell, 4221, 4303, 4362
Howell, Joshua, 4293
Howell, Joshua Ladd, 1228, 2217
Howison, Alexander, 2907
Howland, Joshua, 1631
Hoyt, Ziba, 0058
Hubbard, Joseph, 4195
Hubbs, Zebulon Townsend, 0479
Huckel, Francis, 1205
Hudgins, Robert, 4231
Hudson, Henry O., 2627, 3783
Hudson, William Levereth, 2047
Huffmaster, Joseph, 0804, 0891, 0892
Hufstedler, Jacob, 3997
Hughes, Edward, 0132
Hughes, Thomas, 1513
Hull, Elijah Gaylord, 3962, 4011
Hull, James, 2257
Hull, Lyman, 0299, 0339
Hull, William, 1003, 1638, 1864

Hulse, James P., 2594
Hulse, John, 0427
Hume, Charles, 1128, 1870
Humes, Samuel, 0474
Humrichouse, Frederick, 3301, 3304, 3305
Hunt, Ebenezer, 0101
Hunt, Eustace, 0945
Hunt, James, 3808, 3851
Hunt, Simon, 2147
Huntington, Samuel Howard, 2812
Hurd, Joy, 1898
Hurst, Elijah, Sr., 4315, 4347, 4348
Hush, Samuel, 0178
Huson, Calvin, Sr., 1985
Huster, Gotlieb, 2277
Huston John, Jr., 0787, 1355, 2172
Huston, John, 2728
Hutchins, John, 0808, 0813, 0816, 0818, 0819, 0821
Hutton, Cornelius, 2751
Hutton, John Galt, 0280
Hutton, John S., 3950
Hyde, Eleazar, 3784
Hyde, John, 0143
Hyland, Henry M., 0014
Hyland, Stephen, 0879, 1517, 1656, 3308, 3474
Hynes, William Rose, 3801
Ijams, John, 1887, 2291
Ince, John, 4278, 4615
Ingle, James, 4035
Ingram, Thomas, 1111
Inloes, William, 1635
Inman, Richard, 3595, 3628, 3630
Insall, Thomas, 3740
Irion, George Anderson, 2519
Irvine, Callender, 2466, 2467, 2468, 2469
Irwin, John Lawson, 2581
Irwin, Matthew, 2249
Israel, Fielder, 1487
Ives, Chauncey, 2349
Ives, Elijah, 3785
Jack, John, 1210
Jackson Isaac, 1464
Jackson, Asa, 4314
Jackson, Samuel, 0317
Jackson, Wiley, 2951
Jackson, William, Jr., 2918
Jacobs, Price, 4519

James, Samuel, 0348
James, Thomas Anson, 1328
Jameson, William, 1841
Jarves, Deming, 0538
Jayne, Benaiah, 3665
Jayne, Benajah (Benaar), 1911
Jayne, Morris, 2113
Jefferies, John, 0481
Jeffries, John, 1930
Jenkins (Jinkins), Lewis, 4342
Jenkins, Benedict Joseph, 2537, 4134
Jenkins, Edward, 0613, 0614, 1187
Jenkins, Felix, 1198, 1700, 2965
Jenkins, John I., 0613, 0614
Jenkins, John J., 4113
Jenkins, Thomas, 3312, 3462, 3463, 3708, 3709, 3710, 3711
Jenkins, William, 1164, 2879, 3739
Jenkins, William Smythe, 0260
Jennings, James, 2577
Jennings, Jonathan, 0133
Jennison, Levi, 0330
Jett, Stephen, 1128
Jett, Thomas H., 3274
Jewett, Martin Dewey, 1296
Johnson, Alfred, 0940
Johnson, Alfred, Jr., 0940
Johnson, Friend, 3976
Johnson, James, 0091, 0232
Johnson, Jeremiah, 0547, 0559, 0704, 4057
Johnson, John, 1541, 3182
Johnson, Nathan, 0616
Johnson, Reverdy, 3544
Johnson, Samuel, 0004, 2792
Johnson, Seth, 1034
Johnston, David, 0554
Johnston, Nathan, 4324
Johnston, Nathan, III, 4380
Johnston, William, 0460, 0461
Jones, Bartlett, Sr., 3275
Jones, Branch, 4592
Jones, Daniel, 0331
Jones, David, 2123, 2171, 3267, 4182
Jones, Edward, 1423
Jones, Edward Peters, 0831, 1425
Jones, George W., 3530
Jones, Hugh, 2487
Jones, Hugh Andrew, 2323
Jones, Isaac, 1853
Jones, Jehu, 0257, 2776

Jones, John, 1828
Jones, John Powers, 2938
Jones, Mathew, 3867
Jones, Nathan, 0592
Jones, Richard Yeaton, 2014
Jones, Roger, 2431
Jones, Thomas G., 4421
Jones, Uriah, 0996
Jones, Walter, 3938
Jones, William, 2051
Jones, Wm. Robinson, 0402
Joor, John, 2507, 2533
Jordan, Ephraim, 3003
Jordan, Hugh, 3139
Jordan, Isaac, 3902
Jordan, John, 0412, 0964
Jordan, William, 2164, 2420
Joy, Francis, 0604
Joy, James, 1633
Joy, Zelan, 1330
Joyce, Thomas Boyce, 2606
Judson, Henry, 1953
Kaufman, Jonathan, 0947
Kays, Samuel, 0757
Kearney, John A., 0080, 0106, 0569
Kearney, Stephen Watts, 0650
Keefer, Anthony, 1457
Keen, John, 3512
Keith, John Lee, 3130
Keith, Solomon, 0749
Keithly, William, 3735
Kell, Thomas, 1025
Kelley, Samuel, 4562
Kellogg, Justin, 4240
Kellogg, Lorenzo, 1007
Kellogg, Samuel, 4240
Kellum, Edward, 4330
Kellum, Edward, Sr., 4567, 4578, 4581
Kelly, James, 1251
Kelsey, Francis Hollister, 3495, 4154
Kelso, John, 4395
Kelso, John R., 1500
Kemmerer, John, 1993
Kemp, Joseph, 2851, 3185
Kemp, Thomas, 2733
Kemper, John George, 2833
Kendall, Johnson, 0541, 0621, 0834
Kendrick, Jones, 3368
Kenly, Edward, 0924
Kennedy, Ebenezer Briggs, 0782

224 Ancestor Index

Kennedy, Robert, 4128
Kennedy, Washington, 1192
Kennedy, William Doak, 3653, 3655
Kennon, Erasmus, 4051, 4117
Kent, Robert Wheeler, 4357
Kenyon, Samuel Rogers, 1778, 2357, 2358
Keown (Kown), Nathan Lusk, 3972
Kephart, Jacob, 2958
Kepler, Israel, 3529
Keplinger, George, 3713
Keplinger, Michael, 0489, 3954
Kernan, William, 2777
Kerr, David, 2055, 2056, 2919, 2923
Kerr, David, 2nd., 3144
Kerr, Samuel, 2821, 2828
Ketcham, John, 1900, 2032
Key, Francis Scott, 1540
Keyser, Conrad, 4622
Kidder, Maynard, 1014
Kiersted, Lake, 0684
Killion, Michael, 3676
Kimball, Benjamin, 3990
Kimball, Russell, 4141
Kimberly, Nathaniel, 0011
Kimmis, Samuel, 4410
King Thomas DeVane, 2881
King, Benjamin, III, 2052
King, George, 3985
King, John, 1234
King, John Edwards, 2326
King, Reuben, 2463
King, Samuel, 3164
Kingman, Edward, 1783
Kinney, William Burnet, 3890
Kip, Henry, 1550, 1585, 1586, 1587
Kirk, Thomas, 4268
Kirkpatrick, Andrew, 3264
Kirkpatrick, David, 0738
Klein, Lewis, 0208, 1070
Kleinpeter, Franz, 3436
Kleinpeter, Franz (Francis), 3379
Kline, John George, 2611, 3296
Klinefelter, Michael, 2982
Klock, George T., 0915
Klunk, Peter, 1319, 1368
Knap, Elijah, II, 3095
Knapp, Auren, 2779
Kneass, Christian, 1579
Knickerbocker, James, 0919
Knight, John, 4296

Knight, John Hughes, 3380, 3583
Knight, Joseph, 0880
Knight, Richard, 2272, 2648
Knott, Edward, 0649
Knowles, William, 0558, 0920, 0921
Knox, John, 4214
Kohler, George, 1943
Kolb, John William, 2208, 2343, 2345, 2346, 2551, 4004, 4114
Kollock, James Patriot Wilson, 4440, 4549, 4550
Koons (Kuns, Kuntz), John, 2143
Koons, John, 2144
Koontz, John, 0045
Korn, Charles, 4368
Koser (Keyser), Jonathan, 4067
Kress, Henry, 1658, 1659
Kretzer, John Jost, 3840
Kuns (Koons) (Kuntz), John, 2135
Kuns (Kuntz), Daniel, 4391
Kyes, Laban, 4532, 4546, 4547
LaTourrette, Peter, 0720
Labatut, Jean Baptiste, 2458, 2480, 2494, 2495, 2497, 3331, 3376, 2891, 3032
Labranche, Alexander, 3324, 2632, 2633, 2985, 3034
Labranche, Jacques Hermogene, 3980
Labroquere, Bernard, 3954
Lacey, Ebenezer, 3011
Lafferanderie, Lucien, 3110
Lake, George, 0792, 3654
Lake, Isaac, 1731
Lake, Washington, 0792
Lamb, Jacob, 1944
Lamb, John, 3254, 3580
Lambert, Levi Young, 2638
Lamothe, Jean-Baptiste, 2867, 2882, 2934, 3347
Lanaux, Charles Julian, 3359, 3432
Lanaux, Charles Julien, 2530, 2596, 2623, 3670
Land, Nathaniel Drew, 3471
Landell, George, 1612
Landon, Walsten, 1799
Landrum, Thomas, 4363
Landry, Benjamin, 3758
Landry, Simon Julien, 2890
Landry, Ursin, 3033
Landstreet, John, 0950
Lane, Loring, Sr., 4459

Lang, John, 3118, 3119
Langhorne, Maurice, 0963
Langworthy, Benjamin, 4607
Lardner, Lynford, 0699
Larew, Joseph, 3404
Larkin, Elam, 0595, 1763
Larrabee, Benjamin, 1185, 1186, 1200
Lasere, Jaques, 3588
Lashley, Amos Veach, 3865
Latil(le), Joseph Timebourt, 3435, 3430
Lauck, Isaac Streit, 3284
Lauderdale, Josiah, 4188, 4259
Laughter, John L., 0293
Lawrence, James, 1968
Lawrence, Thomas Leggett, 2340
Lawrence, Watson Effingham, 1327
Lazell, Sylvanus, 1124, 1438, 1450, 1552
LeBarron, James, 0748
LeBeuf, Martial, II, 3076
LeDoux, Zenon, 3408
LeMar, James, 2233
LeMonnier, Yves, 2393
LePretre, Jean Baptiste, 3323, 3412
Leakin, Sheppard Church, 1223
Leary, Peter, 0685, 0932, 1538
Leatherwood, Thomas, 2788
Leaycroft, Viner, 3455
Lebatut, Jean Baptiste, 3799
Leddell, William, II, 4121
Lee, James, 2992
Legg, Otis, 0982
Leidich, Joseph, 3819
Leidy, Philip, 0153
Leiper, George Gray, 3398, 4210, 4493
Leland, Thomas, 1485
Lemar, James, 1979
Lemley, Jacob, 4217
Lemon, Isaac, 1788
Lemon, Mathias, 1912
Lemonnier, Yves, 3321
Lemont, John, 1630
Lentz, Jacob, 0236, 0320
Leonor, Lewis, 0991
Lepretre, Jean Baptiste, 2415, 2428, 2472, 2509, 2848, 2971, 3352
Lester, Lewis, 4159
Levy, Uriah Phillips, 1050

Lewis, Elisha, 0112
Lewis, Jabish York, 4197
Lewis, James, 2475
Lewis, James Martin, 2536
Lewis, John, 0227
Lewis, Jonathan, 1604
Lewis, Morgan, 4013
Lewman, Noah, 4489
Liffberry, John, Jr., 2174
Lile, Malachi, 4086
Lillard, Thomas, 2280
Lillie, Samuel Shaw, 1769
Lilly, William, 0893
Lincoln, Elijah, 4076, 4239
Lincoln, George, 3886
Lindesmith, Daniel, 0214
Lindsley, Abraham Bradley, 1304
Lines, Henry, 3606
Linkous, Adam, 4319
Linnard, William, 0958, 3131
Linthicum, Abner, 1765, 1808, 3624, 4040
Linthicum, Abner Jr., 2763
Linthicum, Charles G., 3088
Linville, James M., 1180
Liswell, Thomas, 0623
Little, John Everett, 3485
Little, Luther, 4627
Livaudais, Jean B. E., 3189
Livingston, John J., 3732
Lloyd, James, III, 2344
Lloyd, Edward, IV, 1492
Lobdell, John, 1508
Lockett, Samuel Locke, 4500
Lockhart, Thomas, 0620
Lockwood, John, 2716
Logan, William, 3929
Logue, John, 3607
London, James, 4049, 4050
Lones, Henry, 3827
Long, Benjamin, 2916
Long, Jesse, 0180, 0184
Lord, Joseph, 1790, 1837
Loring, Perez, 1292, 3013
Lorton, Lewis R., 0902
Lorton, Louis Robert, 2785
Lothrop, Ebenezer, 1590, 1639
Lothrop, Thomas, 0267
Loucks, George G., 1283
Love, Edom C., 4473
Love, Robert, 2444

Lovell, George, 3209
Lovell, Harles Sheaffe, 1072
Lovell, Joseph, 1348
Lovett, Thomas Fens, 4439
Low, Samuel, 1847
Lowd, Allen, 0606
Lowe, Curtis, 4438
Lowell, Moses, 2255
Lowell, Reuben, 2991
Lowry, James, 0210
Lowry, Job T., 1137
Lowther, Robert, 4346
Loyd, Eli, 3096
Lucas, Robert, 2244
Lucas, Simeon, 4229, 4230
Luckett, James, 4554
Ludington, Zalmon, 0005
Luffberry, John, 1815, 2231, 2704
Luffberry, John, Jr., 1977
Lugenbeel, Moses, 1868, 1869
Lutton, William, 4243
Lyman, Silas, 0842
Lynch, James, 0781
Lynch, Patrick of William, 3278
Lynde, Joanathan, 0242, 1169, 1230
Lynde, Jonathan, 1467
Lyon, Asahel Dimic, 2666
Lyon, Asahel Dimick, 3759, 3760
Lyon, John S., 1949
Lyon, Peter, 4078
Lyons, Samuel, 3351
Mabie, Jacob, 0033
MacArthur, Charles Gilderoy, 2808, 0858
MacChesney, Nathan, 1018
MacDonald, John, 0143
MacDonough, Thomas, 0530
Mace, Henry, 3148
Mackenzie (McKenzie), Thomas, 2607
Mackenzie, Thomas, 0203, 1699, 1726
Mackubin, George, 3099
Maclay, John, 1127A
Macomb, Alexander, 0202
Macumber, Ephraim, 1824
Madison, Peyton, 2829
Magee, Alexander, 3203
Magee, Jacob, 4510
Magee, Robert, 4092
Magruder, George, 0690
Magruder, Thomas, 1218
Mahan, Alexander, 0676

Mahool, Thomas, 3766
Major, John, 2103
Malone, Samuel Pinchum, 2795
Manigault, Charles, 0414
Manlove, John, 0134
Manning, Caleb, 3102, 3103, 3104, 3105, 3422, 3568
Mansfield, Leonard Dyre, 1872
Maples, William Cordra, 4184, 4427
Marin, Evariste Pierre Antoine, 2773
Markle, Abraham, 1674, 1696
Marklee, Conrad, 0853
Markley, Philip, 2945
Marks, Alexander, 0952
Marshall, John, 3449
Marshall, Jonathan, 0643
Marshall, Joseph, 0213
Marshall, William, 4206
Marston, Charles, 0437
Marston, John, 0387
Martin, Benjamin, 3741
Martin, Clem, 3698
Martin, David, 2214, 3991
Martin, Jesse, 3014
Martin, Joseph Richard, 2390, 2426, 2838, 3009
Martin, Thomas, 4425
Martin, Valentine, 3130
Martin, Wait, 0487
Martz, George D., 3964
Mason, David, 4191
Mason, Henry, 0438
Mason, James, 1609, 1669
Mason, John, 2036
Massengill, George Washington, 4559, 4560
Massie, John Whitney, 1132
Massie, Peter, 2029
Matheny, Charles Reynolds, 1981
Mathias, Griffith, 1583, 1610, 1611, 2097
Mathiot, Jacob, 2619
Mathis, Gabriel Throckmorton, 4455
Matthews, William, 1002
Maury, Abraham, 0029
McAfee, John, 1751
McArthur, Duncan, 0219
McBride, Charles, 3130
McCall, William, 4359
McCallister, Hugh, 4367
McCartney, John, 0464, 1777

Ancestor Index 227

McCarty, Alfred, 1328
McCarty, Reuben, 4406
McCauley, James, 4213
McCaw, William Henry, 3255
McCay, William, 1834
McClain, John, 3146
McClanahan, Williams, 4021
McCleary, Robert, 1362
McClellan, Hugh, 1444
McClellan, John, 0163
McClendon, Joel, 2304
McClintock, Joseph Allen, 0273
McCluer, Robert, 3006
McCluney, William John, 3450
McCollough, James Brown, 2360
McComas, Elisha, 4339
McComas, Henry Gough, 2209
McComas, Nicholas, 0721
McComas, Zaccheus Onion, 1075, 1393
McConnell, James, 2921
McCorison, William, 2026
McCormack, James, 4157, 2137
McCracken, Robert, 4089
McCrady, William, 2605
McCraw, Oliver B., 4387
McCullah, Alexander, 4058, 4150
McCulloch, Wm. Horsley, 0525
McCullough, Samuel, 4144
McCurdy, Alexander, 0633
McCurdy, Samuel, 4163
McCurley, Felix, 0251, 0252, 1766, 3830
McCurley, John, 2009, 2364, 3018
McCutchen, John, 4037
McDaniel, Matthew, 0350
McDarment, John, 4237
McDonald, Allen, 4506
McDonald, James, 1959
McDonald, John, 3889
McDonald, William, 0828
McFerran, John, 0972
McFerrin, James, 2799
McGarry, William Rodney, 1764
McGaw, John, 1107
McGee, Robert, 4352
McGough, Robert, 4437
McHugh, John, 3800
McKean, James, 4027
McKee, Henry, 4569
McKee, John, 4237

McKim, James, 3297, 3306
McKinney, James, 3900, 4152, 4166
McKinney, Seth, 3477
McKnight, John, 2065, 2116
McLaughlin, Daniel, 3888
McLaughlin, James, Jr., 1562
McLean, John, Jr., 3627
McLemore, Moses, 4602
McMaken (McMahan), Joseph Hamilton, 1905
McMaken (McMahon), Joseph H., 2166
McMaken, Joseph H., 2168
McMaken, Joseph Hamilton, 2698
McMaster, John, 0576, 2920, 3083
McMillan, Alexander, 3528
McMullin, James, 3871
McMurray, Samuel, 1027
McNair, David, 1785
McNair, Thomas, 0237, 1577
McNeal, James, 0693
McNeil, Charles, 0520
McNeil, John, 0108
McNeir, William, 2005, 2022
McPherson, Henry Hendley, 1160, 1830, 1831, 3298
McQuiddy, Benjamin, 3817
McVay, Jacob, 0987
McWillie, Adam, 3895
McWillie, William, 2840
Mead, Artemus, 0140
Mead, Shadrach, 1035
Mead, Smith, 0599
Meaders, Barney, 3140
Meadows (Meadors), Barney, 2642
Meadows, Barney, 3402, 3403
Meadows, Gabriel B., 4237
Means, George, 3100
Medairy, John, 0239, 0247, 3162, 3204
Meigs, Luther, 0877
Melancon, Alexander, 3877
Melancon, Alexandre, 4596
Melvin, Daniel, 4254
Melzard, Benjamin, 1780
Mendenhall, John, 4644
Mengle, Benjamine, 2612
Mengle, Peter, 0975
Meredith, Peter, 3210
Meroney, William, 4509, 4553
Merrell, John, 1318

228 Ancestor Index

Merrikin, Joseph, 0194, 0195
Merrikin, Joseph R., 0177
Merrill, Joseph Annis, 4552
Merritt, Benjamin, 0925
Merritt, John, 2189
Merwin, Miles, 0309, 1947
Merwine, Jacob, 3986
Metcalf, Chandler, 1343
Metcalf, Charles, 0832, 1004, 0852, 0881
Metcalfe, Thomas, 1886, 2080, 2298
Mettee, Martin, 4291
Metzger, Jacob, 3480, 3640
Meunier, Etienne, 4106, 4264
Mickley (Mickly), Jacob, 1974
Middlebrook, Robert, Jr., 0988
Middleton, Richard, 0936
Middleton, Zachariah, 3356, 3357
Mifflin, John Ross, 0490
Mifflin, Thomas, 3996
Milbourne, James, 4080
Miles, Reuben, 1379
Miles, William, 1282
Millard, Bennett, Sr., 4537
Miller, Abraham, 3135, 3537, 3538, 4318
Miller, Andrew, 0010, 2165
Miller, Daniel, 0208
Miller, Ezra, 1349, 1985
Miller, Henry, 2025
Miller, James, II, 2188
Miller, John, 1539, 1919
Miller, Pliny, Jr., 0984
Miller, Thomas, 0591
Miller, Thomas, II, 3115
Miller, William, 2243
Millet, Peter Alexander Maximillian, 3385
Millett, Samuel, 0233
Millholland, Robert Douglas, 2158, 3399
Mills, Ezekiel, 1076, 1341
Mills, Ezekiel, Sr., 0182, 0192, 1711, 1712, 1713, 1730
Mills, William, 4511
Miltenberger, Anthony Felix, 2855
Miltenberger, George, 2757, 2758
Miltenberger, Louis Christian, 2413
Minard, Abel, 1417
Minor, Thomas, II, 2436, 2439
Miranda, Jonathan, 1676

Mitchell, Aden, 4484
Mitchell, David, 1242
Mitchell, George Edward, 1456, 2213
Mitchell, Henry, 0957, 1038
Mix, Elijah, 1225
Moak, Andrew, 3340
Moale, Samuel, 2791, 3445
Monmonier, Francis, 0535
Montague, Thomas C., 3526
Montan, Anthony, 2735, 2737
Montanye, Thomas B., 3049, 4572
Montegut, Jean Raymond, 2488, 2889
Montgomery, John Crathorne, 1660, 2064
Montgomery, William, 1197, 1306
Moody, Andrew, 3637
Moody, Jacob S., 1988
Mooers, Benjamin, 0079, 2106
Mooers, Benjamin Hazen, 0593
Mooers, Benjamin John, 0594
Moon, Nathaniel, 4184
Moore, Asa, 4084
Moore, John B., 1255
Moore, John, II, 1300
Moore, Joseph, 4529
Moore, Lewis, 2804
Moore, Lewis, IV, 3645, 3894
Moore, Noadiah, 1060, 1061, 1262
Moore, Robert Burwell, 4376
Moore, William Walker, 1255
Morgan, Avery, 0105, 0381, 1776
Morgan, Ebenezer, 4295
Morgan, Elias, 3690
Morgan, John, 4064
Morgan, Lodowick, 0785
Morhous, Michael, 0800
Moriarty, John, 1747
Morin, Josiah, 1800
Morris, Charles, 3000
Morris, Garret, 2905
Morris, John B., 3581
Morris, Presley, 0777
Morrison, John, 3896
Morrison, Jonathan, 0564
Morrison, Robert, 2645
Morrow, William, 0600, 1278
Morse, Amasa, 4043
Moses, John Folsom, 4520
Mossburg (Masberg), John, 4641
Mott, Benjamin, 3831
Moulder, John Nicholson, 0766, 0767

Moulton, Abel, 0697, 1551
Moulton, Jacob Smith, 1374
Moyer, Daniel, 0953
Muhlenberg, Peter, 1248
Muhlenberg, Peter, Jr., 0138
Mulholland, Hugh, 2912
Mullany, James Robert, 1354
Mullen, James, 4245
Munson, Augustine, 0462
Murphey, Elijah, 0647
Murray, Dauphin, 0055
Murray, David, 3016
Murray, Elinu, 0055
Murray, Thomas Clinton, 4471
Musser, George, 0311
Myers, Joseph, Sr., 4477
Myers, Michael, Sr., 1973
Myers, Mordecai, 0123, 0675
Myers, Peter, Jr., 1993
Myers, Solomon, 1400
Myers, Stephen, 0023
Napier, John Staples, 3121
Naseby, John, 2307
Nason, Leavitt, 1144
Neal, Sherman M., 4606
Nealey, Ebenezer, 3573
Needham, Calvin, 0884
Neil, John Glidden, 1652, 1667, 1850, 1992
Neilson, John, 1466
Neilson, Robert, 0692, 0772, 1135
Neilson, William Douglas, 4151, 4223
Nellis, Joseph Peter, 0845
Nelson, Benjamin, 0468
Nesbit, Alexander, 4183
Nesbit, James I., 1301
Neven, Thomas, 0012
Nevin, David, 1357
Neving, Thomas, 0250
Newbold, William, 3733
Newby, Elsey, 4045
Newcomb, Elisha, 3930
Newell, Rezon Bryant, 1571
Newkirk, George, 2229, 2230
Newkirk, Matthew, 1978
Newman, Francis, 2419
Newman, Horatio, 2626
Newton, Alvin, 1249
Nichol, John, 1131
Nicholas, Robert Carter, 3472
Nicholls, Thomas Clark, 2400

Nichols, Francis, 3420
Nichols, Francis (Boude), 1580
Nichols, Francis Bonde, 0241, 3768
Nichols, John, 0242
Nichols, Levi, 0597
Nichols, Levi, Jr., 0786
Nichols, Robert Carter, 3488
Nichols, Robert Humphreys, 1546
Nichols, Zadok, 1803
Nicholson, George William, 4601
Nicholson, Orson, 1581
Nickerson, Warren, 0532
Nicoll, Thomas, 0189
Nimocks, Rowland, 1956
Nivin, David, 4496
Nixon, William, 4526
Noble, Daniel, 0641, 1052
Noble, John, 2034
Noble, Ransom, 0520, 0841, 1059
Noel, Jacob, 0560
Noland, Smallwood Turner, 4000
Norman, Robert, 3973
Norrid, Larkin, 4451, 4479
Norris, John Bradford, 1555, 2027, 2234, 2275
Norris, Silas C., 4190, 4215
Northrup, Samuel, 0841
Norton, Carlos Alonzo, 1220
Norton, Zacheus, 1805
Norwood, John, 0302
Nott, William, 2396
Noyes, Daniel Rogers, 0325, 0326
Nugent, David, 1959
Nye, Abraham, 0840
O'Bryant, Joseph, 3677
O'Neale, William, 1970
O'Neill, John, 0089
O'Neill, Robert, 0327
Obenshain, William, 4589
Ogden, Peter Voorhees, 2377, 4029
Oliver, Jean Baptiste, 3177
Oliver, John, 4155, 4460
Oliver, Paul Ambrose, 0149, 1161
Oliver, William George, 0318, 2994
Olivier, Jean Baptist, 3761
Omer, Peter, 1298
Ord, James, 0196
Orebaugh, Jacob, 1472
Orso, Zenon, 2386, 3159
Orton, Timothy, 3901

Orvis, Elihu, 1914, 1915, 1916, 1917, 1936, 1937
Osborn (Osburn), Thomas, 4014
Osborn, Joseph, 4632
Osborne (Osburn), Thomas, 4036
Osborne, Enos A., 0031
Osborne, Henry, 1257
Osborne, Thomas, 3855
Osterhoudt, Simeon, 1415
Ostrander, James, 3762
Otey, Armistead, 1965
Otis, William, 2387
Otto, Jacob S., 0090
Ovenshine, Jacob, 1120
Overstreet, James, 4183, 4571
Owens, Joseph, 0687, 1588, 2274, 2290
Owens, William, 2739
Owin, James, 1807
Owings, Thomas of Richard, 4041
Oxx, William, 3rd., 3747
Packard, Ambrose, 0510
Packard, Hezekiah, 1964
Packer, George, 1621
Packett, John, 0825
Paddison, Samuel, 2557
Paddock, Loveland, 1861
Page, James, 0889, 1150
Palmer, Chillion, 0279
Palmer, David Denham, 0882
Palmer, Noyes, 4091
Palmer, Reuben, Jr., 2118
Palmer, William, 1317
Paramenter, Joseph, 1721
Parish, Levi Hardin, 0215
Park, Russell J., 3287
Parker, William, 1172
Parker, Zachariah, 2752
Parrish, William, 0383, 0384, 1316
Parsons, John, 0677, 4238
Parsons, Luke, 1350
Partlow, Thomas, 3621
Parvis, Joseph, 0809, 0815
Pascal, Francois, 2675, 2832, 2887, 2892, 3499, 3753
Patrick, Ralph, 4088
Patrick, Robert, 4143
Patterson, Charles, 3922
Patterson, James, 1030, 1039
Patterson, Robert, 0495, 0523, 0867
Pattillo, Edward, 4445

Patton, Dorington "Dorn", 4371
Paulding, Hiram, 0256
Paull, George, 3770
Paxton, Robert, 3720
Paynter, Lemuel, 0916
Peale, Charles Linneaeus, 0886
Peale, Rembrandt, 3242
Pearson, Isaac, 3374
Pechin, William, 2078
Peck, John A., 0615
Peck, Josiah J., 2756
Peirce, Joseph Hardy, 4102
Pelot, John Francis, 3898
Pelton, Phineas, 4060
Pendleton, John, 2738, 2742, 2888, 2910, 2933
Pendleton, Nathaniel Greene, 0445
Pendleton, Phineas, 2042, 2288
Pennington, Fredus, 2656
Pennington, James, 2663
Pennington, Josias, 1096
Pentz, Daniel, 0826, 0827, 2657
Pentz, John Joseph, 1884, 2079, 2081, 2299
Percy, Ferdinand Bonaventure Francois, 4333, 4370, 4399, 4400, 4403
Perham, Jonathan, 0301
Perkins, Hardin, 3433
Perkins, John, 0946, 1133, 1134
Perkins, John, Jr., 0533
Perkins, Moses, 1871
Perkins, Richard, 1737
Perrine, Stephen, 3836
Perry, Gad, 2184
Perry, Jabez, 2093
Perry, Melatiah B., 3090
Perry, Oliver Hazard, 3814, 3920
Perry, Ransom, 4153
Perry, Raymond Henry Jones, 1191, 1238
Petefish, George, 3302
Peters, Christian G., 3109
Peterson, Martin, 0542
Petro, Michael, 4160
Pettengill, Elisha, 1253
Pettingell, Cutting, 0985
Pharr (Farr), Henry, 3043
Pharr, Robert, 2438
Phebus, John, 0987
Philbrook, Alfred Spooner, 0117

Philbrook, Benjamin, 0117, 0347, 0355, 1152, 1361, 1497, 3749, 4082
Phillips, Manuel, 3441
Phillips, Solomon, 1839
Philson, Robert, 3750
Pierce, Barnabas C., 1411
Pierce, Lewis, 0656
Pierce, Presevied, 0746
Pierson, Philo, 0798, 1408
Pilie, Louis Philippe, 2524, 2529, 3052, 3056, 3418, 4535
Pinckney, Thomas, 2465
Pinkerton, John White, 0310
Pinkerton, William, 1921
Pinkfield, Samuel, 4635
Pinkney, William, 0228
Pipes, David, 2486, 3502, 4426, 4542
Plascencia, Jean Juan Mathias, 4311
Platt, Zephaniah Pitt, 0041
Plauche, Henry Urbain, 2409, 3631
Plauche, Jacques Henri Urbain, 2521, 2817, 3416, 3778
Plauche, Jean Baptiste, 2396, 2406, 2418, 2425, 2629, 2816, 2935, 3874, 4208
Poindexter, David, 4237
Poindexter, Richard, 4494
Pond, Ashley, 0861, 0862, 1723
Pond, Benjamin, 0861, 0862, 1723
Pond, Moses, 4512
Pond, Preston, 2637
Pontius, Henry, 3175
Pool, William, 0296
Poole, Samuel Hall, 1396
Poore, Andrew, 0161
Pope, James, 4308
Porter, Andrew, 2576
Porter, David, 1821
Porter, James Madison, 2374
Porter, Shadrach, 1816
Porter, Stephen, 0512
Porter, Wrixham Lewis, 1768, 2767
Posey, Joseph Harrison, 4360
Posey, Thornton, 2441
Post, Oliver, 1829
Potter, Isaac, 4476
Potter, Jonathan, 3220
Poulson, John, 2649
Powel, John Hare, 0419
Powell, William, 1031
Powers, Avery, Jr., 3143

Powers, Frederick, 3801, 3228
Prescott, Lewis, 0099
Preston, Archibald, 3503
Preston, William, 1798
Price, Ralph, 4556
Price, Solmon, 4290
Price, Soloman, 4270
Prigmore, Thomas, 2076
Prince, William, 4001
Prince, William Robert, 0871
Prindle, Eleaxer, 0509
Prindle, Eleazer, 0531
Pringle, John, 1471
Provost, Godfroy, Sr., 4262
Pullen, Jenks, 4531
Purdy, Isaac, 2787, 2989
Putnam, Samuel, 1143
Quackenbush, Isaac F., 0959
Quarles, Peter, 4174
Raborg, Christopher, II, 1221
Radabaugh, John, 1993
Radford, Jeremiah Smith, 0859
Ralston, John, 4499, 4516, 4533
Rambin, Francois Augustin, 3674
Ramsdell, Abner, 1845
Randall, Beale, 0398
Randall, Henry Knapp, 0549, 0847, 1406
Randall, Josiah, 0128
Randall, Ornan, 4551
Randall, Thomas, 4115
Randall, William, 3367
Randolph, Charles Carter, 4247
Randolph, Thomas Beverley, 0201, 0679
Ransdall, Zachariah, 4237
Rathbone, William, 3044
Rawle, Francis William, 3136, 3536
Rawle, William, Jr., 0231
Rawlings, Benjamin, 1725
Rawlins, Levi, 4193
Rayburn, James, 2972
Raymond, George Bromley, 0433
Raymond, Josiah, 1939, 2902
Rea, Ebenezer, Jr., 2310
Rea, John, 0266, 1265
Read, Samuel J., 0211, 0758
Read, Sion Spencer, 1904
Reaves, James, 4505
Redding, Samuel, 2315
Reddish, Silas, 1935

Redman, John, 0783
Reed, Henry Ludovicus, 0416
Reed, John, 1371
Reed, Michael, 4418, 4474
Reed, Stephen, 1288
Reed, Thomas, 0837
Reed, William, 0768, 2278
Reeder, Charles, 1589, 1594, 1595, 1596, 1597, 1598, 1599, 1600, 1628, 1647, 1648, 1670, 2324, 4202
Reese, Charles, 4044
Reese, John, 4096
Reeve, Joab, 3182
Regar, Henry, 1895, 2102, 2115, 2126, 2127, 2128, 2129, 2130, 2139, 2140, 2142, 2145, 2146
Reichart, John, 0263
Reid, John Charles, 0835
Reid, Joseph Carmel, 1274
Reid, Samuel Chester, 0435
Reilly, Patrick, 3273, 3969
Reilly, Paul, 0002, 0016, 0017
Reip, Henry, 0167, 0169
Remington, Shadrach, 0040
Reneau, John Fleming, 3586
Reneau, William T., 3684
Renninger, Jacob, 4062
Reno, Benjamin, 1213
Reno, Lewis Thomas, 1213
Rensselaer, Cooms, 0431
Rerick, John, 1449
Reynolds, Abraham, 2270
Reynolds, John, 0238, 0322, 0583, 2033
Reynolds, Joseph, 1608
Reynolds, Samuel, 0719, 4255
Rhinelander, Wm. Christopher, 0578
Rhoades, David, 1269
Rhodes, Ezekiel, 1099
Rice, Edmund, 0032
Rice, Ezekial, 1232
Rice, George, 4074
Rich, Joel, 1774
Rich, Joel, Sr., 2476
Rich, John Jr., 1774, 1913, 2476
Rich, Reuben, 0488
Rich, Thomas Lathrop, 2262
Richards, Ambe, 0359
Richards, Cyrus George, 0757
Richards, John, 0714, 0715, 0860
Richards, Joseph, 1079

Richardson, Alford, 0713
Richardson, Allen, 3999
Richardson, Charles, 1420, 1592
Richardson, Genjamin, 2321
Richardson, Gilman, 3362
Richardson, Jared N., 3153
Richardson, John, 1169, 1230, 1467
Richardson, Phinehas, 4631
Richardson, Rufus, 2844
Richardson, William Hervey, 1687, 3987
Ridgate, Benjamin Cornick, 0603, 1902
Ridgway, Andrews, 2269
Rieman, Henry, 2322
Ries (Reese), Christian, 4301
Rigg, Thomas, 3667
Riggs, Elisha, 1149, 1714
Riggs, Moses, 0751
Rightmyer, John, 4432
Riley, James, 4237
Riley, Ninian, 4237, 4444
Riley, Zachariah, 4237
Rillieux, Vincent, II, 3058
Rimmer, Thomas, 4587
Ripley, Franklin, 0104
Ripley, Uriah, 0301
Risdon, David, 4297
Risley, Eli, Jr., 4583
Risley, James, 1101
Ristine, Henry, 1690, 1691, 1692
Riter, Michael, 4131, 4335
Rivell, Adam, 3863
Roane, John Jones, 1342
Robbins, Asa, Jr., 1145, 1664
Robbins, Josiah, 0482
Robbins, Thomas, Sr., 4570
Robe, Roswell, 0162, 0270
Roberts, Abraham, II, 3787
Roberts, James, 4346, 4470
Roberts, John, 0599, 2560
Roberts, Joseph Gill, 3217
Roberts, Lydia Macdonough, 4112
Roberts, William, 2105
Robertson, Cornelius, 4401
Robertson, John, 4070
Robertson, Julius Caesar, 2966
Robeson, Robert Amay, 0670
Robeson, Thomas, 0939
Robinson, Benjamin Hazel, 0134
Robinson, Edward, 4165

Robinson, George Rogers, 4566
Robinson, Jabez, 4618
Robinson, Jonathan Jehu, 0917
Robinson, Nicholas Nixon, 0134
Robson, Benjamin Ross, 1649
Robson, Robert Amsy, 0566
Roby, Joseph Warren, 0155
Roche, Pierre Felix, 3912
Rockefeller, Henry, 0537, 1033, 1927, 1928
Rockefeller, Peter, 2647
Rodman, Joseph, 0664
Rodney, Daniel, 4393
Roe, Isaac, 0018, 0019, 0042
Rogers, John, 1784, 3081, 3731
Rogers, Joseph, 4624
Rogers, William, 0844, 1771
Rogers, William Charles, 3700, 3737
Rolle, Thomas, 3272
Rollins, Richard, 2834
Rome, Jean Andre, 3835
Roney, William, 0967, 0968
Roosevelt, Thomas Wilton, 1736
Rose, Harmon, 3785
Roseboom, Henry, 1431
Rosenkrans, Benjamin, 4317
Ross, Jonathan, 2635
Ross, Reuben, 0428, 1365
Ross, William, 0407
Rothrock, John, 2553, 2556
Rouse, E. S. S., 2543
Rouse, Peregrine, 0956
Roush, Henry, Sr., 1644
Rover, John, 1833
Rowland, Jonathan, 3193
Rowles, David, 4052, 4053, 4054
Rowlett, Thomas, 3828
Rowntree, Henry, 4417
Roy, Joseph, 3794
Ruby, Peter, III, 4442
Rucker, Richard, 2303
Rucker, William B., 3107
Rumney, John, 1338
Rumph, Jacob, II, 3151
Rumsey, Stephen, 2500, 3325, 3421, 3501
Runyan, Joseph, 0666
Rupley, Simon, 1445
Rush, Lewis, 0728
Rush, Philip, 3236
Rush, Thornton, 1115

Rusk, George, 0712
Russell, George Burr, 2198
Russell, Henry, 1643, 1929
Russell, Isaac F., 0064
Russell, Samuel Hooper, 0907
Russell, William, 0752, 1470
Russell, William, III, 1797
Rust, Samuel, 0899
Ruth, Jacob, 2691
Ryan, Thomas, 1743
Saddler, William, 1443
Sadtler, Philip B., 0186, 0207, 0306, 0334, 0360, 0377, 0765
Sadtler, Philip Benjamin, 1151, 1646, 2731
Safford, Hiram, 1058
Sage, Henry, 1640
Sage, Hezekiah, Jr., 0636, 0653
Salmon, Benjamin, 3957
Salmon, Birsdall, 2835, 3050
Salter, Henry, 2320
Samble (Sipley), Thomas, 0393
Sanborn, Jonathan C., Jr., 3524
Sanders, George, 4344, 4619
Sanders, Malachi, 3743
Sandidge, Garrett Longmire, 4187, 4218, 4302
Sands, James, 0368
Sanford, Elihu Jr., 0113, 0434
Sanford, George, 1407
Sanford, Hervey, 0113, 0434
Sanford, Ruben, 1043
Sangster, James, 3165, 3935
Sanno, George Michael, 0082, 0890
Sappington, Henry, 2559
Sargent, Epes, 2250
Satterfield, Archabald, 3956
Saucier, Severin Descoteaux, 3622
Saunders, Samuel Little, 1958, 2041, 2062, 4518
Sawyer, Horace Bucklin, 0094
Scarborough, Allen, 4453
Schaeffer, Philip, 4065, 4132
Schall, George, 3241
Scheetz, Gerhard Henrich, 4087
Scheetz, Henry, 2053, 3656
Schlosser, John George, 2186, 3197
Schminke, George, 0170
Schnebly, James, 3571
Schneider, Henry, 3572
Scholl, Christian, 2794

Schrum (Shrum), George, 1673, 1681
Schuchtts, John Henry, 1086
Schute, John William, 2077
Schuyler, Peter Philip, 1339, 1358, 1369
Scofield, Jacob Smith, 0642
Scofield, Thomas E., 0197
Scotes, Norton, 1174
Scott, Abraham, Jr., 3224
Scott, Alexander, 4035
Scott, Andrew, 1127, 1662, 1709
Scott, Jeremiah, 1433
Scott, John, 1121, 1206, 1209, 2018, 2125, 2191
Scott, John Baytop, 2928
Scott, John Morin, 1012, 3723, 3729
Scott, William G., 0212
Scott, Winfield, 2120
Scout, Lewis, 2741
Scribner, Samuel, Jr., 1117
Scrivener, John, 0903, 1063
Searl, Jeriah, 3789
Sears, Alfred, 4256
Seavey, Amos, 3852
Sebree, John, 4237
Seghers, Dominique, 2459, 2493, 2526, 2617, 2803, 3360, 3428, 3680, 3915, 3916, 2516, 3344
Sellers, Samuel, 3288
Semmes, Raphael, 0405
Serpa, Antoine, 3589, 3793, 3845
Seth, James, 3882
Severance, Benjamin, 0283
Sewall, Benjamin, 2550
Seymour, Hezehiah, 0055
Shaler, Ephriam, 1383
Shane, Daniel, 1880
Shank, John, 1382
Shannon, William, 2904, 3525
Sharp, George, 3614
Sharp, Isaac, 2199
Sharriot, Abraham, 2074
Sharrock, Everard, 1575, 3951
Shaver, Peter, 1665
Shaw, Abraham, 0870
Shaw, Josiah, 3013
Shaw, Thomas, 4222
Shaw, William Holder, 4420
Shawger, J. Philip, 2659, 2661
Shawger, Philip, 2660
Sheaves, Robert, 0383, 0384

Sheely, George Washington, 3271
Shelby, Isaac, 3101
Sheldon, Ichabod, 1389
Sheldon, James, 1044
Sheldon, Samuel, 0598
Sheldon, Walter, 0598
Shell, George I., 1795
Shelton, Crispin (Chrispian) Eli, Sr., 4220
Shepherd, David, 0503
Shepherd, John, 0503, 4384
Sherman, Aaron, 1698
Sherman, Asaph, 1847
Sherman, Humphrey, 0857, 1059
Sherman, Jacob, 4480
Sherman, Samuel, 2376
Sherman, Solomon, 4411
Shibley, John, Jr., 4098
Shields, Thomas, 2030
Shiffer, John, 3532, 3576
Shinn, John, 1876
Shinn, John, Jr., 0492
Shipley, William, 1104, 1509, 1510
Shirk, John, 1835
Shiry, John, 3818
Shively, Solomon, 4119
Shivers, Thomas Wilson, 3617
Shober, Samuel L., 1655
Shoemaker, Henry, 1266
Shoemaker, Robert, 0429
Shope, Henry Adam, 1616, 1617
Showalter, David, Sr., 3802
Shreffler, John, 1040
Shreve, Israel, 1140
Shubrick, Edward Rutledge, 0118
Shubrick, William Branford, 3366
Shumate, John, 1128
Shumway, Duty, 3361
Shunk, Francis Rawn, 1754, 1755, 1794, 2069, 2293
Shurrager, Conrad, 3699
Shute, Andrew B., 2100
Shute, John William, 0941, 1491, 1507, 2289
Shute, Samuel Moore, 1258
Sias, Nathaniel, 0026
Sibley, Elisha, 2111
Sicard, Marcelin, 4345
Sickles, Daniel, 0157
Sidell, John, Jr., 0556
Silver, Jacob, 4424

Simmons, James, Sr., 1846, 2309, 3952
Simmons, John, 2597, 2711, 2714
Simmons, Noble, 0814
Simons, Levi, 3582
Simpkins, Darius, 4269
Simpson, Joseph, 1339
Simpson, William, 4504
Singleton, Jechonias, 2743
Sitcher, Andrew, 0116
Skelton, Zachariah, 4321
Skelton, Zedock, 4614
Skiddy, William, 0370
Skinner, Daniel, 1576
Slaughter, Francis T., 3039
Slavens, Isaiah, 1923
Slaymaker, Henry Fleming, 3041, 3042, 3714
Slayton, Bucklin, 1419
Slicer, Andrew, 2614
Slingluff, Jesse, 2107, 4286, 4358, 4386
Sloan, John, 1236
Sloane, Samuel, 0868
Sloat, Alexander, 0023
Slocum, Benjamin, 1532, 1534, 1568
Sly, John, 0117
Sly, John, Jr., 0117
Smalley, Francis, 2952
Smalley, Francis, Jr., 1380, 1384
Smartt, William Cheek, 2976
Smick, Peter, 3549, 3771, 3963, 3966
Smith, Adam, 1370
Smith, Ambrose, 0983
Smith, Asaph, 3187
Smith, Augustine Charles, 2504
Smith, Benjamin B., 0013, 0193
Smith, Byrd, 3724
Smith, Christopher, 2328, 2329, 2372
Smith, Ebenezer H., 2112
Smith, Frederick, 1068
Smith, Jacob Sheafe, 4623
Smith, John, 1185, 1186, 1200, 1843, 3746
Smith, John Joseph, 4313
Smith, John Wheeler, 1855
Smith, Joseph Lee, 0121, 1024
Smith, Lucius, 2631
Smith, Moses Rogers, 0548
Smith, Ransford, 2721, 2796
Smith, Sabritt, 2651, 3482

Smith, Samuel, 1145
Smith, Thomas Jarratt, 3438
Smith, Waitstill, 2161
Smith, Walter, 3318
Smith, William, 2511, 3178
Smith, William Rudolph, 0035, 0065, 0878
Smithsom, Gabriel, 1095
Smull, Jacob, 1375, 1376, 1537, 1906, 2222, 2639, 2855
Snell, James, 3928
Snell, John Jacob, 0969
Snider, Nicholas, 0020
Snyder, Adam Vrooman, 1344, 2200
Snyder, David, 1792
Snyder, George, 3001, 3072
Snyder, John C., 1718
Snyder, Simon, 0200
Snyder, Thomas, 1403
Snyder, William, 1311
Solliday, Jacob, 3555
Sommerville, John, 3927
Soule, Howland, 1167, 1181
Southard, John, 1259, 1732
Southard, William, 1677
Souther, Nathan, 1100
Spalding, Joseph, 2859
Spangler, Jacob, 0480
Spann, John, 2546
Sparhawk, Thomas, 0137, 0145
Sparks, Samuel, 1001
Sparks, Solomon, 1284
Sparks, Stephen, 3686
Sparks, Wright Bruce, 3051, 3150, 3395
Sparrow, Patrick (Parrie), 3781
Sparrow, Seth, Sr., 3694
Spaulding, James, 0909
Spears, John, 4294
Spencer, Benjamin, 4418
Spencer, Oliver Hatfield, 0271
Spencer, Silas, 0024
Spering, Henry, 1069
Spigner, Samuel, 4324, 4380
Spilman, John, 3021
Spinks, Raleigh, 2917
Sprague, Joshua, 0797
Springer, Job, 2194
Sproat, James William, 0206
Spurrier, Greenbury, 2856
Squire, Jonathan, 3994

236 Ancestor Index

Stacey, Sam Sewell, 0807
Stadden, John, 0820
Stadelman, William, Jr., 2827, 2961, 2962, 2963
Stadler, John, 4265
Stahl, Harry, 1085, 1271, 1272, 1273
Stanard, John, 1414
Standish, Matthew, 0599
Stanley, James, 2740
Stanley, Page, 1923
Stansbury, Charles, 3873
Stansbury, Elijah, 2318
Stanton, Malachi, 3944
Stanton, William, II, 1706
Stanwood, Ebenezer, 2754, 2904, 3124
Stark, Jonathan, 1351
Starke, William B., 2667
Starne, Joseph, 1614, 1615
Starr, William, 0333
Stecher, John, 1239
Steele, James, 0050
Steele, John, Jr., 0526, 0527
Steele, Samuel, 3739
Steelman, Frederick, 1434
Steely, Gabriel, 1412
Steely, George, 1412
Steers, William, 2259
Steiner, Henry, 0429
Stell, George Washington, 3636, 4577
Stephens, George, 1032
Sterling, Eben, 2138
Stetson, Abner, Jr., 3120
Stetson, Reuben, 1201
Steuart, William, 3084
Stevens, Benjamin F., 3226
Stevens, Ebenezer, 3904
Stevens, Joseph Lowe, 1141
Stevens, Obediah, 4022, 4023
Stevens, William, 0328, 0329
Stevenson, Cornelius, 2094
Stevenson, John E. W., 0332, 0408
Stevenson, William, 4246
Stewart, George H., 0582
Stewart, John, 4646
Stewart, John I., 1049
Stewart, Robert, 1119
Stewart, Simeon, 2915
Stewart, Thomas, 0175
Stickney, Henry, 0366
Stiff, James, 2575

Stiff, William Nelson, 2308
Stiles, Joseph, 1801
Stillwaggon, William, 3945
Stine, George, 0367
Stiness, Samuel, 1533
Stirling, Lewis, 3333, 3590
Stockman, Jacob, 1459
Stockton, John Cox, 1142
Stockton, Robert Field, 1203, 2771
Stone, John, 2922
Stone, Oliver, 0706
Stone, William, 2554
Story, Benjamin, 2592
Story, Benjamin Saxon, 2908, 2937
Stoughton, James, 3936, 3937
Stovall, John, 2869
Stover, Daniel, 4645
Stow, Daniel, 0926, 2232, 1519
Stowe, Frederick, 1293
Stowell, Ration Levings, 1219
Stratton, Alpheus, 2824
Strawbridge, John, 1960
Street, Joseph, 3646
Streett, John, 2998, 3669
Stremback, Jacob, Jr., 0028
Stremback, Jacob, Sr., 0028
Strembeck, Jacob, 0077
Strevey (Streebery), Peter, 2198
Stribling, Erasmus, 0965
Strobel, John Peter, 0380, 1045
Stroh, Benjamin, 4069
Strong, William A., 1109
Strother, Aaron, 2849, 2850, 2914
Strunk, Peter, 3744
Stubblefield, Peter Beverley, 3615
Stucky, John, 1784
Stull, Adam, 0129, 1545
Sturgis, Nathan, 2006, 3238, 3239
Sturtevant, Thomas, 1182
Subte, Lewis, 0622
Sumner, Henry Payson, 0856
Sumwalt, John T., 0185, 0645
Sutherland, Joel B., 0122
Sutliff, Salmon, 4334
Sutton, Smith, 3961
Sutton, Tingley, 3934
Swaim (Swain), William, 3315
Swaim, William, 2054, 3194, 3237, 3240, 3246
Swain, Charles W., 2012
Swan, Benjamin, 0139

Ancestor Index 237

Swan, Nathan, 1291
Swan, William, 2255, 2607
Swartwout, Robert, 0074, 0075, 0341
Swearingen, James Strode, 0471, 0501
Sweeney, Daniel, 0654
Sweetser, Seth, 1771
Swift, Charles, 3929
Swift, John, 2043
Swift, Zebulon, 4454
Swing, Abraham, 1896, 1932, 1933, 2037, 2038
Swisher, Henry Woodrow, 4127
Swisher, Jacob, 2352
Swisher, John, 4492
Swogger, John, Jr., 4258
Swoyer, John, 0367
Synder, Simon, 0269
Sypher, Jacob, 4503
Taggart, John, 3022
Talbott, Richard, 0691, 0838, 0839
Talmadge, Thomas, 3616
Tanner, Christopher, 0718, 1459
Tanner, Nathan, 4343
Tappan, George, 3126
Tate, James, 3121
Tate, Jesse Overton, 3728
Taws, Kenny (McKenna), 3970
Taylor, Elias, 4181
Taylor, Henry, 2046
Taylor, James, 1668
Taylor, James, 5th., 4126
Taylor, John Bradford, 0085, 2332
Taylor, Lemuel, 0398
Taylor, Lemuel Greenberry, 4171
Taylor, Lewis, 1345
Taylor, Robert, 0935, 2600
Taylor, Robert A., 1672, 1674A
Taylor, Thomas, 4101
Taylor, Thompson, 2748
Taylor, Titus, 2260
Taylor, William, 0173, 0291
Teale, John Cranmer, 0747
Teegarden, William, 4580
Tempest, William, 1336, 1427
Ten Broeck, John, 0756, 1082
Ten Eyck, Harmon Hoffman, 2160
TenEyck, Coenradt, 1703
Terry, Nathaniel, Jr., 3511
Tete, Auguste, 4373
Thacker, Allen, 1675

Tharpe, Jeremiah Allen, 2899
Thaxton, Thomas, 4557, 4564
Thayer, Oppolos, 1525
Thibaut, Jean Pierre, 2563, 2564
Thomas, Allen, 2333
Thomas, Andrew, 0797
Thomas, Benjamin, 3634
Thomas, Charles W., 1701
Thomas, David, 2586
Thomas, Elam, 4429
Thomas, Hilliard, 3556
Thomas, John, 2903
Thomas, Philemon, 4408
Thomas, Richard, 1840
Thomas, Samuel, 2718
Thomas, Sterling, 3559
Thomas, William, Jr., 3585
Thompson (Thomson), William, 1952
Thompson, Henry, 1394
Thompson, Isaac, 1544
Thomson, David, 4456
Thornton, James Brown, 0722
Thrall, Walter, 4090
Throckmorton, Josiah, 0998
Tilden, Luther, 0770
Tilley, Reuben Dodson, 3957
Tipton, Luke, 4032
Tipton, Solomon, 3096
Todd, Bernard, 1263
Todd, Robert S., 3429
Todd, William W., 0051
Toledano, Christopher, 3490
Tolin, James, 1799
Tolman, Robert Pierce, 0658
Tomkins, Elijah, 3619
Tompkins, Daniel D., 0125, 1320, 3619
Toothaker, William Rodick, 3905
Torrey, Nathan, Jr., 4534
Tottingham, Joseph, 0637
Tower, Reuben, 2024, 3277
Towle, Joseph, 0021
Towles, Henry, 2510
Town, Stephen, 1862
Town, Thomas, 2621, 3460
Towne, Elijah, 1881
Towne, Stephen, 1924
Townley, Robert, Jr., 3047
Townsend, Daniel S., 0455, 0631, 0843, 2254
Towsend, Jeremiah, 2644

Toxier, Stephen, 1867
Tracy, Dyer, II, 2108
Trenchard, Edward, 0027
Tridel, John, 1216
Trigg, Stephen, 2332
Triplett, William Harrison, 4398
Trites, John, 1760
Trousdale, William, 3031
Trout, Joseph, 0965
Trowbridge, Abner, 4225
Trowbridge, Adonis, 3112, 3113
Trowbridge, Jacob, 4322
Trowbridge, Luther, 1781
Trowbridge, Reuben, 1657
Trowbridge, William Frasier, 3675
True, James Hill, 3117
Trumbo, Matthias, 0197
Tschudy, Samuel, 1468, 1502
Tuck, Levi, 0686
Tucker, Amos Dennis, 4353
Tucker, Benjamin, 1194
Tufford, Philip, 0253
Tuggle, William, Sr., 4185
Tupper, Charles, 0063
Turner, Charles, 0358
Turner, Daniel, 0084
Turner, Henry Edward, 0084
Turner, John Bryant, 1078
Turner, Nathan, 2852
Turner, Peter, 0084, 4561
Turner, Robert, 1312, 2096, 2122
Turner, William, 0084, 1744
Tuttle, John, 2750
Twiggs, David E., 4277
Twining, John, 2995
Tyler, David E., 4521
Tyrrell, Artemas, 3692
Udall, James, 0795
Updegraff, Abner, 2681, 2682, 2683
Urquhart, David, 2416
Urwiler, George, 2220
Usilton, Robert, 3547
Utley, Alvin, 3956
van Schaumburg, Bartholomew, 4015, 4109
Valere, Charles, 4377
Vallandingham, Richard, 4237
Van Boskerck, John, 0761
Van Deman, Henry, 1062
Van Duersen, William, Jr., 0100
Van Etten, Anthony, 0078

Van Meter, John, 3957
Van Pelt, Peter H., 3552
Van Rensselaer, John Sanders, 3841
VanDeren, Godfrey, 4237
VanDeren, Stephen, 4237, 4325, 4326
VanDeventer, Christopher, 1999
VanDuersen, William Jr., 0467
VanHorne, Isaac, 0494
Vananda, Jacob, 3813
Vandenbemden, Joseph, 1752
Vanderslice, Edward, 0793
Vanderslice, Isaac, 4593
Vandever, Wm., 0453
Vanosdol, Robert, 3941
Vanuxem, Lewis Clark, 0137, 0145, 0222
Vaughn, Manoah, 3960
Veillon, Joseph Sylvain, 2561
Verret, Augustin, 2673
Verret, Godfroi, 3679
Vickers, Clement, 2212, 2221
Vickers, Joel, 0674
Vieillon, Joseph Sylvain, 2593
Viele, John L., 0068
Villere, Jacques Philippe, 2379, 2381, 2384, 2385, 2388, 2403, 2427, 2440, 2517, 2544, 2578, 2602, 2780, 2820, 3349, 3424, 3506, 3844, 3911, 3932, 3353
Villere, Rene Gabriel, 2407, 2408, 3417
Villere, Rene Philippe Gabriel, 2837
Vincent, Francis Alva, 3805
Vinnedge, John, 3803
Viven, John, 0199
Vodges, Jacob, 0454, 2703, 3078, 3195, 0465, 1329, 1757, 1758, 1759
Von Trupel, John, 0264
Voorhees, John P., 1256
Voorhies, Cornelius, 3390, 3425
Voorhies, Peter Gordon, 0098
Wack, John Jacob, 3314
Wack, Jacob, 2695
Wack, John Jacob, 3295
Waddell, Littleton, 0965
Wade, James, 4536
Wade, Lewis, 1782
Wade, Zepheniah, 0393
Wadhams, Luman, 0602, 0644, 0799, 3235
Wadleigh, Benjamin Dean, 2311

Ancestor Index 239

Wadsworth, Elijah, 0730
Wagener, Henry, 1447
Wager, Philip, 2013
Waggaman, George Augustus, 2394, 2492, 2736
Waite, Oliver, 4320
Wakefield, Matthew, 1786
Walbridge, Solomon, 0786
Walcott, Silas, 1446
Waldorf, Philip, 3574
Walker, Benjamin, 0115, 1520
Walker, Isaac, 1572, 2017
Walker, Joseph, 2896
Walker, Richard Henry, 4235
Walker, William, 0725
Wallace, Thomas Nesmith, 1378
Waller, Jonathan, 0829
Waller, Robert Page, 3570, 3717, 3718
Waller, William, 0245
Walling, Daniel, 3269, 3281, 3282
Walls, Isaac, 2574
Walpole, Horace, 4189
Walton, Nathaniel, 0561
Walton, William, 3154
Walworth, Hiram, 0043
Ward, Aaron, 0300
Ward, Francis Asbury, 3797
Ward, John Wesley, 2246
Waring, Francis, 1037
Waring, Henry, Jr., 1918
Waring, John, 3257
Waring, John, Jr., 3137
Warne, Elisha Spring, 0927, 1246
Warner, Andrew E., 0171, 0209
Warner, Michael, 0321, 1407, 2048
Warren Benjamin, 2650, 1946, 2124
Warren, Ebenezer, 4104
Warren, Orlando Edgar, 0872
Warterfield, Peter, 4118
Waterman, Barnabas, 4390, 4413
Waters, Richard R., 3065
Waters, Richard Rawlings, 3925, 3926, 3947
Waters, Zebulon, 2853
Watkins, Gassaway, 0390, 0924, 2314
Watkins, John, 4634
Watmough, John Goddard, 0224
Watson, James, 0030
Watson, Thomas, 0398
Watt, John, 3172
Watts, John, 4237

Watts, John T., 4237
Watts, Julius, 4237
Watts, Nathaniel, 0187
Watts, Thomas B., 0176
Wayne, Isaac, 0314
Wear, George, 3695
Wear, Samuel, 1618
Weaver, John, 0362
Weaverling, John, 1891
Webb, Abner, Jr., 1601, 1860
Webb, Adin, 4423
Webb, John, 0278
Webb, Reynold, 0044
Webb, Samuel, 1962, 1987
Webb, William, 3280, 3566, 3689
Webster, John Adams, 0034, 1177, 2238
Webster, Phineas, 2109
Weeks, John Wingate, 0484, 1623
Weeks, Lemuel, 0885
Weeks, Stephen, 2045
Weeks, Wm. Raymond, 0709
Weer, Joseph, 3706
Weigle, Samuel, 1627
Weitzel, George, 0865
Welch, Daniel, 1360
Weller, George, 4123
Wells, Benjamin, 0806
Wells, James, 4167, 4276
Wells, Jonathan, 4481, 4482, 4483
Wells, Sheriff, 2359, 2361, 2362, 2365
Wells, William, 2071
Wells, William John, 3191
Wells, William, Jr., 1015
Wells, William, Sr., 1015
Wentz, Jacob, 1136
Wersler, John Gulden, 1247, 1741
Wessels, John, 0151
West, Henry, 2119
West, Leonard, 1907
West, Lynn, 3608, 3815
Westerbrook, C. D., 0056
Westerbrook, Frederick, 0056
Westmoreland, John, Sr., 2917
Weston, John Whitney, 2725
Wheat, Joseph, 3121
Wheeler, Erastus, 4024
Wheeler, Jonathan Jones, 4124
Wheeler, Joseph, 0702
Wheeler, Nathan, 3444
Wheeler, Thomas, 2283

Whelan, Thomas, 2253
Whipple, John, 0716, 3869
Whitaker, Joseph, 0255, 2057
Whitcomb, Lot, 3183
White, Hugh, 0449, 0726
White, John J., 2978
White, Joshua, 3959
White, Maunsel, 2402, 2726, 2781, 3856, 4031, 2398, 2399
White, Silas Hathaway, 3780
Whiteford, Hugh, Jr., 2789
Whitley, William, 2986, 3509, 3893
Whitman, Henry Nostrand, 4600
Whitney, Abraham Johnson, 3338
Whitney, Joseph, 1804
Whitsett, William, 3919
Whittlesey, Parnell (Parke), 2926
Whittum, Daniel, 3290
Whyte, Joseph, 0228
Wickes, Van Wyck, 1787
Wickwire, Isaac, 4145
Wiegand, Daniel, 1489, 1528
Wier, John Richard, 2287
Wilcox, DeLafayette, 0701
Wilder, Sampson, 1888
Wiley, John, 4204, 4588
Wilkins, Robert, 2327, 2618, 2811, 2941
Wilkinson, Elisha, 0448
Wilkinson, James, 2389, 2464, 2503, 2585, 2946, 3769, 4030
Wilkinson, Samuel, 1493
Wilkinson, Stephen, 4309, 4310
Willcockson, Elijah, 3662, 3885
Willcox, Oliver, 2926
Willey, John, 0081
Williams, Abner Morton, 1686
Williams, James, 3992
Williams, Jonathan, 2640, 2897, 3475, 3476
Williams, Joseph, 1529
Williams, Otho Holland, 0838, 0839
Williams, Ralph, 4186
Williams, Robert Pearce, 0789
Williams, Solomon, Jr., 1838, 1848, 1849
Williams, Wesley, 3693
Williams, William, 3174
Williamson, James, 2764
Willier, Peter, Jr., 3520
Willingham, James, 3215, 3335, 3481

Willis, Daniel, 4548
Willis, James H., Jr., 1982
Willis, John, 0876
Willis, William W., 4467
Wilmer, John Williamson, 0674
Wilson, Andrew, 0572
Wilson, George P., 4565
Wilson, Hiram Isaac, 4383
Wilson, James, 0391, 3180, 3587
Wilson, John, 0268, 0376, 0955, 2944
Wilson, John Sanford, 0557
Wilson, Nicholas, 4356
Wilson, Peter, 1432
Wilson, Thomas, 0308, 0417
Wiltbank, Robert, 2296
Wimberley, Ezekiel, 2321, 3899
Wimberly, Ezekiel, 3567
Winans, William Wanton, 1347, 1548
Winchester, James, 1334
Winchester, Johnadab, 0469
Winder, Levin, 2281, 2331
Winlock, Joseph, 0575, 0580
Winn, James M., 4447
Winne, Francis D., 0088
Winslow, Kenslin, 4300
Winston, Anthony, 3496
Winston, William D., 3611
Winters, Daniel, 1950
Winters, Nathan, 4100
Wintringer, Nathan, 2148
Witherow, David, 4626, 4630
Withers, Thomas W., 3004
Withington, John, 4107
Witt, Silas, 4178
Wittenmeyer, Jacob, 3531
Wolf, George Frederick, 3961
Wood, Aaron, 1163
Wood, Enos Nathan, 2227
Wood, James, 0046
Wood, John, 0154, 0418, 0665, 0698, 3487
Wood, Matthew, 3138
Wood, Thaddeus Mead, 1163
Woodbury, Robert, 1806
Woodman, Moses, 1748, 3591
Woodman, Stephen, 0421, 0823
Woodruff, Ephraim, 4095
Woodruff, Jonathan, 3181
Woodruff, Joseph, 1314
Woods, Andrew Washington, 3918
Woods, Archibald, 3258

Ancestor Index 241

Woodward, Philemon, Jr., 3129
Woodward, Theodore, 0262
Woodyear, Joseph, 3419
Woolverton, Jacob, 4513
Worcester, Samuel, 1975, 1976, 1997, 1998, 2004, 2023, 2190, 2216, 2696, 2697, 2964
Worley, Elijah, 4292
Worrell, Isaac, 3465, 3541
Worth, William Jenkins, 0277
Worthington, Joab, 3705, 4125
Worthington, Rezin Hammond, 1418, 1421, 1475, 1739
Wright, Alpha, 0506
Wright, Benjamin, 0292, 1704, 2292
Wright, Daniel, 1008
Wright, George W., 4639
Wright, James, 4524
Wright, John, 0168, 0174, 0181, 0183, 0508
Wright, Joseph, 0312, 0375
Wright, Lewis, 3644
Wright, Morgan, 2049
Wright, Spencer, 0443, 0540
Wright, William Alfred, 2228
Wyatt, Daniel, 3883

Wyman, John, 2893, 2894, 2895, 3364
Yates, William, 3636
Yeager, Daniel, 0517
Yeager, Jacob, 0634
Yoakley, Richard J., 2940
York, Stephen, 0497
Young, Abraham, 2693
Young, Benjamin S., 2746
Young, Daniel, 3392, 3406
Young, George, Jr., 4402
Young, Jacob, 2337, 2558, 2701
Young, John, 1047
Young, John Jr., 1705, 1812
Young, Peter, 3168, 3231, 3232
Young, Robert, Sr., 4219
Young, William, 0534
Younker, Francis, 0966
Yount, David, 3754, 4331
Zacharias, Daniel, 1147
Zearfoss, Joseph George, 3820
Zenor, George, Sr., 3467
Zieber, Isaac, 0295
Zimmerman, David, 1514
Zimmerman, Joseph, 1123
Zollinger, Jacob, 1503, 2375

GENERAL SOCIETY OF THE WAR OF 1812

Supplement to the 1989 Roster

Compiled and Edited by
Dennis F. Blizzard

CLEARFIELD

SUPPLEMENT TO THE 1989 ROSTER

PREFACE

Following the publication of the 1989 ROSTER, subsequent research for CHRONICLES in 1993 and DESCENDANTS OF VETERANS in 1994 made it possible to amend and add data which extended the membership and ancestor rolls of the General Society. A more sound base and improved record maintenance motivated this ten-year supplementation.

The Supplement's format is changed only by way of presenting the names of members in alphabetical order rather than by sequence of assigned numbers. In the original work it was deemed important to provide the sequential order of induction during the ninety-five year span. The Supplement deals only with the past decade. The second index of veteran ancestors has reference just to the 1999 Supplement.

Recognition needs to be given with thanks to Forrest R. Schaeffer, Albert B. Snapp and William R. Ward for their important assistance in collecting the material required to produce this Supplement.

Lutherville, Maryland   *Dennis F. Blizzard*
February 4, 1999

MEMBER	ANCESTOR	GEN. SOC. NO.
Abbott, Alvin Arthur	Turner, Joseph	5187
Abell, Richard Bender	Adamson, Greenberry	3561
Abney, Louis Oswell	Hogg, Lewis	4987
Adams, Allan Blakely, Jr.	McClure, William	5217
Adams, Robert Donnell II	Adams, John	4736
Akin, Billie Gordon	Gibson, Samuel	5078
Alexander, Milton Judson	Royalty, Henry	5252
Allen, Alfred Lester	Symonds, John D.	5122
Alsup, Alan Kent	Alsup, Asaph	5125
Amos, Eugene Paul	Mix, Ira, Sr.	5170
Anderson, Gregory Thomas	Howard, Cyrus	4655
Anderson, Richard Edward	Russell, Pliny	4732
Anderson, Richard Edward, Jr.	Russell, Pliny	5127
Anderson, Scott Jonathan	Russell, Pliny	5120
Anderson, Vernon Brian	Anderson, William	5281
Armistead, George, Jr.	Armistead, George	1036
Arnaud, John Felix, Jr.	Tinnin, Asa	5246
Arnold, Robert Carter	Woolsey, Melancthon Taylor	4970
Asher, Richard Russell	Russell, Pliny	5337
Ashley, Robert Drew	Flesher, Isaac Newton	5096
Austin, William Charles, Jr.	Shipley, Benjamin, Jr.	4799
Aycock, Harry Tracy IV	Hughes, Benjamin	5226
Bahan, John Baptiste	Macarty, Jean Baptiste Barthelmy	4849
Bahl, Daniel Lee	Wilson, John	4811
Bailey, Russell Bishop	Bailey, William	4863
Baker, Bruce Addison	Kelly, Sims	4877
Baker, Bruce Addison	McNemar, John	4877
Baker, Bruce Addison	Porter, Hugh	4877
Baker, Bruce Addison	Baker, Samuel	4877
Baker, Harrison Scott II	Gaddis, Abner	5035
Baker, Jerry Allen	Bowers, Cornelius	4955
Baldwin, Roger Conant	Perry, Oliver Hazard	4758
Balser, Everett Wayne, Jr.	Balser, Benjamin	4657
Bandel, Littleton C.	Bendel, William	0764
Barnard, Frederick Henry	Keyser, Conrad	4725
Barnard, Kenneth Norman	Keyser, Conrad	5310
Barnes, Charles Homer	Harpold, Solomon	4871
Barnes, William Joseph	Patton, John	4692
Barroll, David Oakley V.	Barroll, James Edmondson	4706
Bartholomew, Robert Eugene	Ohl, John Philip	5206
Baskette, Alvin K.	Gwinn, James	1807
Bates, Gary Walter	Bates, Seth Hurin	4735
Bates, Roma Scott	Bates, Seth Hurin	4734
Bates, Willis Sherman	Bates, Martin	4911

MEMBER	ANCESTOR	GEN. SOC. NO.
Bauman, Kirby Lee	Wiggins, Archibald	5166
Baxter, Hugh Wise	Baxter, James	5089
Bearden, Mike Michael	Bearden, Jeremiah	4926
Beaufait, Richard Thomas	Beaufait, Louis, Jr.	4991
Becker, David Charles	Thomas, Joseph	4648
Begnal, Dorr Buckley Calkins	Calkins, Amos	4981
Beidler, James Michael	Etschberger, Johann Peter	5351
Belisle, Thomas Richard	Vermette, Antoine	4982
Bell, William Duffield	Bell, William Duffield, Sr.	0505
Berg, Robert Henry	Doten, Jacob	4893
Bernard, Thomas Norton	Labranche, Jacques Hermogen	4920
Berry, George Duane Leatherwood	Leppo, Jacob	4968
Bethard, Alvin Young	Bethards, Henry Selby	4919
Beverly, Kermit Eugene	Ramsey, Joel, Jr.	5248
Birchfield, James de Maris	Johnston, David	5224
Bird, Thomas Edward	Moot, John Conrad	4744
Birely, William Cramer	Cramer, Jacob	3440
Bishop, J. Brooks, Jr.	Bright, John	5104
Black, Leslie Edward	Sharp, Aaron	5083
Blair, John Patrick	Lockhart, William	5279
Blair, William Paul	Lillard, Abraham I	5101
Blankenship, Willard J.	Jolliff, Richard	5267
Blauer, James Freeman	Brownnawell, John	5026
Blizzard, Arthur Keith	Blizzard, William of W.	3829
Blizzard, Dennis Craig	Blizzard, William of W.	3696
Bockstruck, Lloyd DeWitt	Davis, John	3637
Bolt, Eugene Albert, Jr.	Stevenson, Hugh	5272
Bolton, Nelson Mott	Thompson, Henry	5010
Bond, Christopher Eugene	Bates, Seth Hurin	4899
Bond, Weldon Eugene, Jr.	Bates, Seth Hurin	4898
Booth, Edwin Russell	Adams, Lemuel Allen	5207
Booth, Robert Early	Booth, Lemuel Early	5215
Booth, Stuart Lee	Adams, Lemuel Allen	5214
Booth, Talmadge Early	Adams, Lemuel Allen	5192
Boothe, Brian James	Clegg, John Polk	5114
Bouis, Charles Elliott	Foreman, Elijah	4804
Bourg, Blaise Bernard	Bourgeois, Jean Baptiste	4777
Bowen, Norman Adelbert	Bowen, Constant	4749
Bowers, Henry Kenneth	Doran, Philip	4768
Bowling, Charles Taylor, Jr.	Long, John Henry	4721
Bozic, William Joseph, Jr.	Green, John	5238
Bozic, William Joseph, Jr.	Ellison, Akis	5138
Bradshaw, Burton Cox, Sr.	Bradshaw, Amos	5287
Brady, Rodney Howard	Richards, Augustus	4761
Brann, James Richard	Lunt, Joseph, Jr.	5044

MEMBER	ANCESTOR	GEN. SOC. NO.
Breithaupt, Richard Hoag, Jr.	Anderson, James	4935
Brent, Paul Leslie, Jr.	Brent, Charles	5220
Bresnehen, Thomas Francis, Jr.	Sinket, Daniel Jr.	3996
Bresnehen, Thomas Francis, Jr.	Sinket, Samuel	3996
Brewer, Gordon Morgan	Morgan, David Bannister	5183
Brewer, John Morgan	Morgan, David Bannister	4953
Brewer, Stephen Morgan	Morgan, David Bannister	5105
Brinker, Brett Thomas	Brinker, George	5074
Brinker, John Thomas	Brinker, George	5073
Brite, William Bradley	Keown, William	4870
Broadbent, Peter Edwin, Jr.	Talbott, Charles Wells	4724
Brockman, Ellis Radan	Ellis, Abraham	4823
Brooke, Dandridge William	Bissell, Daniel Russell	4816
Brown, Byron Winfield	Hall, James	4941
Brown, Robert Athey	Athey, Willis/William	4737
Brown, Vincent Robert	Haught, Joseph	4789
Brown, William Raymond, Jr.	Kepler, Jacob	4884
Brown, William Beckett III	Brown, Wesley, Sr.	4840
Browne, John Prentiss	Brown, John	4818
Browne, Merrick	Merrick, William Duhurst	5345
Buckaway, William Allen, Jr.	Yates, Lewis	4928
Burch, John Thomas, Jr.	Burch, Bazell	4841
Burkey, Noel Aaron, Jr.	Kelley, Samuel	5053
Burkhart, Valentine, Jr.	Burkhart, Valentine	0158
Burnette, Van Tyle	Sellers, Matthew, Jr.	5037
Burr, Richard Marshall	Middleton, Isaac	4750
Burt, Robert Eugene	Hayse, Samuel	5013
Burton, Claude Raymond	Moore, Jacob	5167
Bush, Daniel Byram	Bush, Henry C.	5290
Bush, Gerard David	Bush, Henry C.	5289
Butler, Edward Franklyn II	Butler, Elias	5086
Butler, Edward Franklyn, Sr.	Butler, Elias	5085
Butler, Jeffrey Darrell	Butler, Elias	5087
Butler, William Joseph, Jr.	Torrey, James	5012
Caddel, Elmer George	Derrick, John	4716
Caddel, Elmer George	Derrick, Simon	4716
Caldwell, James Allen	Duff, William	4605
Calhoun, Ernest Clyde, Jr.	Calhoun, Adam, Jr.	4766
Campbell, William Michael	Campbell, Duncan	4878
Carter, John Henry	Carter, Anthony Terry	5147
Carter, Peyton Franklin III	Upshur, Littleton II	5343
Casey, Lawrence King, Jr.	Files, Ebenezer Scott Thomas	5333
Cassell, Hugh Bethel	Cassell, John	5039
Castleberry, Ottis Lamont	Pangle, Andrew	5265
Cavaroc, John Peter	Percy, Ferdinand	3347

MEMBER	ANCESTOR	GEN. SOC. NO.
Cavaroc, John Peter	Bonaventure François	3347
Chace, George Frederick	Chace, James	4722
Chambers, Robert Douglas	Elliot, Abraham James	4704
Choate, John Mark	Dodson, William	5090
Choate, Lee Hampton	Evans, James Hampton, Sr.	5121
Chotard, Richard DeMeyere	Chotard, Henry	4838
Christian, James Milton	Jarrett, Nicholas	5355
Church, David Lent	Rooney, Daniel	4697
Clark, Alan James	Wheeler, Cornelius	5185
Clement, Harrell E.	McCullock, Alexander, Sr.	4673
Cleveland, Kerry Owen	Cleveland, Joseph	4895
Coker, Robert Wayne	Harding, William	5034
Colburn, Berman Eugene	Jeffreys, William	4894
Colburn, Berman E.	Rye, Solomon II	4894
Colburn, Rolland Dale	Whaley, James	5271
Cole, David	Fluker, Robert	5058
Coleman, Robert Sherrill	Billingsley, Clement Turner	5029
Colley, Darrell Edward, Jr.	Colley, James	5302
Colley, Darrell Edward III	Colley, James	5303
Collier, Henry Grady, Jr.	Harper, Enos	4687
Collins, Alvin Eugene	Strawn, Jacob	5038
Collins, Carroll Jefferson	Bramble, Moses	4793
Conn, John Kendall	Lamb, Chester, Sr.	5040
Conner, Robert Jean	Champlin, Francis Cole	5270
Cook, Grafton Hopkins II	Grafton, Ambrose	4967
Corey, George Reece	Nivin, David	4839
Corn, William Stephen, Sr.	Hill, John	4971
Cornwell, Larry Patrick	Cornwell, Charles	4867
Corum, Otto Franklin, Jr.	Major(s), James	4960
Cox, Gregory David	Grim, Jonathan	5156
Cox, Shawn Alan	Grim, Jonathan	5157
Cox, Wayne Norris	Cox, James	5130
Crawford, Victor Lawrence, Jr.	Robinson, Sampson Avent	5273
Crisler, Edgar Theodore, Jr.	Wood, Francis	4792
Crittenden, Wm. Lafayette	Crittenden, Wm. Gatewood	1226
Cummins, Robert Towles, Jr.	Cummins, Robert	5076
Cupp, Michael Charles	Cupp, Frederick	4691
Curfman, David Ralph	Schreck, Andrew	5094
Curtis, Frederick William, Jr.	Bartlett, Luther	5098
Dakin, John Robert	McGrew, John Flood	4755
Daniels, Thomas Sherman	Gries, John	5095
Daniels, Thomas Sherman	Gries, Jacob	5095
Davenport, Robert Ralsey	Kidd, Alexander	4862
Davidson, Kerry Joseph	Davidson, Richard	5348
Davis, Robert Macnider III	Fitchett, James N.	5077

1999 Supplement 247

MEMBER	ANCESTOR	GEN. SOC. NO.
Davis, William Kevin	Howland, Zephaniah	5036
Davis, William Thomas, Jr.	Davis, Richard	4962
Dawley, Raymond Angus	Dawley, Isaac	4656
de Berardinis, Robert Ewing	Lafarque, Francois	5263
de Berardinis, Robert Ewing	Voorhies, Cornelius	5263
Demass, George Robert, Jr.	Demass, Peter	5049
Denger, Mark James	Sayre, William	5222
Derbes, Lewis Joseph	Martin, Joseph Richard	4860
Dibrell, John Thomas	Dibrell, Charles Lee	4980
Dickerson, Laurence Edward	Vanfossen, George	4795
Diehl, George Sandy, Jr.	Smyth, Richard	5197
Dillon, Lester Reed, Jr.	Shenefelt, John	5148
DiStefano, Richard Renato P.	Geyer, Andrew	4709
Divine, Arthur Eugene	Parker, Warren	5014
Dixon, Malcolm R.	Scott, William Coleman	5162
Dobbins, John William	Wansley, Thomas Jefferson	4614
Dodson, Andrew J.	Godbey, William	5317
Doss, Clyde Lance	Pettigrew, George Augustus	5054
Drake, Paul D.	Midlam, Joseph	5102
Drake, Raymond Lawrence	Hammond, Matthew Brown	5344
Drake, Robert Scott	Hoschar, Andrew	5017
du Fossat, Godfrey Meloney Soniat	Bermudez, Joaquin	4954
Dunahay, Lowell Vincent	Easterday, Jacob	4886
Dunavant, Richard Hannah	Yokley, Andrew	4727
Duncan, James Jefferson	Duncan, William	4757
Dunlap, Kenneth A., Sr.	Dunlap, Richard Gilliam	5234
Dunn, Sydney Bullen, Jr.	Riter, Michael	4696
Dunn, Walter Kenny, Jr.	Owings, John	4848
DuPriest, Travis Talmadge, Jr.	Depriest, Austin	5091
Durnin, Richard Gerry	Millett, Israel	4810
Dye, Donald Elbridge, Jr.	Dye, William	4943
Early, Alexander Rieman III	Moale, Samuel	4950
Early, Jack Jones	Early, William	4931
Early, Joseph Derwood	Early, William	5250
East, Donald Paul	Hartley, Hillory	5323
Eckert, John Clarence	Nuss, Frederick	5230
Edwards, Mark Stuart	Gaines, Robert Taliaferro	4979
Elam, Hunter Ashley	Saunders, Hiram	5293
Elder, Paul William	Henning, John	4958
Elliott, James Robert II	Blair, Jesse	5254
Ellis, Estil Lynn	Wilson, Thomas McMackin	5208
Emge, Lawrence Berryman III	Knight, Daniel B.	4939
Epperly, John Moyer	Epperly, John	5103
Epperly, Loyd Lincoln	Epperly, John	5030
Fairley, Albert Langley, Jr.	Burleson, Jonathan	4925

MEMBER	ANCESTOR	GEN. SOC. NO.
Farnet, Samuel Stewart	Destrehan, Nicholas Noel	5107
Farrington, William Prentice	Forstall, Edmond John	4997
Farrow, Samuel Lee, Jr.	Stephenson, John	4986
Fazzini, Philip Anthony	Russell, Moses	5255
Ferrell, James Mansfield	Ferrell, James Mansfield	5339
Ferrell, James Mansfield (son)	Ferrell, James Mansfield	5340
Ferrell, James Michael	Jennings, Martin	4763
Ferry, John Christopher	Crowder, Peterson	4831
Finch, William Calhoun, Sr.	Thomas, James	4684
Fisher, Harold Clyde	Hooter, Michael	4660
Fitzgerald, John Barnard	Barnard, James O.	5332
Flanagan, Patrick Martin	Marcy, Jared	5277
Flint, Adam Polhemus	Flint, Daniel	5274
Folger, Harry Paine 3rd	Beebe, John	5244
Ford, Douglas Felix	Roberts, John (Jackie)	5118
Ford, John Drew	Roberts, John/Jackie	4817
Ford, John Drew	White, William	4817
Ford, John Drew	Thomas, William Benjamin	4817
Ford, John Drew	White, Henry	4817
Ford, Larry Lindell	Ford, William	4885
Ford, Mark Douglas Lederer	Roberts, John/Jackie	4904
Ford, Roland Wilmer	Roberts, John (Jackie)	5203
Forkner, Charles Thomas, Jr.	Forkner, Henry	5016
Forstall, Terrence Christopher	Forstall, Edmond John	5000
Foust, Perry Elihu	Carter, Nathan W.	4636
Freeland, Michael Willis	Bateman, William Birckhead	5327
Freeman, Edward Patric	Yates, William	4813
Freeman, John Fletcher	Barfield, Lewis	4834
Froelich, James Eugene, Jr.	Cappell, Charles	5305
Fry, Charles George	Jeffers, David Seth	5024
Fuller, Harlan Morris	Fuller, Oliver T.	4652
Fuller, Rex Lynn	Fuller, Moses M.	5322
Gafford, Robert Dale	Gafford, William Robert	5212
Gaines, Larry Bradley	Gaines, Richard	4790
Gallagher, David Wilson	Baker, Greenberry	5169
Garrison, David Lacey, Jr.	Lacey, James	4821
Garrison, David Lacey, Jr.	Gardiner, Ignatius Walter	4821
Garrison, David Lacey, Jr.	Price, Reuben	4821
Garrison, James Gardiner	Gardiner, Ignatius Walter	4964
Garroutte, Keith Tyrone	Garroutte, John Sheridan	4859
Gehring, John George, Jr.	Gehring, John George	0415
Gensemer, Richard Lee	Gilbert, Jacob	5259
Gerlander, Lee Alf	Cutler, Jacob	5141
Gerlander, Randal Lee	Cutler, Jacob	5143
Gerlander, Todd Lee	Cutler, Jacob	5142

MEMBER	ANCESTOR	GEN. SOC. NO.
Gillis, Vern David	Primmer, James	4780
Giuffre, Dennis Michael	Baudry, Jean Baptiste	5329
Gluckert, Francis Albert	Willis, John	4742
Goff, David Murlin	Stirling, Lewis	4854
Gowen, Dana Loomis	Blanchard, David	5262
Grace, James Henry, Sr.	Bloodworth, James, Jr.	5190
Green, Alfred Laland	George, John	4801
Green, Gregory Howison	Howison, Alexander	4708
Green, John Richard	Bird, William	4729
Green, Thomas Milton	Hope, Samuel W.	5186
Greene, Ernest Rinaldo, Jr.	Leftwich, Jesse	5153
Grimes, John Francis	Flesher, Isaac Newton	4864
Grissom, John Farrar	Womack, Abner	4775
Groesbeck, Geoffrey Alan Peter	Bickford, Joseph White, Jr.	4949
Gros, Edward Oliver	Toups, Fuselier Tellesfor	5111
Gurley, Donald Horton	Joyner, Amos	4797
Hadsell, James Earl	Dowse, Stephen Burr	5308
Hall, Mark Alan	Ellis, William	4906
Halle, David Philip, Jr.	Love, Richard H.	5081
Hamilton, Harlan Bernhardt	Roberts, Gilman	4665
Hamilton, James Esta	Ballard, Beverly	5123
Hanna, Muriel Keith, Sr.	Hanna, Richard	5312
Hanna, Muriel Keith, Jr.	Hanna, Richard	5313
Hardin, Charles Kelleher	White, Maunsell	4998
Harper, Miles Douglas, Jr.	Harrison, Nathaniel	5298
Harreld, William Edmiston, Jr.	Dinkins, James	4740
Harrington, Charles Robert	Horner, William	4922
Harris, Benjamin Louis	Harris, Tyree	5300
Harris, Hugh Allen	Harris, Benoni	4944
Harris, John Werner II	Wilcoxson, Elijah	5055
Harris, Timothy Charles	Dustin, Eliphalet	4604
Harris, Timothy Charles	Holden, Ambrose	4604
Harris, William Edney III	Chitwood, Richard	5326
Harrison, Benjamin	Harrison, William Henry	0811
Harrison, Warder Ray	Harrison, Tyree	5171
Hartley, Michael William	Hartley, Richard	5007
Hartnett, Will Ford	Conner, John	4650
Hayward, James Bert	Wood, David Robert	5174
Heath, James Edward	Heath, Ryland	5229
Heckert, John Earl, Jr.	Keely, George	4952
Hedstrom, Carlos Augustino, Jr.	Bullock, Joseph Daniel	4808
Helm, Terry Allen	Wale, Martin	4921
Hemming, Charles Gerald II	McLaughlin, John	5033
Hensel, William Foster	Morgan, David Bannister	5110
Henshaw, Thomas Robert	Henshaw, William Slaughter	4783

MEMBER	ANCESTOR	GEN. SOC. NO.
Herring, Ronald Allen	Underwood, David	4827
Hewitt, Robert Lee	Hewitt, Jonathan	4850
Hicks, Audel Harrison, Sr.	Hicks, William	4869
Hicks, Audel Harrison, Sr.	Holbert, Noah	4869
Hill, Jerry Patrick	Chapin, John	4715
Hill, Joe. M., Jr.	Lowrey, Alexander	5051
Hill, Peter Reichner	Fraser, James P.	4814
Hill, Thomas Allen	Allen, Aaron	4846
Hodalski, Francis Xavier, Jr.	Fogler, Henry	5071
Hodge, Roy Garey	Armstrong, Aaron	4868
Hoffman, Richard J.	Keller, Casper	5195
Hogan, Francis Joseph II	Abbey, Shubel	5276
Hogg, John Webb III	Hogg, Samuel	5031
Holbrook, Paul Evans, Jr.	Evans, Meredith	5052
Hollje, John Buford	McCuistion, James	4879
Holloway, R. Ross	Ross, Reuben	5284
Hooper, Trevor Norris	McCravey, Ezekiel	5116
Hoos, Ernest Lou	McKay, Lewis	5294
Hopkins, Charles Michael	Hopkins, Harris	4963
Horner, Ronald George	Horner, Samuel	5295
Howard, Elijah Davis III	Tabor, John Henry	5239
Howe-Cornwell, Gale Thomas	Howe, Solomon	5319
Hudson, Franklin Flynn	Mead, John	4833
Hudson, John Richard, Jr.	Egbert, David	5047
Hugghins, William Rowe	Cleveland, James	5318
Humphrey, David McClure	Hughart, Thomas	4892
Humphrey, Elwood McClure	Hughart, Thomas	4891
Hunter, Richard Gardner	Sprague, Nathaniel	5321
Hurlbut, Franklin J.	Hurlbut, William Harrison	5309
Hurst, William Moore, Jr.	Smith, Bird Bowker	5210
Huss, William Wiseman, Jr.	Hass, Christian	5296
Hutchins, Joseph Ray	Bigley, James	4853
Hyde, Earl McSherry, Jr.	Cunningham, Jesse	4677
Isaac, Richard Barry	Isaac, Joseph of Richard	5331
Israel, Willard Alfred	Hagler, Isaac	5154
Ives, Charles Pomeroy III	Jacobs, Lyman	5342
Jacks, Thomas Edward	Bayless, John	5228
Jackson, Elmer Martin, Jr.	Jackson, David Edward	4786
Jacobs, Ronald Dean	Brandon, Cornelius	5189
James, Charles Henry	James, Enoch	4900
Jefferson, Stockton Bennett	Bennett, Richard	4776
Jenkins, Alfred Dean	Jenkins, Russel	4913
Jinnett, Robert Jefferson	Aycock, Richard, Jr.	4745
Johnson, Ishmael Herman, Jr.	Walraven, John	5205
Johnson, John Hess	Carney, Solomon	5002

1999 Supplement 251

MEMBER	ANCESTOR	GEN. SOC. NO.
Johnson, Kenneth Willard	Seaton, George Clark	5194
Jones, Myron Ellis, Jr.	Jones, Thomas	5158
Jones, Ralph Hugh	Henderson, Alexander	4815
Jones, Richard S.	Niles, Robert R. II	5245
Jones, Thomas Frank	Kaigler, David	5025
Justice, John Rodman	West, Robert	4674
Keedy, Thomas Cornelius, Jr.	Stuckey, Jacob, Jr.	5266
Kellogg, Ira Newell, Jr.	Kellogg, Pearl	4794
Kellogg, Richard Newell	Kellogg, Pearl	4842
Kellogg, Stephen Alan	Kellogg, Pearl	4881
Kelly, Julian Dantzler, Jr.	Glasson, John	4693
Kemp, Charles Edward	Bobst, Daniel	4707
Kemp, Charles Edward	Grove, Reuben	4707
Kemp, Charles Edward	Kemp, Frederick	4707
Kemp, Charles Edward	Ramsburg, Frederick	4707
Kemp, Charles Edward	Shafer, George	4707
Kemp, Charles Edward	Staley, Moses	4707
Key, Francis Scott	Key, Francis Scott	5268
Kielman, Toxie L.	Rimmer, Thomas	4705
Kienzle, Charles Allen, Jr.	Jones, Joseph	5231
Killen, Harry Edward III	Knowles, John	5269
Killian, John Harrison, Sr.	Tidwell, Robert	4733
Kimberlin, Patrick Blaine III	Kimberlin, Daniel	4909
Kinyon, John Hoey	Abshire, James	4972
Kinyon, Paul Joseph	Abshire, James	4989
Kirkland, Daniel Lloyd	Kellum, Edward	4679
Klinck, Daniel Noble	Hammond, Thomas Denny	5131
Knorr, Norman John	Knorr, William	4910
Knorr, Sheldon Henry	Knorr, William	4888
Kratz, Charles Irving, Jr.	Rolfe, Reuben	4676
Kuriger, Richard Charles IV	Smith, Isaac	5100
Kyle, James H.	Kile, Oliver, Sr.	5285
LaBach, William Anderson	Parker, John Evans	4658
LaBreton, Denvrich Charles	Fortier, Michel II	4994
Landers, William Bruce	Valentine, Joseph	4917
Lands, Ronald Herman	Easter, Peter	4773
Lands, Ronald Herman	Walker, John S.	4773
Lane, William Joseph, Jr.	Lane, Richard	5260
Larson, Charles Jeffers	Jeffers, Thomas	5291
Lauda, Billy George	Delong, John Francis	4748
Lawrence, Floyd Harlow	Lawrence, Zachariah IV	5242
Lawson, Ronald Curtis	Lyford, Peter	4738
LeCompte, Harry Lloyd, Jr.	LeCompte, Joseph	4812
Lee, Donald Edwin	Gates, Valentine	5304
Lee, Donald Edwin	Gates, John Valentine	5304

MEMBER	ANCESTOR	GEN. SOC. NO.
Lee, John Claud	Sellers, Benjamin Duncan	5238
Lee, John Claud	Oldham, William	5238
Lemley, Kenneth McRae	McRae, Christopher	4217
Lessa, Robert John	Moses, Elihu	4686
Lines, Jack Milton	Culver, Aaron	5341
Linthicum, George Emory IV	Linthicum, Charles Griffith	5201
Linthicum, John Whitaker	Linthicum, Charles Griffith	5200
Liscombe, Gerald Bruce	Green, David, Jr.	4782
Logan, Fordyce Barker, Jr.	Allen Logan	5328
Long, Paul Marshall, Sr.	Maull, Henry Fisher	5357
Love, Joseph Bland	Love, David	4664
Lyman, Myron Edwin, Sr.	Lyman, William	5297
MacDonald, Brett Allen	Swartwout, Agustus	5349
Mackie, Charles Le Jeune	Lafargue, Francois	5286
Maginnis, Michael John	Garic, François	4689
Mallory, Donald Nelson	Mallory, Samuel	5020
Malone, Ira Ernest, Jr.	Lee, William Carroll	5264
Mamminga, Michael Arthur	Perrin, Calvin	4975
Manning, John Thomas	Quimby, John, Jr.	5324
Manson, Bradlee Robert	Blackington, Benjamin	4668
Marrs, William Marshal II	Marrs, Archibald	4861
Marshall, David Banks	Morrison, Archibald	5082
Martin, Cornwell Crystal	Sampson, John	5249
Martin, Paul Edmond	Joseph, Hezekiah	4425
Martin, Paul Edmond	Bonar, David	4425
Masters, Vernon Edward	Prather, Thomas	4762
Maxwell, Donald Power	Snook, Casper	5117
Maxwell, Donald Power, Jr.	McCormick, William	5109
Maxwell, Donald Power, Jr.	Snook, Casper	5109
Maxwell, Donald Power	McCormick, William	5117
Mayne, Winfield Scott	Mayne, Adam	4923
McAfoos, Louis Garfield, Jr.	McAfoos, Jacob, Jr.	5280
McAlpin, Benjamin Brandreth III	Gansevoort, John	4743
McCall, James Wilson	McCall, James	5243
McCaskey, Thomas Sims	Sims, James	5124
McCloskey, Malcolm Moore	Evans, Thomas	5335
McCormack, Jay Tucker	Clegg, John Polk	5113
McCoy, Robert C.	Hanson, Peter	4845
McCulloch, James Alfred	Miller, William	5003
McDonald, Marcus Lee	McDonald, Thomas Owen	5164
McElroy, Glenn Wallace III	McElroy, James Erwin	4772
McElroy, Glenn Wallace III	Knowles, Freeman	4772
McFadden, Archibald George William	Brown, Eli	4769
McGath, John Hardin	Boyer, John	5165
McGill, Gerald Lee	Milner, William M.	5237

1999 Supplement 253

MEMBER	ANCESTOR	GEN. SOC. NO.
McGuffey, Carroll Wade, Sr.	Wade, Elisha	4699
McGuffin, Robert E., Sr.	Sias, John	5354
McGuire, Charles Danny	Poore, Edward H.	5080
McHale, Gerald Patrick	Sweetland, Luman	4741
McHargue, James Charles	Oneal, Jacob	5247
McInturf, Robert Cecil	Mingus, William E.	4785
McKay, Donald Innis	McKay, Robert	4927
McKown, Barrett Lee	Pickering, Thomas	4905
McPherson, Ronald Gary	Wright, George W.	4933
McWilliams, Douglas Lyman	McWilliams, John	4765
Mead, Daniel J.	Rhodes, James D.	5129
Meadows, Jeffrey Manton	Nicodemus, John	5088
Meeker, Charles Kenneth, Jr.	Meeker, Jonathan	4874
Meinecke, Tommy Jacob	Charles, Solomon I.	5283
Melville, Robert Middleton	Whitaker, William	4802
Merrill, Ted Duane	Morse, Carpenter	4717
Merrill, Ted Duane	Wood, Benjamin	4717
Merrill, Ted Duane	Merrill, Billosti/Belosti	4717
Merryman of J., Nicholas Bosley	Merryman, Nicholas Rogers	4956
Meservy, Steven Paul	Lancaster, Michael	4918
Milam, David Edward	Milam, Bartlet	5178
Milbank, Walter Cornwell	Ver Planck, Abraham	5334
Miles, William Earle	Miles, William	4659
Miller, Ronald Hague	Rudolph, John, Jr.	5057
Millett, Robert Earl	Hyland, William	4805
Miree, James Wimberly Cook	Wimberly, James	4685
Mix, Richard Lawrence	Mix, Amasa Hotchkiss	4551
Monroe, Kenneth Raymond	Monroe, Randal	5092
Moore, Eugene Nelson	Drake, James	4654
Moore, Frank Warren II	Moore, Enoch Biggs	5350
Moore, Jason Hurd, Jr.	Hurd, Joy	5257
Moore, Jerry Jay	Moore, John Skillman	5182
Moore, Jim Donald	Fry, Philip	5325
Moore, Newton Moore	Nash, Reuben	5347
Moore, Pierce	Moore, Hill	4774
Moore, William Harold	Nash, Reuben	5346
Moore, William Arthur	Moore, John	4820
Moore, William Whitney	Moore, William	4856
Moran, Patrick Edward	Moran, Jesse	4771
Morehouse, Elnathan Paul, Jr.	Hetzer, Philip	4632
Morris, Lowell Winston	Keese, Thomas	4781
Morton, Kim Allen	Bugg, Samuel	5097
Morton, Kim Allen	Ashlock, Obediah	5097
Morton, Kim Allen	Hunt, William	5097
Morton, Kim Allen	Sweeney, Bernard W.	5097

MEMBER	ANCESTOR	GEN. SOC. NO.
Morton, Kim Allen	Winter, Othneal	5097
Mossburg, George Washington	Scatterday, Aaron	4641
Motz, Charles	Boyd, Thomas Duckett	5023
Mullane, Joseph Francis	Parker, William	5282
Mullen, Michael Raymond	Mullen, James	4788
Mumaw, Keith Ray, Sr.	Brandenburg, Solomon	5160
Munford, James Benjamin	Branch, Henry	4759
Murrah, Robert Leland, Jr.	Gates, Benjamin	4728
Murrah, Robert Leland	Gates, Benjamin	4694
Mustain, Robert Dennis	Mustain, John	4936
Muthleb, Gregory G.	Etienne Billiot	5219
Myers, Wilbur Thomas	Myers, Charles	5134
Myles, Edmund Neal	Myles, John, Jr.	4800
Mylnechuk, Larry Herbert	Grover, Silas	5006
Neal, William Benjamin	Neal, William	4746
Neel, Thomas Stephen	Alexander, Squire	4966
Neeley, Koy L.	Hendrick, John	4983
Nettles, Charles R., Sr.	Nettles, Zachariah	5188
Nettles, Charles R., Jr.	Nettles, Zachariah	5161
Newman, George Iley	Koonce, George	4807
Niesen, William Crenshaw	Crenshaw, Cornelius Dabney	5177
Nixon, James Fred, Jr.	Nixon, William	4651
Noel, Edgar Estes II	Noell, Caleb	4976
Norris, William Virgil III	Martin, Robert Elkin	4666
Norton, James John	Norton, Benjamin Spooner	4973
O'Brien, Michael Edward	Darby, Samuel	5009
O'Connor, Gaylord Patrick	Ince, John	4872
O'Neil, John Thomas	Applegate, William	4934
Ohlmeyer, Raleigh Lawrence, Jr.	Schlatre, Joseph	5191
Olney, Allen Lee	Olney, Stephen	4932
Omlor, Richard James	Hulse, Richard	4714
Oppenlander, Christopher Eric	Wiley, John	4824
Osgood, Peter Alan, Sr.	Osgood, David	4760
Pace, Edward McKendrick	Pace, John	4649
Pace, Edward McKendrick, Jr.	Pace, John	4930
Park, Lee Crandall	Smith, William	5202
Parker, Keneth Barry	Brock, George	4965
Parker, Malcolm II	Lansdale, John Wesley	5199
Parmer, J. Norman	Martin, Rawley	4988
Partin, James Daryl	Lowry, Robert Mills	4826
Patout, Robert Bernadas	de Gruys, Pierre	4995
Payne, David LeBarron	Franklin, Thomas Jefferson	4835
Peicker, Martin Jacob	Bonawitz, John	5019
Pemberton, Charles Robert	Pemberton, Nathaniel	4825
Penny, Richard George	Erwin, Robert	5353

1999 Supplement 255

MEMBER	ANCESTOR	GEN. SOC. NO.
Perry, Joseph Minos, Jr.	Harrington, Charles	4779
Perry, Tunstall Barker III	Williams, Henry Guston	5209
Peters, E. Hobart	Hobart, Evans	3218
Peters, Thomas Edward	Wisenbaker, John, Jr.	5181
Peters, Thomas Edward	Fletcher, John, Sr.	5181
Phillips, Robert Leroy	Phillips, Adam	4828
Pierce, Robert Francis	Anderson, James	4959
Pippin, James Michael	King, Samuel	4897
Pippin, James Roberts	Fears, James	4753
Pogue, Ronald Dennis	Splane, Thomas Machen	4739
Pohl, Clifford Ralph	Hall, Thomas Graves	4929
Pond, Franklin Sanford	Fish, Jirah, Jr.	5213
Poor, Harold Everette	Toothaker, William Rodick	5070
Poor, Russell Merritt	Toothaker, William Rodick	5069
Pope, Richard Macauley	Kibbe, Amariah, Jr.	5068
Porter, George Weaver	Grants, Marks, Jr.	4698
Potts, Ewell Cardwell III	Garic, François	5042
Potts, Louis Eldren	Morgan, John Henry, Sr.	4837
Potts, Pearson Bahan	Garic, François	5041
Prejean, Edward Joseph 3rd	Bourgeois, Jean Baptiste	5352
Price, William Archer	Napier, Ashford, Jr.	5093
Pritchard, Cannon Hulbert	Cannon, Willis	5135
Rabun, John Parham, Jr.	Covin, John Peter	5176
Ralston, Michael Eugene	Spade, Henry	4819
Ramirez, Emile J.	Duffel, John L.	4996
Rasmussen, Tom Niel	Trovinger, Joseph	4767
Rassel, David Paul	Knight, Jonathan	5145
Rassel, Oakley Lee	Knight, Jonathan	5144
Rassel, Richard Michael	Knight, Jonathan	5145
Rassel, Stephen Edward	Knight, Jonathan	5152
Rawlins, Steven Wayne	Campbell, George K.	4883
Rayfield, Thomas Filmore	Bullard, Henry	4683
Raymond, Wilford Donald	Raymond, Uriah, Jr.	5136
Raywalt, James Kevin	Crumbaker, John, Jr.	5227
Reeves, John Harlan	Beck, John	5119
Reid, Robert Dale	Gamble, William	4719
Reining, Michael Andrew	Zentmire (Sentmire), George	5112
Reynolds, Alexander Garber	Eubank, Robert	5180
Reynolds, Robert Adair	Tucker, John	5306
Richmond, Jack Commodore	Hummel, John Jacob	5168
Ricketts, John Adams	Adams, Roswell	5021
Ricks, Kenneth Eugene	Branch, David	4908
Ridings, Roger Wilton	Tubb, James, Jr.	5211
Riedel, Frederick Leslie, Jr.	North, Hicks	5356
Riekse, Max James	Platt, Nathaniel G.	4678

MEMBER	ANCESTOR	GEN. SOC. NO.
Riley, David Leslie	Clements, Phillip	4237
Riley, David Leslie	Clements, David	4237
Rising, Lucien Edward	Francisco, Henry A.	5196
Robbins, Donald Gray	Millen, John W.	5320
Robbins, Joel Wayne	Choate, Benjamin	5221
Robertson, Charles Ellwood III	Elder, James, Sr.	5056
Robertson, James Grady, Jr.	Sinclair, John	4653
Robertson, Jimmy Kirk	Kellum, Edward, Sr.	4695
Robinett, David Scott	Simmons, John	4902
Robinett, Richard Bruce	Simmons, John	4903
Robinett, Richard Lee	Simmons, Johns	4901
Robinson, Robert Boyd III	Robinson, Sampson Avant	5001
Roddis, Thomas Hamilton	Leddell, William	4942
Roth, Richard Joseph, Jr.	Courcelles, Joachim	4999
Rothrock, Roger Lee	Rothrock, Solomon	4876
Ruby, John Lindley	Patton, Mathew Houston	4442
Rucker, Ernest Carroll	Shaw, Thompson Breckenridge	4730
Rude, Joe Christopher III	Rude, Isaac A.	5258
Rudy, David Robert	Case, Lester	4990
Rupert, Frederick Russell, Sr.	Scheffey, Henry	4912
Rusch, James Allen	Payne, Scammons	4688
Ryland, James Richard	McKinney, James	5233
Sage, Richard Warren	Sage, Philo B.	5338
Sale, Thomas Wirt, Jr.	Westcott, Major P.	4993
Sanders, Patrick Layton, Jr.	McClesky, David Henderson	5140
Sanneman, Everett Heman, Jr.	Barnett, John	4844
Sayre, Jerry Ray	Davis, James	5240
Scarbrough, Wes L.	Scarbrough, Aven	4680
Schaeffer, Ronald Lester	Ball, Edward	4806
Schiaffino, Ashton	Aler, Thomas	4752
Schiaffino, George Ashton	Aler, Thomas	4851
Schoen, John Garic	Garic, Jean Baptiste Francois	5132
Schubert, Glenn Franklin	Holter, George, Jr.	5072
Schwartz, William Dean	Cox, Martin	4784
Schweizer, Charles Benjamin	Willis, Joel, Jr.	4945
Scoggins, Leland Coulter II	Sewall, Samuel	4832
Seegar, John King Beck Emory, Jr.	Seegar, Arthur	4798
Seely, John Robert	Stone, Stephen	4830
Segraves, William Alexander	Pyron, James	5179
Seiple, Stephen Bradley	Sheakley, George	5075
Sells, George Nelson	Sells, William Henry	4723
Seville, Francis Brent	Long, Christian	4969
Seybold, Edward P., Jr.	Duffel, Edward	5108
Shaw, Donald Chace	Patterson, Arthur	5149
Shaw, James Henry	Brandon, William	4947

MEMBER	ANCESTOR	GEN. SOC. NO.
Shelton, Donald Lee	Craig, James H.	5336
Shepherd, Byrd	Fee, David	5018
Shepherd, Robert Sidney	Hiers, Daniel	5175
Shepley, Raymond, Sr.	Sheple, William	4896
Short, Shelton Hardaway III	Massie, Thomas	5218
Showler, John Thomas	Taggart, Cardiff	5137
Showler, John Thomas	McClelland, William	5137
Shreve-Rountree, Robert Ivan	Earnest, Peter	4836
Simler, Francis Lester	Ripperdan/Ripperdon, John	4938
Simons, David Brenton	Rea, John	4948
Simpson, Gustavus Sailer, Jr.	Simpson, Presley	5155
Skelton, Harold Lawrence	Skelton, Zachariah, Sr.	4701
Skelton, John Loring	Skelton, Zachariah, Sr.	5314
Skelton, Lawrence Harold	Skelton, Zachariah, Sr.	4702
Skinner, William Thomas	Skinner, William	4751
Smith, Billy Earle	Robinson, Stephen, Jr.	4726
Smith, Charles Orestus	Hummer, Jacob	5301
Smith, Clinton Wallace, Jr.	Doherty, George	5022
Smith, Dewey James	Clark, Wilson Lucius	5079
Smith, Edwin Milton	Skeels, Cephas	5256
Smith, Hoyt Oron	Douglass, Jones	4984
Smith, Hoyt Oron	Doherty, George	4984
Smith, Richard Dana, Sr.	Leonard, Nathaniel	5198
Snyder, David Geise	Otto, John Bodo	5099
Spade, Timothy Duane	Pontius, John George	5316
Spellman, Daniel Joseph	Spelman, Timothy	5236
Spivey, Scott Jerome	Knight, Samuel	5043
Sporl, Henry Louis	Settoon, James	4690
Spratt, John Stricklin	Spratt, Thomas	5046
Stair, William Stroman, Jr.	Stair/Stoehr, Daniel	4961
Stair, William Stroman, Sr.	Stair/Stoehr, Daniel	4770
Stakelum, Piercy Joseph, Jr.	Guenard, Nicolas	4852
Starrett, Robert Henry	Starrett, Charles	5133
Steiner, Edward E.	Steiner, Stephen	4006
Stern, Duke Nordlinger	Mackenzie, Thomas	4907
Stevenson, William Robert	Mclachlan, James	5139
Stewart, Dennis Craig	Millikan, Elihu	5216
Stewart, Kelly Loyd	Bradley, Pleasant	5128
Stewart, Kelly Loyd	Yeast, Jacob	5128
Stewart, Lee L.	Seale, James	4865
Stewart, Morton Collins, Jr.	Waterman, Barnabas	4413
Stewart, Thomas William	Stewart, John	4662
Stewart, William	Anthony, Philip	4713
Stigler, Stephen Leath	Barnwell, Edward	5115
Stovall, Fred Dalton, Jr.	Abernathy, Charles Clayton	4754

MEMBER	ANCESTOR	GEN. SOC. NO.
Strang, Frank Morton	Strang, William, Jr.	4880
Streit, Alan Michael	Teagarden, Jacob	4796
Sullivan, Andrew Richard	Fitzhugh, Philip	4747
Suplee, Melvyn James	Suplee, Jesse	4681
Sustendal, Charles Don	Chretion, Hypolite	5126
Sympson, James David	Sympson, James Clendenin	5315
Taylor, Charles Frank	Broadwater, Charles	5184
Taylor, Wallace Goodwin	Goodwin, Joseph	4946
Templeton, Wayne Richard	Sherman, Reubel	4978
Thomas, Kuddy Scott	Sears, Thomas M.	4847
Thornton, Reuben Thomas III	Blassingame, John	5015
Thurber, Cleveland, Jr.	Brady, Hugh	5163
Tice, Robert Dean	Waggener, Richard	4672
Tilton, Bradley Alan	Shrum, George	5307
Tjornhom, Christopher Mark	Morgan, James	4667
Tovey, Herman Rennicker, Jr.	Tovey, Henry	5288
Townsend, Laurence Edward	Townsend, Stephen	5193
Trabue, James Duvall	Trabue, Haskins Dupuy	4756
Trabue, James Duvall	Grace, Henry	4756
Traster, Earl Wilbur	Schuck, David	4682
Trefts, Albert Sharpe	Jones, Marquis	5159
Treppa, Jeffrey Allan	Mitchell, Aden	4663
Treppa, Jerry Anthony	Mitchell, Aden	4843
Troyer, Philip Sanders	Gray, Jonathan	5008
Tucker, Leslie Ray	Christian, Nathaniel	5004
Tucker, Robert Gene	Tucker, Nathaniel	3467
Tucker, William Herbert Martin	Idol, Joseph	5028
Tull, John Earle, Jr.	Tull, John Nicholas	4703
Turner, William Thomas	Atwood, James	4957
Valencia, Dominick Michael, Jr.	Delarue, Celestin	5225
Van Dorn, George Milo Sutherland	Van Dorn, John	5032
Van Tassell, Kenneth Walter	Van Tassell, William J.	4916
Van Wormer, David Lee	Carter, Elijah	4992
Vaughn, John Daniel	Crockett, John Daniel	5311
Veselik, William Allen	Cushman, Caleb	4803
Vivian, Robert Pond	Clark, Ebenezer	5275
von Nirschl, David Allen	Copher, Thomas	4985
Waesche, James Frederick	Conner, Levin	5204
Walker, William Thomas II	Walker, Jeremiah	4829
Ward, Jack Cooper	Williams, Abraham L.	5084
Ware, Joseph Milton	Rucker, Benjamin	4873
Wathen, Richard Albert	Jenkins, Felix	5005
Watkins, Darrell Royce, Jr.	Kellum, Edward, Sr.	4822
Watkins, Jennings Edward	Watkins, Gassaway	4791
Watson, Louis Hamner	Jones, Woody	4671

MEMBER	ANCESTOR	GEN. SOC. NO.
Webb, Emrick Adderson	Webb, Adin	4887
Webb, Milton Harry, Jr.	Hoover, Philip	5261
Webber, Charles Robert	Hill, Richard	4890
Webber, George Hawes	Scheffey, Henry	4977
Webster, Walter Edelen, Jr.	Webster, Jacob	5048
Weeden, Kenneth Carl	Weeden, William	5292
Wells, Charles Joseph	Collins, Thomas B.	4857
Wells, Richard Clifford	Crockett, David	5106
West, Thomas Mabson, Jr.	Rennolds, Reuben	4700
Wheat, John Marc	Wheat, Thomas	5172
White, Eldon Lee, Sr.	White, William	5027
White, Ky Wayne	Crockett, William	5173
White, Ky Wayne	Popejoy, Nathaniel	5173
White, Ky Wayne	Spratt, Thomas	5173
White, Ky Wayne	Weatherby, George Washington	5173
White, Ricky Mack	Spratt, Thomas	5235
Whitehouse, Robert Lacue	McKee, Henry	4787
Whitmer, Dietrich Lynn	Durkee, Sheldon	4974
Whitten, Rondald Waye	Robbins, Joel	4670
Widener, Ralph William, Jr.	Widener, Benjamin	4731
Wilbanks, William Heath	Rogers, Peter Bayard	4924
Wilcox, Kenneth Allan	Wilcox, Jehiel	5011
Wilkens, Leon Franklin, Jr.	Twigg, Charles	4858
Wilkerson, Robert Christopher	Nichols, Henry	4855
Wilkinson, John F.B., Jr.	Wilkinson, James	4951
Wilkinson, John F.B., Sr.	Wilkinson, James	4778
Willard, Craig Kenneth	Zimmerman, Jacob, Sr.	3520
Williams, Darrell Eugene	Doty, Ebenezer	4720
Williams, James Douglass	Cabarrus, Augustus, Jr.	4937
Willingham, Douglas Barton	Willingham, Archibald	4675
Willingham, Douglas Barton	Killen, John Bell Newton	4675
Willson, Richard Eugene	Longabaugh, Jacob, Sr.	4875
Wilmeth, John Robert	Ferguson, Joshua	5232
Wilmoth, Harold Edgar	Iglehart, Jesse	4914
Wilson, Dwight Remington, Jr.	Crowder, Peterson	4940
Wilson, James Earl	Wilson, James	5151
Winslow, Caleb, Jr.	Leiper, George Gray	4889
Winslow, John Leiper, Jr.	Baxley, George	4210
Winston, Robert Nathaniel, Sr.	Bullock, Leonard	4764
Wise, Joseph Powell	Magee, Robert	4711
Wise, Robert Powell	Magee, Robert	4712
Wise, Sherwood Willing	Magee, Robert	4710
Withers, Langdon Abbott	Bruce, Horatio	4882
Withers, Langdon Abbott	Withers, Abijah	4882
Witt, Kenneth Henry	Hudnall, John Smith	4718

MEMBER	ANCESTOR	GEN. SOC. NO.
Wiygul, Charles Harrison	Mayfield, Austin B.	5251
Wolf, Donald Joseph	Kepner, John	5050
Wood, Roger Holmes	French, William	5241
Woodaman, Ronald Elliott Hasbrouck	Bloomer, Daniel	5150
Woodward, Joseph Janvier III	Ordronaux, John	5330
Wright, Richard Morgan, Jr.	Barr, James, Jr.	5253
Yeilding, Hollis Clinton	Robbins, Joel	4669
Yielding, Ronald Eugene	Lyon, Isaac	5223
York, William Alton	Funk, Joseph	4661
Yost, Stuart Henri	Gano, John Stites	5045
Young, James Turner	Young, William	5299
Ziemer, Robert Rhys	McCartney, Henry II	4809
Zillion, Jerry William	Foreman, David	5278
Zimmerman, Kenneth Edward	Zimmerman, John	4866
Zimmerman, Raymond Nathan, Jr.	Kershner, Conrad	4915

0158 Burkhart, Valentine, Jr.
0415 Gehring, John George, Jr.
0505 Bell, William Duffield
0764 Bandel, Littleton C.
0811 Harrison, Benjamin
1036 Armistead, George, Jr.
1226 Crittenden, Wm. Lafayette
1807 Baskette, Alvin K.
3218 Peters, E. Hobart
3347 Cavaroc, John Peter
3347 Cavaroc, John Peter
3440 Birely, William Cramer
3467 Tucker, Robert Gene
3520 Willard, Craig Kenneth
3561 Abell, Richard Bender
3637 Bockstruck, Lloyd DeWitt
3696 Blizzard, Dennis Craig
3829 Blizzard, Arthur Keith
3996 Bresnehen, Thomas Francis, Jr.
3996 Bresnehen, Thomas Francis, Jr.
4006 Steiner, Edward E.
4210 Winslow, John Leiper, Jr.
4217 Lemley, Kenneth McRae
4237 Riley, David Leslie
4237 Riley, David Leslie
4413 Stewart, Morton Collins, Jr.
4425 Martin, Paul Edmond
4425 Martin, Paul Edmond
4442 Ruby, John Lindley
4551 Mix, Richard Lawrence
4604 Harris, Timothy Charles
4604 Harris, Timothy Charles
4605 Caldwell, James Allen
4614 Dobbins, John William
4632 Morehouse, Elnathan Paul, Jr.
4636 Foust, Perry Elihu
4641 Mossburg, George Washington
4648 Becker, David Charles
4649 Pace, Edward McKendrick
4650 Hartnett, Will Ford
4651 Nixon, James Fred, Jr.
4652 Fuller, Harlan Morris
4653 Robertson, James Grady, Jr.
4654 Moore, Eugene Nelson
4655 Anderson, Gregory Thomas
4656 Dawley, Raymond Angus
4657 Balser, Everett Wayne, Jr.
4658 LaBach, William Anderson
4659 Miles, William Earle
4660 Fisher, Harold Clyde
4661 York, William Alton
4662 Stewart, Thomas William
4663 Treppa, Jeffrey Allan
4664 Love, Joseph Bland
4665 Hamilton, Harlan Bernhardt
4666 Norris, William Virgil III
4667 Tjornhom, Christopher Mark
4668 Manson, Bradlee Robert
4669 Yeilding, Hollis Clinton
4670 Whitten, Rondald Waye
4671 Watson, Louis Hamner
4672 Tice, Robert Dean
4673 Clement, Harrell E.
4674 Justice, John Rodman
4675 Willingham, Douglas Barton
4675 Willingham, Douglas Barton
4676 Kratz, Charles Irving, Jr.
4677 Hyde, Earl McSherry, Jr.
4678 Rieske, Max James
4679 Kirkland, Daniel Lloyd
4680 Scarbrough, Wes L.
4681 Suplee, Melvyn James
4682 Traster, Earl Wilbur
4683 Rayfield, Thomas Filmore
4684 Finch, William Calhoun, Sr.
4685 Miree, James Wimberly Cook
4686 Lessa, Robert John
4687 Collier, Henry Grady, Jr.
4688 Rusch, James Allen
4689 Maginnis, Michael John
4690 Sporl, Henry Louis
4691 Cupp, Michael Charles
4692 Barnes, William Joseph
4693 Kelly, Julian Dantzler, Jr.
4694 Murrah, Robert Leland
4695 Robertson, Jimmy Kirk
4696 Dunn, Sydney Bullen, Jr.
4697 Church, David Lent
4698 Porter, George Weaver
4699 McGuffey, Carroll Wade, Sr.
4700 West, Thomas Mabson, Jr.
4701 Skelton, Harold Lawrence

4702 Skelton, Lawrence Harold
4703 Tull, John Earle, Jr.
4704 Chambers, Robert Douglas
4705 Kielman, Toxie L.
4706 Barroll, David Oakley V.
4707 Kemp, Charles Edward
4707 Kemp, Charles Edward
4707 Kemp, Charles Edward
4707 Kemp, Charles Edward
4707 Kemp, Charles Edward
4707 Kemp, Charles Edward
4708 Green, Gregory Howison
4709 DiStefano, Richard Renato P.
4710 Wise, Sherwood Willing
4711 Wise, Joseph Powell
4712 Wise, Robert Powell
4713 Stewart, William
4714 Omlor, Richard James
4715 Hill, Jerry Patrick
4716 Caddel, Elmer George
4716 Caddel, Elmer George
4717 Merrill, Ted Duane
4717 Merrill, Ted Duane
4717 Merrill, Ted Duane
4718 Witt, Kenneth Henry
4719 Reid, Robert Dale
4720 Williams, Darrell Eugene
4721 Bowling, Charles Taylor, Jr.
4722 Chace, George Frederick
4723 Sells, George Nelson
4724 Broadbent, Peter Edwin, Jr.
4725 Barnard, Frederick Henry
4726 Smith, Billy Earle
4727 Dunavant, Richard Hannah
4728 Murrah, Robert Leland, Jr.
4729 Green, John Richard
4730 Rucker, Ernest Carroll
4731 Widener, Ralph William, Jr.
4732 Anderson, Richard Edward
4733 Killian, John Harrison, Sr.
4734 Bates, Roma Scott
4735 Bates, Gary Walter
4736 Adams, Robert Donnell II
4737 Brown, Robert Athey
4738 Lawson, Ronald Curtis
4739 Pogue, Ronald Dennis
4740 Harreld, William Edmiston, Jr.

4741 McHale, Gerald Patrick
4742 Gluckert, Francis Albert
4743 McAlpin, Benjamin Brandreth III
4744 Bird, Thomas Edward
4745 Jinnett, Robert Jefferson
4746 Neal, William Benjamin
4747 Sullivan, Andrew Richard
4748 Lauda, Billy George
4749 Bowen, Norman Adelbert
4750 Burr, Richard Marshall
4751 Skinner, William Thomas
4752 Schiaffino, Ashton
4753 Pippin, James Roberts
4754 Stovall, Fred Dalton, Jr.
4755 Dakin, John Robert
4756 Trabue, James Duvall
4756 Trabue, James Duvall
4757 Duncan, James Jefferson
4758 Baldwin, Roger Conant
4759 Munford, James Benjamin
4760 Osgood, Peter Alan, Sr.
4761 Brady, Rodney Howard
4762 Masters, Vernon Edward
4763 Ferrell, James Michael
4764 Winston, Robert Nathaniel, Sr.
4765 McWilliams, Douglas Lyman
4766 Calhoun, Ernest Clyde, Jr.
4767 Rasmussen, Tom Niel
4768 Bowers, Henry Kenneth
4769 McFadden, Archibald George William
4770 Stair, William Stroman, Sr.
4771 Moran, Patrick Edward
4772 McElroy, Glenn Wallace III
4772 McElroy, Glenn Wallace III
4773 Lands, Ronald Herman
4773 Lands, Ronald Herman
4774 Moore, Pierce
4775 Grissom, John Farrar
4776 Jefferson, Stockton Bennett
4777 Bourg, Blaise Bernard
4778 Wilkinson, John F.B., Sr.
4779 Perry, Joseph Minos, Jr.
4780 Gillis, Vern David
4781 Morris, Lowell Winston
4782 Liscombe, Gerald Bruce
4783 Henshaw, Thomas Robert
4784 Schwartz, William Dean

4785 McInturf, Robert Cecil
4786 Jackson, Elmer Martin, Jr.
4787 Whitehouse, Robert Lacue
4788 Mullen, Michael Raymond
4789 Brown, Vincent Robert
4790 Gaines, Larry Bradley
4791 Watkins, Jennings Edward
4792 Crisler, Edgar Theodore, Jr.
4793 Collins, Carroll Jefferson
4794 Kellogg, Ira Newell, Jr.
4795 Dickerson, Laurence Edward
4796 Streit, Alan Michael
4797 Gurley, Donald Horton
4798 Seegar, John King Beck Emory, Jr.
4799 Austin, William Charles, Jr.
4800 Myles, Edmund Neal
4801 Green, Alfred Laland
4802 Melville, Robert Middleton
4803 Veselik, William Allen
4804 Bouis, Charles Elliott
4805 Millett, Robert Earl
4806 Schaeffer, Ronald Lester
4807 Newman, George Iley
4808 Hedstrom, Carlos Augustino, Jr.
4809 Ziemer, Robert Rhys
4810 Durnin, Richard Gerry
4811 Bahl, Daniel Lee
4812 LeCompte, Harry Lloyd, Jr.
4813 Freeman, Edward Patric
4814 Hill, Peter Reichner
4815 Jones, Ralph Hugh
4816 Brooke, Dandridge William
4817 Ford, John Drew
4817 Ford, John Drew
4817 Ford, John Drew
4817 Ford, John Drew
4818 Browne, John Prentiss
4819 Ralston, Michael Eugene
4820 Moore, William Arthur
4821 Garrison, David Lacey, Jr.
4821 Garrison, David Lacey, Jr.
4821 Garrison, David Lacey, Jr.
4822 Watkins, Darrell Royce, Jr.
4823 Brockman, Ellis Radan
4824 Oppenlander, Christopher Eric
4825 Pemberton, Charles Robert
4826 Partin, James Daryl
4827 Herring, Ronald Allen
4828 Phillips, Robert Leroy
4829 Walker, William Thomas II
4830 Seely, John Robert
4831 Ferry, John Christopher
4832 Scoggins, Leland Coulter II
4833 Hudson, Franklin Flynn
4834 Freeman, John Fletcher
4835 Payne, David LeBarron
4836 Shreve-Rountree, Robert Ivan
4837 Potts, Louis Eldren
4838 Chotard, Richard DeMeyere
4839 Corey, George Reece
4840 Brown, William Beckett III
4841 Burch, John Thomas, Jr.
4842 Kellogg, Richard Newell
4843 Treppa, Jerry Anthony
4844 Sanneman, Everett Heman, Jr.
4845 McCoy, Robert C.
4846 Hill, Thomas Allen
4847 Thomas, Kuddy Scott
4848 Dunn, Walter Kenny, Jr.
4849 Bahan, John Baptiste
4850 Hewitt, Robert Lee
4851 Schiaffino, George Ashton
4852 Stakelum, Piercy Joseph, Jr.
4853 Hutchins, Joseph Ray
4854 Goff, David Murlin
4855 Wilkerson, Robert Christopher
4856 Moore, William Whitney
4857 Wells, Charles Joseph
4858 Wilkens, Leon Franklin, Jr.
4859 Garroutte, Keith Tyrone
4860 Derbes, Lewis Joseph
4861 Marrs, William Marshal II
4862 Davenport, Robert Ralsey
4863 Bailey, Russell Bishop
4864 Grimes, John Francis
4865 Stewart, Lee L.
4866 Zimmerman, Kenneth Edward
4867 Cornwell, Larry Patrick
4868 Hodge, Roy Garey
4869 Hicks, Audel Harrison, Sr.
4869 Hicks, Audel Harrison, Sr.
4870 Brite, William Bradley
4871 Barnes, Charles Homer
4872 O'Connor, Gaylord Patrick

4873 Ware, Joseph Milton
4874 Meeker, Charles Kenneth, Jr.
4875 Willson, Richard Eugene
4876 Rothrock, Roger Lee
4877 Baker, Bruce Addison
4877 Baker, Bruce Addison
4877 Baker, Bruce Addison
4877 Baker, Bruce Addison
4878 Campbell, William Michael
4879 Hollje, John Buford
4880 Strang, Frank Morton
4881 Kellogg, Stephen Alan
4882 Withers, Langdon Abbott
4882 Withers, Langdon Abbott
4883 Rawlins, Steven Wayne
4884 Brown, William Raymond, Jr.
4885 Ford, Larry Lindell
4886 Dunahay, Lowell Vincent
4887 Webb, Emrick Adderson
4888 Knorr, Sheldon Henry
4889 Winslow, Caleb, Jr.
4890 Webber, Charles Robert
4891 Humphrey, Elwood McClure
4892 Humphrey, David McClure
4893 Berg, Robert Henry
4894 Colburn, Berman E.
4894 Colburn, Berman Eugene
4895 Cleveland, Kerry Owen
4896 Shepley, Raymond, Sr.
4897 Pippin, James Michael
4898 Bond, Weldon Eugene, Jr.
4899 Bond, Christopher Eugene
4900 James, Charles Henry
4901 Robinett, Richard Lee
4902 Robinett, David Scott
4903 Robinett, Richard Bruce
4904 Ford, Mark Douglas Lederer
4905 McKown, Barrett Lee
4906 Hall, Mark Alan
4907 Stern, Duke Nordlinger
4908 Ricks, Kenneth Eugene
4909 Kimberlin, Patrick Blaine III
4910 Knorr, Norman John
4911 Bates, Willis Sherman
4912 Rupert, Frederick Russell, Sr.
4913 Jenkins, Alfred Dean
4914 Wilmoth, Harold Edgar

4915 Zimmerman, Raymond Nathan, Jr.
4916 Van Tassell, Kenneth Walter
4917 Landers, William Bruce
4918 Meservy, Steven Paul
4919 Bethard, Alvin Young
4920 Bernard, Thomas Norton
4921 Helm, Terry Allen
4922 Harrington, Charles Robert
4923 Mayne, Winfield Scott
4924 Wilbanks, William Heath
4925 Fairley, Albert Langley, Jr.
4926 Bearden, Mike Michael
4927 McKay, Donald Innis
4928 Buckaway, William Allen, Jr.
4929 Pohl, Clifford Ralph
4930 Pace, Edward McKendrick, Jr.
4931 Early, Jack Jones
4932 Olney, Allen Lee
4933 McPherson, Ronald Gary
4934 O'Neil, John Thomas
4935 Breithaupt, Richard Hoag, Jr.
4936 Mustain, Robert Dennis
4937 Williams, James Douglass
4938 Simler, Francis Lester
4939 Emge, Lawrence Berryman III
4940 Wilson, Dwight Remington, Jr.
4941 Brown, Byron Winfield
4942 Roddis, Thomas Hamilton
4943 Dye, Donald Elbridge, Jr.
4944 Harris, Hugh Allen
4945 Schweizer, Charles Benjamin
4946 Taylor, Wallace Goodwin
4947 Shaw, James Henry
4948 Simons, David Brenton
4949 Groesbeck, Geoffrey Alan Peter
4950 Early, Alexander Rieman III
4951 Wilkinson, John F.B., Jr.
4952 Heckert, John Earl, Jr.
4953 Brewer, John Morgan
4954 du Fossat, Godfrey Meloney Soniat
4955 Baker, Jerry Allen
4956 Merryman of J., Nicholas Bosley
4957 Turner, William Thomas
4958 Elder, Paul William
4959 Pierce, Robert Francis
4960 Corum, Otto Franklin, Jr.
4961 Stair, William Stroman, Jr.

4962 Davis, William Thomas, Jr.
4963 Hopkins, Charles Michael
4964 Garrison, James Gardiner
4965 Parker, Kenenth Barry
4966 Neel, Thomas Stephen
4967 Cook, Grafton Hopkins II
4968 Berry, George Duane Leatherwood
4969 Seville, Francis Brent
4970 Arnold, Robert Carter
4971 Corn, William Stephen, Sr.
4972 Kinyon, John Hoey
4973 Norton, James John
4974 Whitmer, Dietrich Lynn
4975 Mamminga, Michael Arthur
4976 Noel, Edgar Estes II
4977 Webber, George Hawes
4978 Templeton, Wayne Richard
4979 Edwards, Mark Stuart
4980 Dibrell, John Thomas
4981 Begnal, Dorr Buckley Calkins
4982 Belisle, Thomas Richard
4983 Neeley, Koy L.
4984 Smith, Hoyt Oron
4984 Smith, Hoyt Oron
4985 von Nirschl, David Allen
4986 Farrow, Samuel Lee, Jr.
4987 Abney, Louis Oswell
4988 Parmer, J. Norman
4989 Kinyon, Paul Joseph
4990 Rudy, David Robert
4991 Beaufait, Richard Thomas
4992 Van Wormer, David Lee
4993 Sale, Thomas Wirt, Jr.
4994 LaBreton, Denvrich Charles
4995 Patout, Robert Bernadas
4996 Ramirez, Emile J.
4997 Farrington, William Prentice
4998 Hardin, Charles Kelleher
4999 Roth, Richard Joseph, Jr.
5000 Forstall, Terrence Christopher
5001 Robinson, Robert Boyd III
5002 Johnson, John Hess
5003 McCulloch, James Alfred
5004 Tucker, Leslie Ray
5005 Wathen, Richard Albert
5006 Mylnechuk, Larry Herbert
5007 Hartley, Michael William
5008 Troyer, Philip Sanders
5009 O'Brien, Michael Edward
5010 Bolton, Nelson Mott
5011 Wilcox, Kenneth Allan
5012 Butler, William Joseph, Jr.
5013 Burt, Robert Eugene
5014 Divine, Arthur Eugene
5015 Thornton, Reuben Thomas III
5016 Forkner, Charles Thomas, Jr.
5017 Drake, Robert Scott
5018 Shepherd, Byrd
5019 Peicker, Martin Jacob
5020 Mallory, Donald Nelson
5021 Ricketts, John Adams
5022 Smith, Clinton Wallace, Jr.
5023 Motz, Charles
5024 Fry, Charles George
5025 Jones, Thomas Frank
5026 Blauer, James Freeman
5027 White, Eldon Lee, Sr.
5028 Tucker, William Herbert Martin
5029 Coleman, Robert Sherrill
5030 Epperly, Loyd Lincoln
5031 Hogg, John Webb III
5032 Van Dorn, George Milo Sutherland
5033 Hemming, Charles Gerald II
5034 Coker, Robert Wayne
5035 Baker, Harrison Scott II
5036 Davis, William Kevin
5037 Burnette, Van Tyle
5038 Collins, Alvin Eugene
5039 Cassell, Hugh Bethel
5040 Conn, John Kendall
5041 Potts, Pearson Bahan
5042 Potts, Ewell Cardwell III
5043 Spivey, Scott Jerome
5044 Brann, James Richard
5045 Yost, Stuart Henri
5046 Spratt, John Stricklin
5047 Hudson, John Richard, Jr.
5048 Webster, Walter Edelen, Jr.
5049 Demass, George Robert, Jr.
5050 Wolf, Donald Joseph
5051 Hill, Joe. M., Jr.
5052 Holbrook, Paul Evans, Jr.
5053 Burkey, Noel Aaron, Jr.
5054 Doss, Clyde Lance

5055 Harris, John Werner II
5056 Robertson, Charles Ellwood III
5057 Miller, Ronald Hague
5058 Cole, David
5068 Pope, Richard Macauley
5069 Poor, Russell Merritt
5070 Poor, Harold Everette
5071 Hodalski, Francis Xavier, Jr.
5072 Schubert, Glenn Franklin
5073 Brinker, John Thomas
5074 Brinker, Brett Thomas
5075 Seiple, Stephen Bradley
5076 Cummins, Robert Towles, Jr.
5077 Davis, Robert Macnider III
5078 Akin, Billie Gordon
5079 Smith, Dewey James
5080 McGuire, Charles Danny
5081 Halle, David Philip, Jr.
5082 Marshall, David Banks
5083 Black, Leslie Edward
5084 Ward, Jack Cooper
5085 Butler, Edward Franklyn, Sr.
5086 Butler, Edward Franklyn II
5087 Butler, Jeffrey Darrell
5088 Meadows, Jeffrey Manton
5089 Baxter, Hugh Wise
5090 Choate, John Mark
5091 DuPriest, Travis Talmadge, Jr.
5092 Monroe, Kenneth Raymond
5093 Price, William Archer
5094 Curfman, David Ralph
5095 Daniels, Thomas Sherman
5095 Daniels, Thomas Sherman
5096 Ashley, Robert Drew
5097 Morton, Kim Allen
5097 Morton, Kim Allen
5097 Morton, Kim Allen
5097 Morton, Kim Allen
5097 Morton, Kim Allen
5098 Curtis, Frederick William, Jr.
5099 Snyder, David Geise
5100 Kuriger, Richard Charles IV
5101 Blair, William Paul
5102 Drake, Paul D.
5103 Epperly, John Moyer
5104 Bishop, J. Brooks, Jr.
5105 Brewer, Stephen Morgan
5106 Wells, Richard Clifford
5107 Farnet, Samuel Stewart
5108 Seybold, Edward P., Jr.
5109 Maxwell, Donald Power, Jr.
5109 Maxwell, Donald Power, Jr.
5110 Hensel, William Foster
5111 Gros, Edward Oliver
5112 Reining, Michael Andrew
5113 McCormack, Jay Tucker
5114 Boothe, Brian James
5115 Stigler, Stephen Leath
5116 Hooper, Trevor Norris
5117 Maxwell, Donald Power
5117 Maxwell, Donald Power
5118 Ford, Douglas Felix
5119 Reeves, John Harlan
5120 Anderson, Scott Jonathan
5121 Choate, Lee Hampton
5122 Allen, Alfred Lester
5123 Hamilton, James Esta
5124 McCaskey, Thomas Sims
5125 Alsup, Alan Kent
5126 Sustendal, Charles Don
5127 Anderson, Richard Edward, Jr.
5128 Stewart, Kelly Loyd
5128 Stewart, Kelly Loyd
5129 Mead, Daniel J.
5130 Cox, Wayne Norris
5131 Klinck, Daniel Noble
5132 Schoen, John Garic
5133 Starrett, Robert Henry
5134 Myers, Wilbur Thomas
5135 Pritchard, Cannon Hulbert
5136 Raymond, Wilford Donald
5137 Showler, John Thomas
5137 Showler, John Thomas
5138 Bozic, William Joseph, Jr.
5139 Stevenson, William Robert
5140 Sanders, Patrick Layton, Jr.
5141 Gerlander, Lee Alf
5142 Gerlander, Todd Lee
5143 Gerlander, Randal Lee
5144 Rassel, Oakley Lee
5145 Rassel, Richard Michael
5145 Rassel, David Paul
5147 Carter, John Henry
5148 Dillon, Lester Reed, Jr.

5149 Shaw, Donald Chace
5150 Woodaman, Ronald Elliott Hasbrouck
5151 Wilson, James Earl
5152 Rassel, Stephen Edward
5153 Greene, Ernest Rinaldo, Jr.
5154 Israel, Willard Alfred
5155 Simpson, Gustavus Sailer, Jr.
5156 Cox, Gregory David
5157 Cox, Shawn Alan
5158 Jones, Myron Ellis, Jr.
5159 Trefts, Albert Sharpe
5160 Mumaw, Keith Ray, Sr.
5161 Nettles, Charles R., Jr.
5162 Dixon, Malcolm R.
5163 Thurber, Cleveland, Jr.
5164 McDonald, Marcus Lee
5165 McGath, John Hardin
5166 Bauman, Kirby Lee
5167 Burton, Claude Raymond
5168 Richmond, Jack Commodore
5169 Gallagher, David Wilson
5170 Amos, Eugene Paul
5171 Harrison, Warder Ray
5172 Wheat, John Marc
5173 White, Ky Wayne
5173 White, Ky Wayne
5173 White, Ky Wayne
5173 White, Ky Wayne
5174 Hayward, James Bert
5175 Shepherd, Robert Sidney
5176 Rabun, John Parham, Jr.
5177 Niesen, William Crenshaw
5178 Milam, David Edward
5179 Segraves, William Alexander
5180 Reynolds, Alexander Garber
5181 Peters, Thomas Edward
5181 Peters, Thomas Edward
5182 Moore, Jerry Jay
5183 Brewer, Gordon Morgan
5184 Taylor, Charles Frank
5185 Clark, Alan James
5186 Green, Thomas Milton
5187 Abbott, Alvin Arthur
5188 Nettles, Charles R., Sr.
5189 Jacobs, Ronald Dean
5190 Grace, James Henry, Sr.
5191 Ohlmeyer, Raleigh Lawrence, Jr.

5192 Booth, Talmadge Early
5193 Townsend, Laurence Edward
5194 Johnson, Kenneth Willard
5195 Hoffman, Richard J.
5196 Rising, Lucien Edward
5197 Diehl, George Sandy, Jr.
5198 Smith, Richard Dana, Sr.
5199 Parker, Malcolm II
5200 Linthicum, John Whitaker
5201 Linthicum, George Emory IV
5202 Park, Lee Crandall
5203 Ford, Roland Wilmer
5204 Waesche, James Frederick
5205 Johnson, Ishmael Herman, Jr.
5206 Bartholomew, Robert Eugene
5207 Booth, Edwin Russell
5208 Ellis, Estil Lynn
5209 Perry, Tunstall Barker III
5210 Hurst, William Moore, Jr.
5211 Ridings, Roger Wilton
5212 Gafford, Robert Dale
5213 Pond, Franklin Sanford
5214 Booth, Stuart Lee
5215 Booth, Robert Early
5216 Stewart, Dennis Craig
5217 Adams, Allan Blakely, Jr.
5218 Short, Shelton Hardaway III
5219 Muthleb, Gregory G.
5220 Brent, Paul Leslie, Jr.
5221 Robbins, Joel Wayne
5222 Denger, Mark James
5223 Yielding, Ronald Eugene
5224 Birchfield, James de Maris
5225 Valencia, Dominick Michael, Jr.
5226 Aycock, Harry Tracy IV
5227 Raywalt, James Kevin
5228 Jacks, Thomas Edward
5229 Heath, James Edward
5230 Eckert, John Clarence
5231 Kienzle, Charles Allen, Jr.
5232 Wilmeth, John Robert
5233 Ryland, James Richard
5234 Dunlap, Kenneth A., Sr.
5235 White, Ricky Mack
5236 Spellman, Daniel Joseph
5237 McGill, Gerald Lee
5238 Bozic, William Joseph, Jr.

5238 Lee, John Claud
5238 Lee, John Claud
5239 Howard, Elijah Davis III
5240 Sayre, Jerry Ray
5241 Wood, Roger Holmes
5242 Lawrence, Floyd Harlow
5243 McCall, James Wilson
5244 Folger, Harry Paine 3rd
5245 Jones, Richard S.
5246 Arnaud, John Felix, Jr.
5247 McHargue, James Charles
5248 Beverly, Kermit Eugene
5249 Martin, Cornwell Crystal
5250 Early, Joseph Derwood
5251 Wiygul, Charles Harrison
5252 Alexander, Milton Judson
5253 Wright, Richard Morgan, Jr.
5254 Elliott, James Robert II
5255 Fazzini, Philip Anthony
5256 Smith, Edwin Milton
5257 Moore, Jason Hurd, Jr.
5258 Rude, Joe Christopher III
5259 Gensemer, Richard Lee
5260 Lane, William Joseph, Jr.
5261 Webb, Milton Harry, Jr.
5262 Gowen, Dana Loomis
5263 de Berardinis, Robert Ewing
5263 de Berardinis, Robert Ewing
5264 Malone, Ira Ernest, Jr.
5265 Castleberry, Ottis Lamont
5266 Keedy, Thomas Cornelius, Jr.
5267 Blankenship, Willard J.
5268 Key, Francis Scott
5269 Killen, Harry Edward III
5270 Conner, Robert Jean
5271 Colburn, Rolland Dale
5272 Bolt, Eugene Albert, Jr.
5273 Crawford, Victor Lawrence, Jr.
5274 Flint, Adam Polhemus
5275 Vivian, Robert Pond
5276 Hogan, Francis Joseph II
5277 Flanagan, Patrick Martin
5278 Zillion, Jerry William
5279 Blair, John Patrick
5280 McAfoos, Louis Garfield, Jr.
5281 Anderson, Vernon Brian
5282 Mullane, Joseph Francis

5283 Meinecke, Tommy Jacob
5284 Holloway, R. Ross
5285 Kyle, James H.
5286 Mackie, Charles Le Jeune
5287 Bradshaw, Burton Cox, Sr.
5288 Tovey, Herman Rennicker, Jr.
5289 Bush, Gerard David
5290 Bush, Daniel Byram
5291 Larson, Charles Jeffers
5292 Weeden, Kenneth Carl
5293 Elam, Hunter Ashley
5294 Hoos, Ernest Lou
5295 Horner, Ronald George
5296 Huss, William Wiseman, Jr.
5297 Lyman, Myron Edwin, Sr.
5298 Harper, Miles Douglas, Jr.
5299 Young, James Turner
5300 Harris, Benjamin Louis
5301 Smith, Charles Orestus
5302 Colley, Darrell Edward, Jr.
5303 Colley, Darrell Edward III
5304 Lee, Donald Edwin
5304 Lee, Donald Edwin
5305 Froelich, James Eugene, Jr.
5306 Reynolds, Robert Adair
5307 Tilton, Bradley Alan
5308 Hadsell, James Earl
5309 Hurlbut, Franklin J.
5310 Barnard, Kenneth Norman
5311 Vaughn, John Daniel
5312 Hanna, Muriel Keith, Sr.
5313 Hanna, Muriel Keith, Jr.
5314 Skelton, John Loring
5315 Sympson, James David
5316 Spade, Timothy Duane
5317 Dodson, Andrew J.
5318 Hugghins, William Rowe
5319 Howe-Cornwell, Gale Thomas
5320 Robbins, Donald Gray
5321 Hunter, Richard Gardner
5322 Fuller, Rex Lynn
5323 East, Donald Paul
5324 Manning, John Thomas
5325 Moore, Jim Donald
5326 Harris, William Edney III
5327 Freeland, Michael Willis
5328 Logan, Fordyce Barker, Jr.

5329 Giuffre, Dennis Michael
5330 Woodward, Joseph Janvier III
5331 Isaac, Richard Barry
5332 Fitzgerald, John Barnard
5333 Casey, Lawrence King, Jr.
5334 Milbank, Walter Cornwell
5335 McCloskey, Malcolm Moore
5336 Shelton, Donald Lee
5337 Asher, Richard Russell
5338 Sage, Richard Warren
5339 Ferrell, James Mansfield
5340 Ferrell, James Mansfield (son)
5341 Lines, Jack Milton
5342 Ives, Charles Pomeroy III
5343 Carter, Peyton Franklin III
5344 Drake, Raymond Lawrence
5345 Browne, Merrick
5346 Moore, William Harold
5347 Moore, Newton Moore
5348 Davidson, Kerry Joseph
5349 MacDonald, Brett Allen
5350 Moore, Frank Warren II
5351 Beidler, James Michael
5352 Prejean, Edward Joseph 3rd
5353 Penny, Richard George
5354 McGuffin, Robert E., Sr.
5355 Christian, James Milton
5356 Riedel, Frederick Leslie, Jr.
5357 Long, Paul Marshall, Sr.

Abbey, Shubel 5276
Abernathy, Charles Clayton 4754
Abshire, James 4989
Abshire, James 4972
Adams, John 4736
Adams, Lemuel Allen 5207
Adams, Lemuel Allen 5214
Adams, Lemuel Allen 5192
Adams, Roswell 5021
Adamson, Greenberry 3561
Aler, Thomas 4851
Aler, Thomas 4752
Alexander, Squire 4966
Allen, Aaron 4846
Allen Logan 5328
Alsup, Asaph 5125
Anderson, James 4935
Anderson, James 4959
Anderson, William 5281
Anthony, Philip 4713
Applegate, William 4934
Armistead, George 1036
Armstrong, Aaron 4868
Ashlock, Obediah 5097
Athey, Willis/William 4737
Atwood, James 4957
Aycock, Richard, Jr. 4745
Bailey, William 4863
Baker, Greenberry 5169
Baker, Samuel 4877
Ball, Edward 4806
Ballard, Beverly 5123
Balser, Benjamin 4657
Barfield, Lewis 4834
Barnard, James Ò. 5332
Barnett, John 4844
Barnwell, Edward 5115
Barr, James, Jr. 5253
Barroll, James Edmondson 4706
Bartlett, Luther 5098
Bateman, William Birckhead 5327
Bates, Martin 4911
Bates, Seth Hurin 4898
Bates, Seth Hurin 4899
Bates, Seth Hurin 4735
Bates, Seth Hurin 4734

Baudry, Jean Baptiste 5329
Baxley, George 4210
Baxter, James 5089
Bayless, John 5228
Bearden, Jeremiah 4926
Beaufait, Louis, Jr. 4991
Beck, John 5119
Beebe, John 5244
Bell, William Duffield, Sr. 0505
Bendel, William 0764
Bennett, Richard 4776
Bermudez, Joaquin 4954
Bethards, Henry Selby 4919
Bickford, Joseph White, Jr. 4949
Bigley, James 4853
Billingsley, Clement Turner 5029
Bird, William 4729
Bissell, Daniel Russell 4816
Blackington, Benjamin 4668
Blair, Jesse 5254
Blanchard, David 5262
Blassingame, John 5015
Blizzard, William of W. 3696
Blizzard, William of W. 3829
Bloodworth, James, Jr. 5190
Bloomer, Daniel 5150
Bobst, Daniel 4707
Bonar, David 4425
Bonaventure François 3347
Bonawitz, John 5019
Booth, Lemuel Early 5215
Bourgeois, Jean Baptiste 5352
Bourgeois, Jean Baptiste 4777
Bowen, Constant 4749
Bowers, Cornelius 4955
Boyd, Thomas Duckett 5023
Boyer, John 5165
Bradley, Pleasant 5128
Bradshaw, Amos 5287
Brady, Hugh 5163
Bramble, Moses 4793
Branch, David 4908
Branch, Henry 4759
Brandenburg, Solomon 5160
Brandon, Cornelius 5189
Brandon, William 4947

Brent, Charles 5220
Bright, John 5104
Brinker, George 5073
Brinker, George 5074
Broadwater, Charles 5184
Brock, George 4965
Brown, Eli 4769
Brown, John 4818
Brown, Wesley, Sr. 4840
Brownnawell, John 5026
Bruce, Horatio 4882
Bugg, Samuel 5097
Bullard, Henry 4683
Bullock, Joseph Daniel 4808
Bullock, Leonard 4764
Burch, Bazell 4841
Burkhart, Valentine 0158
Burleson, Jonathan 4925
Bush, Henry C. 5290
Bush, Henry C. 5289
Butler, Elias 5086
Butler, Elias 5085
Butler, Elias 5087
Cabarrus, Augustus, Jr. 4937
Calhoun, Adam, Jr. 4766
Calkins, Amos 4981
Campbell, Duncan 4878
Campbell, George K. 4883
Cannon, Willis 5135
Cappell, Charles 5305
Carney, Solomon 5002
Carter, Anthony Terry 5147
Carter, Elijah 4992
Carter, Nathan W. 4636
Case, Lester 4990
Cassell, John 5039
Chace, James 4722
Champlin, Francis Cole 5270
Chapin, John 4715
Charles, Solomon I. 5283
Chitwood, Richard 5326
Choate, Benjamin 5221
Chotard, Henry 4838
Chretion, Hypolite 5126
Christian, Nathaniel 5004
Clark, Ebenezer 5275
Clark, Wilson Lucius 5079

Clegg, John Polk 5114
Clegg, John Polk 5113
Clements, David 4237
Clements, Phillip 4237
Cleveland, James 5318
Cleveland, Joseph 4895
Colley, James 5303
Colley, James 5302
Collins, Thomas B. 4857
Conner, John 4650
Conner, Levin 5204
Copher, Thomas 4985
Cornwell, Charles 4867
Courcelles, Joachim 4999
Covin, John Peter 5176
Cox, James 5130
Cox, Martin 4784
Craig, James H. 5336
Cramer, Jacob 3440
Crenshaw, Cornelius Dabney 5177
Crittenden, Wm. Gatewood 1226
Crockett, David 5106
Crockett, John Daniel 5311
Crockett, William 5173
Crowder, Peterson 4831
Crowder, Peterson 4940
Crumbaker, John, Jr. 5227
Culver, Aaron 5341
Cummins, Robert 5076
Cunningham, Jesse 4677
Cupp, Frederick 4691
Cushman, Caleb 4803
Cutler, Jacob 5142
Cutler, Jacob 5143
Cutler, Jacob 5141
Darby, Samuel 5009
Davidson, Richard 5348
Davis, James 5240
Davis, John 3637
Davis, Richard 4962
Dawley, Isaac 4656
de Gruys, Pierre 4995
Delarue, Celestin 5225
Delong, John Francis 4748
Demass, Peter 5049
Depriest, Austin 5091
Derrick, John 4716

Derrick, Simon 4716
Destrehan, Nicholas Noel 5107
Dibrell, Charles Lee 4980
Dinkins, James 4740
Dodson, William 5090
Doherty, George 5022
Doherty, George 4984
Doran, Philip 4768
Doten, Jacob 4893
Doty, Ebenezer 4720
Douglass, Jones 4984
Dowse, Stephen Burr 5308
Drake, James 4654
Duff, William 4605
Duffel, Edward 5108
Duffel, John L. 4996
Duncan, William 4757
Dunlap, Richard Gilliam 5234
Durkee, Sheldon 4974
Dustin, Eliphalet 4604
Dye, William 4943
Early, William 4931
Early, William 5250
Earnest, Peter 4836
Easter, Peter 4773
Easterday, Jacob 4886
Egbert, David 5047
Elder, James, Sr. 5056
Elliot, Abraham James 4704
Ellis, Abraham 4823
Ellis, William 4906
Ellison, Akis 5138
Epperly, John 5030
Epperly, John 5103
Erwin, Robert 5353
Etienne Billiot 5219
Etschberger, Johann Peter 5351
Eubank, Robert 5180
Evans, James Hampton, Sr. 5121
Evans, Meredith 5052
Evans, Thomas 5335
Fears, James 4753
Fee, David 5018
Ferguson, Joshua 5232
Ferrell, James Mansfield 5340
Ferrell, James Mansfield 5339
Files, Ebenezer Scott Thomas 5333

Fish, Jirah, Jr. 5213
Fitchett, James N. 5077
Fitzhugh, Philip 4747
Flesher, Isaac Newton 4864
Flesher, Isaac Newton 5096
Fletcher, John, Sr. 5181
Flint, Daniel 5274
Fluker, Robert 5058
Fogler, Henry 5071
Ford, William 4885
Foreman, David 5278
Foreman, Elijah 4804
Forkner, Henry 5016
Forstall, Edmond John 4997
Forstall, Edmond John 5000
Fortier, Michel II 4994
Francisco, Henry A. 5196
Franklin, Thomas Jefferson 4835
Fraser, James P. 4814
French, William 5241
Fry, Philip 5325
Fuller, Moses M. 5322
Fuller, Oliver T. 4652
Funk, Joseph 4661
Gaddis, Abner 5035
Gafford, William Robert 5212
Gaines, Richard 4790
Gaines, Robert Taliaferro 4979
Gamble, William 4719
Gano, John Stites 5045
Gansevoort, John 4743
Gardiner, Ignatius Walter 4821
Gardiner, Ignatius Walter 4964
Garic, François 4689
Garic, François 5041
Garic, François 5042
Garic, Jean Baptiste Francois 5132
Garroutte, John Sheridan 4859
Gates, Benjamin 4694
Gates, Benjamin 4728
Gates, John Valentine 5304
Gates, Valentine 5304
Gehring, John George 0415
George, John 4801
Geyer, Andrew 4709
Gibson, Samuel 5078
Gilbert, Jacob 5259

Glasson, John 4693
Godbey, William 5317
Goodwin, Joseph 4946
Grace, Henry 4756
Grafton, Ambrose 4967
Grants, Marks, Jr. 4698
Gray, Jonathan 5008
Green, David, Jr. 4782
Green, John 5238
Gries, Jacob 5095
Gries, John 5095
Grim, Jonathan 5156
Grim, Jonathan 5157
Grove, Reuben 4707
Grover, Silas 5006
Guenard, Nicolas 4852
Gwinn, James 1807
Hagler, Isaac 5154
Hall, James 4941
Hall, Thomas Graves 4929
Hammond, Matthew Brown 5344
Hammond, Thomas Denny 5131
Hanna, Richard 5313
Hanna, Richard 5312
Hanson, Peter 4845
Harding, William 5034
Harper, Enos 4687
Harpold, Solomon 4871
Harrington, Charles 4779
Harris, Benoni 4944
Harris, Tyree 5300
Harrison, Nathaniel 5298
Harrison, Tyree 5171
Harrison, William Henry 0811
Hartley, Hillory 5323
Hartley, Richard 5007
Hass, Christian 5296
Haught, Joseph 4789
Hayse, Samuel 5013
Heath, Ryland 5229
Henderson, Alexander 4815
Hendrick, John 4983
Henning, John 4958
Henshaw, William Slaughter 4783
Hetzer, Philip 4632
Hewitt, Jonathan 4850
Hicks, William 4869

Hiers, Daniel 5175
Hill, John 4971
Hill, Richard 4890
Hobart, Evans 3218
Hogg, Lewis 4987
Hogg, Samuel 5031
Holbert, Noah 4869
Holden, Ambrose 4604
Holter, George, Jr. 5072
Hooter, Michael 4660
Hoover, Philip 5261
Hope, Samuel W. 5186
Hopkins, Harris 4963
Horner, Samuel 5295
Horner, William 4922
Hoschar, Andrew 5017
Howard, Cyrus 4655
Howe, Solomon 5319
Howison, Alexander 4708
Howland, Zephaniah 5036
Hudnall, John Smith 4718
Hughart, Thomas 4891
Hughart, Thomas 4892
Hughes, Benjamin 5226
Hulse, Richard 4714
Hummel, John Jacob 5168
Hummer, Jacob 5301
Hunt, William 5097
Hurd, Joy 5257
Hurlbut, William Harrison 5309
Hyland, William 4805
Idol, Joseph 5028
Iglehart, Jesse 4914
Ince, John 4872
Isaac, Joseph of Richard 5331
Jackson, David Edward 4786
Jacobs, Lyman 5342
James, Enoch 4900
Jarrett, Nicholas 5355
Jeffers, David Seth 5024
Jeffers, Thomas 5291
Jeffreys, William 4894
Jenkins, Felix 5005
Jenkins, Russel 4913
Jennings, Martin 4763
Johnston, David 5224
Jolliff, Richard 5267

Jones, Joseph 5231
Jones, Marquis 5159
Jones, Thomas 5158
Jones, Woody 4671
Joseph, Hezekiah 4425
Joyner, Amos 4797
Kaigler, David 5025
Keely, George 4952
Keese, Thomas 4781
Keller, Casper 5195
Kelley, Samuel 5053
Kellogg, Pearl 4794
Kellogg, Pearl 4881
Kellogg, Pearl 4842
Kellum, Edward 4679
Kellum, Edward, Sr. 4822
Kellum, Edward, Sr. 4695
Kelly, Sims 4877
Kemp, Frederick 4707
Keown, William 4870
Kepler, Jacob 4884
Kepner, John 5050
Kershner, Conrad 4915
Key, Francis Scott 5268
Keyser, Conrad 5310
Keyser, Conrad 4725
Kibbe, Amariah, Jr. 5068
Kidd, Alexander 4862
Kile, Oliver, Sr. 5285
Killen, John Bell Newton 4675
Kimberlin, Daniel 4909
King, Samuel 4897
Knight, Daniel B. 4939
Knight, Jonathan 5152
Knight, Jonathan 5144
Knight, Jonathan 5145
Knight, Jonathan 5145
Knight, Samuel 5043
Knorr, William 4910
Knorr, William 4888
Knowles, Freeman 4772
Knowles, John 5269
Koonce, George 4807
Labranche, Jacques Hermogen 4920
Lacey, James 4821
Lafargue, Francois 5286
Lafarque, Francois 5263

Lamb, Chester, Sr. 5040
Lancaster, Michael 4918
Lane, Richard 5260
Lansdale, John Wesley 5199
Lawrence, Zachariah IV 5242
LeCompte, Joseph 4812
Leddell, William 4942
Lee, William Carroll 5264
Leftwich, Jesse 5153
Leiper, George Gray 4889
Leonard, Nathaniel 5198
Leppo, Jacob 4968
Lillard, Abraham I 5101
Linthicum, Charles Griffith 5200
Linthicum, Charles Griffith 5201
Lockhart, William 5279
Long, Christian 4969
Long, John Henry 4721
Longabaugh, Jacob, Sr. 4875
Love, David 4664
Love, Richard H. 5081
Lowrey, Alexander 5051
Lowry, Robert Mills 4826
Lunt, Joseph, Jr. 5044
Lyford, Peter 4738
Lyman, William 5297
Lyon, Isaac 5223
Macarty,Jean Baptiste Barthelmy 4849
Mackenzie, Thomas 4907
Magee, Robert 4710
Magee, Robert 4712
Magee, Robert 4711
Major(s), James 4960
Mallory, Samuel 5020
Marcy, Jared 5277
Marrs, Archibald 4861
Martin, Joseph Richard 4860
Martin, Rawley 4988
Martin, Robert Elkin 4666
Massie, Thomas 5218
Maull, Henry Fisher 5357
Mayfield, Austin B. 5251
Mayne, Adam 4923
McAfoos, Jacob, Jr. 5280
McCall, James 5243
McCartney, Henry II 4809
McClelland, William 5137

McClesky, David Henderson 5140
McClure, William 5217
McCormick, William 5109
McCormick, William 5117
McCravey, Ezekiel 5116
McCuistion, James 4879
McCullock, Alexander, Sr. 4673
McDonald, Thomas Owen 5164
McElroy, James Erwin 4772
McGrew, John Flood 4755
McKay, Lewis 5294
McKay, Robert 4927
McKee, Henry 4787
McKinney, James 5233
Mclachlan, James 5139
McLaughlin, John 5033
McNemar, John 4877
McRae, Christopher 4217
McWilliams, John 4765
Mead, John 4833
Meeker, Jonathan 4874
Merrick, William Duhurst 5345
Merrill, Billosti/Belosti 4717
Merryman, Nicholas Rogers 4956
Middleton, Isaac 4750
Midlam, Joseph 5102
Milam, Bartlet 5178
Miles, William 4659
Millen, John W. 5320
Miller, William 5003
Millett, Israel 4810
Millikan, Elihu 5216
Milner, William M. 5237
Mingus, William E. 4785
Mitchell, Aden 4843
Mitchell, Aden 4663
Mix, Amasa Hotchkiss 4551
Mix, Ira, Sr. 5170
Moale, Samuel 4950
Monroe, Randal 5092
Moore, Enoch Biggs 5350
Moore, Hill 4774
Moore, Jacob 5167
Moore, John 4820
Moore, John Skillman 5182
Moore, William 4856
Moot, John Conrad 4744

Moran, Jesse 4771
Morgan, David Bannister 4953
Morgan, David Bannister 5183
Morgan, David Bannister 5110
Morgan, David Bannister 5105
Morgan, James 4667
Morgan, John Henry, Sr. 4837
Morrison, Archibald 5082
Morse, Carpenter 4717
Moses, Elihu 4686
Mullen, James 4788
Mustain, John 4936
Myers, Charles 5134
Myles, John, Jr. 4800
Napier, Ashford, Jr. 5093
Nash, Reuben 5347
Nash, Reuben 5346
Neal, William 4746
Nettles, Zachariah 5188
Nettles, Zachariah 5161
Nichols, Henry 4855
Nicodemus, John 5088
Niles, Robert R. II 5245
Nivin, David 4839
Nixon, William 4651
Noell, Caleb 4976
North, Hicks 5356
Norton, Benjamin Spooner 4973
Nuss, Frederick 5230
Ohl, John Philip 5206
Oldham, William 5238
Olney, Stephen 4932
Oneal, Jacob 5247
Ordronaux, John 5330
Osgood, David 4760
Otto, John Bodo 5099
Owings, John 4848
Pace, John 4930
Pace, John 4649
Pangle, Andrew 5265
Parker, John Evans 4658
Parker, Warren 5014
Parker, William 5282
Patterson, Arthur 5149
Patton, John 4692
Patton, Mathew Houston 4442
Payne, Scammons 4688

Pemberton, Nathaniel 4825
Percy, Ferdinand 3347
Perrin, Calvin 4975
Perry, Oliver Hazard 4758
Pettigrew, George Augustus 5054
Phillips, Adam 4828
Pickering, Thomas 4905
Platt, Nathaniel G. 4678
Pontius, John George 5316
Poore, Edward H. 5080
Popejoy, Nathaniel 5173
Porter, Hugh 4877
Prather, Thomas 4762
Price, Reuben 4821
Primmer, James 4780
Pyron, James 5179
Quimby, John, Jr. 5324
Ramsburg, Frederick 4707
Ramsey, Joel, Jr. 5248
Raymond, Uriah, Jr. 5136
Rea, John 4948
Rennolds, Reuben 4700
Rhodes, James D. 5129
Richards, Augustus 4761
Rimmer, Thomas 4705
Ripperdan/Ripperdon, John 4938
Riter, Michael 4696
Robbins, Joel 4670
Robbins, Joel 4669
Roberts, Gilman 4665
Roberts, John/Jackie 4817
Roberts, John (Jackie) 5118
Roberts, John (Jackie) 5203
Roberts, John/Jackie 4904
Robinson, Sampson Avant 5001
Robinson, Sampson Avent 5273
Robinson, Stephen, Jr. 4726
Rogers, Peter Bayard 4924
Rolfe, Reuben 4676
Rooney, Daniel 4697
Ross, Reuben 5284
Rothrock, Solomon 4876
Royalty, Henry 5252
Rucker, Benjamin 4873
Rude, Isaac A. 5258
Rudolph, John, Jr. 5057
Russell, Moses 5255

Russell, Pliny 5120
Russell, Pliny 4732
Russell, Pliny 5127
Russell, Pliny 5337
Rye, Solomon II 4894
Sage, Philo B. 5338
Sampson, John 5249
Saunders, Hiram 5293
Sayre, William 5222
Scarbrough, Aven 4680
Scatterday, Aaron 4641
Scheffey, Henry 4977
Scheffey, Henry 4912
Schlatre, Joseph 5191
Schreck, Andrew 5094
Schuck, David 4682
Scott, William Coleman 5162
Seale, James 4865
Sears, Thomas M. 4847
Seaton, George Clark 5194
Seegar, Arthur 4798
Sellers, Benjamin Duncan 5238
Sellers, Matthew, Jr. 5037
Sells, William Henry 4723
Settoon, James 4690
Sewall, Samuel 4832
Shafer, George 4707
Sharp, Aaron 5083
Shaw, Thompson Breckenridge 4730
Sheakley, George 5075
Shenefelt, John 5148
Sheple, William 4896
Sherman, Reubel 4978
Shipley, Benjamin, Jr. 4799
Shrum, George 5307
Sias, John 5354
Simmons, John 4902
Simmons, John 4903
Simmons, Johns 4901
Simpson, Presley 5155
Sims, James 5124
Sinclair, John 4653
Sinket, Daniel Jr. 3996
Sinket, Samuel 3996
Skeels, Cephas 5256
Skelton, Zachariah, Sr. 4702
Skelton, Zachariah, Sr. 5314

1999 Supplement Ancestor Index 277

Skelton, Zachariah, Sr. 4701
Skinner, William 4751
Smith, Bird Bowker 5210
Smith, Isaac 5100
Smith, William 5202
Smyth, Richard 5197
Snook, Casper 5109
Snook, Casper 5117
Spade, Henry 4819
Spelman, Timothy 5236
Splane, Thomas Machen 4739
Sprague, Nathaniel 5321
Spratt, Thomas 5046
Spratt, Thomas 5173
Spratt, Thomas 5235
Stair/Stoehr, Daniel 4770
Stair/Stoehr, Daniel 4961
Staley, Moses 4707
Starrett, Charles 5133
Steiner, Stephen 4006
Stephenson, John 4986
Stevenson, Hugh 5272
Stewart, John 4662
Stirling, Lewis 4854
Stone, Stephen 4830
Strang, William, Jr. 4880
Strawn, Jacob 5038
Stuckey, Jacob, Jr. 5266
Suplee, Jesse 4681
Swartwout, Agustus 5349
Sweeney, Bernard W. 5097
Sweetland, Luman 4741
Symonds, John D. 5122
Sympson, James Clendenin 5315
Tabor, John Henry 5239
Taggart, Cardiff 5137
Talbott, Charles Wells 4724
Teagarden, Jacob 4796
Thomas, James 4684
Thomas, Joseph 4648
Thomas, William Benjamin 4817
Thompson, Henry 5010
Tidwell, Robert 4733
Tinnin, Asa 5246
Toothaker, William Rodick 5070
Toothaker, William Rodick 5069
Torrey, James 5012

Toups, Fuselier Tellesfor 5111
Tovey, Henry 5288
Townsend, Stephen 5193
Trabue, Haskins Dupuy 4756
Trovinger, Joseph 4767
Tubb, James, Jr. 5211
Tucker, John 5306
Tucker, Nathaniel 3467
Tull, John Nicholas 4703
Turner, Joseph 5187
Twigg, Charles 4858
Underwood, David 4827
Upshur, Littleton II 5343
Valentine, Joseph 4917
Van Dorn, John 5032
Van Tassell, William J. 4916
Vanfossen, George 4795
Ver Planck, Abraham 5334
Vermette, Antoine 4982
Voorhies, Cornelius 5263
Wade, Elisha 4699
Waggener, Richard 4672
Wale, Martin 4921
Walker, Jeremiah 4829
Walker, John S. 4773
Walraven, John 5205
Wansley, Thomas Jefferson 4614
Waterman, Barnabas 4413
Watkins, Gassaway 4791
Weatherby, George Washington 5173
Webb, Adin 4887
Webster, Jacob 5048
Weeden, William 5292
West, Robert 4674
Westcott, Major P. 4993
Whaley, James 5271
Wheat, Thomas 5172
Wheeler, Cornelius 5185
Whitaker, William 4802
White, Henry 4817
White, Maunsell 4998
White, William 4817
White, William 5027
Widener, Benjamin 4731
Wiggins, Archibald 5166
Wilcox, Jehiel 5011
Wilcoxson, Elijah 5055

Wiley, John 4824
Wilkinson, James 4778
Wilkinson, James 4951
Williams, Abraham L. 5084
Williams, Henry Guston 5209
Willingham, Archibald 4675
Willis, Joel, Jr. 4945
Willis, John 4742
Wilson, James 5151
Wilson, John 4811
Wilson, Thomas McMackin 5208
Wimberly, James 4685
Winter, Othneal 5097
Wisenbaker, John, Jr. 5181
Withers, Abijah 4882
Womack, Abner 4775
Wood, Benjamin 4717
Wood, David Robert 5174
Wood, Francis 4792
Woolsey, Melancthon Taylor 4970
Wright, George W. 4933
Yates, Lewis 4928
Yates, William 4813
Yeast, Jacob 5128
Yokley, Andrew 4727
Young, William 5299
Zentmire (Sentmire), George 5112
Zimmerman, Jacob, Sr. 3520
Zimmerman, John 4866

www.ingramcontent.com/pod-product-compliance
Lightning Source LLC
Chambersburg PA
CBHW050839230426
43667CB00012B/2073